Routledge Revivals

Southeast Asia

The articles in this edited collection, first published in 1985, consider the competing theories of the nature of development and under-development in Southeast Asia. Each chapter challenges the academic orthodoxies and dominant traditions of Southeast Asian studies, parti-cularly in relation to orientalist history, behaviourist political science and development economics. Overall, the contributions offer an alter-native framework for analysis, which considers the structural changes to the political economy of Southeast Asia, as well as the relationship between the state, economy and class at a domestic level. This is a fascinating collection, of value to students and academics with an interest in Southeast Asian politics, economics and history.

Southeast Asia

Essays in the Political Economy of Structural
Change

Edited by
Richard Higgott and Richard Robison

Routledge
Taylor & Francis Group

First published in 1985
by Routledge & Kegan Paul

This edition first published in 2013 by Routledge
2 Park Square, Milton Park, Abingdon, Oxon, OX14 4RN

Simultaneously published in the USA and Canada
by Routledge
711 Third Avenue, New York, NY 10017
Routledge is an imprint of the Taylor & Francis Group, an informa business

Publisher's Note
The publisher has gone to great lengths to ensure the quality of this reprint but
points out that some imperfections in the original copies may be apparent.

Disclaimer
The publisher has made every effort to trace copyright holders and welcomes
correspondence from those they have been unable to contact.

A Library of Congress record exists under LC control number: 84022860

ISBN 13: 978-0-415-70554-7 (hbk)
ISBN 13: 978-1-315-88586-5 (ebk)
ISBN 13: 978-0-415-70890-6 (pbk)

Southeast Asia

ESSAYS IN THE POLITICAL ECONOMY OF STRUCTURAL CHANGE

Edited by
Richard Higgott and Richard Robison

ROUTLEDGE & KEGAN PAUL
London, Boston, Melbourne and Henley

First published in 1985
by Routledge & Kegan Paul plc

14 Leicester Square, London WC2H 7PH, England

9 Park Street, Boston, Mass. 02108, USA and

464 St Kilda Road, Melbourne,
Victoria 3004, Australia,

Broadway House, Newtown Road,
Henley on Thames, Oxon RG9 1EN, England

Set in Century 9 on 11 point
by Columns Ltd, Reading, Berks.
and printed in Great Britain by
St Edmundsbury Press, Bury St Edmunds, Suffolk.

Library of Congress Cataloging in Publication Data

Southeast Asia: essays in the political economy of
structural change.
Includes index.
1. Asia, Southeastern—Economic conditions—Addresses,
essays, lectures. 2. Asia, Southeastern—Politics and
government—Addresses, essays, lectures. 3. Asia,
Southeastern—Social conditions—Addresses, essays,
lectures. 4. Asia, Southeastern—Foreign economic
relations—Addresses, essays, lectures. I. Higgott,
Richard A. II. Robison, Richard, 1943-
HC441.S68 1985   338.959   84-22860

British Library CIP data also available

ISBN 0-7102-0325-X
ISBN 0-7102-0471-X (pb)

Contents

Contents

PART I *Introduction*

RICHARD HIGGOTT AND RICHARD ROBISON

During the past decade, the Southeast Asian region has entered a new and critical stage of economic, political and social development. This development has been characterised by rapid industrialisation, the emergence of powerful, centralised authoritarian regimes and complex bureaucratic structures together with the accelerated spread of new class relationships in both the town and countryside. The implications of such changes for both the region itself and for its wider economic and political relationships with the rest of the world are enormous. The response of scholarship to these changes, both from within and from outside the region has not, unfortunately, proceeded apace. This becomes particularly apparent when compared with the vigorous and theoretically innovative debates that have been part and parcel of the analysis of change in Latin America since the mid-1960s, and Africa over the last decade.[1]

This relative failure of Southeast Asian scholarship to take up the theoretical challenge presented by the dramatic transformations in the region is largely the consequence, we will try to suggest, of the extraordinary influence of positivist and empiricist traditions upon Southeast Asian studies. Such traditions, which have tended to constitute an orthodoxy, have been constituted by an amalgam of orientalist history, behaviouralism and structural-functional social science. For a variety of reasons, but largely because they have studiously denied the existence of a theoretical or ideological framework to their own corpus of knowledge, these traditions have failed to generate a process of continuing and conscious theoretical reflection and debate. Consequently, disputes and debates within these orthodoxies have centred more or less exclusively on questions of factual accuracy and the interpretation of events rather than questions of epistemology or ideology.[2]

These orthodoxies do, however, have quite clear theoretical and ideological dimensions just the same as any other intellectual tradition, such as Marxism for example. But because these dimensions have generally been unstated, unacknowledged, or even unconscious, the theoretical element has not been advanced or developed within the corpus of Southeast Asian studies. Instead, the theorising of these orthodoxies, such as it is, has been largely derivative. Orthodox social scientists confronting the fundamental transformations underway in the 1980s still seek to explain events in terms of theories – or more precisely, fragments of theories – developed and often disregarded elsewhere decades ago. Such concepts as the bureaucratic state, patrimonialism, patron-client relations and the ubiquitous tradition-modernity dichotomy still constitute the theoretical frontiers for the main body of orthodox social scientists.[3]

Our first task in this book is, therefore, to provide the basis for a critique of these dominant orthodoxies. This task is pursued largely within the framework of Higgott and Robison's extensive theoretical chapter, which provides an overview of the historical development of the study of change in the Third World in general, but with reference to Southeast Asia in particular, and also in the chapters by Sullivan, Brennan and Warren in Part II of the book.

It is, however, our intention to attempt to go beyond simple epistemological critique to show that not only are these orthodoxies selectively and ideologically informed in their own right – a largely uncontested notion nowadays – but that they are also the precursors of quite specific political and economic policy constructs advocated as the logical outcome of 'disinterested' data collection. We attempt to demonstrate this in Chapter 1 by examining the relationship between global and national economic and political systems and the synthesis of theories of economic growth and the free market on the one hand, with political order theory on the other. This synthesis, we suggest, constitutes the new orthodoxy in development theory in the 1980s.

Having done that, we proceed to situate this new orthodoxy in its specific historical context in the last quarter of the twentieth century – namely in the context of the New International Division of Labour (NIDL) in which Southeast Asia is playing an integral part. It is only within this changing international structure that the kind of policies currently being advocated within the planning ministries of Southeast Asia and the major international financial institutions, such as the World Bank, can be understood. Similarly, it is only within this context that the processes of political evolution and class formation that are accompanying these economic processes can be understood. In Chapter 1 we thus go on to discuss the increasing tendency towards corporatist political organisation that has epitomised much of the political evolution of Southeast Asia over the last couple of decades. In particular we scrutinise the role played by the state in the economic process and its relationship to the nature of contemporary class formation. The general theoretical treatment that these themes receive in Chapter 1 is complemented by specific treatment in detailed case studies in Parts III and IV of the book.

It is also within the context of criticising the new orthodoxy that we have tried to fulfil our second task of providing a basis of an approach to the study of Southeast Asia grounded largely, but not exclusively, in a political economy framework utilising such concepts as imperialism, circulation *and* production, and class formation to help explain the processes of change within the region. Whilst analyses which sought to integrate political, social and economic approaches might have been fairly well advanced in the colonial and immediate post-colonial period in the work of scholars such as Schrieke, van Leur and Wertheim,[4] this socio-historical approach was, to a very considerable extent, eclipsed by the growth of 'Western' scholarship influenced by 'orientalism' on the one hand, and the behavioural and empirical 'revolutions' of the 'end of ideology' era of the 1950s and 1960s on the other. Critical theory did not re-emerge until it was reintroduced by dependency theory at the end of the 1960s and, as with orthodox theory, has tended to be theoretically derivative. Although some excellent studies of political, social and economic change within the region have been made within these derived frameworks, they have not resulted in the further development of radical theory in a systematic and sustained form.[5] Radical theory has been applied to the region, albeit in fragmented form, but the development of radical theory has not emerged from the study of the region. No sustained debate has arisen from the study of processes of transformation as they are specifically manifested in Southeast Asia.

We have attempted therefore in Chapter 1, following on from a review of derivative radical theory conducted in a manner similar to our review of orthodox theory, to proceed to a reassessment which will suggest some of the questions to be asked, and indicate some of the theoretical difficulties to be overcome in developing a sustained radical analysis of the transformation in the Southeast Asian region in the 1980s. In this reassessment we suggest the need to place the analysis of political phenomena, such as the state and the nature of class formation, into an economic framework which integrates – as opposed to what we feel has been the prevailing tendency to separate – the analysis of the processes of circulation and production. In particular we feel that very real prospects for a progression beyond a critique of the new orthodoxy, or a radical theory based on dependency theory, are presented by recognition of the evolution of the New International Division of Labour (NIDL). It is within the context of this new international structure that circulationist and productionist approaches and the analysis of the national and the transnational economy can be integrated. Of all the regions of the developing world, it is in Southeast Asia where the New International Division of Labour is having the most significant structural impact and where the theoretical and political conflicts between Import Substitution Industrialisation (ISI) and Export-Oriented Industrialisation (EOI) strategies are being most fiercely contested. It is also the region where the penetration of industrial capitalism is having the most decisive impact upon pre-capitalist modes of production and socio-political relationships. In short, Southeast Asia – possibly more so than Latin America or Africa – is the ideal laboratory for some kind of genuine advance in our understanding of the process of capitalist transformation in the Third World.

This book is an exercise in the investigation of this process of transformation. The first part, as we have already suggested, deals at a macro level with the historical development of theorising about development and underdevelopment in general, and the way in which it relates to the region in particular. Parts II, III and IV take the substance of Part I and break it down for greater scrutiny and illustration in the specific Southeast Asian context. Part II is thus a critique of several of the major aspects of traditional approaches to the study of Southeast Asia. Part III is an examination of Southeast Asia in the international economic order, and Part IV tackles in case-study fashion the relationship between politics and economic development in three Southeast Asian states.

Part II: History and society

The historical tradition in Southeast Asian studies is underpinned by orientalism. Despite the fact that we are now living in the 1980s, the continuing influence of this orientalist scholarship should not be underestimated. It has been one of the dominant influences in shaping the study of Southeast Asia in many British, Dutch, Australian and, to a somewhat lesser extent, American universities. Western students are introduced to the study of texts, languages and 'culture' (often of a somewhat obscure nature) as the most appropriate vehicle for the understanding of 'eastern society'. For the orientalist, language and culture are the keys to a comprehension of an unchanging orient rather than the methodology of specific disciplines. In examining the assumptions of orientalism we can perhaps do no better than to quote extensively from Bryan Turner's excellent discussion of the issue which is generally appropriate, despite its specific reference to the Middle East:

> Orientalism takes as its object of study an entity referred to as 'Islamic civilisation' within which 'classical Islam' is the crucial feature. This 'civilisation' is treated as a bundle of elements of high culture, in particular religion, philosophy, architecture and poetry. The primary aim of 'Orientalism' is to uncover the deep symbolic significance of Islamic cultural expression, of which the Arabic language is the primary vehicle. Hence research has been traditionally focused on the literary outpourings of the ruling institutions . . . . Orientalism is based on an epistemology which is essentialist, empiricist and historicist. The essentialist assumption is present in the notion that 'Islam' is a coherent, homogeneous, global entity, and also in the decline thesis where Islam is seen as declining because of some flaw in its essence. Social and political decline is a consequence of some historically ever present element – authoritarianism, the lack of autonomous oppositional groups or laws, slavish adherence to formal custom or the failure of ruling institutions. This inner, flawed essence unfolds in history as teleological process towards some final end state which is the collapse of Islam and its civilisation. In this historicist approach, the dynamic history of Western civilisation, punctuated by constant, progressive revolutions, is contrasted with the static history of Islam in which popular uprisings are merely an index of despotism and decay. In this kind of orientalist analysis, issues of epistemology and method are avoided. Once the novice has mastered Arabic which the Orientalist, by professional agreement, recognises as a 'difficult language', there are few difficulties involved in research. The major problems of research for Orientalists are matters of philology, not epistemology.[6]

Given the importance of this orientalist, intellectual tradition in Southeast Asian studies we see it as a necessary starting point to attempt to undermine the rationale of its working assumptions. Thus, in Chapter 2 Patrick Sullivan proceeds to question the claims of orientalist historians to be mere gatherers of facts. Rather, he suggests that they are presenting a form of history underpinned by the ideological perspectives of the pre-colonial court and/or the colonial residency. From this perspective history becomes a cavalcade of princes, governors, generals, religious and rebel leaders whilst the social and economic forces at work within a society are reduced to mere epiphenomena. For example, the political and economic realities of landownership, tenancy and rent relationships, which have formed the basis of the power and wealth of the sultans and other leaders, receive little or no attention in the writings of the orientalist historians or in their documentary sources such as the court chronicles, various literary and artistic records and works and the later official colonial records. As Sullivan suggests, orientalist history must be considered a dubious basis for those seeking to provide an historical context for contemporary events, and must be read with an awareness of its specific ideological underpinnings.

A further major feature of the orientalist tradition is the tendency to argue that non-Western societies cannot be understood in materialist terms, but rather, we should understand the actions of individuals as being primarily motivated by spiritual and/or religious factors.[7] The obvious implication of such a perspective is a denial of economic interests of class action as factors seriously affecting the social structure or the processes of conflict and change. In Chapter 3, Martin Brennan challenges such assumptions in his discussion of the economic and political dimensions of race and the manner in which they have an impact on the political process in Malaysia.

Structural-functional social science is the second issue that we consider in our critique of the positivist orthodoxy. Sociologists and political scientists since the Second World War have primarily approached the study of Southeast Asia from an analytical standpoint underwritten by an abstract and ahistorical model of a social system in a state of tension between the values of tradition and modernity. In this model, deriving its intellectual strength from the work of Talcott Parsons, society is a mechanism or an organism constituted by roles, norms and values and progressing from tradition to modernity in a process of oscillation between integration and disintegration. Too much has been written to warrant any lengthy discussion of these issues here.[8] Higgott and Robison outline some of the issues and criticisms in Chapter 1 to the extent that the philosophical underpinnings of structural-functional analysis still find their way into the policy-making process in Southeast Asia. The main critique of structural-functionalism in this work is, however, carried forward by Carol Warren in Chapter 4 where she demonstrates how the ahistoricism of this approach ignores the crucial dynamic of social organisation. In her examination of rural change in Southeast Asia she highlights the importance of the penetration of colonial and post-colonial capitalism upon the processes of everyday production and social structure.

The final construct of the current orthodoxy we mention only briefly here since it is the subject of considerable scrutiny in Chapter 1. We would like to suggest that growth economics – the central element in development economics in the post-Second World War period – has tended to see the problems of growth and economic development in the Third World as primarily technical problems open for examination in a largely apolitical environment. We suggest in Chapter 1, however, that the claims of growth economics to operate 'outside' or 'above' the realm of politics have to be discounted. Rather we suggest that growth economics implies a specific social structure and in effect operates as a powerful political ideology for regimes which wish to legitimise authority in terms of 'development'. The trend towards 'technocratic authoritarianism' has justified the exclusion of political opponents and the suppression of debate in the name of order and stability as the precursors of efficiency and as motors of economic growth.

Part III: Development strategies and the global economic order

As we also show in Chapter I, the question of the relationship between development, underdevelopment and the world economy has now been on the political agenda since the Economic Commission for Latin America (ECLA) began to articulate the structuralist critique of the asymmetrical exchange relationship between the developed and the developing world in the late 1950s. The four chapters in Part III of this book tap into this debate in a variety of ways. In Chapter 5, Richard Leaver examines the prospects of reformist development. He takes dependency theorists to task for assuming that development will inevitably be stunted and dependent, and that political regimes must consequently be oppressive. He does this by placing Import Substitution Industrialisation strategies, so common to many Third World regimes in the 1950s and 1960s, in their historical context and suggests that these strategies are inappropriate to the era of the New International Division of Labour, characterised as it is by what Leaver calls the 'de-domiciling' of capital. Instead, Leaver suggests that market-oriented strategies represent a realistic understanding of the global accumulation process at this historical juncture and offer the best, or at least a more feasible, option for realising the potential productive forces of states such as those under scrutiny in this book. Leaver is not oblivious to the problems implicit in the adoption of these new strategies – as, for example, the World Bank would appear to be in its largely uncritical advocacy of Export-Oriented Industrialisation of late – but this is not really the issue for Leaver. The real issue is that we understand the historical changes taking place. In this context his broad discussion of the passing of ISI in favour of EOI strategies in developmental thinking is most opportune.

In his discussion of the role of the state in the implementation of export-oriented industrialisation strategies in Singapore in Chapter 6, Garry Rodan deals at a micro-analytic level with the issues that were raised by Leaver at the macro-analytic level. Rodan, too, attests to the popularity of EOI strategies, but questions many of the unstated assumptions of recent EOI advocates. In particular he provides a vast amount of data to suggest that EOI and 'free market' strategies are not necessarily synonymous. The movement into, and success of, EOI is not dictated by rational, or free market, economic considerations but rather by the logic of the New International Division of Labour on the one hand, and the intrusion of the state into the 'free market' on the other. The state in Singapore is shown by Rodan to have provided the necessary economic infrastructure and political control to permit the implementation of EOI.

Again, in Chapter 7, the link between the particular state under scrutiny – in this case Indonesia – and the international economic order is shown to be paramount. Looking at the context of foreign investment in Indonesia (specifically that of Japan) Wayne Robinson tackles the question of autonomous development within a peripheral state of the international economic order. Examining the influential thesis of the late Bill Warren (outlined in Chapter 1 by Higgott and Robison) he concludes, contrary to Warren, that Indonesia's economic relations with Japan constitute a form of dependency in which Indonesia is impelled to follow the logic established by Japan's energy needs rather than by the logic of a perceived Indonesian national economic interest. The development of productive forces in Indonesia and the flow of 'investment capital' move more in accordance with pressures emanating from Japan and only to a limited extent in response to domestic Indonesian dynamics.

Finally, in Part III, Robyn Lim looks from an Australian perspective at the variety of theoretical interpretations devoted to explaining the economic restructuring of Australia's relations with the Association of Southeast Asian Nations (ASEAN). That a chapter on 'white developed Australia' should appear in a book devoted to the study of Southeast Asia is a reflection of both global and regional economic and political reality. The last quarter of the twentieth century has seen a growing recognition of the anachronistic nature of the traditional analysis of Australia as an outpost of the former British empire or, more recently, as an appendage of the advanced industrial bloc. Recent events have also led to a reassessment of the assumption that there is an immutable division of labour in which a technologically backward Southeast Asia is confined to agriculture and the export of primary products whilst Australia, by comparison, will continue to be a technologically advanced and industrialised economy. Of late the relationship has undergone a process of transformation to the extent that Southeast Asian political leaders are now placing increasing pressures on their Australian counterparts to reduce tariff barriers and open Australia as a market for the cheaper products emanating from the region's burgeoning manufacturing sector.

Australia's response to these structural changes and new political pressures has been confused, partly because they have upset long-held images of the way in which societies are divided into industrial and non-industrial. Lim's chapter is particularly useful in highlighting this state of affairs from the Australian point of view, particularly when policy-makers attempt to separate economic from political factors in the analysis of the relationship between Australia and its Southeast Asian neighbours. Yet also implicit in her analysis is the suggestion that whilst policy-makers might not recognise a New International Division of Labour in the way in which it is portrayed in this book, their response to policy questions is in fact a tacit acknowledgment of this reality. Such policy suggestions are basically defensive rather than altruistic. Despite rhetorical support for notions of regional structural adjustment, Australia's policy is in reality geared towards protecting its industries from the fundamental restructuring of the division of labour which is in train within the region.

Part IV: Politics, the state and economic development in Southeast Asia – selected cases

The role that is, or could be, or should be, played by the state is at the heart of contemporary debates about political and economic development in the Third World. Orientalist historians treated politics in isolation from its social and economic contexts. Politics for them was more a matter of the individual wisdom, political cunning and/or administrative efficiency of leaders. Indeed, much contemporary political history has been little more than an attempt to analyse personal or factional conflicts or the ability of regimes to build powerful state apparatuses. In contrast, structural-functional sociology and political science, especially during the heyday of the behavioural revolution in the 1960s, tended to use a variety of criteria for analysing and measuring political development.[9] The major criteria in this form of analysis were yardsticks of the degree of 'modernity' of the political system, particularly the extent of 'institutionalisation'[10] that had taken place, and the ability of the political system to 'integrate' previously heterogeneous societies into an approximation of a Western nation state. In the mid-1970s dependency theory has tended to reduce politics, and particularly the organs of politics such as the state, to an instrument in the process of surplus extraction from the periphery to the centre.[11] Such a quick review of these three perspectives on politics is of course a caricature and Higgott and Robison use Chapter 1 to elaborate on them accordingly. All three approaches do, however, have one thing in common, and that is that they all tended to reduce politics to the status of epiphenomena within the framework of their own particular priorities.

Needless to say, the process of intellectual advance has seen us come to question all three perspectives in turn, and the last few years have produced a process of quite profound reassessment of the political process in the periphery.[12] Questions of power, the role of the state and the nature and role of class formation are now recognised as having a much more central and complex role in the political economy of Third World states than was previously assumed. Three related questions, among many, stand out as being especially important in the current debate. Firstly, the nature of the relationship between the process of class formation and the state and particularly the extent to which the state is an instrument – for mediation or confrontation – in class conflict; secondly, what is the role of the state in the process of capital accumulation; and thirdly, what is the relationship between authoritarianism and the various stages or types of peripheral capitalist development?

The significance of these questions for an understanding of the current political economy of Southeast Asia is again addressed in a general theoretical fashion in Chapter 1 and in much more detailed fashion in the last section of the book. Robert Stauffer in his chapter on the Philippine state under Marcos looks specifically at the relationship between the form of the state and the nature of capitalist development in the Philippines, paying particular attention to the utility of the notion of corporatist political behaviour as it has emerged from recent analyses of Latin America. His assessment suggests that the increasingly corporatist nature of the Philippine state is directly related to the process of Philippine integration into the global political economy and the incorporation of the Philippine bourgeoisie into a transnational bourgeoisie with which it identifies. Kevin Hewison in his discussion of Thailand addresses himself more to the domestic end of that set of linkages which Stauffer had treated in their more specifically global context. Hewison focuses his discussion on the relationship between the Thai bourgeoisie and the local state. In contrast to the traditional line of argument of the dependency theorist of the mid-1970s and more in keeping with the line of argument of authors such as Colin Leys writing on Kenya at the end of the 1970s,[13] Hewison suggests that the state in Thailand has functioned as the cutting edge of an emerging national bourgeoisie rather than as the tool of a comprador bourgeoisie defending the interests of international capital.

In the last chapter of this book, Dick Robison takes a longer view of the New Order State in Indonesia, explaining its evolution in terms of a lengthy process of class formation and political struggle which has its origins in the colonial political economy. In particular, this chapter focuses on the tensions between the politico-bureaucratic alliance that controls the apparatus of the state on the one hand, and the various sections of a broader alliance of the bourgeoisie consisting of international, national and petty bourgeois elements on the other hand. This tension is examined within the context of the political, economic and fiscal crises and contradictions that confront the New Order State.

Notes

1 While Southeast Asia is used in a generally illustrative manner in some of the major, radical, theoretical analyses of development and under-development, there has been little or no Southeast Asian scholarship to date that can claim to have attempted to advance the study of the region in a theoretically specific and systematic manner comparable to that of authors such as Baran, Frank, Laclau, Cardoso, Dos Santos, Furtado, Sunkel, O'Donnell or Evans writing on Latin America, or Amin, Rodney, Ake, Meillassoux, Mamdani, Leys or Shivji writing on Africa. Neither has there been a journal devoted to the study of Southeast Asia that has acted as the vehicle for *systematic debate* about the state of development, theorising from a critical perspective in a manner comparable to the *Review of African Political Economy* or *Latin American Perspectives*. The significance of this work emanating from other regions is discussed in Chapter 1.

2 There are, of course, exceptions to this. R. William Liddle, for example, has written several reflective pieces on theory, looking at the turmoil within comparative politics caused by challenges from political order theory and dependency theory. See R. William Liddle, 'Modernizing Indonesian Politics' in R. William Liddle (ed.), *Political Participation in Modern Indonesia*, Monograph Series, Yale University, Southeast Asian Studies, 1973; R. William Liddle, *Cultural and Class Politics in New Order Indonesia*, Research Notes and Discussion Series No.2, March 1977.

For a critique of 'orthodox' research on Indonesia and Thailand, see Ben Anderson, 'American Values and Research on Indonesia', American Association of Asian Studies, USA, March 1971; and 'Studies of the Thai State', in Ayal, B. (ed.), *The Study of Thailand*, Ohio University, SEA Studies Programme, 1979.

3 For example, despite their age there are two works in particular of

continuing influence in political analysis in Southeast Asia: Carl Lande's work on patron/client politics, Lande, C., *Leaders, Factions and Parties. The Structure of Philippine Politics*, Yale University, Southeast Asian Studies, 1964; and Fred Riggs' work on the bureaucratic state, Riggs, F., *Thailand, the Modernization of a Bureaucratic Polity*, (Honolulu, East West Centre Press, 1966).

See also Robison's critique of approaches which use these notions as a theoretical framework, Robison, R., 'Culture, Politics and Economy in the Political History of the New Order', *Indonesia*, No. 31, 1980.

4 Schrieke, B., *Indonesian Sociological Studies: Selected Writings of B. Schrieke*, Vols 1 and 2, Bandung, Royal Tropical Institute, 1960; van Leur, J. C., *Indonesian Trade and Society: Essays in Indonesian Social and Economic History*, The Hague, van Hoeve, 1956; Wertheim, W. F., *Indonesian Society in Transition: A Study of Social Change*, (The Hague, van Hoeve, 1956).

5 Probably the most important sources of radical and critical analysis of the region are the *Journal of Contemporary Asia* and, from about 1982, editions of the *Bulletin of Concerned Asian Scholars*, although the latter has tended to concentrate on East Asia and Vietnam. See also Mortimer, R. (ed.), *Showcase State*, Sydney, Angus & Robertson, 1973; Chatthip Nartsupha and Suthy Prasartset, (eds), *The Political Economy of Siam, 1851-1910*, and *1910-1932*, Bangkok, Social Science Association of Thailand, 1976 and 1978; Elliott, D., *Thailand, The Origins of Military Rule*, (London, Zed, 1978); Sritua Arief and Adi Sasono, *Indonesia: Dependency and Underdevelopment*, Jakarta, Institute For Development Studies, 1980.

6 Bryan Turner, *Marx and the End of Orientalism*, (London, George Allen & Unwin, 1978), pp. 6-7.

7 Since the work of Clifford Geertz, a significant emphasis has been placed upon cultural/religious traditions as a means of explaining the structure and dynamics of Indonesia. This is dealt with by Carol Warren in Chapter 4. Another focus of analysis of Indonesian politics and society has been the tendency to explain contemporary politics in terms of survival or resurgence of traditional cultural perspectives. For a critique of the cultural politics school, including the works of Anne Ruth Willner and Don Emmerson, see R. Robison, 1980, *op.cit.*

8 See *inter alia*, Kothari, R., 'Tradition and Modernity Revisited', *Government and Oppositions*, 3 (2) 1968; Gusfield, J., 'Misplaced Polarities in the Study of Social Change', in Finkle, J. and Gable, R. (eds), *Political Development and Social Change*, (New York, Wiley, 1971); and Bendix, R., 'Tradition and Modernity Reconsidered', *Comparative Studies in Society and History*, 9, 1967.

9 See, for example, the work of the Social Science Research Council's Committee on Comparative Politics which devised numerous criteria for measuring political development. For reviews of their work see Montgomery, J., 'The Quest for Political Development', *Comparative Politics*, 1 (2) 1969; Milne, R.S., 'The Overdeveloped Study of Political Development', *Canadian Journal of Political Science*, 5 (4) 1972 and

Holt, R.T. and Turner, J.E., 'Crises and Sequences in Collective Development Theory', *American Political Science Review*, 64 (3) 1975.

10 The chief exponent of 'institutionalisation' as political development is Samuel Huntington. See the discussion of this issue in Chapter 1 pp. 19-24.

11 For a review of this 'sucking out of surplus' process see Andrew Mack and Richard Leaver, 'Radical Theories of Development: An Assessment', in A. Mack, D. Plant and U. Doyle (eds), *Imperialism, Intervention and Development*, (London, Croom Helm, 1979).

12 For a detailed study of this reassessment, see Richard Higgott, *Political Development Theory: The Contemporary Debate* (London, Croom Helm, 1983).

13 Colin Leys, 'Capital Accumulation, Class Formation and Dependency: The Significance of the Kenyan Case', *Socialist Register*, 1978.

1 Theories of development and underdevelopment: implications for the study of Southeast Asia

RICHARD HIGGOTT AND RICHARD ROBISON
WITH KEVIN J. HEWISON AND GARRY RODAN –
Murdoch University

1 Introduction

Since World War II theoretical approaches to the question of development and underdevelopment have been modified and transformed as the result of a series of debates both within and between two major intellectual traditions which we might call positivist and Marxist.[1] The first stage in this transformation process was characterised by the initial optimism and dominance of modernisation theory in the 1950s and 1960s. The second stage, the late 1960s and early 1970s, was characterised on the one hand by a conservative reassessment of modernisation theory resulting in a modification of its very intellectual foundations. The conservative reassessment represented a switch in emphasis from cultural transformation to political order as the crucial ingredient of development. On the other hand we saw the emergence of radical structuralists (Latin American dependency theorists), who drew the intellectual basis of their critique from Marxist theories of imperialism and the economic components of modernisation theory. The third stage, dating from the mid-1970s, is perhaps the most intellectually complex. It can be characterised by the growth of a process of critical evaluation of modernisation and dependency theory from both the left and the right, resulting in an acknowledgment of the complexity of the nature and causes of underdevelopment noticeably absent from the earlier phases.

It is important to stress that modernisation theory's intellectual crises in the 1960s did not result in its replacement by neo-Marxist analysis (whatever the variant) as the dominant manner of studying the Third World in some kind of Kuhnianesque paradigm change.[2] Instead the development of theory is best seen as the development of contiguous and parallel streams of competing descriptive and prescriptive traditions. Within each stream, however, analysis continues to revolve around the same fundamental theoretical questions. However, modernisation theory, particularly its economic growth theory component, has continued to constitute the orthodoxy at both the analytical and policy levels for Western scholars, political leaders, officials and corporate managers dealing with the Third World.

Unlike the rest of this book, therefore, which is more specifically Southeast Asian oriented, this introduction is essentially a macro-theoretical analysis of these competing theories as they have evolved over the past twenty years or so and as they are applicable, explicitly or implicitly, to Southeast Asia. It constitutes the thematic framework of a book in which each of the chapters seeks to consider specific issues or questions in the context of one or more aspects of the broader theoretical debate. This chapter is divided into two main sections, both of which adopt a common methodology. In the first section we review the nature of both orthodox and radical thinking on development as they evolved up to about the end of the 1970s. In the second section we address ourselves to the contemporary situation as we examine the current orthodoxy as it pertains to development policy in the Third World in general, but Southeast Asia in particular, and then proceed to provide what we feel is a sustained and logically argued critique of this orthodoxy.

2 Theories of development and underdevelopment: a review

The first stage of orthodoxy: modernisation theory and growth theory

Modernisation theory and growth theory are not simply intellectual constructs transformed by a process of scholarly debate. They are also an explanation and a description of policies and processes which have accompanied intervention by the industrial West in the Third World. Consequently, modernisation theory and growth theory must be regarded as both the ideology and strategy of capitalism in the Third World, addressing themselves to concrete as well as intellectual problems. It could be argued that modernisation and growth theory have actually followed and described the capitalist penetration of the Third World, presenting as theory what was already a concrete reality.

Much has been written about the early modernisation theory of political and social change, and it is our intention here to outline only some of its major characteristics and some of the most significant critiques which have confronted it.[3] Central to early modernisation theory was the notion of a dichotomy between traditional and modern societies, conceptualised in essentially Weberian terms. Traditional societies were defined as being prestate, pre-rational and pre-industrial. Most Third World societies were seen as exhibiting pattern variables which approximated to the traditional ideal type. In the optimistic period of the 1950s, modernisation theorists believed that for development to take place, it was merely necessary to bridge the gap between tradition and modernity through the acquisition of the appropriate modern pattern variables.[4] Further, it was felt that such a process was primarily a technical one in which problems could be overcome on the basis of guidance and diffusion from the advanced industrial societies of the West. As such, modernisation was seen essentially as a unilinear and inevitable process.[5]

There are a variety of explanations for what appears to have been a naive belief in the inevitability of the process of modernisation that prevailed in this first phase. Paramount is the influence on modernisation of what has been referred to variously as the 'American Liberal Ideology',[6] or the 'ideology of developmentalism'.[7]

As Packenham has pointed out, this social and cultural orthodoxy was based on four central tenets: change and development are easy; all good things, such as economic growth and democracy, go together; radicalism and revolution are bad; and distributing power (pluralism) is more important than centralising power.[8] From such an intellectual heritage was derived the belief of modernisation theorists in the role of *diffusion* as the motor for bridging the gap between tradition and modernity.

The optimism of the first phase, especially the belief in the modernising capabilities of diffusion, be it the diffusion of capital and technology as advocated by economists such as Rostow, Hoselitz, Higgins *et al.*,[9] the diffusion of cultural values advocated by sociologists such as Daniel Lerner,[10] or the diffusion of Western political values advocated in the literature of the Committee on Comparative Politics of the Social Science Research Council[11] was, however, to be shortlived.

A crisis in modernisation theory emerged as it became increasingly apparent that economic, social and political conditions on the ground in the Third World did not approximate to the expectations generated by the models emanating from Western (primarily North American) universities. Quite clearly, the process of diffusion was producing neither economic take-off nor flourishing indigenous bourgeoisies and, most glaringly, political systems were becoming increasingly authoritarian rather than democratic.[12]

Whilst some modernisation theorists soldiered on bravely, ignoring economic, social and political realities, the majority turned their energies towards explaining the failures.[13] Scholars of political change in Southeast Asia tended, for example, to adopt a behaviouralist approach and laid the blame at the feet of resurgent traditional culture, victorious over the new, secular, modernising culture.[14] Such a reaction provided neither an intellectual way out of the problem nor a solution for policy-makers. A major reassessment of modernisation theory was required, and it came in the middle of the 1960s.

The second stage of orthodoxy: economic growth, political order and public policy

The conservative reassessment of modernisation theory, previously outlined, questioned the basic assumptions that the process of economic and political modernisation in the Third World would necessarily and specifically reproduce the industrial capitalism or the liberal democracies of the industrial West. During the 1950s and early 1960s modernisation theory outlined development not only as a process but also as a set of ends or *achievements*. These specific end products were, however, put aside in the second half of the 1960s as development came increasingly to be regarded almost exclusively as a *process*. The major implications of such a shift in epistemological orientation meant that economic development came to be measured in terms of growth rather than in terms of the reproduction of the specific forms of Western industrial capitalism. Similarly, political development came to be viewed as a process of creating political institutions able to solve specific problems pertaining to stability and regime maintenance rather than the reproduction of democracy. Indeed, it came to be argued that strong government was a prerequisite of economic growth. This shift in political analysis was made necessary by the widespread collapse of the liberal democratic form within the Third World and its replacement by authoritarian regimes. In addition, Western policy-makers found themselves entering increasingly into partnership with such regimes as, for example, those of Goulart in Brazil, Mobutu in Zaire and, more relevantly for this book, Thieu, Suharto, Marcos and Lon Nol in the Asian region, in order to maintain their influential economic and political positions.

While modernisation theorists may have been concerned to achieve the diffusion of the values of 'modernity' – particularly liberalism – such obligations were never as important for policy-makers. They had quickly come to the conclusion that it was just as often strategically and politically necessary to underpin authoritarian regimes as to defend liberal democracies. This situation was illustrated in Southeast Asia as early as 1947–8 by US support for the avowedly authoritarian military government of Thailand led by

Marshal Phibun who, a few years previously, as an ally of the Japanese, had declared war on the US and Great Britain.[15] Western support for Diem in South Vietnam and Roxas in the Philippines should be viewed in a similar light.

These political realities were mirrored at the theoretical level in the shift, outlined by Donal Cruise O'Brien, from liberal to conservative dominance within the mainstream of academic development studies.[16] Of particular importance was the downgrading of emphasis by political scientists of the establishment and preservation of liberal democratic political institutions in the Third World, and an upgrading of the importance attached to the preservation of *order*. This shift was epitomised in the influential work of Samuel Huntington.[17]

Writing in the second half of the 1960s, Huntington challenged the prevailing idea of the unilinearity of modernisation theory and its minimising of the *dislocations* that arise out of the process of modernisation. Defining political stability in the normative sense as the absence of open conflict, he saw political development as the growth of institutions competent to deal with the strains of social mobilisation and political participation. Similarly, Ithiel de Sola Pool in a widely used quotation also epitomises this order-based literature:

> it is clear that order depends on somehow compelling newly mobilized strata to return to a measure of passivity and defeatism from which they have been aroused by the process of modernization. At least temporarily, the maintenance of order requires a lowering of newly acquired expectations and levels of political activity.[18]

Under this new formulation political development came to be seen as a political system's ability to cope with the array of 'crises' it was likely to face.[19] Governmental capacity referred specifically to governing 'elites' and crises were seen therefore from the perspective of threats to the position of those elites for the maintenance of order. In its desire to safeguard the position of ruling elites, the literature of political development had supported a view of order as the *end* not the *means* to good society. In so doing, modernisation theory deemed it unimportant to measure the costs involved in the preservation of order.[20]

Theories of political order were, and indeed still are, extremely attractive at an ideological level to authoritarian regimes. In Indonesia, the New Order regime of President Suharto developed an extensive rationale for its increasingly authoritarian form of rule by blending political order theory with modernisation theories of economic development. Essentially, New Order ideologues argue that an extended period of authoritarian rule is necessary to implement development programmes in the volatile period of economic transformation. More importantly, it is argued that development policies are matters of scientific knowledge most appropriately devised and implemented by technocrats and soldiers. Open political competition is consequently dismissed as obsolete.[21] A similar position was taken by various authoritarian regimes in Thailand from as early as 1851-8 to 1973 and again in 1976-7, and was proposed, to varying degrees, by the National Operations Council in Malaysia after the 1969 riots, and by President Marcos in the Philippines as a justification for martial law.[22] The debts to the conservative reaction in North American political science and particularly to the end of ideology school, are obvious.[23] This notion of authoritarian developmentalism or technocratic authoritarianism has become the ideology of Third World states wishing to equate authoritarian rule with economic development and scientific decision-making as opposed to the political chaos and economic stagnation typical of the first parliamentary governments of the Third World.

Perhaps we can recapitulate upon what we see as the two major steps in the intellectual development of modernisation theory. First, we see a stage wherein it was assumed that the process of diffusion of capital, technology, values and ideas from the industrial West to the Third World would replicate the historical experience of the Western democracies. Second, we see a stage wherein the process of social and economic change in the Third World was considered to produce a disintegrative interregnum which required strong, authoritarian rule to achieve political reintegration and economic development.[24]

In contrast to the changes in political development theory, the basic thrust of developmentalist economic theory has remained fairly stable throughout this period of reconstitution. This is, in large part, due to the fact that the mainstream developmentalist economic assumptions were in reality an attempt to present as a prescriptive set of policies and as theoretical analysis the autonomous process of capital accumulation in the Third World. Given time, and political order as the essential prerequisite, it was felt that the implementation of appropriate economic development strategies would still be proven to be correct.[25]

The increasing integration of growth and political order theory occurred in response to another aspect of the frailty of modernisation theory. Not only was it weak at an analytico-prescriptive level, it was also largely policy-irrelevant. As a form of grand theory, the modernisation approach was not geared to dealing with policy questions. Consequently, the last decade has seen attempts to integrate the theoretical aspects of the political order concept with empirically-based public policy approaches to development. The concentration and centralisation of power and authority becomes a necessary factor in the modernisation process. The tasks of modernisation have become defined in terms of problem-solving and policy management rather than in terms of reproducing Western political and cultural forms. In this context, public policy theory is the logical consequence of the integration of political order theory and growth theory.

In large part, the increasing importance of policy-making is a consequence of the changing nature of Western economic involvement in the Third World. Since the mid-1960s, Western capital investment has changed from being almost exclusively concerned with mining and plantation crops to greater emphasis upon industrial investment and a greater involvement of international finance capital through agencies such as the International Monetary Fund (IMF), the World Bank, and such regional organisations as the African and Asian Development Banks. Over the past decade capital investment has not only become significantly larger in scale, but has also become more complex, requiring the provision of effective management of specific projects. Investment in agriculture, for example, is no longer simply a matter of plantation production; it involves huge sales of pesticides, fertilisers, machinery and the provision of credit by international corporations and financial institutions. Governments are required to provide the legislative means, the infrastructure and the political apparatus to deal with the massive social restructuring which follows in the wake of such projects as the Green Revolution.[26]

Similarly, the governments of industrial economies and the administrators of the international finance agencies are able to make broader demands on fiscal policies of Third World states through their control of finance for both long-term government borrowings and specific projects. In the Southeast Asian context, for example, the Indonesian Government, throughout the mid-1960s, conducted negotiations with major creditor nations through the Intergovernmental Group on Indonesia. The result was a package, fairly universal throughout the Third World, which saw the rescheduling of existing debts and, in return, the implementation by the Indonesian Government of policies designed to encourage foreign capital investment, currency stabilisation and a reduced role for the public sector. In Thailand, the redirection of economic strategy in the late 1950s and early 1960s under Sarit, was closely attuned to IRBD reports and recommendations that Thailand abandon policies of economic nationalism which favoured state enterprise and state-led development for policies advantageous to private and foreign investment as the generator of economic growth.[27]

An important feature of the public policy approach is that it is often seen as synonymous with 'state activity',[28] and for most analysts of the Third World nowadays, the role of the state in the developmental process is deemed to be pivotal. This emphasis on the state, and the institutions of government, stands in marked contrast to the first phase of modernisation theory which emphasised the centrality of the political system and its socio-psychological environment rather than specific processes and policy outputs.[29] Put another way, the policy approach represents a shift of emphasis from the system *within* which politics operates to the strategy *of* and *for* political activity.[30]

These general changes have specific relevance for the analysis, and practice, of politics in the Third World. Public policy-making is primarily a problem-solving and management activity but within the specifically limited confines of regime maintenance. Gone is the naive optimism of the 1950s and 1960s. The basic problems to which policy-makers now address themselves are not of the grand 'how does development come about?' variety but rather questions like 'how can Third World states, under existing circumstances, *with existing decision-makers*, obtain some kind of optimum deal for their states?[31] In such a context the *degree* of government not the *form* of government is the key distinction in deciding whether policy will be implemented or not.[32] Political order theorists, such as Huntington, emphasising the level of institutionalisation, had the opportunity to see the implementation of policies based on their theories during the period of US involvement in Vietnam. Urbanisation and centralisation of political authority was urged (forced?) on South Vietnamese society in the belief that such a government, with its US backers of course, could control the population in the long term given that it was denying power to the revolutionaries whose support was in the countryside.[33]

In similar vein it is worth noting that the recent policy-oriented literature takes little account of the need for radical political reform. Rather, echoing the order theory of the likes of Huntington, Weiner, Pool *et al.*, it argues for a return to passivity and moderate (low) rates of social and economic progress as necessary prerequisites for order and elite maintenance. One author has argued, for example, that it is necessary to devise policy-making systems for Third World states that do not threaten the security of existing regimes and that do not promise only long-term benefits.[34] Such an emphasis, of course, has the effect of institutionalising the position of the group that occupies the major decision-making roles in the community on behalf of their own and external interests. These generalised notions about the nature of political development in what we may call orthodox political science have quite clearly manifested themselves at the policy level in Southeast Asia over the last decade or so. Particularly noticeable has been the emphasis on order and regime maintenance in Indonesia from the mid-1960s, Malaysia in 1969, Thailand from 1958 to 1973 and again in 1976-7, and the Philippines in 1972.

At a general level the preceding discussion represents an overview of the approach to economic, political and social change located within the modernisation framework in the post-World War II period. Most analysis of Southeast Asia in this period is firmly located within this intellectual tradition and should perhaps be considered in more detailed fashion at this stage. For purposes of clarity, and following the process of their actual separation within the corpus of modernisation theory, theories of economic and political development will be considered as discrete entities.

Economic development theory and Southeast Asia

Whilst theories of political development have undergone important changes as a result of theoretical debate amongst political scientists, the approach to economic development has, until the last decade, been largely unencumbered by problems of theoretical disputation. The dominant orthodoxy has been that of growth theory, first proposed by W. Arthur Lewis in the 1950s and pursued by such economists as Gerald Meier, H. Myint and P.T. Bauer.[35] This is not, of course, to suggest that there is a uniform view of how growth is best achieved. One needs, for example, to distinguish between those development economists such as Bauer, who emphasises the primacy of market forces, and those such as Lewis and Seers, who have adopted an essentially Keynesian approach, built on Harrod models, to development economics.[36] Growth theory operates on the (generally unstated) assumption that economic growth will spontaneously generate a reproduction of the historical experiences of the industrial West. Further, capital formation and corporate structures necessary for growth can best be provided by the already developed Western economies. Hence the primary concern of economists has been to devise policies most able to implement growth. This is seen as a technical problem, involving management of monetary and fiscal policy, designed to maximise foreign capital investment, foreign exchange earnings and productivity. In other words, economic growth theorists were essentially concerned with fine-tuning the existing process of capital accumulation.

Until the late 1960s, the theoretical assumptions remained unchallenged, and the apparent failure of growth strategies to cope with problems of poverty and unemployment or to produce viable domestic industrial economies were ascribed to a variety of endogenous factors including the incompetence and corruption of the state bureaucracies and the intrusion of nationalist and socialist policies into what was supposedly a scientific and rational economic decision-making process. The period of Guided Economy in Indonesia from 1958-65, or that of Phibun in Thailand from 1948-57, were considered major examples of such interference. Indeed, Western economists have continued to express disquiet at any attempts by Southeast Asian governments, particularly in Indonesia, to subsidise and protect specific national economic interests.[37] As we shall shortly suggest, the current enthusiasm amongst growth economists for Export-Oriented Industrialisation (EOI) is based upon what we feel is the fallacious belief that it is a process in harmony with market forces requiring no expensive state subsidies or controls, and fully exploits the Third World's national comparative advantage in low wage levels. Import Substitution Industrialisation (ISI) is justified only where it can compete without protection. (One may wonder what form the Japanese economy would now take if the Meiji oligarchs had been given, and taken, such advice.)[38]

Here then we see most clearly the view of the mainstream of economists that economic policy-making can, and indeed should, be determined by objective economic criteria (amongst which market forces figure prominently) free from the interference of *political* interests. Social and political factors tend to be seen as temporary irritants. This view stands in sharp contrast to a political economy position which regards economic policy as one dimension of a broader political and social conflict.[39] From the mid-1960s onwards, the intellectual assumptions of growth theory began to sustain challenges from both within and without. Growth economists, such as Heinz Arndt, became embroiled in debates with dependency theorists who argued that the economic policies which accord with the prescriptions of growth theory simply serve to enrich foreign capital investors and their local compradors whilst entrenching mass poverty and the broad structures of 'dependence' and 'under-development'.[40] Arndt admits that there is an unfortunate economic necessity, at least in the early stages of growth, for trade-offs between development and equality as well as a tendency for strong political forces to seize a disproportionate share of wealth. In any case, Arndt argues that despite a possible decline in the relative position of the bottom 40 per cent of the population of Indonesia, their absolute position has probably improved.[41] His position reflects the general growth economics thesis that long-term increases in production and productivity are the only viable basis for the achievement of broader goals of social and economic welfare even though this generally involves an unfortunate concentration of wealth and power in the short term.[42]

Nevertheless, it is clear that at least some of the economists writing for the *Bulletin of Indonesian Economic Studies* (BIES) were well aware that the spontaneous mechanisms of 'trickle down' and diffusion were faulty; that growth did not automatically lead to development in any wider social sense.[43] It is also clear that several of the growth economists most prominent in the analysis of Indonesia have seriously considered policy initiatives that involve land reform, employment generating investment, appropriate technology and investment in Basic Needs.[44] At the same time it is clear that the type of liberal reformist reaction to growth economics noted earlier did not take place amongst the economists who dealt with Indonesia. The type of theses embodied in the New International Economic Order (NIEO) or the Basic Needs approaches have not taken hold in any systematic or cohesive fashion.[45]

Growth economics in the case of those economists concerned with Southeast Asia turned not to liberal reformism but to the free market, small government ideology so popular with the supply-side economists of the major Western powers in the last few years. In terms of policy, the free market approach implied reduction of the role of government in the market place, the removal of protection and subsidy for costly and inefficient production and a process of structural adjustment to benefit from comparative advantage. This approach will receive closer treatment in section 3 of this chapter. At this stage it is simply sufficient to note that such policies are in stark contrast to those advocated in the growth with equity approaches. Peter McCawley, one of the most influential marketeers amongst the BIES economists, indeed argues that government intervention in the Indonesian economy has largely served to enrich that small group of well-connected businessmen in the Import Substitution Industrialisation sector to the advantage of no one else. He is as a consequence a staunch advocate of the deregulation of the economy at the domestic level, but he has stopped short of a similar deregulation advocacy at the international level because of its likely impact on Indonesia's fragile infant manufacturing sector in the immediate future.[46]

In the long term, however, the dominant tendency in growth economics in Southeast Asia does not stop at national boundaries. Increasingly, growth economists – be they in universities, the World

Bank or the policy branches of government – urge economic restructuring at both the global and the regional level. In terms of specific policy recommendations this means a concerted move into Export-Oriented Industrialisation[47] – again a subject to receive greater treatment in section 3 of this chapter.

Political science and Southeast Asia
Although the ideological and theoretical assumptions of structural functionalism have underwritten the work of Southeast Asian political scientists, the most important feature of this political science has been the general emphasis upon the centrality of culture as the determining factor of power and conflict – rather than the systems approach developed by the Committee on Comparative Politics of the Social Science Research Council under the leadership of Gabriel Almond in the late 1950s and early 1960s.[48] Nor has there been much emphasis upon political relationships between groups or classes. In the Thai case, for example, Wilson and Riggs decided that class analysis was inappropriate for the analysis of Thai political reality. They tended instead to fall back upon the concept of 'loosely structured' society to explain a polity they saw as being based upon personal and inter-clique rivalry amongst a small group of politically active individuals who stood apart from the vast mass of apolitical, harmony-seeking individuals who comprise Thai society.[49] In somewhat similar vein in Indonesia, Willner, Jackson, Emmerson and Liddle all view politics largely in terms of a personal client-patron relationship structured by the psychological or cultural attachments of individuals.[50] In the case of the Philippines, Lande also provides a picture of political relationships dominated by the mutual needs of patrons and clients.[51] His approach explains patron-client networks in terms of political and economic needs rather than cultural or psychological attachments but nevertheless emphasises politics as a process of the integration of individuals rather than the conflict of groups. Within such a methodological framework the study of politics becomes a study of attempts by factions and cliques to maintain power and to divide the spoils of office, minimising socio-economic aspects of political identity and conflict.

As the science of the struggle of 'elites' to maintain power, secure spoils and structure support on the basis of networks of individual loyalties, political science neglected the role of the state as a political institution interacting with a specific social and economic formation. It was, nevertheless, aware of the role of the elites, the bureaucracy and the 'government' as providers of both political and economic 'modernisation'. Failure to achieve Huntington's prescriptions for effective political organisation or to cope with economic problems (usually as defined by growth economists) was generally ascribed, as we have mentioned, to the persistence of patrimonial political culture and forms within the elite. In this sense, the focus of political analysis, especially in Indonesia, turned upon the conflict between secular modernisers and patrimonial traditionalists.[52] The policy implications of such a theoretical approach are twofold. First, they imply the reorganisation of bureaucratic structures to enable more effective political authority. Second, they suggest the cultural transformation of the 'elite', replacing patrimonial patrons and clients with 'secular modernisers' able to provide and implement scientific and objective public policies of social and economic development.

Certainly, there are political scientists who have recognised the importance of class conflict and economic structure in the general process of political structure and conflict. The problem is that structural-functionalism does not provide a theoretical basis for systematically achieving the integration of political and economic analysis. Yet while such deficiencies may have seen modernisation theory give ground to a variety of radical forms of analysis as the most useful *descriptive* models with which to look at the Third World in general, or Southeast Asia in particular, at a *prescriptive* level the major tenets of its public policy-oriented modifications would appear to have been adopted almost totally by its governments, as much of the evidence in this book would appear to suggest.

The radical alternative in development thinking and its relevance for Southeast Asia

The modifications that have taken place in modernisation theory over the last decade have occurred, as we have suggested, largely in isolation from what we might call the radical alternatives. These alternatives have been many and varied, ranging through liberal, structuralist, neo-Marxist and more orthodox Marxist. This pluralistic tendency of radical theory should of course warn us of the dangers inherent in discussing bodies of knowledge utilising shared terminologies as if they were a homogeneous school of thought. This warning is reinforced by the fact that many of the leaders of Southeast Asia, recognising that many aspects of radical theory seem descriptively superior to much modernisation theory, have been able to utilise radical rhetoric for their own political ends. This has been especially so in the international context, where these leaders have been able to bemoan the problems of 'surplus extraction', 'imperialism' and 'dependency' whilst at the same time maintaining domestic political and economic systems which owed much to the rhetoric and theories of growth economics and the political order theorists. It is in this context that the demands for a New International Economic Order must be seen. By blaming most of the ills of their countries on the inegalitarian structures of international economic relations in existence *outside* of their national boundaries, governing Third World regimes are able to shed much of their responsibility for many of the problems that exist *within* their national boundaries. It is thus necessary to pick our way briefly through the various debates as they have emerged in radical theory and as they would appear relevant to the current political economy of Southeast Asia. For such purposes, there would appear to be three major phases of radical thought in need of examination here:

a) The historical evolution of dependency theory from its radical structuralist origins and the rekindling of and interest in, older theories of imperialism.

b) The debate that has sprung up as a reaction to the increasingly populist appeal of the 'development of under-development' conceptualisation of André Gunder Frank and his supporters.

c) The development in the late 1970s of the debate over the nature of class formation and the role of the state in development society, which has emanated from the perceived weaknesses of the dependency debate and which will be tackled in the last section of the chapter.

The discussion that follows introduces a variety of concepts in *sequential* fashion. It is not the intention to suggest that these concepts were not 'known' prior to their introduction, but rather that their introduction into the discussion is a chronological representation of their importance to the development debate at a particular point in time. For example, it is not until the end of this section that consideration is given to the role of class formation and the post-colonial state. This is not an oversight but a reflection of the way the debate was to develop throughout the 1970s.

The early development of radical development theory
As is now well known, the impetus for the development of dependency theory evolved out of the growing dissatisfaction with the role of the Economic Commission for Latin America (ECLA) and particularly with its failure, during the first UN development decade, to comprehend the growing problems of the 1960s. In 1963 Raul Prebisch outlined the essentials of what was to be known as a 'structuralist' position in economic development[53] which rejected the

diffusionist capabilities of international trade, and the possibility of capital and technology transfer from the developed to the developing world. It was not, however, until the work of Gunder Frank began to appear in the mid-1960s that the structuralist position began to gain popular acceptance. It was Frank who initially articulated the view that the development studies of the 1950s and 1960s had been little more than an elaborate apology for neo-colonialism – particularly in its assertions that underdevelopment was an *original* condition predating capitalism and for which capitalism, therefore, could not be held responsible. Along with Paul Baran,[54] Frank pioneered the view that the inherited productive structures of the Third World 'blocked' capitalist development. Adopting much of the structuralist perspective, Frank formulated his own ideas into the 'development of underdevelopment' hypothesis. Looking at Latin America, Frank, and his contemporaries, argued that while it may have been *un*developed before Western penetration, it only became *under*developed after incorporation into the international capitalist system. Development and underdevelopment were seen as linked in a causal relationship in which the advanced industrial West was able to develop primarily because it was underdeveloping the Third World. The basic point about the type of dependence outlined by such theorists is that it is *dependent* development or underdevelopment, not *interdependent* development. Dependent development is a by-product of the expansion of dominant nations and tied to the needs of the dominant economy as opposed to the needs of the dependent economy. Frank's predominant image was that of the metropolis-satellite relationship in which the satellite was kept dependent by a sucking out of economic surplus to the metropole. Such a description is in many ways a caricature of Frank's work but it is at the heart of much early dependency theory.[55]

Thus, boldly stated, was the essence of dependency theory as it stood in the first half of the 1970s. While it never achieved the paradigmatic status that some observers have suggested, it did have an influence on development thinking sufficient to make both Marxists and modernisation theorists keen to refute its essence. The popular and populist nature of the development of underdevelopment hypothesis, especially its identification of capitalism as the cause of underdevelopment, forced both schools to respond to a theory that contradicted the teleological and unilinear assumptions they both shared. The outcome of this process, somewhat ironically, has been the emergence of some kind of consensus in development studies greater than at any other time since the heady days of early modernisation theory. The critiques of dependency theory that have emerged, from both the left and the right, are in fact quite similar in empirical substance – if not in normative assumptions.

If we consider orthodox critiques first, our starting point must be their attack on the vagueness and generality of the development of underdevelopment hypothesis. While the near universality of Frank's metropolis-satellite dichotomy was one of the major attractions, it was also its major weakness. In descriptive terms it differed little from modernisation theory's tradition-modernity dichotomy. Consequently, dependency theory was as difficult to refute at the macro-level, or apply at the micro-level, as in fact was modernisation theory. The orthodox critique went on to argue the ambiquity of the distinctions between dependency and inter-dependence. No country, it was contested, was autarchic. Developed as well as underdeveloped states have a high reliance on foreign trade, investment and technology, etc. Dependency must, therefore, be seen as a sliding scale from rich, capitalist states at one end of the scale to poor, small, underdeveloped states at the other. Dependent growth is not unique to the Third World and must be seen as an essential feature of capitalist growth in general.[56] What we have seen from modernisation theorists of late has been an attempt to harness an international political economy, operating in a liberal mould and stressing transnationalism and interdependence[57] as the exogenous variable for a revamped modernisation theory. It was generally argued that those states receptive to integration into the existing economic order were the ones undergoing the most rapid rates of economic growth.

Beyond the sociology of underdevelopment

If conventional critiques were an attempt to draw back from dependency theory then recent developments in radical theory must be seen as an attempt to go beyond the initial dependency conceptualisation. There would appear to be two related, but nevertheless identifiable, streams in this movement. First, attempts to modify and refine, but not reject in essence, early Latin American dependency theory's emphasis on the inequality of exchange relationships between the First and Third World – what we may call 'circulationism'. Second, a theoretical rejection of circulation for a stress on the importance of historical materialism and modes of production – which we may call 'productionism'. Both approaches, however, are based on a series of general criticisms of dependency theory that became popular in the second half of the 1970s.

The most important criticism related to the inadequacies of dependency theory's conception of capitalism. Frank, for example, was unable to distinguish adequately between different modes of production, leading him to the conclusion that *any* production for a market meant the existence of capitalism. As Laclau pointed out, the existence of capital and a market did not define a capitalist mode of production.[58] This theoretical critique was later expanded by Bill Warren. He argued that the assertion that capitalism caused underdevelopment was logical nonsense since this seemed to deny the possibility of development taking place along capitalist lines in the Third World at all.

Warren extended this criticism empirically. By aggregating data he suggested that *per capita* growth rates in the Third World had in fact outstripped population growth. Furthermore, and in contrast to the view of many a dependency theorist, not all of this had been growth without development and that capitalist development had taken place under the influence of imperialism. Significantly, Warren emphasised that industrialisation (his yardstick for development) was advancing at a much greater rate in areas of the Third World than many dependency theorists were prepared to concede. As such, Warren was undermining the metropolis-satellite conceptualisation so central to dependency theory.[59]

Quite clearly the industrialisation of many Third World countries posed problems to dependency theorists. Nevertheless, they attempted to incorporate this development into their theoretical framework in a way that did not appear to contradict their notion of underdevelopment as the consequence of surplus extraction. Cardoso's notion of Associated Dependent Development is the best example of the dependency adjustment to the fact of Third World industrialisation. Essentially, he argues that dependence and surplus extraction is not expressed solely through the export of primary products and the import of manufactures but within the very structure of a manufacturing industry dependent on Western technology and forced to import the means of production.[60]

At the same time the 'development of underdevelopment' hypothesis has been criticised for its insistence that underdevelopment is a capitalist phenomenon. Numerous studies have indicated that pre-colonial modes of production were not always completely destroyed by capitalist penetration. Indeed, in some areas, colonial policy effectively built upon pre-capitalist structures. Such a situation is relevant for Southeast Asia where dependency theorists have placed much emphasis on colonialism at the expense of an analysis of indigenous social, cultural, economic and political factors in inducing change. This relationship between colonial and indigenous structures has been illustrated in the relationship between commercial plantation agriculture and pre-capitalist village society during the colonial transformation of Indonesia.[61]

Despite criticisms of the inegalitarian nature of the type of development Warren identified, both he and Laclau undermined the notion evident in dependency theory that formal political independence made little or no difference to the development process in the Third World. Some Third World states have clearly demonstrated a capacity for sustained growth and a consequent improvement in their structural position in the international economy.

For our purposes, it matters little that such Third World industrialisation was largely isolated to urban areas, lopsided and extremely uneven in respect to those who were its beneficiaries. More important is that an acceptance, or rather recognition, of the existence of a group of semi-peripheral states has necessitated some distinction between that group of states where some kind of national system of economic power was being built and those states where capitalist penetration and consequent industrialisation had been much less influential. Such a distinction, as we shall see, is particularly relevant to the Southeast Asian context.

To review briefly our discussion to this stage, radical critiques of dependency theory to the mid-1970s revolved around the supposed ability, or otherwise, of capitalism to generate capitalist growth at the periphery. Dependency theorists emphasised economic stagnation at the periphery and the extraction of surplus[62] from the Third World – particularly important were the perceived mechanisms of surplus extraction: trade, aid, finance and investment controls, profit repatriation, debt servicing, etc. Marxists, on the other hand, came to express a contradictory point of view. In mounting a challenge to dependency theorists they joined with more orthodox theorists to question the reliability of a development of underdeveloped hypothesis in the works of Arghiri Emmanuel, Immanuel Wallerstein and Samir Amin.[63] At the risk of oversimplification they, like most dependency theorists, see an outflow of capital – a sucking out of surplus – from the periphery to the centre, but they explain this as a complex process of 'unequal exchange',[64] a considerably more sophisticated device than the earlier conceptions of dependency theory had envisaged.

Like Warren, they have played an important role in outlining the alternative varieties of development possible in the periphery. Wallerstein, for example, outlines the rise of semi-peripheral states which occupy an intermediary position between the ubiquitous core and periphery of the early 1970s;[65] and Amin recognises the possible variety of modes of production that can exist at the periphery.[66] For Amin, the capitalist world system is a combination of capitalist (in its pure form at the centre) and non-capitalist modes of production (in albeit distorted form) which are combined at the periphery in a variety of social formations. It is instructive here to compare the detail Amin provides on the uniqueness of peripheral social formations in *Unequal Development* with Frank's early rudimentary distinction between metropolis and satellite. This spatial distinction in their work can also be contrasted with a comparable temporal distinction. Amin, along with Wallerstein, has also been at the forefront of that group of radical scholars who see the need to 'periodise' the stages of capitalism – unlike Frankian analysis which envisaged only feudalism and capitalism.[67]

The importance of this more refined analysis has been that it has focused attention on a situation in which stratification in the Third World is undergoing a stretching out process and thereby necessitating an analytical distinction between *types* of Third World states as opposed to looking for similarities conducive to building universal theory. The latter approach has characterised development studies in all but the last few years. The former, we feel, will characterise the next few years. But to understand the nature of what we might call 'dependent development' we do of course need a much better understanding of the 'production' aspects of Third World states, as opposed to the 'circulation' aspects which tend to be the focal point of much dependency theory.[68] Indeed we have, of late, seen a much greater emphasis in the analytical literature on the importance of understanding the way in which capitalist and non-capitalist modes of production 'articulate' at the periphery. In contrast to the early work of dependency theorists, we now accept that elements of capitalist and non-capitalist modes can exist side by side in the periphery, and that the penetration of capitalism does not immediately eradicate pre-capitalist forms. The process of transformation of pre-capitalist modes is often a drawn out and fitful process which may, for example, simply begin with the penetration of exchange relationships. In the long haul to the full establishment of capitalist relations of production, pre-capitalist social and political structures may indeed persist and interact with capitalist structures. We would stress, however, that it is not our intention to suggest the permanent dual existence of capitalist and non-capitalist modes. The capitalist mode, we would argue, will inevitably achieve dominance in the long run.

In accepting such views we should not, as has happened often in development studies in the past, throw out the baby with the bath water. It is important to incorporate analyses of global exchange relationships into the reformulated theory of imperialism which has emanated from the macro-analytical approaches of dependency theory and world systems theory. The tendency to swing from macro-analytical circulation theory to micro-analytical production theory has to be avoided at all costs.[69] We must certainly avoid relegating the influence of foreign or international capital, foreign political power and international exchange relationships to a position of insignificance, as, for example, Warren does in a bout of overreaction typical of development thinking.[70] The development of forces and relations of production in *both* industrial capitalist and partly-industrial, partly-capitalist societies constitutes the basis for the logic which underlies the global division of labour. The capacity of transnational corporate entities to locate and relocate capital and to plan accumulation on a global scale is crucial for individual peripheral social formations. The decisions to invest or not to invest, to invest in industry or agriculture, are not only determined by specific social and economic structures of the peripheral society but by political or strategic factors or by developments in the accumulation process within the industrial 'centres'.

Dependency theory embodies very specific implications for policy. At both a methodological and an ideological level, it undermined the assumptions of modernisation theory and highlighted the uneven nature of the development of capitalism on a global scale. For dependency theorists the logical solution to the problems of underdevelopment came to be seen as the eradication of capitalism as a world system of unequal exchange relations. The battle lines for the eradication of this system were, therefore, to be between world capitalism as the oppressor and the Third World as the oppressed. While theorists like Amin and Frank saw socialism and/or autarchic development as the solution to dependency, the ideological element of dependency theory has had quite specific implications at the policy level in Southeast Asia, and indeed in the Third World generally. Dependency theory's identification of exogenous factors, particularly an inequitable economic system, as the major problem facing developing countries has led to great stress being placed on designs for a New International Economic Order. Ironically, such designs are often championed by authoritarian regimes militantly opposed to socialism. It is not our intention to question the importance of such a policy initiative but rather to point to the effect it has on minimising endogenous issues, particularly with regard to the nature of stratification and the distribution of power within states. In short, dependency theory, by the very nature of its concerns, precluded any *meaningful* analysis of such issues within Third World states. For dependency theory and world systems theory, with their emphasis on unequal exchange relations between a core and a periphery, social classes have tended to become synonymous with geographical entities and problems of inequality and deprivation, thus making the prospect of any useful class analysis extremely unlikely. It was only with the appearance of productionist critiques of dependency theory and specific critiques of the banality of dependency theory's class categories[71] that it became possible to perceive a system of class relationships more complex than that of a dependent Third World bourgeoisie in a comprador relationship with international capital as conceptualised by dependency theorists.

Dependency theory's impact on Southeast Asian studies and politics was brief but influential, and we can perhaps best illustrate this impact by a discussion of its application in a particular context. In 1973 Rex Mortimer's edited volume on Indonesia entitled *Showcase State* was published.[72] This book was a frontal attack on growth theorists and political scientists who had dominated the study of Southeast Asia in the post-war period. The harnessing of dependency theory to the study of Indonesia provided a basis for intellectual and political attacks on hitherto sacred cows such as transnational corporate capital, international finance capital (IMF, World Bank) and the domestic ruling groups. Until the early 1970s this three-way, politico-economic alliance, propped up by modernisation and economic growth theory, had been portrayed as 'modernisers' and 'dynamisers'. With the advent of dependency theory there now existed at least a basis for criticism of such regimes as Suharto's – as agents of the underdevelopment process and foreign economic interest and appropriators of the wealth generated by economic activity within Southeast Asia.

Transnational corporate and finance capital came under particular scrutiny. Whereas modernisation theorists had looked at foreign capital in terms of the infusion of the capital and technological bases for development, critics argued that foreign capital was creating massive external debts for Southeast Asian countries, sucking out surplus capital, providing little employment, effecting little technology transfer, monopolising economic decision-making and extending foreign ownership of the productive forces.[73] At the same time, domestic ruling groups, whose economic and political alliances with foreign capital and whose corruption, conspicuous wealth and authoritarian rule had previously been justified on the grounds of the necessary concentration of power and wealth in the initial stages of growth, could now be criticised as comprador.

Dependency theory, or selected elements of it, became a very potent political and ideological weapon for a whole host of political groups. Its value lay in its clear, if somewhat populist, identification of an enemy – foreign capital and their domestic compradors. Such a critique was useful to those social forces shouldered aside by the alliance of domestic military regimes and foreign capital. In

Indonesia, for example, the disintegrating Muslim petty bourgeoisie believed the crucial cause of their difficulties to be the collusion of the New Order with foreign capital and Chinese business, and the utilisation of state policy in the furtherance of this alliance.[74] A similar response came also from those sections of the middle classes excluded politically from the centres of wealth and power who were anxious to press their case for selective protection and subsidy by the state. This was made especially clear in the events of 1972-3 in Thailand. Various middle-class opposition groups came together to attack the role of foreign capital in bolstering a repressive political regime. Such a view proved to be politically potent, and in 1973 the middle-class alliance was able to bring down the military dictatorship.[75]

As an intellectual basis for political and economic analysis, however, the fatal flaws of dependency theory had been revealed almost as soon as it was being applied to the study of the region. Amongst students of Southeast Asia, dependency theory remained a central influence for only a few years in the early to mid-1970s. By this time, critiques of dependency theory by both productionist and circulationist schools had taken root. Indeed, the pure circulationist form of the Frankian dependency school never really established itself in Southeast Asian studies as it did in Latin American studies and briefly in African studies. Class struggle continued to be a major focus for radical analysis. By the mid-1970s in Southeast Asia it was clear that industrialisation of various sorts and to varying degrees was taking place, that indigenous bourgeoisies were emerging and were *both* integrating with the confronting foreign capital. It was also clear that *all* Southeast Asian social formations could not be understood in simple terms of dependence. For example, little could be understood of the nature of the political or ruling classes if they were categorised simply as comprador. The political predominance of the military in Indonesia and Thailand and of landed families in the Philippines could only be explained by reference to the processes of social and economic transformation specific to each country – in particular the development of the Hacienda in the Philippines as a major unit of agricultural production compared with variations of articulation between landlord/tenancy farming and something akin to the model of the Asiatic mode of production in central Thailand and Java.

3 The current phase: orthodox development strategy and the Marxist critique in the 1980s

In the first half of this chapter we reviewed the way in which

Introduction

development thinking had emerged up until the last few years of the 1970s. In this second half, we wish to bring the picture up to date. Using a similar methodology to that adopted so far, we will examine what appears to be the predominant approach in policy-making circles – what we call the current orthodoxy – and then proceed to what we feel is the necessary critique of these prevailing approaches.

Export-Oriented Industrialisation, structural adjustment and the corporate state

To recapitulate, thinking on economic development passed from its growth-oriented phase of the late 1950s and 1960s into a period of self-doubt in the early 1970s. The upshot of this self-doubt, brought about by the failure of Third World societies to 'take off' and the failure of a 'trickledown' of benefits to the poor to occur, was a move towards Redistribution with Growth and Basic Needs strategies – initially articulated by the then chairman of the World Bank, Robert McNamara, in 1973.[76] By a process of deliberate intervention into the policy process, these strategies, it was felt, would direct attention to the needs of the poorest sections of society. Of course Basic Needs strategies were to some extent, although not exclusively so, counter-strategies to the increasingly vociferous call from the Third World for a New International Economic Order. Whilst there is evidence to suggest that Basic Needs strategies were taken seriously in some quarters,[77] their life span has in fact been quite short. The passing of Basic Needs, and interestingly its major supporters at the World Bank, is not of itself a major event. It is, however, symptomatic of the decline in policy circles of what we might call the 'social democratic' perspective or international welfare state approach to development.[78] More important for the purposes of our current analysis are the policy prescriptions that attend on these new strategies. The policy approaches of the World Bank discussed in the following section, whilst of interest in their own right, take on greater significance when it is acknowledged that they have considerable influence on the policy-making groups of Southeast Asia – as we shall endeavour to demonstrate in subsequent chapters of this book.

In sharp contrast to the Basic Needs strategy of the latter part of the 1970s, the 1980s have seen 'the goddess of growth . . . [returned] . . . to her pedestal'.[79] In the context of development and practice two specific aspects of contemporary theory are of particular currency in the early 1980s and in need of some discussion. The two issues are the growing, indeed predominant, influence of Export-Oriented Industrialisation strategies and the kinds of structural adjustment policies required to bring them about. In addition we also need to consider the kinds of political arrangements which seem to be developing to organise the socio-political environment in which these strategies can be pursued.

The increasing advocacy of EOI has to be seen in the context of the declining importance of Import Substitution Industrialisation. ISI failed to facilitate the kinds of beneficial changes in the trade patterns of developing countries that were envisaged in the first instance. Also, and probably more importantly, it was rejected because of the limits on production that inevitably accompanied a policy geared almost exclusively to serving the needs of local markets in the Third World countries.

At the risk of digression it is important, we feel, to understand the changes that have come about in the intellectual climate in which development strategy is planned. It is no coincidence that ISI strategies became popular during a period when there was a questioning of the previously unquestioned benefits of Third World participation in international trade. We pointed out in an earlier section the initial influence of the radical structuralists of the ECLA and subsequent theorists of varieties of 'unequal change'. The acceptance of such assumptions does of course lead to policies geared towards self-reliance or at least withdrawal, to the best of a state's ability, from reliance on the international market for manufactured goods. Such was the basic mood of pessimism in the wake of the failures of development 'take-off' in the first UN development decade. It was in this period that notions of unequal exchange, or more generally the asymmetry of dealing between the developed and the developing world, held brief sway in the development community. We have, however, seen the intellectual climate change somewhat over the last few years. Particularly important has been the reversal in fortunes of the notion of 'comparative advantage' amongst students of international trade.[80] The 'miracle of the NICs (Newly Industrialising Countries)' has allowed growth theorists to argue the benefits of incorporation into the world's economy – or from a different perspective, Marxists to argue that imperialism can cause capitalist development. As the popular Marxist anecdote would have it 'if there is one thing worse than being exploited by international capital in the Third World, it is not being exploited by international capital!!' It is in this changing intellectual climate that the growing popularity of EOI strategies needs to be understood. Export-led growth or growth through trade is clearly the orthodoxy in development thinking in the first half of the 1980s.

The way such strategies are to be brought about is through the implementation of structural adjustment policies. Adjustment is basically a codeword for a variety of overlapping and long-term actions such as practising fiscal 'responsibility', controlling inflation, controlling the money supply, 'pricing reform' (a euphemism for devaluation), having a reasonable balance of payments ratio, or to paraphrase the World Bank – restoring the external accounts of developing countries. There are, of course, other aspects of an adjustment package, especially diminishing the role of parastatals and encouraging the private sector, as well as the introduction of a variety of austerity measures geared to cutting down public sector expenditure.[81]

The economic philosophy underpinning structural adjustment is pure 'supply side' whereas the Basic Needs approaches of the previous decade were 'demand side' – or consumption-oriented. To take the argument one stage further structural adjustment means, in the words of Bela Balassa, an economist closely associated with recent World Bank policy:

> [that] growth objectives will need to be given greater weight as compared to income distributional objectives . . . [further] policies to alleviate poverty should give emphasis to measures that raise the productivity of the poor rather than increase consumption through the provision of public services or government subsidies.[82]

In simple terms structural adjustment is really about developing countries 'putting their economic houses in order' in a manner similar to the desire which seems to preoccupy many Western governments in the 1980s. The rationale for such adjustment is its supposed facilitation of export-led growth.

In the 1981 *World Development Report*, the World Bank points to several countries that are model proponents of these policies and which have thus benefited accordingly. Of middle-income countries, South Korea is the one above all, though not the only one, that has achieved 'spectacular results through export led growth'.[83] Of the primary producing nations with agriculturally based economies, Ivory Coast and Thailand are prime examples of a fairly successful process of a diversification of exports to earn foreign exchange for investment in the development of manufacturing industries.[84] In general terms, 'outward'-oriented economies are applauded by the World Bank for having been the most successful of the last decade in responding to dislocations such as those caused by rapid increases in the cost of energy. Consequently, the World Bank's 'Policy Lessons' for the 1980s are geared towards adjustment for outward-oriented strategies. As such, the World Bank loans policy is undergoing a considerable change from the second half of the 1970s. Much less emphasis will be given to project lending in the pursuit of Basic

Needs. Instead 'Structural Adjustment Lending' will see funds: 'applied toward productive investments which enhance the country's capacity to produce exports and curb imports. For this reason, the uses to which external finance are put required *careful* monitoring [our emphasis].'[85] In 1980 the Philippines, by way of brief example, received one of the World Bank's first Structural Adjustment Loans. This US$600 million loan was geared towards securing the 'reform' of the Philippine tariff structure in the form of an overall reduction from the average rate of 42 per cent in 1978 to 28 per cent in 1985 and the 'rehabilitation' of selected Philippines industries. It was aimed particularly at increasing international competitiveness through the improvement of managerial and technical assistance, the injection of capital and the establishment of trading corporations to improve export potential.[86] Similarly, restrictive lending policies have also been applied in the Thai case.

If economic policy could be implemented in isolation from social and political concerns then nothing relating to structural adjustment policy discussed so far would seem exceptional. Such a situation is, however, not the case. There are several very evident social and political concerns which have to be confronted with the implementation of such policies. The first concern is the impact of such policies on Basic Needs. As even the World Bank is prepared to acknowledge, albeit obliquely, it is the 'human development programs which are obviously at risk at a time of budgetary stringency'.[87] Structural adjustment's emphasis on productivity and growth takes funds away from those sectors of public spending which have no *immediate* returns but which were at the core of Basic Needs strategy. Education and health policy are two areas which have only an intangible relationship with productivity but which are high cost areas which offer instant prospects of 'savings' – especially salaries. All structural adjustment policies inevitably rein in on public sector spending – as the World Bank acknowledges: 'There is no reason to single out social programs for cuts during an adjustment period. In many cases, however, budgetary constraints will force cuts in spending, and a share of this burden will fall on human development programs.'[88]

Secondly, structural adjustment, given its primary emphasis on economic policies with an outward – or international – focus, takes very little account of its political implications at the domestic level, particularly the prospects for political instability emanating from the initial dislocations such policies can cause. Cuts in basic needs programs may be expected to create disaffections in the poorest sections of the community. Yet these cuts may not have as severe political consequences as those emanating from the more powerful and articulate members of the political community who may be affected by these policies. For example, we have noted that structural adjustment entails a cutting back in public sector spending. Where this does not actually amount to retrenchment in the public service in every case, it almost certainly means less rapid upward mobility and fewer avenues of potential employment in the state sector. Incorporation into the public sector as a traditional avenue of reward or patronage for a government is thus closed off. This can, and indeed often does, lead to disaffection with government policy in those educated sections of the community that are the usual beneficiaries of such spoils.

Thirdly, whilst structural adjustment policies may indeed benefit some industries, others are invariably affected in an adverse manner with a resulting increase in unrest in these quarters. The 1981 period in the Philippines, for example, has seen exactly such a process occur. There has been considerable opposition from those sectors of the economy accustomed to operating behind the high tariff walls but who have recently seen their protection reduced.[89]

The World Bank recognises the potential political difficulties facing Third World states implementing structural adjustment policies. As the *World Development Report* indicates: 'policy reform is not easy ... it is important to persist with the above policies in the face of possible short term setbacks'.[90] To this end, Third World governments embarking on structural adjustment need to receive support, the World Bank suggests, especially of a financial nature: 'without external borrowing, governments may avoid domestic reform for fear of precipitating internal unrest'.[91]

The Bank's report does not, however, indicate the specific ways in which external lending may prevent potential unrest. There are, of course, a variety of issues that are important in this context but of particular concern, given the preceding discussion in earlier sections of this chapter, is the issue of the relationship between public policy implementation, order and regime maintenance. Export-Oriented Industrialisation and structural adjustment policies have important repercussions for the nature of political organisation required to ensure the implementation of such economic policies. To put it bluntly, there has to date tended to be strong correlation in the Third World between Export-Oriented Industrialisation, structural adjustment and what has been referred to variously as repressive developmentalism, bureaucratic-authoritarianism, neo-fascism, organic statism or, more generally, corporatism.[92]

The chapters in this book on the state in Indonesia, Singapore, Thailand and the Philippines are excellent discussions of this relationship between economic policy and the growth of this form of political organisation. The relationship can, of course, be overstated and all care should be taken not to do so. The important factor is not the existence of a one-to-one relationship between Export-Oriented Industrialisation and varieties of corporatist political organisation, rather the crucial issue is the strengthening of the corporatist form over the last decade or so. As was suggested earlier in this chapter, order and regime maintenance have flourished as policy priorities since the recognition of the frailty of Third World political institutions in the mid-1960s.[93] Furthermore, it is not unreasonable to suggest that underlying the advocacy of Basic Needs policies during the 1970s was the belief that they would enhance the potential for political stability by forestalling demands for a much more radical kind of social reform from below. There is therefore a continuity with the previous periods that needs to be noted.

At the risk of overgeneralisation we might suggest that attraction of the corporatist form of government in some of the more rapidly developing countries of the Third World is its ability to accommodate, in fairly unfettered fashion, the market-oriented demands of growth theory on the one hand, and the demands for political order, elite security and regime maintenance on the other. In essence, corporatism is a system of politico-economic organisation in which 'the state directs and controls predominantly privately owned businesses according to four principles: unit, order, nationalism and success'.[94] In such a context, corporatism exhibits a tendency to *over*control at the political level and *under*control at the economic level. The aim is to provide a fairly unrestricted degree of freedom to a society's entrepreneurial groups while providing strong control over the workforce – especially with regard to wage rates and union activity.

These controls are deemed essential if a Third World state is to capitalise on its few real aspects of comparative advantage in the current international economic order – namely a cheap and plentiful supply of labour unfettered by such inconvenient factors as politically organised labour, environmental protection legislation, pollution controls or safety regulations. It is these factors, along with the removal of import restrictions, undervalued currencies and a variety of concessional incentives that attracts international capital to the developing countries, or some of them at least, to invest in ventures geared to producing low cost competitive exports. If Export-Oriented Industrialisation strategies are having the success in some Third World countries that their protagonists suggest they are, then it is only because those strategies are taking place in a political environment approximating to the one sketched out above. It is the necessity of this kind of political environment that 'supply siders' are all too ready to ignore.

There is one other important temporal dimension of the current complementarity of export-oriented growth strategies and corporatism that is worth mentioning here. As Richard Leaver demonstrates at some length in Chapter 5, different strategies are appropriate, or are at least deemed to be appropriate, to specific sets of international economic circumstances. Without pre-empting Leaver it is useful to note here that Import Substitution Industrialisation seemed appropriate as a 'defensive' strategy for Third World countries to adopt as a way of 'protecting' nascent industries against competition from developed countries in the 1960s and early 1970s. We are, however, now in a period which Leaver suggests is epitomised by the 'de-domiciling' of capital and in which ruling groups, by taking advantage of their countries' somewhat dubious comparative advantages, can profit by pursuing 'offensive' outward-oriented industrialisation strategies.

The preceding discussion is a fairly straightforward and largely uncontentious account of what we might call the current orthodoxy – Export-Oriented Industrialisation strategies, carried out by the implementation of structural adjustment policies underpinned by the support of the growing, albeit unacknowledged, apparatus of the corporate state. Our review was necessarily brief but the chapters in this book on Thailand, Singapore, Indonesia and the Philippines provide explicit and well-documented discussions of the corporatist tendency in Third World state behaviour. Our brief in the remainder of this introductory chapter is to push farther our general theoretical discussion by tackling some of the unanswered questions that are raised by the current orthodoxy, particularly as they have been addressed in some of the Marxist literature on development and underdevelopment.

Contemporary Marxist theory has, of late, had to deal with the growing predominance of this orthodoxy at the policy level on the one hand, and the influence of dependency theory at the rhetorical and populist level on the other hand. In so doing, we feel it has provided us with useful insights into two very important areas of concern that are ignored almost entirely by the current orthodoxy, or treated in simplistic and reductionist fashion by dependency theory. These two issue areas, the subjects of the final section of this chapter, are the nature of class formation in the Third World and the position of the Third World state in the wider international economic order.

Class formation, the state and the New International Division of Labour

The advocacy of EOI and structural adjustment policies by the World Bank has been discussed at some length and in largely *narrative* fashion since that, we suggest, is the very essence of their weaknesses – namely that they have been considered merely as 'strategies' developed in some kind of ideological and theoretical vacuum and then served up as alternatives to the less than successful ISI strategies of a previous era. Such an approach is both unsatisfactory at a theoretical level and disturbing at a policy level to the extent that such policies are being widely implemented in many parts of the Third World. Such strategies have not just been 'plucked out of the air' but rather they have emerged as part of the growth of a New International Division of Labour (NIDL) brought about by the dramatic structural changes in the world economy over the last decade. The 'miracle of the NICs' – the World Bank's model export-industrialising countries – has not come about simply because of the implementation of EOI strategies. Quite to the contrary such strategies are a symptom of a qualitatively distinct stage in the process of international capital accumulation.

The industrialisation of these countries has to a large extent been facilitated by the internationalisation of production – a process which has involved the relocation of entire industries (such as textiles) as well as specific aspects of industrial production (such as component manufacture and assembly) from industrialised to developing countries. This relocation has been enhanced by techno-logical innovation providing for the disaggregation of the production process so that labour intensive aspect of the production of complex products can be carried out in countries providing cheap and largely unskilled and semi-skilled labour; in the words of some of the most prescient observers of the New International Division of Labour: '[it] entails a growing fragmentation of the production process into a variety of partial operations performed world-wide at different production locations.'[95]

This qualitatively new stage in international capital accumula-tion constitutes a tendency towards redefining not only the position of developing countries, but also the already industrialised ones. The essence of the new division is greater specialisation in the production process and the ensuing facility for location and relocation of productive activity. The process of refinement still continues with investors now drawing the distinction between varying categories of developing countries. For example, some labour intensive industrial activities are nowadays being moved from Hong Kong and Singapore into countries of even lower wage costs such as Malaysia or, more recently, Sri Lanka. The increasing sophistication of this international specialisation depends very much on an ongoing supply of new entrants to the cause of EOI to compensate for the rising production costs in already established production sites.

That it is only in the last few years that we have come to recognise the growth of this New International Division of Labour, despite the fact that its evolution has been taking place for a decade or so, is due in no small part, we would suggest, to the blinkering effect of the rhetoric of dependency theory. The appeal of dependency theory as a critique of modernisation theory caused us to ignore the deficiencies in its own analytical concepts – as we have already, to a certain degree, suggested. In this particular context dependency theory's traditional view of the international division of labour has been very misleading, organised as it was around a dichotomy of a few highly industrialised countries supplying the bulk of the world's manufactured goods on the one hand, and a large number of developing countries acting as the suppliers of the world's raw materials and primary produce on the other. That dependency theory had an essentially geographical or spatial view of the division of labour stems inevitably from what we called its circulationist intellectual origins in an earlier section of this chapter. It is only since the growth of the productionist critiques of dependency theory in the latter part of the 1970s that we have been able to recognise the more complex structure of the international division of labour. With production as our starting point – as opposed to exchange, or circulation – we can put the spatial or geographical components of the division of labour, which we would not wish to dismiss entirely, into their proper but secondary perspective. Production is quite clearly a global, not national, process in the last quarter of the twentieth century.[96] We must treat the international political economy as a whole for the purposes of analysis. Different parts of the productive process interact with one another and change in response to one another, they do not remain geographically distinct or separate.

The recognition of this situation has been important for our understanding of the nature of class formation and the role of the state in the Third World. With the growth of the productionist critique it was no longer satisfactory to assert that the dominant classes of peripheral formations could operate only within a comprador framework. The analysis of class formation in the periphery has become contingent on an understanding of the historical conditions of specific cases of capitalist penetration. In the early part of the 1970s the popular appeal of dependency theory and its subsequent modifications effectively prevented the recognition of such a viewpoint. Rather, the view of class and the state that emanated from dependency theory was one which perceived ruling groups in the Third World – be they industrial/commercial or political/bureaucratic/military and whether knowing or not – as agents of foreign domination. Working from a simple economic determinism, dependency theory perceived Third World countries, given their dependence, as incapable of producing as indigenous dominant class capable of serving other than foreign interests. Such theory does not, for example, allow us to explain the variation in the form of peripheral social formations, from central American banana republics or the impoverished land-locked states of francophone Africa on the one hand, through to the industrialised societies with highly technocratic, authoritarian regimes such as South Korea or Brazil on the other.

Indeed, when we look at how the NICs have increased their share of the world market over the last decade or so, and when we compare that increase with the decline in the share of the non-oil-producing developing countries we can see what one observer has called 'an explosive fragmentation of the old periphery'.[97]

The conception of the state which grew out of dependency theory was one in which the state was a hinge between international capital and Third World social formations – in effect a staging point in the syphoning of surplus.[98] Such a state exhibited a certain autonomy[99] from the indigenous class structure *per se* at the same time as it exhibited control over the production process. In this context the state was seen as a mediator between local and international capital and as a security agent for international capital.[100] This conception of the Third World state, referred to by some as 'overdeveloped', was further characterised by a large military and administration/bureaucratic apparatus inherited from the colonial period and responsible for expropriating and utilising a substantial proportion of the state's economic surplus.[101] The consequence of such activity is that the personnel of the state apparatus who took on these functions were thought to develop a specific class interest of their own. This group has been referred to by Shivji, for example, as the 'bureaucratic bourgeoisie' – a class of well-paid administrators, military officers and/or party officials appropriating or controlling production. Not the least significant outcome of this has been the personal acquisition of private capital.[102] As a nascent class, the bureaucratic bourgeoisie was perceived as having a vested interest in preserving its client role with international capital.

The productionist critiques of dependency theory over the last few years have, however, caused us to refine substantially these essentially reductionist views which clearly offered little or no prospect for the autonomy of the 'political' from the 'economic' and must consequently be rejected as too narrow. We are not suggesting that the dominant economic forces in most Third World states are not exogenous. Rather we wish to question the inappropriateness and restrictiveness of a class analysis based on the notion of a structurally determined bourgeoisie, be it 'bureaucratic' or whatever. Such views of class, especially notions of the burgeoning of a bureaucratic bourgeoisie as a functional or structural class, are simply too narrow. The dominant classes of many Third World states now exhibit significant entrepreneurial and professional sectors as well as bureaucratic and military ones. A bureaucratic section of a dominant class cannot, by itself, be the sole constitutent.[103] Consequently, we need to ask more important questions about a more numerous general dominant class and its relations to the post-colonial state – particular questions about the extent to which the dominant class undermined, as opposed to supported, external interests. As Colin Leys has suggested, in sharp distinction to dependency theorists, the dominant class in many Third World states may in fact use state power for its own purposes and not simply for the benefit of international capital.[104] The state apparatus may well be harnessed on behalf of the national bourgeoisie in any conflict between global and local accumulation. It is also, it goes without saying, capable of utilisation on behalf of international capital when the interests of international capital and those of domestic capital coincide. We have suggested, already, a number of ways in which the state may perform such an important role in our discussion of the political support systems of EOI strategies. The chapters of this book on Thailand, Indonesia, and Philippines and Singapore provide, we feel, ample documentation to back up the assertions made here.[105]

In retrospect such an interpretation appears self-evident, yet to accept such an assumption is not, *ipso facto*, to accept that the way is open for development centred on the economic nationalism of a growing bourgeoisie. It should be noted that these processes may well be limited to specific states or limited in extent to particular sections of individual Third World states. Imperialism, as Warren suggested, does allow for the spread of indigenous capitalist development, but again we should note that such a spread is contingent on variables such as the size of a state's initial factor endowments, the degree of imperial penetration, and so on. We also need to note that there are vast disparities in the allocation of such variables, not only between the three major regions of the Third

World, but also within these regions. It is in this context that attempts to assess which states are, and which states are not, achieving or likely to achieve, significant development are important. It is a strange irony that while the levels of capitalist development in Asia are certainly higher than those in Africa, the level of analysis of these respective rates of development are reversed. There would appear to be a much greater theoretical understanding of the processes taking place in Africa, than Asia, if the recent literature is any yardstick. Particularly insightful has been the debate that has taken place over the nature of capitalist development in Kenya[106] over the last few years and the general line of analysis of Southeast Asia taken in this work has been usefully informed by it.

It behoves us to recognise the important influence of the different historical and socio-economic considerations of respective peripheral states. Such a conclusion leaves the debate at a stage where it is difficult to attempt to formulate generalisations at all, with any degree of certainty, apart from the need to see the dominant class in holistic terms (despite its acknowledged fractions) as opposed to seeing the dominant class in a structural sense of being a specific functioning group, in the fashion favoured by the radical structuralist framework of the dependency theorist in the mid-1970s.

To urge this holistic approach to the dominant class is not, however, to assert a relatively straightforward process of analysis of class formation in the Third World. Discussions of the nature of class formation and the role of the post-colonial state have specific 'levels of analysis' criteria which need to be applied. The national bourgeoisies of Third World states, as we would hope to show in this book in the Southeast Asian context, are in an ambiguous relationship, exhibiting both confrontation and alliance with foreign/ international capital. To talk about a dominant class that interacts with the international environment requires a different perspective to an analysis which focuses on that dominant class's domestic relationship within the specific social formation. In this latter context the class frequently looks less dominant than it does when involved in a process of international interaction. In the Third World, classes can often appear more complex than classes in the advanced industrial societies. This is so because many fractionalised classes exist in societies where pre-capitalist relations of production have not been entirely eliminated, and where capitalism might be at only an immature stage of development. In such contexts, the behaviour of nascent classes is therefore often conditional on their interaction with groups exhibiting forms of group solidarity, other than class affiliation, in a given society.[107]

As with class, then similarly with the role of the post-colonial state, we need to recognise the variety of levels of development and the subsequent range of options open. The peripheral state is neither economically determinist nor politically voluntarist. The economic structure may well be the dominant factor, but it does not preclude the state, or rather the personnel of the state, behaving with varying degrees of political or ideological independence. It is important to avoid the pitfall of attempting to build up some kind of generalised hypotheses around the nature of the state in post-colonial societies. This pitfall is the danger inherent in the creation of one or possibly two abstract models of the 'state-in-general'. It would seem to us methodologically absurd to make generalisations about the peripheral state when our data and knowledge of its functioning in individual cases are almost always inferior to those which we possess about the advanced industrial state, but about which we are far less ready to make sweeping statements.

4 Concluding remarks: Southeast Asia, development theory and the international order

Given the length of this chapter and the wide range of ideas it has tried to canvass, it probably makes sense by way of conclusion to draw out what we feel are the major issues in development thinking that need to be borne in mind in any attempt to understand the current political economy of Southeast Asia. Perhaps the first point that needs to be made related to what we have referred to as the current orthodoxy. Contrary to the views of the initial variant of growth theory that assumed that economic growth led to spin-offs in the implantation of democratic forms of government, the current orthodoxy makes no such assumption. Rather, the corollary of current growth theory is authoritarian government – or what we have referred to as corporatism. The major difference between growth theorists of the last 1950s and those of the present is that earlier theorists were liberal minded optimists while present policy analysts and theorists seem to show little or no anxiety at the strength of the relationship between economic growth and authoritarianism. While growth theory may have a preference for growth with equity and democracy, where possible, it will acquiesce in growth with inequality and authoritarianism where necessary – especially, not to put too fine a point on it, where the preservation of Western interests are concerned. The influence of the political order approaches to political development have been grafted on to growth theory in no uncertain manner.[108]

The other aspect of the current orthodoxy to which we devoted considerable attention is the prominence of Export-Oriented Industrialisation strategies amongst developmental policy-makers, be they in the Third World or in the corridors of the world's major financial institutions – especially the World Bank. We are not suggesting that such strategies are already predominant in all the states to be studied in this work. Whilst EOI might have developed to its purest form in Singapore, Import Substitution Industrialis-ation still largely predominates in Indonesia, Thailand and Malyasia. Rather we are suggesting that the popularity of EOI should be understood by the manner in which it optimises the growth of the New International Division of Labour. It is in this context that we allocated particular importance to the analysis of the nature of class formation and the role of the state in the Third World, that has developed as a response to dependency theory over the last few years. Such analysis has highlighted for us the way in which the state can be harnessed in the interests of international capital, but also more importantly the way in which it can also be used by the dominant class in a given society in any potential conflict of interest between domestic and international capital. Class and state behav-iour is a much more complex phenomenon than was assumed in the early dependency literature.

Similarly, the kind of post-dependency radical theory we have outlined provides the basis, we feel, for a much more complex analysis of the structure of capital be it merchant, industrial or financial – as with the various elements of the dominant class, be they foreign, domestic, industrial, financial, merchant or petty bourgeois. It provides a means of explaining and analysing the huge variety of capitalist transformations occurring in Southeast Asia through the analysis of the specific historical development of domestic relations and forces of production and their relationships with specific forms of foreign capital intrusion.[109] Perhaps the major weakness of radical theory is still its tendency to treat foreign or transnational capital in largely polemical terms and with implicit circulationist assumptions about its function as an exploiting agency. We are, however, striving towards some reconciliation of the productionist and circulationist poles.

It is in this context that we feel the most promising development to flow from the analysis of production rather than exchange is the recent utilisation of the concept of the international division of labour. Within this concept it is the dynamic of accumulation rather than the logic of unequal exchange which determines the levels of industrialisation in specific social formations. The notion of exploi-tative economic relationships between two countries, or the centre and the periphery in common radical parlance, is replaced by the working assumption of a common subjection of *all* nations (including the advanced industrial West) to decisions about the movements of capital taken in those decision-making situations which do not draw on the concept of national interest for their impetus. Consequently, the advanced industrial economies have been progressively divested of more labour-intensive manufacturing processes as profitability considerations force a concentration of capital and technology-intensive industries in high-wage countries. The industrialisation of the Third World is a complex interaction of these waves of industrial investment, technological diffusion and specific developments in the class formation and political structures of individual Third World states. Post-dependency radical theory has yet to provide a systematic analysis of the industrialisation process in Southeast Asia in terms of the relationship between these domestic transformations in the relations of production and the global division of labour. We hope that the chapters in this volume can go some way towards advancing such an analytical tradition.

Notes

1 We use these broad generic terms simply to note the distinction between intellectual traditions emanating from Comte, Durkheim, Weber and Parsons on the one hand, and Marx and Lenin on the other.

2 A view contested by Aidan Foster-Carter. See his 'From Rostow to Gunder Frank? Conflicting Paradigms in the Analysis of Underdevelopment', *World Development* 4(3) 1976.

3 Of the many general reviews see *inter alia*, Higgott, R.A., 'Competing Theories of Development and Underdevelopment: A Recent Intellectual History', *Politics* 13(1) 1978; Bernstein, H., 'Modernisation Theory and the Sociological Study of Development', *Journal of Development Studies* 7(2) 1971 and Tipps, D.C., 'Modernisation Theory and the Comparative Study of Societies: A Critical Perspective', *Comparative Studies in Society and History*, 15, 1973.

4 It is, of course, important not to caricature modernisation theory and, whilst conscious of Raymond Grew's warning, in this context we feel that the ideal-typical dichotomy was indeed at the heart of modernisation theory. See Grew, R., 'More on Modernisation', *Comparative Studies in Society and History*, 14(2) 1980.

5 See, for example, Eisenstadt, S., *Modernisation: Protest and Change*, (New Jersey, Englewood Cliffs, 1966), p.1.

6 Packenham, R., *Liberal America and the Third World*, (New Jersey, Princeton University Press, 1973) points to the importance of Louis Hartz' analysis in this regard.

7 Bodenheimer, S.J., *The Ideology of Developmentalism: The American Paradigm Surrogate for Latin American Studies*, (Beverly Hills, Sage, 1971).

8 Packenham, *op. cit.*

9 The list of economists of this school is simply too numerous to mention. See above all Rostow, W.W., *Politics and the Stages of Growth*, (Cambridge, Cambridge University Press, 1960). For a critical review of the leading luminaries of the diffusionist school see Nafziger, W., 'A Critique of Development Economics in the U.S.', *Journal of Development Studies*, 13(1), 1976.

10 Lerner, D., *The Passing of Traditional Society*, (New York, Free Press, 1968).

11 Again the literature is too numerous to list. It is listed and analysed in Higgott, R.A., 'From Modernisation Theory to Public Policy: Continuity and Change in the Political Science of Political Development', *Studies in Comparative International Development* 15(4) 1980. See also Leys, C., 'Introduction' in Leys (ed.), *Politics and Change in Developing Countries*, (Cambridge, Cambridge University Press, 1969).

12 Of the numerous critiques to emerge see *inter alia*: Frank, A.G., *The Sociology of Development and the Underdevelopment of Sociology*, (London, Pluto Press, 1971); O'Brien, D.C., 'Modernisation, Order and the Erosion of a Democratic Ideal: American Political Science 1960-1970', *Journal of Development Studies* 8(2) 1972; Bernstein, *op. cit.* For specific critiques of the tradition-modernity dichotomy see Gusfield, J.R., 'Tradition and Modernity: Misplaced Polarities in the Study of Social Change', *American Journal of Sociology* 72, 1967 and Kothari, R., 'Tradition and Modernity Revisited', *Government and Opposition* 3(2) 1968.

13 See, for example, Grossholtz, J., *The Philippines*, (Boston Little Brown, 1964); Pye, L., *Southeast Asia's Political Systems*, (New Jersey, Prentice Hall, 1974) and Riggs, F., *Thailand: The Modernisation of a Bureaucratic Polity*, (Honolulu, East West Center Press, 1966).

14 See Willner, R., 'Neo-traditional Accommodation to Political Independence: the Case of Indonesia' in McAlister, J. (ed.), *Southeast Asia, the Politics of National Integration*, (New York, Random, 1973). Indeed, throughout the McAlister volume the dominant theme is the struggle between traditional and modern political culture. More recently see Mulder, N., *Everyday Life in Thailand*, (Bangkok, Editions Duang Karoul, 1978), for a culturalist approach.

15 See Bell, P., 'Cycles of Class Struggle in Thailand', *Journal of Contemporary Asia* 8(1) 1978, and Vengkataramani, M.S., ' "The United States and Thailand": The Anatomy of Super-power policy-making, 1948-1963', *International Studies* 12(1) 1973.

16 O'Brien, *op. cit.*

17 See Huntington, S., 'Political Development and Political Decay', *World Politics* 17(3) 1965 and *Political Order in Changing Societies*, (New Haven, Yale University Press, 1968).

18 Pool, I. de Sola (ed.), *Contemporary Political Science: Towards Empirical Theory*, (New York, McGraw-Hill, 1967), p.26.

19 These crises were: legitimacy, identity, participation, penetration and distribution. See Binder, L. *et al.*, *Crises and Sequences in Political Development*, (Princeton, Princeton University Press, 1971).

20 See Kesselman, M., 'Order or Movement: The Literature of Political Development as Ideology', *World Politics* 26(1) 1973.

21 This approach is best expressed in Moertopo, A., *The Acceleration and Modernization of 25 Years Development*, (Jakarta, Yayasan Proklamasi, 1973), and Moertopo, A., *Strategi Politik Nasional*, (Jakarta, Yayasan Proklamasi, 1974).

22 Other examples of this ideological approach are to be found in Marcos, F. *et al.*, *Towards the New Society: Essays on Aspects of Philippines Development*, (Manila, National Media Production Centre, 1974), and *National Operations Council: The May 13 Tragedy; A Report*, (Kuala Lumpur, NOC, 1969). On Sarit and the Thai case, Thak Chaloemitiavana, *Thailand: The Politics of Despotic Paternalism*, (Bangkok, Thai Khadi Research Institute, 1979).

23 This ideological connection is pointed out by Ward, K., 'Indonesia's Modernization: Ideology and Practice' in Mortimer, R. (ed.), *Showcase State*, (Sydney, A & R., 1973).

24 Apart from Huntington's work, this theme is stressed by Johnson, C., *Revolutionary Change*, (Boston, Little Brown, 1966), and Riggs, F., *Administration in Developing Countries: The Theory of Prismatic Society* (Boston, Houghton Mifflin, 1964).

25 For examples of this position see Myint, H., *Southeast Asia's Economy: Development Policies in the 1970s*, (Harmondsworth, Penguin, 1972), and Arndt, H., 'Development and Equality: the Indonesia Case', *World Development* 3(2/3) 1975.

26 See Ho Kwon Ping, 'Profits and Poverty in the Plantations', *Far Eastern Economic Review*, 11.7.80 and 'Thailand, Broken Rice Bowl', *ibid.*, 1.12.78. For a more general look at the problem see Doner, R., 'The Development of Agri business in Thailand', *Bulletin of Concerned Asian Scholars* 6(1) 1974 and George, S., *How the Other Half Dies*, (Harmondsworth, Penguin, 1976).

27 See Hewison's chapter of this book: 'The State and Capitalist Development in Thailand'.

28 Feldman, E.J., 'Comparative Public Policy', *Comparative Politics* 10(2) 1978, pp.228-9.

29 Heclo, H., 'Policy Analysis', *British Journal of Political Science* 2(1) 1972, p.87.

30 See Higgott, *op. cit.*, pp.35-88.

31 For a good illustration of this emphasis in the African context see Rothchild, D. and Curry, R., *Scarcity, Choice and Public Policy in Middle Africa*, (Berkeley, University of California Press, 1978). See also Grindle, M.S., *Politics and Policy Implementation in the Third World*, (New Jersey, Princeton University Press, 1980).

32 Huntington, *Political Order*, *op. cit.*, pp.1-2.

33 Chomsky, N., *At War With Asia*, (London, Fontana, 1971), pp.44-7.

34 See, for example, Rothstein, R., *The Weak in the World of the Strong: Developing Countries in the International System*, (New York, Columbia University Press, 1977), p.199.

35 Lewis, W.A., *The Theory of Economic Growth*, (London, Allen and

Unwin, 1955); Meier, G. (ed.), *Leading Issues in Economic Development*, (Oxford, Oxford University Press, 1970); Myint, H., *Southeast Asia's Economy*, (Harmondsworth, Penguin, 1972); Bauer, P.T., *Dissent on Development*, (London, Weidenfeld & Nicholson, 1976).

36 See the review of the rise and demise of development economics by Dudley Seers, 'The Birth, Life and Death of Development Economics', *Development and Change* 10(4) 1979.

37 A comprehensive collection of the economist/political science critique of the Sukarno regime is Tan, T.K. (ed.), *Sukarno's Guided Indonesia*, (Brisbane, Jacaranda, 1967). In Chapter 11, Arndt, H., 'Economic Disorder and the Task Ahead', looks forward to a return to the freeing of the market and the reconstruction of the Indonesian economy on the basis of rational economic decision-making. McCawley, P., *Industrialization in Indonesia*, (Occasional Paper No. 13, Development Studies Centre, Australian National University, 1979), continues to deplore political and government intervention in economic planning, especially in relation to state subsidy and protection of important substitution industry.

38 See Chapter 5.

39 For a view of the political economy/economics debate from an economist's perspective see Glassburner, B., 'Political Economy and the Suharto Regime', *Bulletin of Indonesian Economic Studies* 14(3) 1978.

40 The central dependency work in this debate is Mortimer, R., 'Indonesia: Growth or Development' in Mortimer, R. (ed.), *op. cit.*

41 Arndt's views are best set out in the earlier version of his previously cited paper on development and equality presented as a work in progress paper in the Department of Economics, Research School of Pacific Studies, Australian National University, 1974.

42 For the best review of the debate about growth and equality see Adelman, I. and Taft Morris, C., *Economic Growth and Social Equity in Developing Countries*, (Palo Alto, Stanford University Press, 1973).

43 One of the most cohesive and influential groups of analysts dealing with Southeast Asia, and particularly Indonesia, is located within the Research School of Pacific Studies at the Australian National University. *The Bulletin of Indonesia Economic Studies*, until recently edited by Heinz Arndt, has been an important barometer of developments within the growth economics school and for this reason is worthy of close attention.

44 Sundrum, R.M. and Booth, E.A., 'Income Distribution in Indonesia: Trends and Determinants', in Garnaut, R.G. and McCawley, P. (eds), *Indonesia: Dualism, Growth and Poverty*, (Canberra, Australian National University, 1980). Glassburner, B., 'Indonesia's New Economic Policy and Its Socio-Political Implications', in Jackson, K. (ed.), *Political Power and Communications in Indonesia*, (Berkeley, University of California Press, 1978).

45 One of the few who have enthusiastically embraced the liberal reformist approach is the political scientist Phillip Eldridge. See his *Indonesia and Australia: The Politics of Aid and Development Since 1966*, (Canberra,

Development Studies Centre, Australian National University, 1979).

46 McCawley, P., 'Stability, Equity, Growth and Devaluation', in Garnaut and McCawley (eds), *op. cit.*

47 Perhaps one of the strongest statements of advocacy of EOI policies is to be found in a collection of essays edited by Ross Garnaut. See Garnaut, R. (ed.), *ASEAN in a Changing Pacific and World Economy*, (Canberra, Australian National University Press, 1980).

48 See especially Almond, G. and Powell, B.J., *Comparative Politics: A Developmental Approach*, (Boston, Little Brown, 1966).

49 The analyses of Riggs, F., *Thailand, op. cit.*, and Wilson, D., *Politics in Thailand*, (Ithaca, Cornell University Press, 1962) are based upon the concept of a loosely structured society characterised by personal interaction between individuals. This concept, based clearly upon structural-functional notions of roles and norms was first applied specifically to Thailand by John Embree in his article, 'Thailand – A Loosely Structured Social System', *American Anthropologist* 52(2) 1950.

50 Jackson, K., 'Bureaucratic Polity: A Theoretical Framework for the Analysis of Power and Communications in Indonesia' and 'The Political Implications of Structure and Culture in Indonesia', and Emmerson, D., 'The Bureaucracy in Political Context: Weakness in Strength' in Jackson, K., *op. cit.*

51 Lande, C., 'Parties and Politics in the Philippines', *Asian Survey* 8(9) 1968.

52 The conflict between political forces representing modern, rational, secular, political values and those representing traditional, patrimonial values as a central theme in Indonesian political history is treated by Crouch, H., 'Patrimonialism and Indonesian Politics', *World Politics* 31(4) 1979 and by Feith, H., 'Political Control, Class Formation and Legitimacy in Suharto's Indonesia', *Kabar Seberang* 2, 1977. See also Roth, G., 'Personal Rulership, Patrimonialism and Empire Building in New States', *World Politics* 20(2) 1968.

53 See Prebisch, R., *Towards a Dynamic Development Policy for Latin America*, (New York, United Nations, 1963), and Love, J., 'Raul Prebisch and the Doctrine of Unequal Exchange', *Latin American Research Review* 15, November 1980.

54 Baran, P., *The Political Economy of Growth*, (Harmondsworth, Penguin, 1957).

55 It would be too arduous a task to list the voluminous amounts of recent Latin American dependency literature. By far the most comprehensive review of Latin American theories of dependency to date is Gabriel di Palma's 'Dependency: A Formal Theory of Underdevelopment or a Methodology for the Analysis of Concrete situations?', *World Development* 6, 1978. For a general review of the literature and themes pursued in this section see Higgott, R.A., 'Beyond the Sociology of Underdevelopment: An Historiographical Analysis of Marxist and Dependency Theories of Development and Underdevelopment', *Social Analysis*, 7 April 1981.

56 Of the numerous critiques couched in this vein see Nove, A., 'On

Reading André Gunder Frank', *Journal of Development Studies* 10(3/4) 1974. Lall, S., 'Is "Dependence" a useful concept in analysing underdevelopment?', *World Development* 3, 1975 pp.801-8 and Ray, D., 'The Dependency Model of Latin American Underdevelopment: Three Basic Fallacies', *Journal of Inter-American Studies and World Affairs* 15, 1973.

57 For a discussion of these linkages see Petras, J. and Trachte, K., 'Liberal, Structural and Radical Approaches to Political Economy: An Assessment and an Alternative' in Petras, J., *Critical Perspectives on Social Class in the Third World*, (New York, Monthly Review Press, 1978).

58 See Laclau, E., 'Feudalism and Capitalism in Latin America', *New Left Review* 67, 1971.

59 Warren, B., 'Imperialism and Capitalist Industrialisation', *New Left Review* 81, September-October 1973.

60 Cardoso, F.H., 'Associated Dependent Development: Theoretical and Practical Implications', in Stepan, A. (ed.), *Authoritarian Brazil*, (New Haven, Yale University Press, 1973).

61 Clearly colonial economic penetration based upon political control of trade and forced deliveries of crops and labour worked through and depended upon existing social and political structures. Even in the period of corporate plantation production, wage levels could be kept low because they were not intended as a social wage – part of the burden of maintaining the families of workers was borne by the subsistence village sector. However, we do not wish to push this concept of dualism to the extent that some writers have by claiming that capitalism may permanently shore up pre-capitalist modes. Articulation of the two modes at the same time involves the introduction of wage labour, commodity production and money which erodes the old structures. See, for example, Elson, R., 'The Cultivation System and Agricultural Involution', *Monash University, Centre of South East Asian Studies Working Paper* 14 (n.d.) for criticisms of Geertz' thesis that the intensification of colonial exploitation under the cultural system in Java actually created a retrogression to homogenous, communally dominated village social structures outlined in Geertz, C., *Agricultural Involution*, (University of California Press, 1963).

62 See the excellent review of the 'Sucking out of Surplus' arguments in Mack, A. and Leaver, R., 'Radical Theories of Underdevelopment: An Assessment' in Mack, A., Doyle, U. and Plant, D. (eds), *Imperialism: Intervention and Development*, (London, Croom Helm, 1979).

63 Especially Amin, S., *Unequal Development: An Essay on the Social Formation of Peripheral Capitalism* (Sussex, Harvester Press 1976); Emmanuel, A., *Unequal Exchange: A Study of the Imperialism of Trade*, (London, New Left Books, 1972) and Wallerstein, I., *The Capitalist World Economy*, (Cambridge, Cambridge University Press, 1979).

64 For an excellent discussion of this concept see Mack, A., 'Theories of Imperialism: The European Perspective', *Journal of Conflict Resolution* 18, 1974.

65 Wallerstein, *op. cit.*, Chapter 4.

66 Amin, *op. cit.*, especially Chapter 5.

67 See, for example, Amin, *op. cit.*, and Wallerstein, I., 'The Three Stages of African Involvement in the World Economy' in Gutkind, P. and Wallerstein, I. (eds), *The Political Economy of Contemporary Africa*, (Beverly Hills, Sage, 1976).

68 For a good discussion of the distinction between productionist and circulationist approaches see Crompton, R. and Gubbay, J., *Economy and Class Structure*, (London, Macmillan, 1977), especially Chapter 1.

69 See Foster-Carter, A., 'The Modes of Production Controversy', *New Left Review* 107, 1978, p.55.

70 See the excellent critique of Warren by Alain Leipitz 'Marx or Rostow', *New Left Review*, 132, March-April 1982.

71 See, for example, the critiques established by Leys, C., 'Underdevelopment and Dependency: Critical Notes', *Journal of Contemporary Asia* 7(1) 1977; Phillips, A., 'The Concept of Development', *Review of African Political Economy* 8, January-April 1977; Luton, H., 'The Satellite Metropolis Model: A Critique', *Theory and Society* 3(4) 1976 and Roxborough, I., 'Dependency Theory and the Sociology of Development: Some Theoretical Problems', *West African Journal of Sociology and Political Science* 9(2) 1976.

72 *Showcase State, op. cit.* was certainly not the first work to confront the Weberian/Modernisation theory orthodoxy. There have been many scholars of Southeast Asia who have worked within a broad Marxist tradition, or who have at least attempted to integrate political and economic factors into their analysis. See Wertheim, W., *Indonesian Society in Transition*, (The Hague, van Hoeve, 1964). Even Clifford Geertz offered a dependency type explanation of Indonesia's economic backwardness when he argued that Dutch colonialism had syphoned out the wealth generated by the sugar industry to finance manufacturing industry in Holland. In contrast Japan had developed because the surplus squeezed from agricultural produce in the late nineteenth century had been invested in manufacture *within* Japan. See Geertz, *op. cit.* For a discussion of theoretical approaches to the question of Thai political history see Anderson, B., *Studies of the Thai State*, paper submitted to the conference on The State of Thai Studies, Chicago, 30 March 1978. Of other early influential attempts to apply dependency theory to Southeast Asia see Bell, P., *The Historical Determinants of Underdevelopment in Thailand*, (New Haven, Yale University Economic Growth Center, Discussion Paper No. 84, 1970) and Resnick, S., 'The Decline of Rural Industry Under Export Expansion: A Comparison of Burma, Thailand and the Philippines, 1870-1938', *Journal of Economic History*, 30, 1970.

73 Works deriving inspiration from dependency critiques are numerous indeed. The journals, *Bulletin of Concerned Asian Scholars* and *Prisma* constitute the main course of works which combine elements of dependency theory with what we might call a reformist liberal/modernisation approach. *The Journal of Contemporary Asia*, on the other hand,

has generally been the forum for the interface of dependency theory with more orthodox Marxist theories of imperialism and class.

74 Robison, R., *Capitalism and the Bureaucratic State in Indonesia*, unpublished Ph.D. Thesis, Sydney University, 1977, pp.416-47.

75 Pizzia, R. and Sinsawasdi, N., *Thailand: Student Activism and Political Change*, (Bangkok, Editions Duang Kamol, 1974).

76 Chenery, H. *et al.*, *Redistribution with Growth*, (London, Oxford University Press, 1974), and Ul Haq, M., *The Poverty Curtain*, (New York, Columbia University Press, 1976) are the most fundamental statements of these two approaches.

77 Hayter, T., *The Creation of World Poverty*, (London, Pluto Press, 1981), p.90.

78 Cox, R., 'Ideologies and the New International Economic Order', *International Organisation*, 30(2) 1979, discusses these perspectives.

79 Righter, R., 'World Bank Betrays Poor Says Official', *The Sunday Times*, 7 March 1982, p.10.

80 See Hollis Chenery's publication for the World Bank, *Structural Change and Development Policy*, (New York, Oxford University Press, 1979).

81 *World Development Report*, 1981, (New York, Oxford University Press, 1981), p.4.

82 Balassa, B., 'Structural Adjustment Policies in Developing Countries', *World Development*, 10(1) 1982, p.23.

83 *World Development Report*, *op. cit.*, p.87.

84 *Ibid.*, p.71.

85 *Ibid.*, p.76.

86 Hill, H., 'The Philippine Economy Under Marcos: A Balance Sheet', *Australian Outlook*, 36(3) 1982, pp.32-9.

87 *World Development Report*, *op. cit.*, p.5.

88 *Ibid.*, p.98.

89 Hill, *op. cit.*

90 *World Development Report*, *op. cit.*, p.76.

91 *Ibid.*, p.78.

92 Feith, H., 'Repressive-Developmentalist Regimes in Asia: Old Strengths, New Vulnerabilities', *Prisma* 19, December 1980; Collier, D., 'The Bureaucratic Authoritarian Model', in Collier, D. (ed.), *The New Authoritarianism in Latin America*, (Princeton, Princeton University Press, 1979); Petras, J., 'Neo-Fascism: Capital Accumulation and Class Struggle in the Third World', *Journal of Contemporary Asia*, 10(1/2) 1980; Stepan, A., *The State and Society: Peru in Comparative Perspective*, (Princeton, Princeton University Press, 1978) and Higgott, R., 'The State in Africa: Some Thoughts on the Future Drawn From the Past' in Shaw, T. (ed.), *Africa Projected: From Dependence to Self-Reliance by the Year 2000?*, (London, Macmillan, 1984).

93 It is worth noting that Huntington's 'Political Development and Political Decay', *op. cit.* was first published as early as 1965.

94 Pahl, R. and Winckler, J.T., 'Corporatism in Britain' in Raison, T. (ed.), *The Corporate State – Reality or Myth?*, (London, Centre for Studies in Public Policy, 1976), p.6.

95 Frobel, F., Heinrichs, J. and Krey, O., 'The New International Division of Labour', *Social Science Information*, 17(1) 1978, p.123. This article is an excellent summary of the New International Division of Labour. See also, however, by the same authors 'Export Oriented Industrialisation of Underdeveloped Countries', *Monthly Review*, November 1978 and Leipietz, A., 'Towards Global Fordism', *New Left Review*, 132, March-April, 1982.

96 For an excellent discussion see Barkan, D., 'The Internationalization of Capital: An Alternative Approach', *Latin American Perspectives* 8(3/4) 1981.

97 Leipietz, *op. cit.*, p.39.

98 See, for example, Alavi, H., 'The State in Post-Colonial Societies: Pakistan and Bangladesh', *New Left Review* 74, 1972; Saul, J., 'The State in Post-Colonial Societies: Tanzania', *Socialist Register* 1974; Leys, C., *Underdevelopment in Kenya: The Political Economy of Colonialism*, (London, Heinemann, 1974); Shivji, I., *Class Struggles in Tanzania*, (London, Heinemann, 1976) and Petras, J., 'New Perspectives on Imperialism; Social Classes in the Periphery', *Journal of Contemporary Asia* 5(3) 1975.

99 See Miliband, R., *Marxism and Politics*, (London, Oxford University Press, 1977), pp.106ff.

100 Petras, *op. cit.*, p.302.

101 See, for example, Ake, C., 'Explanatory Notes on the Political Economy of Africa', *Journal of Modern Africa Studies* 14(1) 1976.

102 Shivji, I., *op. cit.*

103 See Sklar, R., 'The Nature of Class Domination in Africa', *Journal of Modern African Studies* 17(4) 1979, pp.544-5.

104 Leys, C., 'Capital Accumulation, Class Formation and Dependency: The Significance of the Kenyan Case', *Socialist Register*, 1978, pp.251-3.

105 See also Caporaso, J., 'The States Role in Third World Economic Growth', *Annals of the American Academy of Political Science* 459, January 1982.

106 For a useful review of this debate which has occurred through the pages of the *Review of African Political Economy* see Chapman, P., *The Development Debate: Some Theoretical Implications of the Kenyan Case*, MA Thesis, Graduate School of Arts and Social Studies, Sussex University, 1980.

107 Some of those problems are well discussed in Ian Roxborough's *Theories of Underdevelopment*, (London, Macmillan, 1979), pp.72-8.

108 Donal Cruise O'Brien in his study of American political science in the 1960s makes the distinction between the liberal-minded optimism of the Social Science Research Council (SSRC) Committee on Comparative Politics under the chairmanship of Gabriel Almond in its early days and its order-oriented focus in the later days under the growing influence of Lucien Pye and Samuel Huntington. See O'Brien, 'Modernisation, Order and the Erosion of a Democratic Ideal . . . ', *op. cit.*

109 We have yet to see any substantial attempt to analyse the historical development of any specific country in Southeast Asia using mode of

production and social formation as the central theoretical concepts. Two very tentative steps in this direction are: Gordon, A., 'Stages in the Development of Java's Socio-Economic Formations, 700-1979', *Journal of Contemporary Asia* 9(2) 1979 and Elliott, D., 'The Socio-Economic Formation of Modern Thailand', *Journal of Contemporary Asia* 8(1) 1978.

PART II *History and society*

2 A critical appraisal of historians of Malaya: the theory of society implicit in their work

PATRICK SULLIVAN –
Australian National University

i) Introduction

This chapter critically examines the writing of Malay history from the earliest texts to the present day, uncovers and criticises a common view of society in these writings, and examines the way this view has been transmitted through generations of historians. No history writing is possible without a theory of what constitutes society and what changes it. It is my contention that the sociological theory implicit in historical works on the Malay Peninsula takes the manifestations of society, social institutions such as law and sovereignty, for the whole substance. Institutions are seen as having an ideal, natural and traditional mode of functioning and implicit in this view is the assumption that their purpose is the perpetuation of these same institutions. Necessary, also, is the antithesis of ideal functioning – deviance.[1] The origin of this approach is twofold: firstly, the sources themselves direct the historian's attention to institutional aspects of society. Secondly, the social and political position of the historian, whether court chronicler, imperialist administrator, or modern intellectual, requires (to a greater or lesser extent in each case) a politically conservative viewpoint, one that places great importance on constituted authority. This is evident in the earlier cases, but is contentious when applied to modern researchers. Nevertheless, the fact that Asian Studies have been founded on political involvement in the subject of study must lead scholars to question the origins and the implications of their sociological perspective.

Because the view of society that is prevalent in Malayan history writing offers a static morphology instead of a system of underlying structure, it is singularly incapable of dealing theoretically with social change. Change, which should be the stock-in-trade of the historian, must be explained by factors extrinsic to the social system such as accident or personality. It is a theory, also, that neglects the experience of the people, their social and economic relations and the conflicting interests embodied in them. Instead, it celebrates the imposition of a changeless structure of authority over the historical landscape and is incapable of revealing the vibrant interaction that is the real basis of societies.

Before examining the nature and origins of the functionalist perspective in Malayan history it is necessary to set out my view of the purpose of history writing, its relationship to social theory and the kind of social theory I consider useful. This done, the chapter will examine three stages of history writing in Malaya: (1) traditional writings and their uses for both traditional and more recent historians; (2) the works of colonial scholar-administrators; and (3) post-colonial works. Although much of what I will say is true of Malayan history writing in general, I will be concentrating on the construction of Perak history up to the early years of British intervention. The final section of the chapter will explore the possibility, and difficulties, of a more useful approach to the reconstruction of past societies.

ii) The purpose of history and its relationship to social theory

Historical works cannot simply be a neutral record of 'what happened' for two reasons. Firstly, because the historian is selective, he or she chooses to transmit the most important facts and events. The question then arises – important to whom? In the case of Malaya, history has usually been written by and for the ruling class to legitimate its rule.[2] Secondly, facts and events do not exist independently of consciousness. As Thompson points out, the simple statement of fact 'King Zed died in 1100 A.D.' embodies a concept of kingship which cannot exist without a set of related concepts.[3] It often unconsciously occurs that the concept 'king' is made to subsume such titles as the 'Yang di Pertuan Agong', and so further assumptions are made about the relationship of 'our' society to 'their' society, and an act of appropriation is perpetrated by linguistic substitution. These assumptions about the structure of society (and of reality), which are necessary for the selection and ordering of data, tend to be 'proven' by the presentation of the same historical facts. It is in this sense that history writing must be seen as always partial, never neutral. Even the most insignificant story of past events must, by what it includes and leaves out, adopt a partisan stance towards the existing social order.

History writing, then, cannot escape the necessity for a theory of society; if this theory does not explicitly inform a particular work, it is implicit throughout it and, not being subject to debate, is quite likely to be inconsistent or plainly wrong.[4] Many writers have put forward a plea for the unity of the human disciplines.[5] Anthropology, sociology, history and philosophy, for example, are founded on discredited distinctions between primitive and complex, past and present, thought and reality. Given this unity of subject matter, just as history cannot escape the need for theory neither can theory ignore the demands of the 'empirical' disciplines such as history.[6] Theories of society that ignore history distort reality, presenting a specific historical conjuncture as a timeless, natural and inevitable fact; they are conservative in the true sense of the word. The kind of theory which I have labelled functionalist, has been especially guilty of ignoring history, and yet exists in a complex relationship to the process of writing history, both drawing on it and informing it.

The overwhelming concern of many historians with relationships within the aristocracy, affairs of state, and institutions of violence and control has stemmed from the source of their patronage (similar institutional structures) and leads to the 'common-sense' assumption that social institutions *are* society. It is this assumption that is the basis of the sociological theories of Talcott Parsons and Radcliffe-Brown. Their method of analysing a particular society is to lay out a morphology of the most readily observed mechanisms of control of human beings, and it is by these mechanisms that a society is said to function. The concept 'function' implies a purpose. Since functionalist methodology is necessarily synchronic, the only purpose that can be ascribed to the social structure is self-perpetuation. This approach, then, favours those with an interest in preserving the particular structure described, however much certain of its elements (groups of real human beings) may be adversely affected. Historians of Malaya usually concentrate on sovereignty and the state, for reasons that will be examined, so when called upon to make theoretical generalisations about their work they almost automatically fall into the functionalist approach. In this way history and sociology reinforce each other in the service of the status quo.[7]

There is, of course, an alternative approach to both history and sociology. It is the description and analysis of social relations as opposed to social institutions, and it must embody a concept of 'dynamic' – a system in motion even while reproducing itself over time. This alternative receives attention in the conclusion to this chapter. Two themes inform this work: one is the uncovering of an inexplicit view of society in the writings examined, and relating this view to the writer's social and political position. This is inevitably subject to discussion as contentions can be supported but not conclusively proved. The other is the revisionist task of questioning the standard interpretation of events. This is an easier task and, although not my main purpose, a necessary one if the study of Malaya is to free itself of the influence of colonial scholarship. The two themes are complimentary if they are viewed as a contribution to a reconstruction of Malay history, and to a revolution in methodology and theory necessary if that reconstruction is to succeed.

iii) Traditional Malay tests and their uses

Traditional Malay writings are frustrating for the social historian, firstly because of their paucity, secondly in their subject matter, and thirdly in their accuracy. Although Winstedt, in his *History of Classical Malay Literature* tells us 'the Malay Peninsula is particularly rich in histories',[8] he lists only eight, and several of these draw on each other.[9] This replication is also a problem with the other major written source on pre-colonial social relations, the legal texts. The Malacca laws are, according to Hooker 'the original of all the island South-East Asian texts ...'.[10] They reappear as the *Undang-Undang Kerajaan* of Perak, Johor and Pahang,[11] the *Undang-Undang* of Kedah,[12] and part of the laws of Selangor.[13] When this overlapping of manuscript sources is taken into account, the amount of material shrinks to even less than that of its apparent proportions. Although it may be argued that one good source is worth hundreds of poor ones, in our case the subject matter of the material promotes a one-sided view of traditional Malay society. Furthermore, this ruling class view of society, which presents the superstructure as the whole, is notorious for idealising even the limited subject matter it encompasses.

Winstedt's comment on the *Misa Melayu* that 'much space is devoted to court ceremonies, marriages, funerals and picnics ...' is true of most Malay texts, even the popular *Hikayat Hang Tuah*.[14] Much space in *hikayat* is given over to official genealogies.[15] Legal texts also tend to concentrate on the right and duties of rulers, paying much attention to trade and little to agriculture.[16] As Hooker points out, there is a danger of assuming that existing legal texts constituted all the law there was. Actually there was a strong and conflicting unwritten legal tradition; this, and the area of 'private law', was a matter of local custom. The primary concern of Southeast Asian legal texts was to set out the nature of sovereignty.[17]

Both the legal texts and *hikayat* were written for, and sometimes by, the Malay rulers.[18] The *Misa Melayu* and the *Tufhat al Nafis* were written by the aristocrats Raja Culan and Raja Ali of Riau respectively. Maxwell's Perak manuscripts, on which he based part of his 'History of Perak from Native Sources' were obtained from Bendahara Osman[19] and Raja Haji Yahya, a descendant of Raja

Culan.[20] Often in these traditional works genealogies are manufactured,[21] and, as Barbara Andaya has noted, events in which the ruler acted in an unbecoming manner are glossed over.[22] Distortions, sometimes of ludicrous dimensions, frequently occur.[23] Malay historians were not concerned with whether a ruler, or his actions, were fictional. They were concerned with presenting an image of the ideal ruler. 'It is the re-shaping of historical reality in terms of this ideal which is the concern of a text such as the Misa Melayu.'[24] Historical reality, of course, cannot be reshaped, although historical myth may be perpetuated. What Andaya has drawn attention to here is in agreement with Sujatmoko's suggestion that Malay and Javanese historiography had a non-historical function.[25] In reality, that function was to give traditional rulers a place as natural as the sun, the moon and the stars, and to misrepresent the means and the consequences of their rule for their slaves and subjects.

Poor in quantity and quality (from the social historian's point of view) and overwhelmingly concerned with court ceremonies, aristocratic lineages and the prerogatives of rulers, these texts should be used cautiously. Yet Hooker is not alone in assuring us that the legal texts 'truly reflect the historical reality of the Islamic legal word [sic] in South-East Asia'.[26] It is on the basis of such sources that the 'Malay World' is constructed – geographically, culturally and even psychologically. Said's criticism of Orientalism is truly applicable to its Malay manifestation:

> It remains the professional orientalist's job to piece together a portrait, a restored picture as it were, of the Orient or the Oriental; fragments ... supply the material, but the narrative shape, continuity, and figure are constructed by the scholar, for whom scholarship consists of circumventing the unruly (unoccidental) non-history of the Orient with orderly chronicle, portraits, and plots.[27]

Undoubtedly a common language, religious tradition and close contact throughout the ages means there was, in a sense, a Malay World. Yet 'our' Malay World is largely based on a homogeneity of *texts*, not social practice, and these texts have been 'doctored' in favour of the ruling class. Common representations of the state between societies often mask fundamentally different social relations.[28] It is a methodological error to assume a homogeneous culture from apparently common state ideologies. Such comparisons can only be made on the basis of an analysis of social practice.

It is clear that the concerns of traditional texts lend themselves to a functionalist social analysis. The social relations of the working population are harder to discern and 'the real Malay' appears in later scholars' work as an ideal-typic caricature. It is in the absence of an analysis of social relations that Gullick is able to tell us that Malaya was a two-class society, the rulers and the ruled.[29] The ruled, to judge from traditional texts, are not much more than a necessary inference from the fact of rulers,[30] and to represent them we have only the ruler's perception. Wilkinson may have been the first to offer a portrait of the fiercely loyal Malay *rakyat* drawn from traditional literature.[31] Rubin carries on this tradition on the assumption that 'nothing is more revealing about a people's concepts of right behaviour than the descriptions of admirable characters and noteworthy events contained in *their own* historical writings'.[32] Building on C.C. Brown's introduction to the *Malay Annals*, Rubin tells us the distinguishing characteristics of the Malay are (1) admiration of quick wit in dealing with foreigners, (2) concern for genealogy, and (3) loyalty to the ruler. Courage and fighting spirit were also admired.[33] The authors and patrons of Malay manuscripts would certainly have nothing to quarrel with here, but would those so characterised have agreed with this representation? There are frequent indications in other sources that it has little truth.[34]

This fantastic reconstruction of the Malay psyche as a substitute for an examination of social relations reaches its apogee in Shelley Errington's literary analysis of the *Hikayat Hang Tuah*. She finds it impossible to situate this work in its social context because the social structure of Malacca, where the *Hikayat* was composed at the end of the sixteenth century, is not susceptible to the kind of analysis developed by the Radcliffe-Brown school,[35] and therefore cannot be understood at all.[36] This uncritical acceptance of the genesis of the text allows her to suggest that the *Hikayat Hang Tuah* is 'predicated on the notion of the sultan as an organizing principle for experience'. He was a symbol in the sense of 'an object or event within the world which serves to make sense of experience'.[37] Like the Javanese ruler, as 'the unpredicated reference point around which everything else was organised; he provided the terms in which the world made sense'.[38] For the Malay, then, the sultan performed an ontological function which in our society is filled by Newtonian physics.[39] Although Errington's work is explicitly textual analysis rather than a social or historical study, it shows clearly how the Oriental becomes the Occident's intellectual plaything, and ruling class perceptions are uncritically exchanged in this process.

Indigenous texts, then, are used on the one hand to depict an ideal state mechanism, on the other an ideal Malay mentality. Yet are these indigenous texts completely useless as sources for a history of the Malay people, or have they simply been misused? Wilkinson suggested that we may not be specially interested in the fate of Tun Mi Hairy Caterpillar [a noble at the court of Sultan Mahmud Shah in the *Sejarah Melayu*] . . . but we are deeply concerned in the setting of the tales – the details that come out incidentally . . . . Such matters are of very real importance to the scientific historian who cares more about the condition of the people than about the biographies of individual kings.[40]

Bottoms, who cites this passage, also feels that, if the material is examined with imaginative care, social historians may produce such 'entrancing titles' as 'A Social History of the Malays' and 'Everyday Life in Fifteenth Century Malacca'.[41] My own feeling is that, armed with a dynamic theory of social relations rather than a concern for timeless structure, status and personality, a reappraisal of traditional texts would be fruitful. Theory, in a sense, 'creates' empirical facts out of material prior approaches found irrelevant, redundant or simply puzzling. Yet the kind of work Wilkinson and Bottoms looked forward to has yet to be attempted. To understand why, we must turn to the work of the colonial scholar/administrators, who found traditional history writing peculiarly appropriate for their own purposes and whose 'work laid the foundation for Malay studies and to whom the modern student owes a particular debt.'[42]

iv) Colonial scholar/administrators

The works referred to as traditional histories (which for my purposes include *hikayat, sejarah, silisilah* and *undang-undang*) were collated and translated by European scholar/administrators for several interrelated reasons. Firstly, there was the orientalist project itself in which the 'Orient' was constructed as an object of exclusively European discourse.[43] Raffles' offer of a reward for delivery of an indiscriminate variety of native flora, fauna and manuscripts was a Malayan manifestation of this grand project which still exerts its influence today.[44] This ostensibly academic exercise was everywhere allied to political intervention in the countries whose history (one could say entire being) was thus appropriated. Malay historiography proved particularly suitable to the demands of colonial intervention; it was by the manipulation of royal pedigree that Europeans first gained a lever to prise open the Malay Peninsula, and court ceremonies and state ritual were all that was to be left to those in whose name they ruled.[45] Traditional history served a third purpose: by concentrating on politics, on the struggles of ruling cliques and factions and matching this 'deviant' behaviour against the ideal, a picture of pre-colonial anarchy and decay could be built up that is still accepted today.[46] This view was supported by the use of Dutch East India Company records, again almost wholly concerned with courts and rulers, which tend to be most abundant for times of conflict and disruption of trade.[47]

In this section of the chapter I want to show how the political and military involvement of early colonial scholars dictated their limitations, both as historians and sources of historical material. Their involvement inevitably led to a distortion of the record. While not losing sight of my principal purpose (the notion of society embodied in their works) placing these historians within their own historical context necessarily involves a reexamination of the events they were involved in. The principle theme can be returned to when this has been done.

Some scholar/administrators were reticent about writing a history of their own times, or of events that had led to their position of authority. Sir W.E. Maxwell, KCMG CMG (1846-97) wrote much on Malay law and custom but stopped short at 'A History of the Dutch in Perak'.[48] R.J. Wilkinson, CMG (1847-1941) declined to write an account of British intervention in Malaya until 1923 (some fifty years later) as he felt it was the 'subject of bitter controversy' and to do so might 'arouse further bitterness'.[49] Others were not so reticent. Sir Frank Athelstane Swettenham, GCMG KCMG CMG (1851-1945) wrote prolifically on events with which he had been involved from the time he was a cadet in the Malayan Civil Service to his retirement as Governor of the Straits Settlements and High Commissioner for the Malay States in 1904. Sir Richard Winstedt, KBE CMG FBA DLitt Hon LLD (1878-1966) drew heavily on Swettenham's work and also official Dutch and British correspondence. An examination of these scholars' position in Malayan society, and of their work, will show firstly the uses to which a knowledge of traditional Malaya was put, and secondly that their own function as scholars was very little different from that of the court chronicler engaged in 'reshaping historical reality'. While some attention has been given to correcting colonial bias in history writing, the imperialist view of what constitutes society and history has still not been shaken off.

Members of the Malayan Civil Service were predominantly public school educated even in the early days of British rule, and this tendency was more firmly established with the introduction of Civil Service examinations requiring a classical education in 1882.[50] This background 'bred a respect for versatility and the amateur style of the English gentleman and a distrust of technical specialization'.[51] It bred also a respect for 'custom and etiquette, stress on teamwork, deference to authority . . .'[52] and, I would suggest, a sense of their own authority over Malays of any class. This rested firstly, and especially in the nineteenth century, on a kind of Darwinian genetic myth. Governor Weld, writing in 1882, was convinced that

> it would be beyond the powers of a despotism entirely to stamp out ideas engrained in these races – Chinese and Malays – from prehistorical times, and those ideas will bear fruit until they fade before a purer religion and a higher civilization.[53]

Swettenham was convinced that criminality could be transferred by 'the fatal inheritance of blood'.[54] Even 'the gentle Hugh Clifford' who realised that 'the moral qualities he admired . . . were not exclusively European but were possessed by the common people of Malaya as well'[55] came to believe that Malay ignorance and lack of enterprise was inherent in the race.[56] Although Butcher shows that racial explanations of inferiority were not more widespread than environmental or cultural explanations,[57] his work also shows why this was so. A belief in the Malay's ability to change was necessary for the implementation of British policy in the early years, and a recourse to the idea of genetic inferiority readily explained its failure.[58]

This authority over the Malays, that expresses itself in the need to represent on their behalf their history, culture and character, rested in the last instance on the British political position. Thus, when the decision was taken in London to 'rescue, if possible, these fertile and productive countries from the ruin which must befall them . . .'[59] it was decided that Raja Muda Abdullah was the rightful heir to the throne of Perak and should replace the constitutionally appointed Sultan Ismail. Abdullah was related to the previous ruler in the male line while Ismail claimed descent on his mother's side.[60] Ignorant that there was precedent for the 'distaff' line holding the sultanate in Perak,[61] and that Abdullah's claims to royal benefice had not been favoured by Sultan Ali before his death,[62] Governor Clarke arranged a meeting of Perak chiefs and had Abdullah elected in Ismail's place. It remained only to cajole the Perak state regalia from Sultan Ismail to give this pantomime some kind of Malay legitimacy. This was not accomplished, however, until after the killing of the first British Resident, appointed by authority of Abdullah, and the subsequent invasion of Perak by British troops.[63]

These events, the first steps towards control of the whole peninsula, presented some problems for colonial historians, and we shall see how they dealt with them later in this chapter. With the establishment of British Residents and their staff in Perak, Selangor, Negri Sembilan and Pahang, by the turn of the century, the collection of historical data could proceed on a much firmer basis. It was at all times both an academic and political exercise, the two aspects inseparably united in the person of the scholar/administrator. The *Journal of the Royal Asiatic Society (Straits Branch*, later the *Malayan Branch*) was the supreme repository of Malayan data, publishing essays on subjects ranging from penis pins in Borneo[64] to the shape of Chinese coolies' hats in Malaya.[65] The Journal (*JMBRAS*) published little history in its early years; the first, a dynastic history of Brunei, was contributed by Hugh Low, Resident of Perak.[66] The most regular contributor in the 1880s was W.E. Maxwell, Low's Assistant Resident.[67] The topics treated in *JMBRAS* could only be an orientalist potpourri as the contributors 'lacked a framework of history which would have enabled them to relate to each other the scraps of material they thus acquired'.[68]

Many of the earliest histories to appear in *JMBRAS* were adapted from official reports. These reports, to the Residents and to the Governor, were intended to establish precedent in matters of royal succession, law and finance.

> It was practical history, undertaken to serve the needs of the present and the demands of European officials for facts. It was a narrow form of history . . . tracing the antecedents of political and administrative questions of contemporary importance.[69]

This is no less true of the later works, for instance of R.J. Wilkinson's *Papers on Malay Subjects*, a series begun under government auspices at the turn of the century to aid the education of Malayan Colonial Service (MCS) cadets.[70] R.O. Winstedt, a colleague of Wilkinson's, contributed both to *JMBRAS* and *Papers on Malay Subjects*, and it is with him 'the doyen of Malay Studies'[71] that the need to justify British control of Malaya appears in its most seemingly erudite form. Swettenham also responded to this need, more personal in his case, in his many omnibus works on the Malays and Malaya. These last two scholar/administrators will be examined here, before proceeding to an analysis of their heritage.

Swettenham's works are riddled with minor errors of fact that stem from the casual authority with which he treats everything in the Malay Peninsula. Yet these errors are not his most important fault; it is his grossly partisan interpretation of events that wrongs both the Malays and the student of their history. Swettenham's justification of British intervention, and of his own manipulation of Malay affairs, has three main thrusts: firstly, he paints a picture of anarchy and oppression under native rule. Secondly, he stresses that Britain was invited to take control of states they previously had neither knowledge of nor interest in. Thirdly, he lists the benefits the modern world had to offer. His presentation of the first two arguments will be dealt with here.

In *About Perak* (1893) Swettenham tells us that prior to 1874 'murders were unpunished, robbery unnoticed, whole villages defied the authority of their own rajas, and the will of the strongest was the law of the land'.[72] Perak was in a state of 'bewildering chaos'.[73] Any person who could muster twenty followers 'sat down on the bank of some river and extracted toll from every passing boat'.[74] Debt-slavery, an 'ever-spreading sore', was rife.[75] Writing shortly after the turn of the century Swettenham is not so detailed in his calumny; he contents himself with the simple assertion that all the Malay states had been in a state of anarchy and strife for many years.[76] He does, however, mention the Chinese factional fighting in the Perak province of Larut[77] and the dispute over the succession to the sultanate in Perak Besar.[78] These are linked together in his *Footprints in Malaya* (1942), but by this time the original condition of the Malay population is less harshly described, taking on more of the attributes of a bucolic yeomanry.[79]

That Swettenham's picture of Perak is a gross distortion of the state of affairs can be seen from Birch's journal where it is recorded that both small and large scale trade is being carried on, rice continues to be grown and tin mined.[80] As Adas points out, the 'before and after' dichotomy is a feature of all imperialist history writing and continues to be accepted uncritically even by anti-colonialist writers. His own work on Burma has shown it to be a lie, and mine on Perak indicates a re-examination of the Western Malay states would show the same.[81] Admittedly, Perak did not conform to the British idea of a state, and their cultural blindness led them to suppose a situation of anarchy in all Malay states not directly under their control. No doubt the situation did seem to verge on 'bewildering chaos' to Birch and Swettenham as the Malays tended to bamboozle both of them, offering aid that never materialised and making appointments that were never kept.[82] As for actual warfare, its relatively mild character among Malays can be seen from Munshi Abdullah's account of the Kelantan dispute,[83] although the only fighting to take place between Malays in Perak in these years was Raja Muda Abdullah's attack on the Raja Mahkota at Sungai Durian in 1872.[84] Swettenham himself suggests that it was the Chinese who fought 'with a fury and carnage unknown to Malay warfare'.[85] Having described a state of anarchy and oppression in Perak, Abdullah's request that the British send someone to 'teach him how to rule this unruly country'[86] appears as natural as the British ability to do so. Nevertheless, 'it has been shown that Malay Sultans, far from welcoming the British to their states, were usually suspicious of their intentions' and rulers of the west-coast states 'were appalled by the consequences of the treaties that they had signed with Britain . . .'.[87]

If we are to believe Swettenham, nothing was known of the Malay Peninsula until Abdullah came requesting assistance in ruling his country.[88] British financiers were ignorant of the mineral wealth of the country, and not especially interested even after the treaty of 1874.[89] It was the ferocity of the Chinese feuding in Larut, not the consequent interruption of tin supplies that made 'interference the duty of the paramount power ...'.[90] By a happy coincidence the rightful claimant of the Perak throne also saw things the British way; at the meeting of chiefs on the island of Pangkor, the Chinese disturbances, the disputed succession, and the future administration of Perak were settled amicably. All the necessary Malay chiefs were present except 'Raja Ismail' (actually Sultan Ismail) and one other.[91] It was only later that Abdullah 'proved faithless' and conspired with Ismail and another powerful chief to have Birch killed.[92] The guilty parties were rounded up and either exiled, imprisoned, or executed,[93] 'a severe, but merited penalty...'[94] (and one that removed at a stroke the most respected and powerful leaders of Perak). This military operation reveals the nature of a Resident's 'advice' as, Swettenham tells us, it gave them 'that material support which was necessary to enforce respect for their advice in trying to introduce a better form of government'.[95]

It is hardly necessary to refute Swettenham's interpretation of events, although it has been the basis for much influential scholarship on traditional Malay society. Yet the involvement of British and Chinese financiers in the succession disputes of the nineteenth century has been documented by Khoo;[96] and even Sir William Jervoice who, on succeeding Clarke as Governor in 1875, saw events in a somewhat different light:

> In a British vessel, with a British man-of-war alongside, we collected together some Perak chiefs, to 'elect' a Sultan, when we just put down one who was absent and set up another who was present, that other being the wretched individual I have now described. [i.e. Abdullah][97]

As this extract indicates, colonial administrators are usually more useful to the historian in their official correspondence than in their published works.[98] Swettenham's bias as an historian is perhaps not as relevant as his bias as an historical source, a participant observer in events. This bias is twofold: firstly, in the interpretation of facts; secondly, and more insidiously, in the hierarchical and elitist view of what constitutes history. The people of Malaya are reduced to 'the Malay', sometimes an object of interest similar to a thoroughbred horse, at other times simply a homogenous mass subject to the whim of the rulers. The people have no power, not even of a reactionary kind, they have no part in either 'society' or 'state'. This twofold bias is repeated by Winstedt, whose influence in Malay historiography far exceeds that of Swettenham.

Winstedt's thesis so closely parallels Swettenham's that it need only be briefly indicated. He links together the violent Chinese dispute in Larut and the non-violent succession dispute in Perak Besar to give a picture of complete unrest.[99] He begins his chapter on British intervention with a catalogue of the misery of the common people 'in a society where might only counted'.[100] He tells us that famine was frequent, and the population was constantly worried about having enough to eat.[101] He even reminds us that there were no anaesthetics for people injured 'in the constant fighting'.[102] While Swettenham was content to confine himself to the period just prior to his own involvement, Winstedt's 'History of Perak' draws on Dutch and Malay sources to present a catalogue of conflict and confusion since Perak's inception. On this basis he can declare

> The most bigoted little Englander, the most convinced supporter of the rights and customs of small people, must admire the *pax Britannica* in Perak and bless the work of British protection in bringing out of centuries of great tribulation this rich and beautiful country and her ancient line.[103]

Winstedt's influence continues to be felt in Malay historiography; while his faults are recognised, so is his authority. Andaya calls him the doyen of Malay studies and, while indicating the 'severe shortcomings'[104] of his work, she also tells us that both Malaysian and Western writers continue to depend on it heavily.[105] Her own interpretation of Malay texts shows that the eighteenth century was regarded by (ruling class) Malays as a period of tranquillity and prosperity,[106] yet she appears willing to accept the conventional wisdom that the nineteenth century was a period in which the political system had been undermined.[107] Something of the dilemma of contemporary writers dependent on Winstedt is conveyed by Rubin in a footnote:

> Some demonstrably misleading assertions cast doubt upon the reliability of some assertions whose [unattributed] sources cannot be found and checked. However, since Dr. Winstedt is recognised as a leading authority on Malayan history, it has seemed wisest to accept his assertions of fact throughout except where convincing contrary evidence is available.[108]

Such deference to authority, we have seen, is a characteristic of both native and colonial historians, but should it also be a trait of the modern scholar? It remains to be shown that this deference does more than transmit wrong information, it replicates a view of society and history that is essentially not useful. In this view the motive power of society lies not with the people, in their relationship to their means of livelihood and the multiform systems of authority this gives rise to. Rather, it proposes that society is a simple hierarchy, that power flows in one direction only, and that social change is dependent on the personality of great figures or accidents. The colonial scholar's concern with ruling cliques and factions, state ceremony and ideology, and the exercise of power, underplays or even neglects the very basis of power – namely the direct unmediated control of people and the appropriation of their surplus produce. This was not a simple process but one operating under a variety of constraints and producing its own contradictions.[109] An examination of this level of activity goes a long way to explaining, rather than simply categorising, the state institutions that so preoccupied colonial scholarship. It was this preoccupation that in later years facilitated the development of structural-functional anthropology, and historians of Malaya still to a great extent accept it as the proper object of their discipline.

v) Post-colonial historians

It is useful to see Gullick's 'Indigenous Political Systems of Western Malaya' as a bridge between colonial and post-colonial scholarship. One of the last scholar/administrators, Gullick began this work in 1948 and completed it in 1956.[110] It is avowedly a work of structural-functionalist anthropology, although Gullick quite naturally has reservations about the anti-historical dogma of this school.[111] While the monograph does place more importance on the value of history than the theory itself is capable of, it is limited by the primary assumption of this school that society *is* its manifest institutions, in this case institutions observed by early colonial administrators. Since 'Frank Swettenham is quoted more in this study than all other sources put together'[112] the process by which colonial bias becomes sociological fact, and colonial concerns become wedded to academic theories, is revealed in Gullick's work. It is uniquely influential in post-colonial studies of Malaya, providing a general introduction to numerous specialised studies, and the theoretical underpinning to historian's reflections on their data.

Gullick conceives of a political system as a set of institutions of social control adapted to the social system's need for organised defence, trade and law.[113] If Gullick's only purpose was to describe these institutions as they apparently functioned in the states of Perak, Selangor, Pahang and Negeri Sembilan, the work would perhaps be useful, at least for students of comparative government. He goes further, however, and tries to draw from these disparate states a general picture of the functioning of the abstract 'Malay State'. It is this abstraction, this state that nowhere existed, that he has bequeathed to countless students of Malaya. Gullick is aware that an 'account in general terms must to some extent be an abstraction and simplification which ceases to correspond exactly with the complicated facts of the situation'.[114] He seeks to compensate for this either by setting aside exceptions to his general rules for separate discussion, or by ignoring them as insignificant. Thus, almost every general statement Gullick makes needs to be supplemented with a caveat concerning Negeri Sembilan, which is referred to separately.[115] The implication is that Negeri Sembilan is a renegade while Perak, Pahang and Selangor mirror each other in all essentials. Research on Perak in the nineteenth century shows that it bears little resemblance to Gullick's abstract model,[116] and there is no reason to believe an examination of other states would not show the same.

In Gullick's classic characterisation, the power of the sultan rested on control of the principal river mouth. The states relied on trade for supplies of rice and the sultan exercised his power by taxing and controlling this trade.[117] However, Gullick is less than rigorous when he argues that the Perak capital in 1874 was called Bandar (Port) and was near the mouth of the river, as was the capital of Selangor, Bandar Termasa.[118] Bandar Bahru (New Port) in Perak, about twenty-five miles from the river mouth, was actually one of several sites proposed to Abdullah as his capital by Birch;[119] the Malay capital at this time was Kuala Kangsar, about sixty miles inland. Perak's capital had always been situated at least fifty miles inland and, in times of war, often further.[120] Gullick is also wrong to suggest that Perak farmers could not grow enough for their needs because of the ravages of war and the oppression of their rulers.[121] Rice was only imported into Perak to meet the needs of Chinese miners, it was abundant in Malay areas.[122] Gullick here relies on false information and partially presented facts to vastly oversimplify the ruler's involvement in trade,[123] presenting it as little more than highway robbery, though he has to relocate the sultan's seat to do so.

Nor was it universally true that:

> the sparse Malay population of the 1870s lived in villages on the banks of rivers. This riverain pattern of settlement was dictated by the fact that the rivers were the only convenient communications.[124]

Bukit Gantang, a long-standing settlement in Larut, was situated inland, as were several *kampungs* between it and Kuala Kangsar.[125] Although most villages were on river banks, the evidence supports McNair's information that 'many Malays reside in the interior, and on the pathways and tracks through the jungle'.[126] This passage also indicates that rivers were not 'the only convenient communications'; far from being convenient, Ulu Perak was unnavigable for much of the year.[127] Some overland routes connected Blanja to the Jurumas and Dinding Rivers, Blanja to Kinta, Bota to Dinding, and Kuala Kangsar to Larut. There were also overland routes between states; from Bidor to Ulu Langat in Selangor, from Kuala Bernam into Pahang, and from northern Perak into Kedah and Patani.[128] These tracks were not simply a means of communication between jungle settlements, they also carried substantial trade in tin, opium, gold and ivory.[129] It is evident, then, that the image of state structure Gullick has put forward, in which political and economic power was ideally centralised in the sultan who controlled a river mouth, is not only simplified but untrue. Its corollary, the anarchy that ensued when district rulers usurped the sultan's prerogative by controlling the trade of their own districts, must also be questioned. This situation was not a deviation from the ideal mode of functioning; it was an intrinsic part of the states economic and political system.

While Malay scholarship has not stood still since Gullick's day, the revisions that have been made are often still within the same theoretical framework, and still tied to the concerns that we have traced as those of the Malay, and later the British, ruling class. This can be demonstrated by briefly considering two more works before concluding this chapter.

Barbara Andaya, whose *Perak, the Abode of Grace* is the only detailed study of a single period in the state's history, is a good example of what modern scientific, balanced and objective history can be about. She argues for the uniqueness of each Malay state and calls for detailed studies before generalisations are made.[130] She seems to regret the fact that in her sources 'only rarely is there a glimpse into the lives of the ordinary people ...'.[131] She is suitably critical of the bias of her sources, both Malay and Dutch, and is aware that 'by their very nature they have delineated and, to a degree, limited the scope of research'.[132] Yet this critical, reflective approach, which one expects of the trained historian, is matched by a curious absence. She appears unaware that her two purposes 'to organize and simply record what occurred ...' and 'to supply a case study of the manner in which an eighteenth century Malay state functioned'[133] cannot simply be a matter of *description* but must simultaneously be an exercise in *interpretation*. The limits and biases of her sources do more than restrict the amount of information she can present; they contribute to the intrinsic meaning of that information, as does her own historical existence, her training, and her social and political position.

It is not difficult to uncover in Andaya's work a view of society that has escaped her own scrutiny, one which is in part transmitted by sultans and imperialists via their chroniclers, but within which may also be discerned the influence of the structure of the university which insidiously moulds the modern intellectual.[134] Andaya conforms well to Chesneaux's observation that historians invariably present civil war as the supreme catastrophy, while foreign war is glorified.[135] At its inception Perak was all set to 'dominate its neighbours and make some impact on the course of Malay history. Yet this bright future did not eventuate.'[136] The reasons for this are threefold: its small population, its lack of entrepot wealth, and the difficulty experienced by the sultan in controlling the resources of the state.[137] Central control is desirable as an end in itself as well as a prerequisite for 'development of a powerful kingdom'[138] as can be seen from Andaya's choice of vocabulary: 'the smooth functioning of the Perak political system was constantly endangered' by the potential power of territorial chiefs.[139] That this 'smooth functioning' is dependent on their loyalty[140] is a source of 'inner tension' in the political system,[141] it 'aggravates' the problems involved in becoming a powerful kingdom,[142] and is an 'inherent weakness'.[143] Territorial chiefs who managed to control the resources of their own territory were 'perpetual trouble spots'[144] and the Raja Huda was another 'focus for dissidence'.[145] 'Because of this potential or actual opposition of the *orang besar*, the Perak political system was constantly endangered.'[146]

This last sentence shows us the extent to which Andaya has adopted the sultan's point of view;[147] this state of 'inner tension' actually *was* the political system. It was not the system itself but the sultan's power that was endangered. Centralised power may be a feature of history departments, colonial domination, city-states such as Malacca (on which Perak's constitution was *apparently* based), but it is not a universal characteristic of political systems (especially in the world beyond Europe), nor is it an acceptable form of power to all social classes. Apart from state ceremony and some court nomenclature, Perak diverged from the Malacca model and more nearly approaches Weber's ideal-typic 'patrimonial bureaucratic state' in which 'the ties which held the various parts of the realm together were always comparatively loose'.[148] In Andaya's case, as in many others, the historian leads us to see as natural and universal that which is culturally and temporally specific. It is no accident, also, that the abolition of the Perak political system in the nineteenth century results, in Andaya's view, from its own inherent weakness and not from the inexorable advance of outside forces: industrial capitalism under the aegis of British military intervention.

It is in the work of Khoo Kay Kim that we should expect this process to be stripped bare, subtitled as it is 'The Effects of Commercial Development on Malay Politics'.[149] As a Malaysian national Khoo lends support to D.G.E. Hall's claim that imperialist administrators (such as himself) gave their subject peoples both history and nationalism.[150] However, Stockwell is unfortunately right in saying:

> Just as in domestic and international affairs the arrangements inherited from the British were continued into the post-independence period, so in the academic field, scholarship was not overturned by a school of historians eager to rewrite the history of the country in nationalist terms.[151]

It is not surprising, then, that Khoo accepts Gullick's two-class division of Malay society into rulers and subjects. However, finding it an 'oversimplification' he offers us a rundown of the 'elaborate system of gradation' of the ruling class.[152] This by now familiar approach also informs his analysis of links between the Malay ruling class and Chinese and British financiers, which in other respects breaks new ground. In these chapters[153] the continual concern with Malay rulers finds its counterpart in dredging up the names of influential Straits financiers and company directors and recording the early history of various influential Straits companies. Occasionally Khoo is able to show how one was in competition or partnership with the other,[154] but he goes no further. This work may be a useful source material for anyone wishing to investigate the dynamics of capitalist expansion, but if it makes any point of its own, it is only that British and Chinese financiers conspired to seize control of Malay resources.

It is almost superfluous to add that Khoo, whose study has earned him an influential position in Malaysian society, is working in a society where economic relations are still significantly influenced by the structure of the Straits Settlements in the nineteenth century. A society, moreover, where mildly dissident political opinions may be punished by indefinite imprisonment without trial.[155] It would be naive, then, to expect a thoroughgoing critique of capitalist expansion to be undertaken under such circumstances. It is less clear why Western researchers are constrained to adopt a conservative, elitist and static view of Malayan history. This problem, and the suggestion of an alternative approach, is dealt with in the conclusion. Doubtless there are works on the Malay Peninsula that would not prove susceptible to the criticisms offered in this chapter; this survey does not pretend to be complete; it is limited by my own interest in Perak. Strong undercurrents that are common in much Malay history have, however, been charted here. It is necessary for historians to question the theoretical perspective and preconceptions that underlie their work, to question the origin of these assumptions and relate this to their own social position as intellectuals, and to unite with social theorists in developing a more effective representation of societies past and present.

vi) Conclusion

This chapter has proceeded from the assumption that the historian is as much the product as the producer of history. The social setting of the Malay chronicler was compatible with an essentially non-historical view of the world; each ruler was portrayed as an embodiment of the ideal ruler. Recent historians also reflect the myths that hold their society together. Much stress is laid on the power of the individual to affect the course of events, and so the object of analysis is often personal motive rather than impersonal forces. This freedom of the individual extends, in popular myth, to the intellectual who pursues truth without fear or favour in magnificent isolation from social, cultural or political forces. For this reason the documenting of class interest in supposedly objective works is often interpreted as a personal insult. Yet Chesneaux is correct when he says:

> The real function of historiography (the history of history) should be to identify and describe the specific relationship between historical knowledge and the prevailing mode of production. Yet few professional historians take an interest in this task . . . . History is viewed as an autonomous intellectual activity moving in a kind of closed circuit.[156]

It is not an autonomous activity; it is an activity with its own history and it is embedded in the institutions of contemporary society. In our case its history is one of absolute authority over the subject matter, the Malay people, and it is carried out today within similarly authoritarian structures. These institutions have been not simply the refuge of colonial ideas, but frequently of the ousted colonialists themselves. There are exceptions, but in general the student of Southeast Asia has been constrained to adopt the position of the acknowledged authorities, or not to succeed at all.

This situation is changing, while it remains true that historical representations must be 'embedded first in the language and then in the culture, institutions, and political ambience of the representer',[157] within these limits new approaches may develop out of critical reaction against entrenched schools of thought. The approach that is advocated here is not new in other fields, it is the study of social relations at the mass level, as opposed to institutions of the elite. The relationship found to be most useful for social analysis is one in which a transfer of labour occurs, whether embodied in goods, services or symbols. When societies are analysed in terms of the transfer of labour, a number of systems of labour-exploitation can be uncovered, each with its own reproductive structures. This necessarily entails an examination of the process of production of social necessities, but should not be confined to it. Such an analysis reveals classes of people whose interests, according to their position in the mode of production and its regulatory mechanisms, often fundamentally differ. The systems of exploitation operating in a society may have conflicting requirements for their reproduction. Thus, contradictions occur within a society as contradictions between classes, and within and between systems of labour exploitation. In this way change and conflict are seen not as aberrant, but as endemic to some types of societies.

This is basically a historical materialist approach. In concrete terms it means we need to examine the way members of a community gain their living, the forms of cooperation they enter into. We need to know how their product is appropriated and distributed, whether through relations of kinship, personal bondage, taxation or commerce. We should be interested also in the connection between various spheres of economic life; mining and agriculture, for instance, were inseparably linked in Perak. When the various forms of production are mapped out, and the means by which surplus is appropriated and used to reproduce productive relations is clear, state institutions and ideology acquire new meaning. Their form is partially explained. Partially, because there are elements of culture that must enter our analysis at the beginning and cannot be explained *post hoc*.[158] This is one of the problems of the materialist approach, there are others, for instance, its determinism.

However, one consequence of this approach is to give the community the history that scholarship has so often denied, to offer the antecedents of daily life as a basis for changing it. Another consequence is that by uncovering underlying structures, societies may be compared without simplified and general statements, and our knowledge of social dynamics advance. The historian is necessarily involved in this task, not as a merely passive provider of data – we have seen that is impossible – but as an active participant in the complex dialectic of empirical and theoretical research, and of intellectual and social practice.

Notes

This chapter was originally prepared as a paper as an academic exercise for the Southeast Asian Studies Programme, Murdoch University, Western Australia. It was presented to the seminar of honours students in 1980 and benefited from the critical appraisal of Dr Jim Warren. A subsequent draft was presented to the Third Malaysia Society Colloquium at Adelaide University in August 1981.

1 For a very brief summation of structural-functionalism and an alternative view similar to the one I propose, see David Baker, 'Theory as a Cultural System' in Joseph Fischer (ed.), *Foreign Values and Southeast Asian Scholarship*, (Research Monograph No. 11, Berkeley, 1973). For a more detailed critique see Marvin Harris in A.R. Radcliffe-Brown, *The Rise of Anthropological Theory* (London, Routledge & Kegan Paul, 1972), Chapter 19.

2 See below pp.68-71.

3 E.P. Thompson, *The Poverty of Theory and Other Essays*, (London, Merlin Press, 1978), pp. 210-11. The criticism of empiricism owes much to Sir Karl Popper, lucidly presented in Brian Magee, *Popper*, (Glasgow, Fontana/Collins, 1975), pp.33-4.

4 This argument is put forward by Hindess and Hirst in *Precapitalist Modes of Production*, (London, Routledge & Kegan Paul, 1975), pp.1-5. For a very useful argument against the Althusserians' dogmatic rejection of the value of history writing, see Thompson's *Poverty of Theory, op. cit.*, pp.205-29.

5 David Seddon, *Relations of Production*, (London, Frank Cass, 1978), pp.1-2. E.J. Hobsbawn, 'From Social History to the History of Society', *Daedalus*, (n.d.), pp.24-5. Louis Althusser cited in Thompson, *Poverty of Theory, op. cit.*, p.215.

6 See C. Wright Mills, *The Sociological Imagination*, (Harmondsworth, Penguin, 1969), pp.162-71.

7 This is true not only of those who call themselves structural-functionalists; it is true of much American social science with its endless manipulation of superficial categories. It is true, also, of the structuralist Marxists, Althusser and Balibar, who deal with 'concepts' in precisely the same manner as structural-functionalists deal with social institutions.

8 R.O. Winstedt, *A History of Classical Malay Literature*, (London, Hutchinson, 1968), p.155. One of these, the *Hikayat Raja-Raja Pasai* is not a peninsular *hikayat*.

9 Particularly the *Marong Mahawangsa* or *Kedah Annals* (*ibid.*, p.163), but also the *Sejarah Malayu* (p.159). Bottoms' 'Malay Historical Works' in Treggoning, K.C. (ed.), *Malaysian Historical Studies*, (Singapore, Singapore University Press, 1962) lists more than Windstedt, but many of these are probably copies of each other, see p.40, footnotes j and k.

10 M.B. Hooker, *A Concise Legal History of South-East Asia*, (Oxford, Clarendon Press, 1978), p.62.

11 *Ibid.*, p.65.

12 *Ibid.*, p.54.

13 *Ibid.*, p.65.

14 R.O. Winstedt, *Classical Literature, op. cit.*, p.152. Sir William Maxwell, not notably a social historian, had reason to complain of the *Misa Melayu* that 'accounts of palace festivities, the installation of chiefs, the amusement of youthful princes, the superstitious ceremonies in cases of illness, religious observances and royal progress fill page after page while events of historical interest receive comparatively little notice', cited in Barbara Andaya, *Perak, the Abode of Grace*, (Kuala Lumpur, Oxford University Press, 1979), p.9.

15 See e.g. Winstedt on the Bustan a's-Salatin, *op. cit.*, p.162. Maxwell apologises for the second part of his 'History of Perak from Native Sources', *JSBRAS*, (14) 1884, that it 'does not profess to be more than a genealogical record . . .', *JSBRAS* 14, Dec. 1884, p.305.

16 See e.g. Hooker, *Concise Legal History, op. cit.*, on the *Undang-Undang Kerajaan*, p.53 and *passim*.

17 *Ibid.*, pp.2, 3, 49.

18 Nearly all the texts used in Matheson's analysis of Malay conceptions of ethnicity are described objectively as 'a court based text of ruler legitimation'. Virginia Matheson, 'Concepts of Malay Ethos in Indigenous Malay Writings', *Journal of Southeast Asian Studies* 10 (2) 1979, pp.352-5, 369.

19 Andaya, *Abode of Grace, op. cit.*, p.7 and fn.35.

20 Maxwell, 'Native Sources', *op. cit.*, p.305.

21 R.J. Wilkinson (ed.), *Papers on Malay Subjects*, (Kuala Lumpur, Oxford University Press, 1971), pp.28-9.

22 Barbara Andaya, 'The Nature of the State in Eighteenth Century Perak', in Reid, A. and Castles, L. (eds), *Pre-Colonial State Systems in Southeast Asia*, (Kuala Lumpur, Royal Asiatic Society, Monograph No.6, 1975), p.23.

23 Winstedt, *Classical Literature, op. cit.*, pp.163-4 and *passim*.

24 Andaya, 'Nature of the State', *op. cit.*, p.24. See also Teeuw cited in Bottoms, J.C., 'Malay Historical Works', in Tregonning, K. (ed.), *Malaysian Historical Sources*, (Singapore, Singapore University Press, 1962).

25 Sujatmoko (Soedjatmoko), 'The Indonesian Historian and His Time', in Soedjatmoko *et al.* (eds), *An Introduction to Indonesian Historiography*, (Ithaca, Cornell University Press, 1965).

26 Hooker, *Concise Legal History, op. cit.*, p.51. Andaya also feels that Malay texts can be used to 'give an added dimension and to help the twentieth-century historian to see events as they might have appeared to Perak Malays in the eighteenth', *Abode of Grace, op. cit.*, p.6.

27 Edward Said, *Orientalism*, (London, Routledge & Kegan Paul, 1978), p.151.

28 See e.g. Maurice Bloch, 'Property and the End of Affinity', in Bloch, M. (ed.), *Marxist Analyses and Social Anthropology*, (London, Malaby Press, 1975), pp.203-22.

29 J.M. Gullick, *Indigenous Political Systems of Western Malaya*, (London,

Athlone Press, 1968), p.65. This two-class division, which derives from Swettenham, is so simple as to be of no analytical value at all. Using purely political criteria every society can be divided into rulers and ruled. This approach takes no account of those who were both rulers and ruled, nor does it include those whose authority was not expressed through political institutions, slave-owners for example. Gullick's own analysis of status distinctions belies this simplistic division of rulers and ruled so often repeated. Yet a class analysis based on economic relations would be far more explanatory.

30 This is not mere sarcasm. Winstedt, citing 'a Malay history' tells us that after Sultan Iskandar Muda's invasion of Perak in 1634 'in Perak were left only Maharaja Lela and Paduka Raja'. R.O. Winstedt and R.J. Wilkinson, 'A History of Perak', *JMBRAS*, 12(1) 1934, p.21.

31 Wilkinson, *Papers, op. cit.*, pp.39-40.

32 Alfred P. Rubin, *The International Personality of the Malay Peninsula*, (Kuala Lumpur, Penerbit Universiti Malaya, 1974), p.12 (emphasis added).

33 *Ibid.*, pp.12, 13.

34 For example, Peter Burns (ed.), *The Journals of J.W.W. Birch 1874-1875*, (Kuala Lumpur, Oxford University Press, 1976) *passim*. See also Sika's evidence, CO 273/88. 'The people hate the rajas because they constantly are extorting money from them without reason'. For an earlier period Andaya, using traditional texts, reconstructs an age when an 'unbroken chain of loyalty' extended from the sultan to the *rakyat* (Andaya, 'Nature of the State' *op. cit.*, p.35), yet Dutch representatives in Perak at this time were specifically instructed not to let disaffected subjects hide on their ships and escape the country. Wilkinson and Winstedt, 'A History of Perak', *op. cit.*, p.44.

35 Shelley Errington, 'A Study of Genre: Meaning and Form in the Malay Hikayat Hang Tuah', Ph.D Thesis, Cornell University, (Michigan, University Microfilms, 1978), pp.12-13.

36 *Ibid.*, p.15.

37 *Ibid.*, p.30.

38 *Ibid.*, p.29.

39 See Errington, 'Study of Genre', *op. cit.*, p.5.

40 Wilkinson, *Papers*, cited in Bottoms, 'Malay Historical Works', *op. cit.*, pp.41-2.

41 Bottoms, 'Malay Historical Works', *op. cit.*, p.51.

42 Andaya, *Abode of Grace, op. cit.*, p.3.

43 See the Introduction to Said's *Orientalism, op. cit.*, especially p.6.

44 A.H. Hill (trans.), 'The Hikayat Abdullah', *JMBRAS* 28(3) 1955, pp.73-4. Abdullah tells us: 'With my own hands I packed his books, manuscripts and collections of verses .... I filled three leather cases each six feet long with Malay works alone. After that I packed two more cases with letters from Java, Bali, and Celebes .... There were thousands of different creatures whose insides and bones had been taken out and which had been stuffed with cotton wool .... There were hundreds of bottles, large and small, tall and short, filled with snakes,

centipedes, scorpions, worms and so on . . . . Mr. Raffles prizes all these specimens very highly, more than gold or diamonds'. (pp.169-70). Fifty miles out of Bencoolen on the return voyage to England, Raffles' ship took fire and all these artefacts were lost (p.310, fn.8).

45 See Article VI of the Pangkor Engagement of 1874 in Burns (ed.), *Journals*, p.375.

46 Politics always involves conflict (see Ranney cited in Khoo *Western Malay States, 1850-1873*, (Kuala Lumpur, Oxford University Press, 1975, p.109). Concentrating on the ruling class, whose normal activity was considered deviant, led colonial scholars to ignore the orderly progress of economic life among other classes. Total disruption was assumed to follow from highly localised ruling class contests.

47 Andaya, *Abode of Grace, op. cit.*, pp.5-6.

48 W.E. Maxwell, 'A History of the Dutch in Perak', *JMBRAS* (10), Dec. 1882, pp.245-68a. For a list of Maxwell's work in the Royal Asiatic Society's journals see Lim Huck Tee and K.E.K. Wijasuriya, *Index Malaysiana, JMBRAS*, 1970, pp.84-5.

49 Wilkinson cited in Burns' introduction to Wilkinson, *Papers*, p.7.

50 John Butcher, 'Attitudes of British Colonial Officials Towards Malays 1888-1928', MA Thesis, (Madison, University of Wisconsin, 1971), p.23.

51 *Ibid.*

52 *Ibid.*, p.22.

53 CO273/115, *Colonial Office Records, Straits Settlements, Original Correspondence*, (London, PRO).

54 Sir Frank Athelstane Swettenham, *The Real Malay*, (London, Bodley Head, 1900), p.295.

55 Peter Wicks, 'The Gentle Hugh Clifford', (Queensland, Darling Downs History Teachers Association, April 1980).

56 Butcher, 'Attitudes', *op. cit.*, p.52.

57 *Ibid.*, p.61.

58 *Ibid.*, pp.52, 53, 54.

59 Colonial Office to Governor Straits Settlements cited in Winstedt and Wilkinson, 'History of Perak', *op. cit.*, p.96.

60 Burns, *Journals, op. cit.*, pp.11-12.

61 Andaya, *Abode of Grace, op. cit.*, p.75.

62 Winstedt and Wilkinson, 'History of Perak', *op. cit.*, p.84.

63 *British Sessionary Papers*, (Malay Peninsula) C1501, (Vol.54:287, 1876), p.50.

64 Harrison, T., 'The "Palang" its History and Proto-History in West Borneo and the Philippines', *JMBRAS* 37(2), 1964.

65 C.A. Gibson-Hill, 'Chinese Labourers Hats Used in Malaya', *JMBRAS* 25(1), pp.35-47.

66 C.D. Cowan, 'Ideas of History in the Journal of the Malayan (Straits) Branch of the Royal Asiatic Society, 1874-1941', in Hall, D.G.E. (ed.), *Historians of South East Asia*, (Kuala Lumpur, 1963), p.279.

67 *Ibid.*

68 *Ibid.*, p.280.

69 *Ibid.*, p.282.

70 Burns' introduction to Wilkinson, *Papers, op. cit.*, p.1. Burns feels the papers should be seen in the wider context of a new school of British administrators who hoped better information about the Malays would promote greater concern for their welfare.

71 Andaya, *Abode of Grace, op. cit.*, p.3.

72 Frank Swettenham, *About Perak*, (Singapore, Straits Times Press, 1893), p.10. In his *Footprints in Malaya* (London, Hutchinson, 1942) he contradicts this statement. In 1874 'the Rajas and Chiefs ruled, the people obeyed. The people had no initiative whatever: they were there to do the will of the Raja or Chief under whose authority they lived; with a general understanding that the commands of the ruler must be followed by all'. (p.48).

73 Swettenham, *About Perak, op. cit.*, p.11.

74 *Ibid.*, p.9.

75 *Ibid.*

76 Swettenham, *The Real Malay, op. cit.*, p.16. This chapter is based on the first chapter of his *About Perak, op. cit.*

77 Swettenham, *The Real Malay, op. cit.*, pp.10, 11.

78 *Ibid.*, p.12.

79 Swettenham, *Footprints, op. cit.*, pp.28, 32, 48-9.

80 Burns, *Journal, op. cit.*, pp.65, 116, 119, 238 and *passim*.

81 Michael Adas, 'Imperialist Rhetoric and Modern Historiography. The Case of Lower Burma Before and After Conquest', *Journal of Southeast Asian Studies* 3(2) 1972, p.177. Patrick Sullivan, 'Social Relations of Dependence in a Malay Sate; Nineteenth Century Perak', *MBRAS Monograph*, 1982, p.37 and *passim*.

82 Swettenham, *About Perak, op. cit.*, p.10 (on Birch; for his own experience, see P.L. Burns and C.D. Cowan, *Swettenham's Malayan Journals 1874-1876*, (Kuala Lumpur, Oxford University Press, 1975) especially the entries for 12 and 13 February 1874, pp.29, 30.).

83 Abdullah, asked by the Panglima Besar how his side can overthrow their rivals' stockade, advises them to blow it up. This advice is relayed to the Raja Bendahara, and the reply comes back: 'If we do this probably many of our people on that side will be hurt. If it were only the Raja who was killed it wouldn't matter . . . . The people in the stockade over there and in the stockade here are not strangers; there are wives on that side whose husbands are over here; fathers are on that side and mothers here; older brothers there, younger here. Thus each regards the face of the other, how may they have the heart to kill them?' Kassim Ahmad (ed.), *Kisah Pelayaran Abdullah*, (Kuala Lumpur, Oxford University Press, 1960), pp.87-91. (My translation from p.91. See fn.156.)

84 Burns, *Journal, op. cit.*, p.19.

85 Swettenham, *The Real Malay, op. cit.*. p.10.

86 Swettenham, *About Perak, op. cit.*, p.9.

87 A.J. Stockwell, 'The Historiography of Malaysia: Recent Writings in English on the History of the Area Since 1874', *Journal of Imperial and Commonwealth History*, 1 (1976).

88 Swettenham, *Footprints, op. cit.*, p.25.

89 *Ibid.*, p.31.
90 Swettenham, *About Perak, op. cit.*, p.5.
91 Swettenham, *Footprints, op. cit.*, p.33.
92 Swettenham, *The Real Malay, op. cit.*, p.13.
93 Swettenham, *Footprints, op. cit.*, p.66.
94 Swettenham, *The Real Malay, op. cit.*, p.14.
95 *Ibid.*, p.13.
96 Khoo, *Western Malay States, op. cit.*, Chapters 7 and 8, especially pp.210-17.
97 Jervois to Carnarvon, 16 November 1875, cited in Emily Sadka (ed.), 'The Journal of Sir Hugh Low', *JMBRAS* 27(4) 1954, p.11.
98 This statement is made with some reservations. Jervois himself was not averse to rewriting history. After Birch's death and the successful reprisal on the village of Pasir Salak, Jervois ordered that the report be amended, telling Swettenham: 'You don't suppose that I am going to allow the report of a successful operation like this to be made without saying that it was done under my instructions.' (*Footprints, op. cit.*, p.63); and this is the way the event is recorded in McNair's *Perak and the Malays*, published in 1878, (Kuala Lumpur, Oxford University Press, 1878), p.387.
99 Winstedt, *Malaya and Its History, op. cit.*, p.64.
100 Winstedt and Wilkinson, 'History of Perak', *op. cit.*, p.91.
101 *Ibid.*, p.92.
102 *Ibid.*, p.93. Winstedt in his preface to the 'History of Perak' says that this chapter 'in its original form' was the work of Wilkinson. It may be true that the information itself was Wilkinson's but an examination of his 'History of the Peninsular Malays' on which this chapter is based shows that the uses to which it was put were entirely Winstedt's. See Wilkinson, *Papers, op. cit.*, pp.89-118.
103 Winstedt and Wilkinson, 'History of Perak', *op. cit.*, p.2.
104 Andaya, *Abode of Grace, op. cit.*, p.3.
105 *Ibid.*, p.4.
106 *Ibid.*, p.1.
107 Andaya, 'Nature of the State', *op. cit.*, p.29.
108 Rubin, *International Personality, op. cit.*, p.52.
109 Sullivan, 'Social Relations', *op. cit.*, pp.58, 93-5, and *passim*.
110 Gullick, *Political Systems, op. cit.*, Preface.
111 *Ibid.*, pp.18-19.
112 *Ibid.*, p.145.
113 *Ibid.*, p.43.
114 *Ibid.*, p.20.
115 *Ibid.* See e.g., pp.9, 22, 26, 37, 43, 45, 48, 68, 74, 75, 86 and 105.
116 Sullivan, 'Social Relations', *op. cit.*, pp.33-8.
117 Gullick, *Political Systems, op. cit.*, pp.21, 29.
118 *Ibid.*, pp.27-8, fn.5.
119 Burns, *Journal, op. cit.*, pp.204, 209.
120 Andaya, *Abode of Grace, op. cit.*, p.24.
121 Gullick, *Political Systems, op. cit.*, p.29.

122 Sullivan, 'Social Relations', *op. cit.*, pp.37-8, 48.
123 For an indication of the complexity of an *Orang Besar's* interests see Sullivan, 'Social Relations', *op. cit.*, p.56.
124 Gullick, *Political Systems*, *op. cit.*, p.28.
125 See *British Sessionary Papers. Further Correspondence*, (Vol.54:287 C1505-I, 1876).
126 McNair, *Perak and the Malays*, *op. cit.*, p.157. See also Sullivan, 'Social Relations', *op. cit.*, pp.34-5.
127 Andaya, *Abode of Grace*, *op. cit.*, p.25.
128 See C1505-I, 1876, *op. cit.*, and Harrison, C.W. (ed.), 'Perak Council Minutes', in Wilkinson, R.J., *Papers on Malay Subjects*, (Kuala Lumpur, Oxford University Press, 1971), p.178. Leech, 'Slim and Bernam', *JSBRAS* (4)1879, p.41. Maxwell, 'Journey on Foot to the Patani Frontier in 1876', *JSBRAS* (9)1882, pp.54-63.
129 Burns, *Journal*, *op. cit.*, p.212, fn.2. Harrison, 'Perak Council Minutes', *op. cit.*, p.178.
130 Andaya, *Abode of Grace*, *op. cit.*, p.10.
131 *Ibid.*, p.6.
132 *Ibid.*, p.9.
133 *Ibid.*, p.10.
134 Dennis Altman, on resigning from Sydney University, said: 'The basic structure of Australian universities is feudal, with the vice-chancellor at the apex ... presiding over a large group of small fiefs or departments, administered by professors.' Jean Chesneaux, on the other hand, sees history departments as operating more on the model of capitalist enterprise. The basic point about centralisation of power, and its consequences for staff members, is the same. *Past and Futures*, (London, Thames & Hudson, 1978), pp.56-62.
135 *Ibid.*, p.17.
136 Andaya, *Abode of Grace*, *op. cit.*, p.22.
137 *Ibid.*, pp.23-7, 34.
138 *Ibid.*, p.23.
139 Andaya, 'Nature of the State', *op. cit.*, p.29.
140 Andaya, *Abode of Grace*, *op. cit.*, p.28.
141 Andaya, 'Nature of the State', *op. cit.*, p.35.
142 Andaya, *Abode of Grace*, *op. cit.*, p.27.
143 *Ibid.*, p.27.
144 *Ibid.*, p.23.
145 Andaya, 'Nature of the State', *op. cit.*, p.33.
146 Andaya, *Abode of Grace*, *op. cit.*, p.31.
147 'The Zaman Mas [Golden Age] is seen as a time when power is concentrated in the hands of one who then shares it with his faithful ministers and chiefs.' Andaya, 'Nature of the State', *op. cit.*, p.35.
148 B. Schrieke cited in W.F. Wertheim, 'The Sociological Approach', in Soedjatmoko, *op. cit.*, p.348. Yet even this approach is more descriptive than explanatory. Pronouncements on the nature of the state are possible only after an examination of the mode of life of the population; they should not be a substitute for it.

149 Khoo Kay Kim, *The Western Malay States 1850-1873, op. cit.*

150 D.G.E. Hall, introduction to *Historians of Southeast Asia, op. cit.*, p.2.

151 Stockwell, 'Historiography', *op. cit.*, p.90. Khoo himself admits this point in a recent conference paper, indicating he would not be out of sympathy with many of the criticisms offered here. He feels, though, that the solution is not to overturn past approaches to Malaysian history, but to 'fill in the gaps', and that recent Malaysian history graduates are now engaged in this task. Khoo Kay Kim, 'History Writing by Malaysians since 1945: Perspectives, Emphases, Themes', *op. cit.*, pp.17-9, 21-5.

152 Khoo, *Western Malay States, op. cit.*, pp.15-22.

153 Parts II and III of *Western Malay States, op. cit.*, Chapters 3-8.

154 It is interesting, though, that in capitalist history the equivalent of war is not anathema: competition between the Patent Slip and Dock Co. and the Tanjong Pagar Dock Co. for permission to build a railway in Singapore had the result that 'neither party succeeded in its scheme'. Khoo, *Western Malay States, op. cit.*, pp.90-100. The railway was not built, but this is not seen as dysfunctional conflict in an unstable system.

155 Amnesty International Report, pp.9-13. Kassim Ahmad, whose edition of Kisah Pelayaran Abdullah is cited in this paper, has been imprisoned without trial since November 1976 (p.47).

156 Chesneaux, *Pasts and Futures, op. cit.*, p.23.

157 Said, *Orientalism, op. cit.*, p.272.

158 'Any material productive force contains in it, right from the outset, a complex *idéel* element which is not a passive, a posteriori, representation of this productive force in the mind, but, from the very beginning, an active ingredient, an internal condition of its very emergence.' Maurice Godelier, 'Infrastructures, Societies, and History', *Current Anthropology* 19(4) 1978, p.766.

3 Class, politics and race in modern Malaysia

MARTIN BRENNAN –
King Alfred's College, Winchester

Introduction

The Malaysian social formation is a recent and complex phenomenon which came into existence as a direct result of imperialism and colonialism. In the pre-colonial period the Malay Peninsula was politically divided into a number of small sultanates based on the control of river basins[1] while the northern part of the island of Borneo was inhabited by a series of tribes and came under the sway of political entities based upon Sulu and Brunei at various periods.[2] Social formations thus existed under semi-feudal and lineage modes of production,[3] but these formations were of a scattered and fragmented nature and in no way resembled the modern Malaysian state in their precise extent or in the delimitation of their political boundaries. These formations were, however, the arenas in which the penetration of capitalism occurred particularly during the late nineteenth and early twentieth centuries.

This penetration of the capitalist mode of production was uneven and restricted; thus while parts of Malaysia became fully integrated into the world market under the sway of plantation and mining capital, other areas remained virtually untouched.[4] The penetration of capitalism was accompanied by the establishment of a British colonial state but the influence of this political apparatus was again varied and the Malay Peninsula and northern Borneo were administered under a complex and confusing array of different political units.

However, the articulation of several modes of production created by imperialist penetration gave rise to a complex, multi-racial social formation characterised by a rapid economic growth, large-scale immigration, rootlessness, a lack of social cohesion and the general atmosphere of a frontier society. The composition of the population was changed radically in a short space of time as imperialism ensured that labour was shifted from India and China to create surplus value on the basis of British capital.[5] Thus by the Second World War a society had been created which appeared to be a vast medley of peoples which on the one hand 'mixed but did not combine',[6] while on the other hand was divided into discrete ethnic blocs composed of Malays, Chinese and Indians. The official ideology of the colonial state which presided over this arrangement was that its task was to maintain a harmonious, plural society,[7] a task reflected in the endeavours of colonial and neo-colonial academics who adopted a mode of analysis which mirrored this ideology.[8]

The image of harmony and consensus which was cultivated by the British and latterly their heirs in the immediate post-Merdeka period was rudely shattered by the traumatic experience of the 1969 race riots, an experience which has set in train a series of social, economic and political policies which will form a background to the present chapter. However, the post-1969 period has also been one of reassessment on the part of the social analysts with the outcome that a pluralistic approach is increasingly being rejected as an inadequate framework for confronting Malaysian social reality. Whilst not denying the significance of racial categories in their explanations, many social scientists have called for a more sophisticated incorporation of both the race and class dimensions.[9] Indeed, the task facing us now appears to be one of identifying the intersection of race and class and of spelling out and clarifying the relationship between these two structural variables.

In this chapter I will attempt to identify the classes which intersect and occasionally coincide with racial groups of the Malaysian social formation. Underpinning my approach will be the notion of Malaysia as a dependent neo-colony within the world economic system. Despite formal political independence in 1957, the country, by virtue of its reliance upon the export of primary products and the state's strategy of export-oriented industrialisation utilising foreign capital, remains firmly locked into the structure of international capitalism. This relationship between Malaysian society and the international social and economic system has its own specific economic, political and ideological effects. I will argue that the articulation of particular modes of production has led to the reproduction of politics which both preserves elements of the old feudal order and simultaneously paves the way for further imperialist penetration. I will attempt to delineate the classes which result from this articulation, and to identify the alliances and contradictions within the power-bloc. I will seek to expose the race/class nexus by examining the strategy of the dominant class in maintaining control through the repressive and ideological apparatuses.[10] Finally, I will demonstrate the methods used by particular class fractions to legitimate their positions by the invocation of racial ideologies. In short, I will attempt to show that racial conflict in Malaysia has its origins in the struggle between classes.

Class in the Malaysian social formation

Class analyses of Malaysian society are still comparatively rare but it may be useful to review some recent attempts at constructing a class framework before presenting our own formulation. Most writers agree that the peasantry and the urban proletariat constitute the two major dominated classes although there is disagreement as to the degree of differentiation and the various fractions which make up these two classes. Rather than focusing on these classes the tendency has been to concentrate on the ruling classes and the middle strata. This is partly because a power stuggle between the fractions within these classes is believed to hold the key to an understanding of the way that race is deployed in the political arena. Thus, for Lim Mah Hui[11] the Malaysian dominant class or power-bloc faces a crisis of hegemony in which there is a divergence between what he calls 'political hegemony' and 'economic hegemony'. This divergence results in conflict between the three 'fragments' of the dominant class which are the Malay governing class, the non-Malay (mainly Chinese) capitalist class and the metropolitan or international bourgeoisie. For Lim the metropolitan bourgeoisie is conceived of as an almost domestic class within the Malaysian social formation, and its presence is measured by the degree of foreign control of the economy. However, it is doubtful whether the metropolitan bourgeoisie can be considered to be an indigenous class in that presumably foreigners cannot have any direct political representation although their interests can of course be politically represented through the local bourgeoisie.

In Hashim Hussin Yaacob's[12] formulation the Malaysian ruling class is composed of the following groups: (a) a land-owning class exploiting the cheap labour in the countryside for the production of cash crops; (b) former members of the aristocratic and noble families; (c) the owners of estates and mines; and (d) a commercial group of financial and industrial magnates. Below the ruling class, according to Hashim, is a middle class which is of crucial strategic and political importance because it is pushing for greater political and economic power and utilises race in order to gain support for its aims. This middle class is composed of (a) an urban commercial group, (b) the rural bourgeoisie (often teachers and government officials), (c) a bureaucratic class and (d) a technocratic/managerial class allied with the multinational companies.

Michael Stenson characterised the Malaysian class system as one in which an urban aristocratic/administrative elite, a capitalist elite, a salariat and a rural landlord and administrative class face an urban proletariat and a mass of impoverished peasants,[13] while for Selveratnam the ruling class is composed of foreign capitalists, a bureaucratic and technocratic elite, the local bourgeoisie and the large landowners.[14]

Although the emphases differ in the above formulations, all seem to be agreed that an alliance of local aristocrats, bureaucrats, urban capitalists and rural landlords is in collusion with foreign capital to exploit and oppress the Malaysian peasant and worker. With the exception of Lim, the role of the state (or even a definition of the state) is left fairly vague although there is virtual unanimity that a bureaucratic or administrative class or elite exists and that it is of considerable and increasing importance. However, it is little wonder that these writers bypass an extensive analysis of the state given the confusion that abounds in the literature (particularly on the state in peripheral societies).[15] Nevertheless, there are indications that whilst a crudely instrumentalist view of the state as the executive committee of the bourgeoisie may have been replaced by the state as the 'condensation of the balance of forces' (between fractions of the bourgeoisie), there remains the conviction that in the last analysis the state represents the power-bloc.[16] In short the state as the site of political and class struggle where the conditions for that struggle are constantly changing due to the state's own activities has not been opened up as a key question for analysis.

At this point and given the above reservations we will indicate our broad agreement with the gist of the class analysis briefly reviewed so far. Our task is to build upon these approaches, to perhaps specify more clearly the classes and class fractions in the Malaysian social formation and to relate these classes and their political and ideological representation to the articulation of specific modes of production. Only by rooting our analysis in the complex class structure of Malaysian society will we be able to explain the rapid changes which are occurring, and thus escape the trap of characterising Malaysia as a plural society beset by ethnic and cultural antagonisms, the roots and persistence of which remain inexplicable.

In Figure 3.1 we represent diagrammatically the class structure of the Malaysian social formation. It will be apparent that class divisions cross-cut all racial blocs within the formation representing a clear division of labour within each bloc, and therefore within the formation as a whole. We will now move on to provide a sketch of each of these classes and class fractions and to develop a theory of

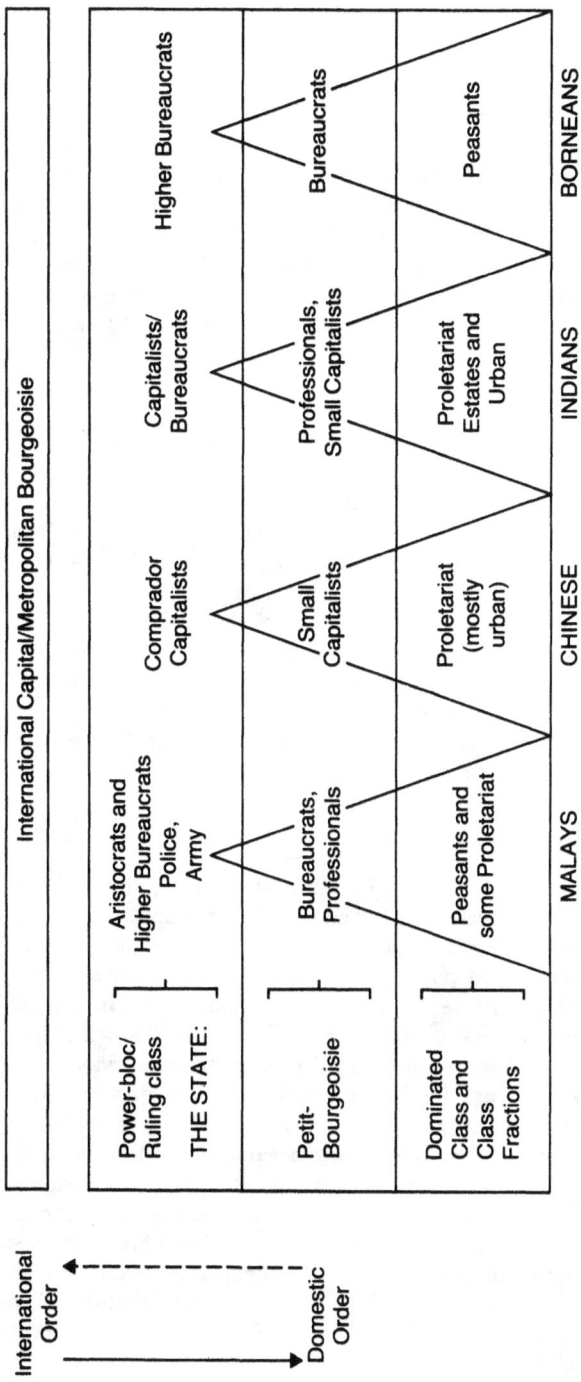

Figure 3.1 Malaysia: class and race structure

Notes

1 Each racial group is divided into classes.
2 Each class is divided into fractions. (These are defined and discussed in the body of the chapter.)
3 The state is conceptualised as a 'condensation of the balance of forces within the power-bloc' (Poulantzas).

their oppositions or alliances in explaining social change. Classes are defined in terms of their relationship to the means of production, distribution and exchange while a class fraction is part of a class which has an ideological coherence and political effectiveness.[17]

In Figure 3.2 we outline some of the assumptions underlying our analysis in terms of the complex relationships between the international system and the Malaysian formation. These relationships involve representation and correspondence not only at the economic base but also in the political and ideological superstructures.

The dominant ruling class

The composition of the Malaysian ruling class results from its genesis in the pre-capitalist and pre-colonial period, its transformation during the colonial era and its present day relation with the metropolitan bourgeoisie or international monopoly capital. Thus, the Malaysian national bourgeoisie is a dependent and subservient bourgeoisie which relies upon international capital for its existence. This class has evolved as a consequence of the articulation of the (Malay) semi-feudal mode of production with the (British and international) capitalist mode of production. The various fractions within it derive from both modes, but given its dominance in the present conjuncture, they fundamentally serve to ensure the reproduction of capitalism.

i The Malay aristocracy

This is a significant fraction of the Malaysian ruling class with its origins deep in the pre-colonial period and the pre-capitalist mode of production. The important point about this fraction is that, historically, it possessed both political and economic power. Malay sultans and rajas collected tribute as a result of their political control over the river basins of the Malay Peninsula.[18] Much of their economic and most of their political power was stripped away during the British colonial period, but the aristocrats themselves were institutionalised and given special roles and privileges under the system of indirect rule. In short, they became dependent upon the colonialists in that they were the group effectively co-opted and utilised by the British in maintaining control. Independence came late to Malaya partly because this group remained ambivalent about losing the protection of the British. When independence did arrive it was led and therefore controlled by the aristocrats themselves as symbolised by the country's first Prime Minister, Tunku Abdul Rahman, a Kedah prince.

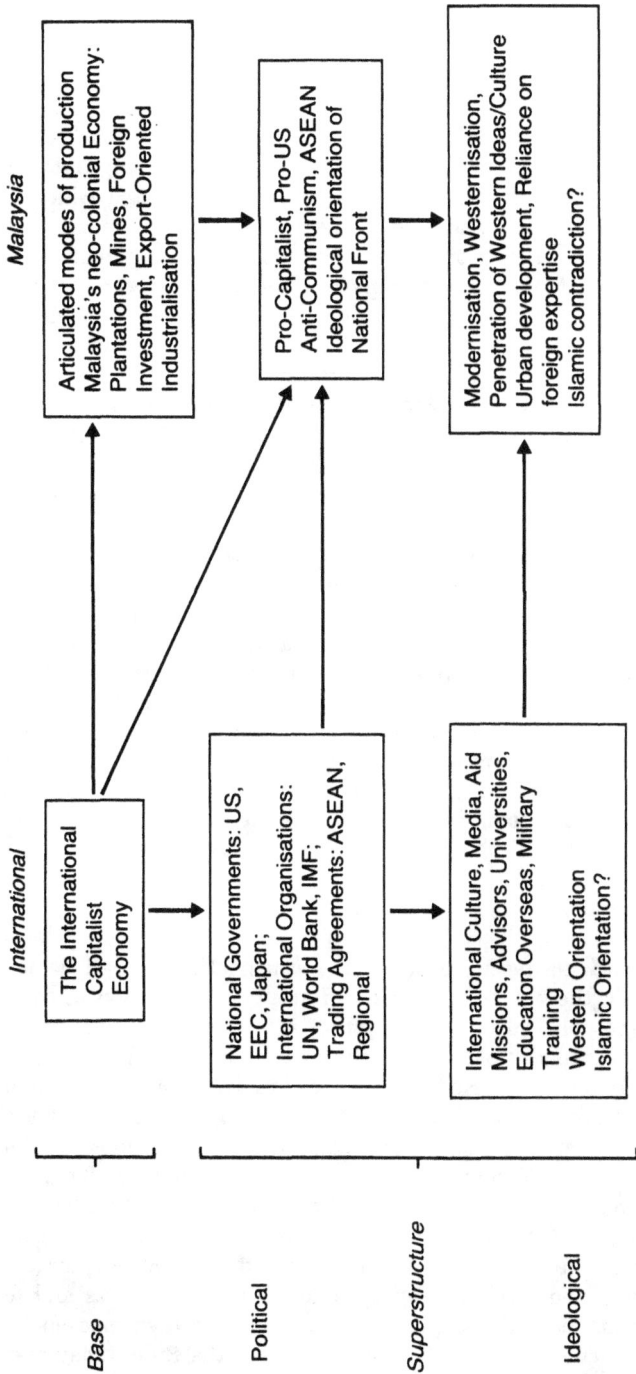

Malaysia

Articulated modes of production Malaysia's neo-colonial Economy: Plantations, Mines, Foreign Investment, Export-Oriented Industrialisation

Pro-Capitalist, Pro-US Anti-Communism, ASEAN Ideological orientation of National Front

Modernisation, Westernisation, Penetration of Western Ideas/Culture Urban development, Reliance on foreign expertise Islamic contradiction?

International

The International Capitalist Economy

National Governments: US, EEC, Japan; International Organisations: UN, World Bank, IMF; Trading Agreements: ASEAN, Regional

International Culture, Media, Aid Missions, Advisors, Universities, Education Overseas, Military Training Western Orientation Islamic Orientation?

Base

Political

Superstructure

Ideological

Note

The notion of an Islamic contradiction refers to Malaysia's growing links with the Islamic world whose interests can differ from those of the West e.g. over Israel or Iran.

Figure 3.2 Base and superstructure at the international and local level

99

In the post-Merdeka period this fraction has sought to recapture economic as well as political control thus harking back atavistically to the pre-colonial period when feudal rule was undisturbed by either the Europeans or the Chinese or Indian immigrants. A cumbersome and contradictory ideology has been erected which is designed to legitimate the rule of the aristocrats by appealing to tradition, race and religion. This is the ideology of 'bumiputraism' which sees the Malays as the only truly indigenous people of the Peninsula owing unswerving allegiance to the sultans, the Malay race and Islam. This Malay feudal fraction has not, however, been able to retain its power without forging alliances both with the rising Malay bureaucratic stratum of state functionaries and with dominant class fractions from other racial groups. Relationships of interdependence thus exist within the local ruling class, relationships which are cemented by this class's adherence to the demands of international capital.

Because the maintenance of their constitutional position has suited the legitimising needs of other class fractions, the Malay feudal aristocrats now find themselves in an enviable and seemingly impregnable position, a position protected by laws which place the sultans above criticism. A position in which their ownership of land and timber stands has made them excessively wealthy; and a position in which the state is prepared to finance their lavish, conspicuous consumption while turning a blind eye to corruption and increasing interference in the political system.[19] The sultans dispense patronage to an extraordinary degree thus acting as a vital ingredient in cementing the unity of the Malaysian bourgeoisie.[20] The role of the Malay aristocracy is justified by local as well as Western academic apologists as follows:

It is hard to piece together the constitutional shell which surrounds the rulers and make an accurate evaluation of their social and political role. Clearly they retain influence over many Malays, especially older ones, through tradition and because of their religious authority. The Rulers are Western-educated and several attended the Malay College at Kuala Kangsar. Many are also 'Western' as judged, for example, by their interests in Western sports. The fact that the Rulers continue to confer titles and honours strengthens their positions inside their states. It may be argued that, to many Malays, the Rulers are a necessary part of the social fabric. It is expensive to maintain the Rulers, largely because of the need to keep up a number of residences and to provide for members of the royal family or the royal household, but conspicuous consumption on the part of the Rulers may give vicarious pleasure to poorer Malays, who may not in the foreseeable future be able to derive pleasure from their own consumption.[21]

Not surprisingly this notion of the masses deriving 'vicarious pleasure' from the wealth of the ruling classes is also put forward by those in control of the New Economic Policy in Malaysia today when they advocate the creation of a class of Malay 'millionaires'.[22]

ii The landlords

The penetration of capitalist relations of production into the rural areas of Malaysia during the colonial period naturally led to new forms of social differentiation. As land and labour became commodities for purchase and sale, a class structure evolved in the village based on the processes of exploitation and accumulation. The British introduced the concept of private property to replace the pre-colonial system under which land was owned by the aristocracy and operated by the peasantry on a fairly 'free' basis, i.e. a peasant would work as much land as he needed for subsistence. The British also introduced cash crops on land they acquired and thereby began the integration of the Malaysian economy into the world economic system with all that this implied.[23]

Class formation in the Malaysian countryside has proceeded since the capitalist mode of production was introduced in colonial times, and there is mounting evidence that polarisation has increased during the post-colonial period.[24] There can be little doubt that a powerful land-owning class has emerged in the kampongs, a class which has been highly significant in its political interventions,[25] and a class which, in stark contrast to many Third World countries, has kept itself hidden from the development-planning process.[26] Kessler has argued that this landlord class has given the ruling United Malays National Organisation (UMNO) its strongest support in Kelantanthus leading to class antagonisms and an electoral pattern whereby the poorer peasants consistently voted for the Partai Islam (PAS) despite pressure which was exerted upon them. Thus in 1959:

> Village landlords threatened not to renew tenancies of their sharecroppers who supported PAS (and ensured that they did not vote for it by requiring them to surrender their identity cards, without which polling officers – generally schoolteachers sympathetic to UMNO – would not permit them to vote) . . . the very control landlords had over tenants, which the UMNO sought to use was also the major source of antagonism and resentment.[27]

Stenson argues that Kessler's work on Kelantan makes an illuminating case study because the relative absence of other ethnic groups has allowed class conflict to emerge without the deflecting mechanism of ethnic conflict.[28] On the other hand it cannot be argued that Kelantan is entirely a special case, for rural unrest is never far below the surface as witnessed by events in Kedah in 1974 and 1980.[29]

In any case what is clear is that a significant landlord class exists in Malaysian society, a class whose degree of landownership and control has been quantified in recent studies.[30]

iii The state bureaucracy

There is a great deal of debate in various theorisations of the state as to how the stratum of state functionaries relates to the overall class system. Here we are considering the senior state functionaries to be a fraction of the ruling class for:

> The state bureaucracy's interests (maintaining and extending their privileges) are realised through the state revenue, which means they must guarantee and promote the process of value creation in the economy to provide a source of state finance.[31]

In short we are taking a view of the state which reflects the fact that:

> The task of the state is to maintain the unity and cohesion of a social formation divided into classes, and it focuses and epitomises the class contradictions of the whole social formation in such a way as to sanction and legitimise the interests of the dominant classes and fractions as against other classes of the formation, in a context of world class contradictions.[32]

Thus the state is not an instrument to be captured by a social class and then wielded to its advantage, still less a neutral arbiter, umpire or referee which exists above or external to society as the democratic pluralists would have it. Rather the state is a 'condensation of the balance of forces'.[33] These forces are the fractions of the dominant class or bourgeoisie and at any specific moment one fraction will be hegemonic and organise the other fractions and the relationship between the bourgeoisie and the proletariat. The relative autonomy of the state is thus a relative autonomy vis-à-vis the fractions within the bourgeoisie and not a relative autonomy with regard to the whole social formation. Further we would argue that in peripheral capitalist formations such as Malaysia, the importance of the state will inevitably grow as a site of class struggle for:

the heterogeneous, world-market dependent reproduction process produces and reproduces a fragmented and unstable class structure and a relative social weakness of the classes, fractions of classes and groupings in the nation. The consequence is that interests are realised and accommodated less and less within the social process and are mediated more and more by the state. Thus the state becomes the natural forum of the class struggle and class relations.[34]

The higher state bureaucrats are thus in a crucial position not only in organising and directing production on a certain level but also in creating the terrain on which the class struggle is fought.

In Malaysia this bureaucratic fraction of the ruling class was orginally created by the colonial power in order to service the needs of the colonial state. The members of this group were drawn from the ranks of the traditional Malay elite referred to above, and although initially barred from its higher reaches, they were eventually fully absorbed into the colonial bureaucracy i.e. the Malayan Civil Service (MCS).[35] This group became deeply involved in Malay nationalist politics and formed the backbone of the United Malay Nationalist Organisation which came to power as the leading partner in the Alliance government in 1957. Since independence the civil service has not been exclusively Malay, although recruitment policies have assured that Malays are in a majority. This trend has increased since 1969 with the proliferation of new government organisations at national and state level. The members of this bureaucratic class fraction[36] are now drawn from a wider social background than simply the aristocracy as a result of expanded educational opportunities and the possibilities of rapid promotion from university-educated Malays.[37]

Other areas of the state apparatus which have identified with the dominant class and in particular (on a racial, Malay basis) with the state bureaucracy are the institutions of the military and the police.[38] Taylor has argued that the 'rapid increase in the number of state functionaries during the independence period must be related to the growth of the semi-proletariat in the urban areas'[39] and here we may find part of the explanation for the largely Malay nature of state employees, for the vast majority of migration into Malaysian towns and cities in recent times has been of Malay peasants. Thrown off the land by the very processes of land accumulation we have described above, their support must nonetheless be retained by the Malay aristocratic and bureaucratic classes thus reflecting essentially pre-capitalist social relations in their ideological forms. A Malay nationalism which is essentially conservative and populist is thus utilised by the Malay ruling class to satisfy peasants transformed into semi-proletariat, and secure their allegiance through government employment.

The political expression of these three fractions – the Malay feudal aristocracy, the rural landlords and the Malays who man the higher reaches of the state apparatuses – is the UMNO which has held effective political power since 'merdeka' in 1957. We can thus characterise this group as being composed of dispossessed feudal rulers in alliance with landlords seeking to further their opportunities for accumulation plus an insurgent bureaucratic and military fraction which seeks economic ownership to match its political control. It is the activities of this class and the alliances it has forged with both foreign and local capital that provide us with the key to the explanations of racial conflict in Malaysia. The mechanisms by which this class has maintained and increased its control will be examined in the final section of this chapter.

iv The comprador capitalists

As with other groups in the class structure of the Malaysian social formation, this fraction emerged during the colonial period. Composed mainly of Chinese merchants, small, industrial capitalists and the owners of some mining and plantation capital, the comprador capitalists acted as middlemen between the giant British agency houses and the mass of workers and peasants who provided the labour from which surplus value could be extracted.[40] Under the protection of the British whose official ideology was to keep the Malays in rice production,[41] Chinese and Indian immigrants were encouraged to establish themselves in the intricate network of wholesale and retail activities which was necessary for the reproduction of the labour force and the smooth functioning of an economy geared to the export of mineral and agricultural products to the metropolitan country. From the very start then, this fraction was reliant upon imperialist penetration, and as Taylor has pointed out, its political ideology and economic strategy is inevitably dominated by this fact. In contrast to a national capitalist fraction, this group will always argue for 'the importance to economic development of the value accruing to the state from foreign investment in the export sector, the importance of linkage industries, the increase in reliance upon the use of imported technology etc.'.[42] Historically this reliance upon foreign penetration has been exacerbated by the fact that the comprador fraction has been almost entirely non-Malay and therefore has come into conflict with those who control the state apparatus, mainly Malays. Because of this division, no coherent 'national capitalist class' has emerged in Malaysia, although there are signs that one could emerge as a result of the New Economic Policy (NEP).[43]

During the 1950s this comprador fraction of the Malaysian bourgeoisie formed an alliance with the Malay bureaucratic class so as to protect its interests as independence approached, and to provide a united front of local ruling classes and colonial power against the liberation efforts of the Malayan Communist Party (MCP).[44] In the event this triangular alliance of British colonial interests, the local non-Malay comprador capitalists and the Malay feudal class was outstandingly successful. In fact the struggles of the 1950s provided the basis for the continued rule of the Alliance (sic), now the National Front, and the continued protection of this local power-bloc by international capital. The mainly non-Malay bourgeoisie has, however, been forced to adopt a racial strategy in order to legitimate its position with the non-Malay masses.[45] This strategy has inevitably led to contradictions and conflict between the various fractions of the power-bloc and it is these intra-power-bloc struggles which have eventually surfaced as racial conflict.

The petit-bourgeoisie

A major feature of post-war Malaysian society has been the emergence of an urban petit-bourgeoisie. This class is composed of middle-ranking bureaucrats, teachers, workers in the social agencies, professionals and small-scale capitalists mainly in retailing and distribution. It is a multi-racial class although a certain congruence of race with occupation has occurred, i.e. Chinese in business and shopkeeping, Malays in government service. The expansion of the petit-bourgeoisie is a result of capitalist economic growth providing an increased role for the state and thus employment in a vast range of government agencies such as PERNAS, MARA, UDA and the SEDCs.[46]

The major feature of the Malaysian middle class has been its unswerving support for the ruling class power-bloc adumbrated above. This is hardly surprising for its very existence is dependent on the patronage of particular racial fractions of the ruling class. Thus government employees are dependent upon government ministers and senior civil servants, while given the highly integrated, clan-and-dialect-based vertical structure of Malaysian Chinese society, shopkeepers owe allegiance to the large-scale Chinese capitalists. Because of this dependency, but also through its growing influence derived from electoral politics, the petit-bourgeoisie has supported the Alliance party and pressurised the state to continue its pro-capitalist, anti-socialist and racialist policies in a bid to increase its own share of the cake at the expense of the mass workers and peasants. Thus commenting on the New Economic Policy, Hashim Hussin Yaacob has concluded that:

> Given their past historical role, it seems quite clear that a profound cleavage between the middle class and the working class and peasantry will develop. Their unwillingness to develop a social and reform programme directed towards the needs of the workers and peasants will be a living testimony of their presence as an inhibiting force in the eradication of poverty. On the other hand they will develop closer links with the military and the police force to maintain economic position and their social status.[47]

This is not to argue that in conditions of class polarisation the petit-bourgeoisie will not mount a political alternative to the political representation of the power-bloc. This of course will be 'social democracy' as witnessed by the rise of parties such as the Gerakan and the DAP.[48] These parties basically support the existing order but challenge its implementation in terms of alleged racial hegemony and a maldistribution of the rewards of the accumulation process amongst fractions of the petit-bourgeoisie. A small minority of professionals and others will side with the proletariat and peasants as witnessed within certain factions of the Labour Party in the 1960s[49] and more recently the Partai Sosialis Rakyat Malaysia (PSRM). But by and large the Malaysian ruling class has been able to rely wholeheartedly on the urban (and rural) middle classes in its desperate crusade against militant labour[50] and revolutionary socialism.

The contradictions which exist within the petit-bourgeoisie have tended to erupt along racial lines. The expansion of the state in the 1970s has brought an increasing number of Malays flooding into the cities, and tensions have arisen between them and the non-Malay middle class over the allocation of educational privileges, employment in the civil service and the operation of business enterprises under the terms of the third Malaysian Plan (TMP) and the New Economic Policy in general.[51]

The dominated classes

The dominated classes in the Malaysian social formation can be divided into three major fractions – the peasantry (mainly Malay and indigenous Boreans), a rural proletariat of plantation and mine workers (mainly Indian and Chinese), and a multi-racial urban proletariat. Given the articulation of several modes of production and the uneven and restricted development of capitalism, this broad sub-division could be differentiated further as we will indicate below. But for the purpose of analysis here we will focus on these three main groups.

i The peasantry

The origins of the Malaysian peasant lie in the semi-feudal mode of production established in pre-colonial times as we indicated in our discussion of the Malay feudal rulers. The majority of peasants are still Malay but their economic situation has been drastically changed by the penetration of capitalism into the rural areas of the country. Thus the sale of land and the introduction of cash crops has led to a situation in which:

> The Malaysian peasantry exhibits a distinct pattern of social differentiation and polarisation. On the one hand there is a rich land-owning group who are also middle-men-wholesalers-creditors having farms of more than 10 acres in size, and on the other, there are many groups having less than that, and still others, about 60 per cent, who have no land at all.[52]

On the other hand, social relationships between peasants, landless labourers and landlords are overlain by feudal and religious ideologies derived from the pre-capitalist mode of production. Thus a patron-client relationship exists in which:

> The landowner (patron) is free to choose who will operate his land, be its tenant, sharecropper or labourer. Since the amount of land in the village is often small compared to the supply of labour, clients must depend on the landlord's 'kindness and goodwill' and oblige and support him in order to retain their means of livelihood. This may take the form of supporting the landlord when he stands for election to the committee of any of the local social or political organizations. The result is the creation of a strong relationship of obligation and dependence between the patron (landlords) and clients (landless peasants). The landlords are able to mobilize and influence the majority of the peasants, especially those who are operating their land, thus determining to a certain extent the socio-political behaviour of the landless peasants.[53]

As we saw in our discussion in the tenant-landlord class, UMNO has attempted to institutionalise this patron-client relationship into one of political allegiance. In doing this it has been aided by the support of the aristocracy with the implication that a peasant who does not vote for the government is in fact displaying disloyalty to the sultan. The use of Islam by UMNO has been far more difficult, for traditionally it has met fierce opposition from PAS which has its own base amongst the peasants.[54] How UMNO has coped with this problem, particularly in Kelantan, provides an instructive case study in the politics of repression and manipulation and the attempted destruction of political opponents.[55] But of course the trump card in ensuring the support of the peasantry for the ruling Malay elites has been race. By drumming up fear of the 'immigrant races' and appealing to a crudely populist Malay nationalism, the Malay ruling class has been able, very effectively, to keep race consciousness high and class consciousness low. This job has been made easier by the fact that the majority of Malays are concentrated in the countryside while the Chinese and Indians reside in the towns. Secondly, through its control of the repressive state apparatus, UMNO has been able to harass a class-based political party like the PSRM[56] and prevent its political message from getting across. We will return again to consideration of these strategies of social control below.

ii Plantation and mineworkers

The export of tin and rubber was the basis on which the Malaysian social formation was developed under British control. In essence the 'Malay States' were one gigantic unit for the extraction of these two commodities which were of vital importance to the expansion of British (and international) capitalism. Looked at in this way, the towns, industries, roads and railways of Malaya were all ancillary to this central task of exploitation. But of course labour was needed for this mammoth enterprise and in the case of Malaya it was readily obtained from India and China. Or as Stenson has put it:

> The West Malaysian case is an excellent illustration of the social and political mechanisms by which imperial capitalism established and maintained its supremacy in the colonial and neo-colonial world. The plural society was devised for the systematic extraction of surplus value from a large mass of cheap, Asian labour.[57]

The Indians who worked in the rubber plantations and to some extent the Chinese who worked in tin mining were isolated from other fractions of the Malaysian dominated classes by their location and attachment to particular production units. This was particularly true of the Indians because:

Production on the Malayan plantations was organised on military/industrial lines with up to 1,000 labourers employed on one plantation, but the labourers consciousness as a wage-earning proletariat was retarded by their incorporation into closed, productive societies headed by Europeans.[58]

However, this early isolation did not prevent the eventual awakening of class consciousness amongst plantation workers faced with the appalling conditions of the depression, and by the 1930s some of the militant industrial action was based in these estates. Mineworkers were also involved during this period, as Stenson has documented in his account of industrial conflict in Malaya.[59] But Malayan trade unionism was to have a brief life, for its rise was interrupted by the Japanese occupation and later brought to a halt as the British first sought to re-establish control and then to destroy the Malayan Communist Party after the war.

Today plantation and mineworkers are closely under government control as quiescent unions have been inherited from the colonial power, remodelled and virtually assimilated into the state apparatus. The political representation of this fraction of the Malaysian proletariat is fragmented and weak. Formally, and in terms of electoral politics, it is aligned with the Malaysian Indian Congress (MIC), the Indian partner in the National Front, the MCA, or the DAP,[60] the strongest non-Malay opposition party. However, as with the peasantry reviewed above, the chances of a political force emerging based on its real material interests are slim indeed in the present conjuncture.

iii The urban proletariat

This is a group which has grown substantially in size in the last ten or fifteen years as the processes of industrialisation, urbanisation and rural-urban migration have accelerated. Malaysian towns and cities were characteristically 'Chinese' in the colonial period and right up to the 1960s, but since that time there has been a substantial inflow of rural Malays especially to Kuala Lumpur.[61] Thus Malaysian urban centres are becoming increasingly multiracial, a demographic change which some observers feel could have strong implications for the political and class struggle.[62] As we have already indicated, many of the Malay section of this urban proletariat throng to the cities in search of government employment. They seek their share of the 'bargain' offered to them by those who control the state in exchange for their political support and social acquiescence. The state in its turn, despite having expanded significantly, is unable to satisfy all these job-seeking aspirants thus leading to the growth of a class of rural-migrants cum urban-unemployed who find themselves housed in squatter settlements around the major cities. Nevertheless, an increasing number of Malays working in government organisations and in industry and commerce are coming face to face with a Malay bourgeoisie, thus leading to the possibility that class consciousness will begin to erode and subsume ethnic consciousness.[63]

The non-Malay working class is differentiated in complex and significant ways, in particular because of the organisation of Chinese businesses. These have traditionally been based narrowly on the family and more widely on the clan and dialect group. A worker in such a system is thus not selling his labour directly to a capitalist but is locked into an almost feudal familial system. On the other hand, with the development of the distribution of commodities under colonialism vast numbers of Chinese and Indians were proletarianised as they were forced to sell their labour-power to the infrastructural institutions of the colonial state (ports, railways, etc.) or to private capital (the agency houses). This process of proletarianisation has speeded up in recent years with the advent of multinational companies setting up plants in areas such as Petaling Jaya and Penang.[64]

As with plantation and mineworkers, the urban proletariat experienced its moment of greatest militancy during the 1930s and just after the Second World War. Often led and inspired by the Malayan Communist Party, workers were able to stage strikes and other forms of industrial action in an attempt to force capital to concede better wages and working conditions.[65] However, as we have already suggested, this militant phase was shortlived and ended with the military defeat of the MCP and the emasculation of the unions, a series of events which one observer has not failed to connect with the rise and consolidation of racial politics:

> The socio-political identity of any working class is first and foremost incarnate in its trade unions. It experiences itself as a class only through its collective institutions of which the most elementary one is the trade union. The destruction of the Malayan labour movement in the years 1945-48 meant that the British were able to successfully determine the structure of communal politics that has prevailed in Malaysia ever since.[66]

The Alliance and National Front governments of the post-colonial period have been fierce in their determination to prevent the development of an autonomous labour or socialist movement.[67] Thus, the Malaysian working class remains organisationally weak and racially fragmented.

The MCP has been outlawed, the unions remain cowed by draconian labour laws and the populace is divided by racial politics. Thus, Malaysia's urban proletariat has no effective political representation and the prospects for such a development in the near future are not bright.

We can now turn, in order to explain further the above, to the strategies employed by the power-bloc through the state to ensure its own dominance and to an investigation of racial conflict through an exploration of the contradictions within the power-bloc.

Strategies of social control: race, class and the state

So far in this chapter we have attempted to identify the classes and class fractions that constitute the modern Malaysian social formation. We have indicated that in the present conjunction this formation is based upon a dominant capitalist mode of production articulated with a basically Malay semi-feudal mode. We have also suggested that the Malaysian bourgeoisie is in the last analysis responsive to the demands of international capital. Malaysia remains a neo-colony whose state revenues are overwhelmingly gleaned from the export of rubber, tin, palm oil, petroleum and timber,[68] and whose nascent industrialisation programme is almost totally dependent upon foreign investment and multinational companies.[69]

We have attempted to show that class formation in Malaysia proceeded apace during the colonial period as imperialism created a social formation in which a vast mass of Asian cheap labour could be exploited in order to provide the raw materials needed for the growth of industrial capitalism. As part of this process, a ruling class was created, nurtured and protected by the British and eventually bequeathed with the reward of independence. Since independence social and economic changes including land accumulation, urbanisation and industrialisation borne of a close integration of Malaysia into the world economy have resulted not only in class polarisation between the Malaysian bourgeoisie and workers and peasants but also in the creation of an urban petit-bourgeoisie which is increasingly playing a decisive political role.

The articulation of modes of production and uneven development in Malaysia which has given rise to conflict between fractions of the ruling class has in turn led to the burgeoning of a strongly interventionist state. We are thus arguing that Malaysia is a class society structured in dominance by capitalism and that the state represents the interests of the ruling power-bloc, not as a simple 'executive committee', but:

in a complex fashion depending on the class contradiction, by means of a whole chain involving the subordination of certain apparatuses to others which particularly condense the power of the hegemonic fraction . . . shifts of apparatuses from the ideological field to the field of the repressive apparatus and vice-versa; finally, significant cleavages within each apparatus itself.[70]

What then is the hegemonic fraction[71] of the ruling class within the Malaysian social formation? We would suggest that it is an alliance of the Malay aristocratic, bureaucratic and landlord classes[72] which by virtue of its dominance within the state (politics, civil service, police, army) is able increasingly to determine the conditions of capital accumulation and also the political terrain on which the class struggle is to be fought. However, it is crucial to emphasise here that this hegemonic fraction is almost totally dependent upon international capital which supports it as a class because it allows the further penetration of imperialism into the formation.[73] Thus, in the present conjuncture and especially since 1969, this Malay hegemonic fraction has been in alliance with international capital in order to resolve the contradiction between it and Chinese comprador capital. Because the very basis of legitimacy of this Malay fraction relies upon a populist, nationalist and racialist appeal to the Malay peasant and worker, it must be seen to be (at least partly) opposed to Chinese capital, otherwise the entire ideology underpinning its position would be in danger of collapse. The Malay hegemonic fraction must therefore create and advance the conditions for international capital accumulation within the social formation, thereby creating a whole host of further contradictions arising from subsequent and concomitant class formation and polarisation. These it can only resolve through the use of the repressive state apparatus as we shall see below.

For its part local Chinese (mainly comprador) capital is also caught in a dilemma. Historically its inevitable support has been international capital as we have seen above. This must continue to be the case but the degree of its support has lessened due to international capital's need to curry favour with the state which essentially 'created the space' for capital accumulation. This non-Malay fraction is therefore forced into partial acquiescence and compromise with the Malay hegemonic fraction or into exporting its capital outside of the Malaysian formation to more politically favourable locations such as Singapore, Hong Kong or Taiwan.[74] In a similar fashion to the Malay ruling class, its legitimacy rests upon mobilising the support of Malaysian Chinese through chauvinist and racialist appeals. It must therefore be seen to be defending 'Chinese interests' against an apparent onslaught from the Malays.

All these contradictions and compromises are present in the political representation of the ruling class – the National Front and indeed the state. The first priority of the state is to protect the conditions for capital accumulation and thus its activities will involve first and foremost the prevention of any form of 'social instability' which could endanger this exercise. On the other hand, the internal contradictions within the power-bloc must also be mediated and resolved. This is achieved by a precarious process of racial bargaining which can occasionally go badly wrong and erupt with disastrous effect.

The state is therefore involved in two vital tasks. Firstly, to prevent the development of class-based labour and political movements which could threaten the accumulation process through demands for improved wages and conditions. And secondly, to damp down and prevent racial conflict and indeed explosion which result from its own political strategy. The answer is straightforward: a situation of potential social conflagration can only be addressed by increased repression. It is to this strategy that we will now turn.

UMNO, state power and repression

The hegemony of the Malay aristocratic, bureaucratic and landlord fractions within the power-bloc is demonstrated not only by their general racial domination of the state apparatuses but also by the particular dominance of the United Malays National Organisation within the National Front. UMNO is a party whose leadership tends to be dominated by Malay aristocrats and bureaucrats and whose grass-roots support is derived from the landlords and peasants through the type of social processes we have described above. In the last decade the clamour from the emerging Malay petit-bourgeoisie has been added to these fractions creating a dynamic and ruthless social force. A force which has given rise to the New Economic Policy which is designed to shift 30 per cent of wealth to the Malay community by 1990 and which has been accompanied by educational, language and social policies which have created a marked degree of racial tension.[75]

Politically the National Front is overwhelmingly dominated by UMNO for of the ninety-four seats won by the Front in Peninsular Malaysia in 1978, it holds seventy. Of the 240 state Assembly seats won in the same election, it holds 175. The MCA remains the only other significant party in the Front and even then the number of seats it holds is tiny (seventeen and forty-three in national and state respectively). However, UMNO's power cannot be measured in seats alone. Its supremacy is even more apparent if we examine the distribution of ministerial and other government posts. After the 1978 General Elections, out of twenty-two Cabinet Ministers, eighteen were from UMNO, while eleven of the seventeen Deputy Ministers were also UMNO.[76] Furthermore, the key posts of Prime Minister, Deputy Prime Minister, Minister of Home Affairs, Minister of Foreign Affairs, Minister of Finance and Minister of Defence were all held by UMNO politicians. This power of UMNO is readily conceded by other ministers: 'I think I still believe in the notion of constitutional democracy but I do admit that the influence of UMNO is overwhelming...'[77] and, 'The MCA is in the worst state it has ever been in and if it goes on like this it will simply be the "political parasite" of UMNO'.[78] Or in the words of one political commentator discussing the organisation of the National Front: 'The linchpin of this political arrangement is UMNO whose dominance is accepted unquestionably by the other ten component parties.'[79]

When one considers its recent origins and the fairly late development of Malay political awareness, it is remarkable how UMNO has increased and consolidated its power with such speed and thoroughness. UMNO has attempted to become the cement which holds the Malaysian polity together, indeed the 'stability' of Malaysian society as a whole has become increasingly dependent upon the machinations of, and developments which occur within, UMNO.

It would therefore present a distorted picture if we viewed the National Front as a genuine coalition of parties reflecting racial and regional interests within Malaysia. Rather the Front is UMNO plus a series of subsidiary and dependent parties which are under UMNO's close control. Indeed UMNO's senior politician and party managers constantly interfere in and influence the affairs of other parties.[80]

There are several advantages of this strategy of UMNO. Firstly, it can keep a close eye on what is going on and indeed control events in the other 'communities'. Secondly, by having representatives of other races in the Front, it can present the official ideology of multi-racialism, and thirdly, it can ensure that political events are consistently managed to favour those Malays loyal to UMNO.

There are of course always risks that UMNO will overreach itself in pursuing this strategy, risks that were exposed only too clearly in 1969, under the auspices of the Alliance. However, the Alliance, although UMNO-dominated was much more of a laissez-faire arrangement allowing room for manoeuvre for its non-Malay components, the MCA and MIC. The National Front is a very different coalition which operates in an UMNO authoritarian straitjacket. The danger now is that, at least in Peninsular Malaysia, the Chinese will become so alienated from the National Front, that it will cease to represent their interests at all.

But what of the more specific strategies of social and political control pursued by those who manage Malaysia's state apparatus? Broadly they can be grouped under three headings: constitutional, repressive and ideological.

The most blatant aspect of UMNO's control and management strategy related to the Constitution is the constant amending of that document. For:

> It cannot be denied that the Malaysian Constitution has earned for itself the distinction of being the most amended Constitution in the World . . . it is not an exaggeration to say that the history of the constitutional Amendments in Malaysia is the history of a progressive erosion of Democracy in our country.[81]

Its two-thirds majority in Parliament is a key weapon in the National Front's armoury for if it is losing the game, it can simply change the rules, as Means has observed:

> Opposition can be effectively undercut by alteration of the 'rules of the game' in the form of boundary adjustment or constitutional amendment. Under such conditions, politics acquires a rigidity which makes it difficult to achieve changes in the allocation of power since those who have power can control the political environment to perpetuate their supremacy.[82]

The other major area of disputation is over the size of parliamentary constituencies and the weightage given to rural areas. This weightage was originally devised by the British to give greater representation to the Malays. However, there have been numerous boundary changes over the years which have invariably favoured UMNO. Thus one non-Malay Government Minister was moved to remark out of sheer frustration:

> Let me speak to you frankly . . . there is never any chance of the Chinese and the Indians winning a large number of seats in this country because UMNO has always gone in for rampant gerrymandering particularly after 1969 when the constituencies have been changed and boundaries altered so much that they are always ensured of a majority.[83]

In fact, the discrepancies in size between urban (largely non-Malay) constituencies and rural (largely Malay) constituencies are extreme, and for this reason opposition leaders such as Lim Kit Siang see no chance of ever gaining power in Malaysia.[84]

Another aspect of the abuse of the Constitution by the Malaysian government is the fairly frequent suspension of Federal or State parliaments and the imposition of 'Emergency Rule'. This has happened three times in recent years – nationally from 1969 to 1971, in Sarawak in 1966 and in Kelantan in 1977. It could be argued that the 1969 'emergency' was a necessity given the scale of civil unrest although the reasons for suspending Parliament for such a long period are debatable. However, in Kelantan and Sarawak there is considerable evidence that the ruling party was disadvantaged politically and dispensed with normal democratic processes in order to regain control.[85] Indeed, the leader of the opposition has suggested in Parliament that:

> The question that is uppermost in the minds of the people today is whether the Proclamation of Emergency under Article 150 and the imposition of NOC-type rule is dictated by weighty considerations 'whereby the security or economic life of the Federation or any part thereof is threatened' or whether it is being used indiscriminately and even frivolously to further certain partisan political interests.[86]

The repressive activities of the Malaysian government over a number of years have been well documented in a report by Amnesty International.[87] A chapter of the report entitled 'Harassment of Dissent in Malaysia: The Political Parties and Trade Unions' details the way in which opposition leaders and party members have frequently been arrested and detained under the Internal Security Act (ISA). The multi-racial Socialist Front was hardest hit in the 1960s and early 1970s, perhaps because its programme posed the greatest long-term threat to UMNO and the power-bloc.[88]

Members of the DAP, at present the strongest opposition party, have also been imprisoned, including its leader, Lim Kit Siang, who was detained without trial from May 1969 to October 1970. Trade unions have not been immune from government interference for as Amnesty records:

> Trade Unions, like opposition political parties, have been badly hit by the provision of the Internal Security Act. Moreover the Registrar of Societies has broad power over the registration of unions, which the Government has not hesitated to use in the past to curb legitimate trade union activities.[89]

The government's standard response to criticisms of its use of the ISA is that it is being employed to stamp out 'communist subversion'. This tends to reflect the government's analysis of virtually any social unrest that occurs whether it be the race riots of 1969 or the activities of trade unions.

The final aspect of UMNO's strategy of social control lies in the management of ideology. There are many facets of this which include the operation of the education system; the activities of the Rulers and the promulgation of Islam as the state religion. However, here we will concentrate on the mass media.

Radio and television is government-owned and broadcasts in four languages, Bahasa Malaysian, Chinese, Tamil and English. It exists to diffuse government policies and programmes. Thus: 'All aspects of programming, especially the news, emphasise promotion of national unity and the creation of a Malaysian identity'.[90]

Since 1969 an increasing number of broadcasts have been in Bahasa Malaysian and more Malay newsreaders have been employed. The government's handling of radio and television clearly illustrates its intention to restructure society in a more 'Malay' image, a policy which is reinforced by the frequent interruption of programmes for Islamic prayers. Radio and television are thus straightforward government mouthpieces and giving air-time to opposition political parties of dissenting social groups is simply unheard of.

The press is more interesting as it is not directly government controlled and therefore has the potential to encourage or allow 'freedom of expression'. However, the press labours under severe difficulties and constraints. Firstly, every newspaper must obtain an annual licence to publish under the 1971 Printing Press Act. Secondly, journalists and editors must be acutely aware of the provisions of the Sedition Act and the Rukunegara. These pressures tend to lead to a climate in which editors feel that: 'It is not the newspaper's role to check on government. The papers here are not pro- or anti-government, but supporters of government'[91] and

> You must remember the context in which we are working, the environment. After 13 May, controlling ourselves within the press became very important. Many sensitive issues were and are about and we don't want to feel responsible for tipping the balance: we want to play it safe and if we are accused of being cautious this is true.[92]

Editors are wise to be cautious – the previous Managing Editor of the *New Straits Times*, Samad Ismail, is currently detained under the ISA.

The press is therefore effectively muzzled although opposition politicians' activities are occasionally reported. When this is done it tends to be in a derogatory fashion or as a small item on an inside page. Also, while newspapers are not directly owned by the government, they are often controlled by political parties which make up the National Front or by government-controlled statutory bodies. For instance, of the main English language newspapers, the *New Straits Times* is 51 per cent owned by PERNAS (a government trading corporation), the *Star* is owned by the MCA and the *Echo* by Gerakan and Berjaya, two Front parties.[93]

Messages reaching people in Malaysian society through the mass media are thus overwhelmingly pro-government and pro-UMNO. Statements by UMNO leaders are given special prominence and disputes within UMNO (which are frequent) are played down or not mentioned at all. The official ideology of the benevolent government striving to build a prosperous multi-racial society is hammered home relentlessly.

Dissenting groups are portrayed as 'communally-inclined' or 'anti-national' elements and their activities are disparaged. To opposition leaders, the most disturbing aspects of these distortions is the constant branding of their parties as 'communal' when in fact their membership is open to all racial groups in sharp contrast to UMNO where race is an essential badge of admittance. The mass media can therefore be used as a major ideological tool for keeping race-consciousness high and preventing the growth and development of class-consciousness.

Conclusion

In a paper written over nine years ago Michael Stenson suggested that: 'it would not be too much to argue that the Malay-instigated race riots of May 1969 arose from a form of transferred frustration having its roots in intra-Malay class conflict'.[94] We have sought to demonstrate a wider but related proposition, namely that all racial conflict in the Malaysian social formation has its origins in the struggle between classes. Primarily this is a struggle between capital and labour, between the ruling power-bloc and the workers and peasants. But secondarily and crucially for our analysis, the contradictions between fractions of the power-bloc have given rise to a specific conjunctural context in which race is deployed as a vehicle of legitimation and a mechanism of social control and domination.

Further, the Malaysian social formation is a product of imperialism and colonialism, of the penetration of the capitalist mode of production into formations previously dominated by the feudal and lineage modes. Thus, although capitalist relations of production now dominate there are many political and ideological effects which relate to the pre-capitalist period and which have been institutionalised because of their usefulness in paving the way for and facilitating further imperialist penetration. The class structure which has emerged as a result of this articulation and uneven and restricted development is one which encompasses shifting alliances between fractions of the power-bloc and international capital. Race intersects and influences the nature of these alliances whose contradiction become more apparent over time thus revealing the potential for further racial conflict. At the same time imperialist penetration leads to increased social differentiation thus raising the possibility of greater class conflict and indeed eventually revolution.

In the first phase of independence from 1957 to 1969 Malaysia pursued an essentially laissez-faire economic policy under which foreign capital and local comprador capital was allowed a more or less free hand. State intervention was confined to providing the infrastructure which facilitated capital accumulation. The alliance of Malay aristocratic, bureaucratic and landed interests with Chinese comprador capital was a successful one in the sense that overt tensions only occasionally became apparent. However, even during the 1960s pressure was building up from the Malay aristocratic and bureaucratic groups who demanded a greater control of the economy to match their political power. Dissatisfaction also grew amongst the Malay peasantry as a laissez-faire capitalism led to increasing class polarisation in the countryside.[95]

At the same time the non-Malay population was becoming disaffected over the failure of the state's social policies, the compromises required by racial politics and the brief inclusion and subsequent expulsion of Singapore from the Federation.

The 'racial' explosion of 13 May 1969 must be seen against this background of increasing social tension, but our concern here has been with the class configuration which has emerged since. The most significant aspect of this has been the increased intervention of the state and the rise of the (mostly Malay) bureaucratic class. We have attempted to show that this class in alliance with aristocratic and landed class fractions has sought to enhance its control over the economy and also to spawn a new Malay capitalist class through the NEP. The traditional alliance with Chinese comprador capital remains but has come under increasing strain as a result of the need to invoke legitimising racial ideologies. In the late 1970s then, the Malay hegemonic faction within the power-bloc has been forced into a closer alliance with foreign capital.

The above class is a shifting alliance which has led to an unstable situation in which the dominant class, and indeed fractions of it, have less and less room for manoeuvre. Unwilling or unable to promote progressive social change the regime in power has effectively sought to resolve these conflicts, contradictions and inconsistencies by ideological manipulation and repression, a state of affairs which is admirably summed up by M.J. Rajakumar:

> The poor are a threatening but disorganized constituency. To prevent them gaining their objectives it is necessary to keep them divided by communal politics, to turn their minds away from scientific and modernizing ideals to religion and the hereafter and to keep their organizations weak. Trade unions and peasant organizations can be powerful lobbies for the relatively poor sections of the people. Extreme repressive measures are needed to prevent trade unions and peasants organizations from successfully fighting for greater shares. Greater repression is needed to prevent the even poorer sections from joining them in an endeavour to recast society closer to their heart's desire.[96]

In conclusion then, we would suggest that Malaysia's official image as an harmonious and prosperous plural society is an illusion. In addition the government's policies and statements in favour of national unity[97] do nothing to alter the facts of class compromise and class domination which underline the existence of racial tension. Indeed, beneath the surface there lurks the potential for social conflict immeasurably greater than that which occurred on 13 May 1969.

Notes

1   For an account of the pre-colonial political systems of the Malay Peninsula see Gullick, J.M., *Indigenous Political Systems of Western Malaya*, London, Athlone Press, 1968.
2   A discussion of the history of north Borneo can be found in Wang Gungwu (ed.), *Malaysia: A Survey*, Praeger, New York, 1964.
3   The evidence on class relations in pre-colonial Malay society is scanty but we are using the term 'semi-feudal' to describe the mode of production in the Malay sultanates and 'lineage' to describe that obtaining amongst the Orang Sali and the various tribal groups of northern Borneo.
4   This penetration is analysed in Emerson, Rupert, *Malaysia: A Study in Direct and Indirect Rule*, Macmillan, London, 1937.
5   See Stenson, Michael, *Class, Race and Colonialism in West Malaysia*, University of Queensland Press, Queensland, 1980, for a discussion of immigration particularly from India.
6   A phrase used by J.S. Furnivall in his work on Southeast Asian plural societies. See his *Colonial Policy and Practice*, London, Cambridge University Press, 1948.
7   For a discussion of the colonial ideology of harmony and consensus

combined with a policy of racial divide and rule see Abraham, C.E.R., 'Race Relations in West Malaysia – With Special Reference to Modern Political and Economic Development', unpublished D.Phil. Thesis, University of Oxford, 1976.

8 Strong criticism of these academic approaches is contained in a short paper by Abdul Rahman Haji Embong, 'A Comment on the State of the Sociology of Race Relations and Political Sociology in Malaya', *Jernal Antropoloji dan Sosioloji*, Jil.III 1974, pp.63-8.

9 An increasing number of works in this school are appearing but see particularly Stenson, Michael, 'Class and Race in West Malaysia', *Bulletin of Concerned Asian Scholars*, Vol.8, No.2, 1976, pp.45-54; Selveratnam, V., 'Decolonisation, the Ruling Elite and Ethnic Relations in Peninsula Malaysia', *IDS Discussion Paper No.44*, Institute of Development Studies, University of Sussex, 1974; Cham, B.N., 'Class and Communal Conflict in Malaysia', *Journal of Contemporary Asia*, Vol.5, No.4, 1975; and Lim Mah Hui, 'Ethnic and Class Relations in Malaysia', *Journal of Contemporary Asia*, Vol.10, No.1/2, 1980, pp.130-55; and for a comprehensive account of class formation see Sundaram, Jomo Kwame, 'Class Formation in Malaya: Capital, the State and Uneven Development', unpublished Ph.D. Thesis, Harvard University, 1977.

10 These phrases originate in the work of Louis Althusser. The repressive state apparatus includes the police, army, bureaucracy and so on while the ideological state apparatuses are those institutions which ensure the reproduction of the ideologies of the dominant class – such as the education system and the mass media.

11 Lim Mah Hui, 'Political Economy of the State in Malaysia', paper presented at the Annual Meeting of the Association of Asian Studies, March 1980, Washington, D.C., USA.

12 Hashim Hussin Yaacob, 'Development and Restructuring of Society: Some Social and Cultural Dilemmas in a Transitional State', paper presented at the Fourth Malaysian Economic Convention Agenda for the Nation: Public Policies for Restructuring of Society, published by Pertsatuan Ekonomi Malaysia, Kuala Lumpur, May 1977, pp.394-416.

13 Stenson (1976), *op. cit.*

14 Selveratnam, *op. cit.*

15 For a full review and critique of various approaches to the state in peripheral societies see Ziemann, W. and Lanzendorfer, M., 'The State in Peripheral Societies' in Milibrand, R. and Saville, J. (eds), *The Socialist Register*, 1977, The Merlin Press, London, 1977, pp.143-77.

16 Here we are employing terminology derived from the work of Nicos Poulantzas, some of which will be referred to below.

17 For a discussion of the concept of class fractions see Massey, Doreen and Catalano, Alejandrina, *Capital and Land: Landownership by Capital in Great Britain*, Edward Arnold, London, 1978, pp.22-54. In some circumstances a fraction of a class can come into conflict with another fraction of the same class, particularly if, as in the Malaysian case, it is racially based.

18 Husin Ali, Syed, *Malay Peasant Society and Leadership*, Oxford University Press, Kuala Lumpur, 1975, p.19.

19 For some examples of the political role of the sultans see Milne, R.S. and Mauzy, Diane K., *Politics and Government in Malaysia*, Federal Publications, Kuala Lumpur, 1978, pp.257-61.

20 The number of Tuns, Tan Sris, Datuks, etc., is remarkable, far exceeding the pretensions of the British honours system.

21 Milne and Mauzy, *op. cit.*, p.259.

22 The way in which Malays from the United Malays National Organisation (UMNO) have encouraged the idea that the Malays as a whole will be uplifted by the creation of a class of Malay millionaires is critically reviewed by Syed Hussein Slatas in his book *The Myth of the Lazy Native*, Frank Cass, London, 1977, especially Chapter 10, 'Mental Revolution and Indolence of the Malays', pp.147-65.

23 For a description of this process see Shamsul Amri Baharuddin, 'The Development of the Underdevelopment of the Malaysian Peasantry', *Journal of Contemporary Asia*, Vol.9, No.4, 1979, pp.434-55.

24 See Stenson, *op. cit.*, (1976), pp.45-54.

25 Baharuddin and Stenson suggest that teachers and other officials have used their positions to accumulate land and have joined moneylenders and middlemen as part of the landowning class. See Baharuddin *op. cit.*, and Stenson, *ibid.*

26 None of Malaysia's development plans including the *Third Malaysia Plan* contain any serious proposals for land reform.

27 Kessler, Clive, S., *Islam and Politics in a Malay State: Kelantan 1838-1969*, Cornell University Press, Ithaca, 1978, p.165.

28 Stenson, *op. cit.*, (1976), p.47. Kelantan's population is over 90 per cent Malay, and Kessler and Stenson argue that given a racially homogeneous population, processes of social differentiation based on the ownership of land became more apparent than on the west coast of the Peninsula where the population is mixed and political leaders can therefore indulge in racial politics.

29 For a report of riots by 10,000 farmers in Kedah on 23 January 1980, see *Far Eastern Economic Review*, 8 February 1980, p.20.

30 See Baharuddin, *op. cit.*, and Fatimah Halim, 'Differentiation of the Peasantry: A Study of Rural Communities in West Malaysia', *Journal of Contemporary Asia*, Vol.10, No.4, 1980.

31 Ziemann, W. and Lanzendorfer, M., *op. cit.*, p.165.

32 Poulantzas, Nicos, *Classes in Contemporary Capitalism*, Verso, London, 1978, p.78.

33 A phrase used by Poulantzas to indicate that social forces condensed within the state reflect the structure of a class society.

34 Ziemann, W. and Lanzendorfer, M., *op. cit.*, pp.161-2.

35 For a description of this process see Puthucheary, Mavis, *The Politics of Administration: The Malaysian Experience*, East Asian Social Science Monographs, Oxford University Press, Kuala Lumpur, 1978, pp.25-38.

36 For a discussion of the formation of a 'bureaucratic class' see Hashim Hussin Yaacob, *op. cit.*, and Lim Mah Hui, *op. cit.*, 1980.

37   For a comprehensive analysis of the functioning of the Malaysian bureaucracy see Puthucheary, *op. cit.*

38   See Enloe, Cynthia, H., 'Malaysia's Military in the Interplay of Economic and Ethnic Change', in Lent, John A. (ed.), *Cultural Pluralism in Malaysia: Polity, Military, Mass Media, Education, Religion and Social Class*, Center for Southeast Asian Studies, Special Report Number 14, Northern Illinois University, 1977, pp.17-31.

39   Taylor, John G., *From Modernization to Modes of Production: A Critique of the Sociologies of Development and Underdevelopment*, Macmillan, London, 1979, p.250. Several of John Taylor's ideas particularly on the class structure of Third World formations have helped me to clarify my analysis in writing this chapter.

40   Here we are avoiding the difficult question of attempting to distinguish between 'comprador' capitalists and 'national' capitalists. While the existence of purely 'national' capitalists is not ruled out, in the Malaysian case the vast majority of capitalists are involved in the circulation of commodities tied to the international market. One of the aims of the New Economic Policy appears to be to create a class of 'national' (Malay) capitalists who may, in certain circumstances, advocate policies against the interests of foreign capital, or may form alliances with new sectors of foreign capital originating in the Islamic world (e.g. links with Saudi Arabia or Libya). For a full discussion of the problems of differentiating between national and comprador capital see Sundaram, *op. cit.*, (1977), pp.282-305 who comments: 'The proportion of local capital which is neither subordinate to foreign capital nor tied into the international commodity circuits is small' (p.304).

41   According to Malcolm Caldwell: 'It was indeed, conscious British policy to "protect" Malay traditional subsistence society, and in pursuit of this aim obstacles were put in the way of Malays seeking to obtain footholds in the commercial sector'. Caldwell, M., 'The British "Forward Movement", 1874-1914' in Mohamed Amin and Malcolm Caldwell, *Malaya: The Making of a Neo-Colony*, Spokesman, Nottingham, 1977, pp.13-38, 23.

42   Taylor, *op. cit.*, p.249.

43   Potential Chinese national capitalists find it difficult to identify with the state in the present conjuncture dominated by racial ideology and are likely to identify with regional 'overseas Chinese' capitals. However, the NEP is already creating a small Malay capitalist class.

44   For an account of this liberation war or 'Emergency' which lasted from 1948-60, see Hanrahan, Gene, Z., *The Communist Struggle in Malaya*, University of Malaya Press, Kuala Lumpur, 1971.

45   This racial strategy is embodied in the activities of the Malaysian Chinese Association (MCA), a senior partner in the National Front Government with membership open only to the Chinese. Chinese culture, language and education are emphasised as well as vertical clan and dialect group ties in order to persuade Chinese workers that the racial group should be the focus of their allegiance.

46   PERNAS (Perbandan Nasional), MARA (Majis Amanah Rakyat), UDA

(Urban Development Authority), SEDC's (State Economic Development Corporations).

47 Hashim Hussin Yaacob, *op. cit.*, p.410-11.

48 The DAP (Democratic Action Party) was originally an off-shoot of the PAP (People's Action Party) of Singapore and was formed after Singapore's exit from Malaysia in 1965. It is now the largest opposition party in the Federal Parliament and adopts a social democratic and pro-Chinese set of policies. Gerkan Rakyat Malaysia was founded in 1969 by middle-class professionals (doctors, university lecturers, etc.).

49 For an account of the Labour Party and indeed other 'non-communal' parties see Vasil, R.K., *Politics in a Plural Society: A Study of Non-Communal Political Parties in West Malaysia*, Oxford University Press for the Australian Institute of International Affairs, Kuala Lumpur, 1971.

50 I say 'militant labour' because the middle class has been cooperative in the creation of a compliant and subservient trade union movement such as exists today in Malaysia. For a more detailed discussion of this see Stenson M., *op. cit.*, (1980); Stenson, M., *Industrial Conflict in Malaya: Prelude to the Communist Revolt of 1948*, Oxford University Press, London, 1970; and Morgan, Michael, 'The Rise and Fall of Malayan Trade Unionism, 1945-50', in Amin, Mohamed and Caldwell, Malcolm, *Malaya: The Making of a Neo-Colony*, Spokesman, Nottingham, 1977, pp.150-99.

51 We shall not discuss the New Economic Policy (NEP) in detail in this chapter although clearly its operation is symptomatic of the conflict between class fractions within the power-bloc and the petit-bourgeoisie. For a further analysis of this question see Sundaram, J.K., 'Restructuring Society: The New Economic Policy Revisited', *Persatuan Ekonomi Malaysia Conference*, Kuala Lumpur, 1978, Lim Mah Hui, *op. cit.*, (1980), and Chandra Muzaffar, 'Some Political Perspectives on the New Economic Policy', *Fourth Malaysian Economic Convention*: Agenda for the Nation: Public Policies for Restructuring Society, 19-21 May 1977, published by PEM.

52 Baharuddin, *op. cit.*, p.443.

53 *Ibid.*, p.444.

54 At the time of writing the Malay class which controls the state is threatened on its Islamic wing not only by PAS but by the rise of other Islamic groups and by their links with the Islamic world in general. Many government ministers are more worried by this development than by any others within Malaysia. For an account on the rise of radical Islamic groups see 'Islam's Rising Cry', *Asiaweek*, 24 August 1979, pp.21-31; Tasker, Rodney, 'The Explosive Mix of Muhammad and Modernity', *Far Eastern Economic Review*, 9 February 1979, pp.22-9; and Kessler, Clive S., 'Malaysia: Islamic Revivalism and Political Disaffection in a Divided Society', *Southeast Asia Chronicle*, Issue No.75, October 1980, pp.3-11.

55 For an account of the ruling party's activities in Kelantan in 1978 see Lim Kit Siang, 'NOC Rule in Kelantan' in Lim Kit Siang, *Time Bombs*

in Malaysia, Democratic Action Party, Petaling Jaya, 1978, pp.247-59.

56 The PSRM has made strenuous efforts to gain Malay support in states such as Pahang and Trengganu.

57 Stenson, *op. cit.*, (1980), p.214.

58 *Ibid.*, p.25.

59 Stenson, *Industrial Conflict in Malaya, op. cit.*, (1970).

60 The MIC and the MCA are both partners in the ruling National Front, and formed the original Alliance Government with UMNO.

61 For an analysis of these processes see Hans Dieter Evers, 'Race and Class: The Structure of Malaysian Urban Society', paper presented to the Department of Malay Studies, Universiti Malaya, September 1979.

62 See Stenson, *op. cit.*, (1976).

63 Here we are arguing that only when the Malay proletariat is faced with a Malay bourgeoisie will class antagonisms begin to replace ethnic conflict and resentment. This can occur in the government departments and statutory authorities. For a discussion of ethnic and class consciousness see Lim Kah Cheng, 'Class and Ethnic Consciousness Among Women Factory Workers in Penang – A Case Study', unpublished M.Soc.Sc. Thesis, Universiti Sains Malaysia, Pulau Pinang, 1979.

64 For a discussion of modern, multinational penetration see Sivanandan, A., 'Imperialism and Disorganic Development in the Silicon Age', *Race and Class*, Vol.XXI, No.2, Autumn 1979, p.111-27.

65 Stenson, *op. cit.* (1970), describes this struggle in detail.

66 Michael Morgan, *op. cit.*, p.192.

67 See the final part of this chapter for a brief discussion of the government's repressive measures.

68

Product	% of Malaysia's Export Earnings
Natural Rubber	28.3
Tin	14.9
Palm Oil	10.7
Timber	14.4
Petroleum	6.6

Source: *Malaysia in Brief*, Ministry of Foreign Affairs, Kuala Lumpur, 1976.

69 For an analysis of the role of multinational corporations see Lim Mah Hui, *Multinational Corporations and Development in Malaysia*, Department of Anthropology and Sociology, University of Malaya, October 1975 (mimeo). And for the effect of this economic strategy upon the labour force see *Southeast Asian Chronicle*, Issue No.66, January/February 1979, 'Changing Role of SE Asian Women: The Global Assembly Line and the Social Manipulation of Women on the Job' and Lau, Esther, 'Why Miss Free Trade Zone is a Soft Touch', *Guardian*, 4 March 1981, p.8.

70 Poulantzas, *op. cit.*, p.164.

71 The hegemonic fraction is that fraction of the ruling class which is politically and ideologically dominant at a particular time. Given the attempt of the (Malay-controlled) state to promote Islam and Malay

culture as well as the political predominance of UMNO, a strong case can be argued that this group is, (at least domestically) hegemonic.

72   It would be incorrect to see these class fractions as entirely discrete. For example, both aristocrats and bureaucrats own land while many aristocrats work in the state apparatuses.

73   Foreign interests own 54.9 per cent of all share capital in limited companies in Malaysia. The Chinese share is 27.9 per cent and the Malay 2.3 per cent. See *Third Malaysia Plan*, Government Printer, Kuala Lumpur, 1976, Table 4.16, p.86.

74   For a discussion of the investment of domestic capital overseas by the Chinese and the private investment drought in Malaysia see *Far Eastern Economic Review*, 13 April 1979, pp.36-9. In this article, Ho Kown Ping argues that 'The smaller pool of private savings is one reason for the investment drought. But the other reason is simply the massive rate of capital flight, the exodus of private wealth abroad'. From an original estimate of M$2.45 billion for the plan period (third Malaysia Plan), the actual amount of capital outflow is expected to be two and a half times higher at M$7.57 billion. Ho argues that the government has used the windfall of petroleum revenues to 'foot the bill for investment shortfalls in the private sector' and that this 'results in the curious anomaly where the state is the dominant investor in private enterprise'.

75   Reflected in a series of seventy interviews which the author carried out with Malaysian politicians, bureaucrats, capitalists and trade unionists in 1979.

76   Source of data: *Information Malaysia 78/79*, Berita Publishing Sdn., Bhd. Kuala Lumpur, 1979, p.49.

77   Interview with Dr Goh Cheng Teik, Deputy Minister of Transport, October 1979.

78   Interview with Tan Sri Lee Siok Yew, former Minister of Health, September 1979.

79   Ismail Kassim, *Race, Politics and Modernisation: A Study of the Malaysian Electoral Process*, Time Books International, Singapore, 1979, p.9.

80   For dramatic examples of this interference during the 1970s see Bruce Ross-Larson, *The Politics of Federalism*, Singapore, Singapore University Press, 1976.

81   Encik Lee Lam Thye, Director of the Political Bureau of the DAP, speaking at the Foram Rakyat on 'Democracy in Malaysia', organised by Aliran, 10-11 December 1977 in Penang. Reprinted in the booklet *Whither Democracy? An Analysis of the Malaysian Experience*, Aliran Publications, May 1978.

82   Means, Gordon P., *Malaysian Politics*, New York University Press, New York, 1970, p.415.

83   Personal interview in Kuala Lumpur, October 1979.

84   Interview with Encik Lim Kit Siang, Secretary-General of the DAP in Kuala Lumpur, September 1979.

    Some examples of 'Chinese' compared with 'bumipurtra' constituencies in Sarawak are as follows:

Maling: 23,096: Dr Wong Soon Kai
Padungan: 20,941: Datuk Haji Shahbuddin Cheng Yew Kiew
Stampin: 20,146: Datuk Amar Sim Kheng Hong
Katibas: 6,686: Ambrose Blikan Anak Enttwan
Sebandi: 6,537: Sharifah Mordiah bte Tku Haji Fauzi
Machan: 6,888: Gramong Juna
Source: *New Straits Times*, 24 September 1979.

85 See Bruce Ross-Larson, *op. cit.*, p.45 for an account of government constitutional manoeuverings in Sarawak.

86 Speech by Lim Kit Siang in the Federal Parliament on 8 November 1978 reprinted in Lim Kit Siang, *Time Bombs in Malaysia*, Democratic Action Party, Petaling Jaya, 1978, p.250.

87 Amnesty International British Section, *Report of an Amnesty International Mission to the Federation of Malaysia 18 November-20 November, 1978*, London, July 1979.

88 *Ibid.*, pp.9-10. Interestingly from our point of view the most prominent Malaysian sociologist of race relations, Syed Husin Ali, Professor of Sociology at the University of Malaya, was detained from 1974 until 1980.

89 *Ibid.*, pp.11-12.

90 Lent, John A., 'The Mass Media in Malaysia', in Lent, John A. (ed.), 1977,*Cultural Pluralism in Malaysia, op. cit.*

91 Quoted in *ibid.*, p.39.

92 Interview with Dr Mohamed Noordin Sopiee, Managing Editor of the *New Straits Times* in Kuala Lumpur, October 1979.

93 Data supplied by Dr Mohamed Noordin Sopiee.

94 Stenson, *op. cit.*, (1976), p.48.

95 For a more detailed account of these changes see Sundaram (1978), *op. cit.*, and Lim Mah Hui, *op. cit.*

96 Rajakumar, M.K., 'Conflict Resolution and National Progress', paper delivered at the Fourth Malaysian Economic Convention Agenda for the Nation: Public Policies for Restructuring Society, Persatuan Ekonomi Malasia, Kuala Lumpur, May 1977, pp.423-41.

97 Examples of the apparent promotion of national unity include the existence of the National Unity Board within the Prime Minister's Department in Kuala Lumpur and the 1979 National Day Slogan of 'Bersattu, Berdisiplin' (Unity and Discipline).

This chapter first appeared as an article in the *Journal of Contemporary Asia*. The editors would like to thank *JCA* for allowing them to republish it here.

4 Class and change in rural Southeast Asia

CAROL WARREN – *Murdoch University*

Any analysis of the transformation of Southeast Asian societies must include consideration of changing relations of production at the rural base. It is the rural peasantry who bore the brunt of colonial exploitation, whose 'conservatism' has been blamed for the failure of modernization in the post-colonial era, and who have been the most apparent victims of the contradictions of the development process in the last two decades.

Tradition and modernity: the orthodox interpretation

Post-war sociology of development theory supposed that the economic advancement of former colonies was largely a matter of stimulating the same evolutionary pattern of social change that had taken place in the West. The conceptual emphasis on a rigid traditional/modern dichotomy stereotyped the peasant world squarely in the 'traditional' sphere. In the Weberian terms adopted by modernization theorists the modern social type was epitomized by formal economic rationality[1] – the unfettered operation of calculating decision-making, geared to efficiency and maximization of profit. By contrast, the socially and culturally bounded world of the peasant, in which ties of kinship, religion and social and political dependence dominate productive and distributive relations, represented the antithesis of modernity.

The fetishization of this typology has had two consequences in the modernization literature. First, it led to an exaggerated view of the static nature of the traditional village community and the conservatism of the social values that characterized it. The ideal typical 'closed corporate' village community has been an anthropological truism. The peasant world view was described as a finite one of 'limited good' in which the economic advancement of some was assumed to be at the expense of others. In this zero-sum situation, a range of constraining social mechanisms to counterbalance or control, if not quite level, differences within the community were generated. The classic analyses of peasant social and cultural systems by Wolf and Foster at least recognize the structural context within which such behaviour had a practical economic logic.[2] Not so with the stereotyped treatment of tradition in the writings of Rostow, McClelland and Lerner.[3]

A second consequence has been a corollary focus in modernization theory and policy, particularly in its early phase, on the importance of the dissolution of traditional cultural values and social relations. In so far as these were perceived to impede the full play of optimum supply-demand competition in the market, and to be inimical to the accumulation of capital, they were considered an obstacle to the potential for unlimited economic growth.

Certainly the most provocative treatment of rural underdevelopment in the Southeast Asian context has been Clifford Geertz' classic study, *Agricultural Involution*. It is all the more interesting in that, while focusing on the historical roots of the contemporary Indonesian dilemma in the colonial experience (as dependency theory would do), its basic premises and conclusions ultimately hinge on the polarity between tradition and modernity and the tenets subscribed to by modernization theorists regarding the role of cultural values in economic development.

Geertz analyses the complex interrelationship between the ecological characteristics of wet-rice agriculture, the correlated socio-cultural values of Javanese peasant society and the effects of Dutch colonial policies. The thesis of *Agricultural Involution* is that the forced cultivation system[4] imposed by the Dutch from 1830 to 1870 reinforced traditional authority, increased Javanese dependence on labour-intensive agricultural practices and intensified reciprocal and redistributive social systems. Javanese society became involuted – that is, introverted, increasingly complex and rigid.

Taking up the work of a number of Dutch scholars, Geertz described the process of change in the Javanese agricultural sphere as one of 'treading water', a 'static expansion' through population growth and increase in the absolute size of the labour force which contributed to colonial capital accumulation without any return from the capitalist sector to enable regular improvements in the productivity of indigenous labour.[5] Involution in the subsistence sphere was paralleled by social and cultural involution as the Javanese adapted to the land-labour-population squeeze by intensifying community redistributive mechanisms. By share-cropping, subcontracting, communal harvesting and other means of work-spreading, the peasant ethic of 'limited good', according to Geertz, became one of 'shared poverty' in which an enormous population was held on the land 'at a comparatively very homogeneous, if grim, level of living'.[6] In this way some minimum security was assured by sharing out access to subsistence, though at the cost of limiting productivity.

Involution in Javanese economy and society is contrasted explicitly with what 'could have been' – an evolution like that which took place in Japan, where a developing industrial sector absorbed excess population and contributed to capital intensified development in the agrarian sphere, or that which he believed was incipient in the Outer Islands of Indonesia. There, for ecological reasons, the rural population was incorporated more fully into commercial production and the appropriate 'economic mentality' and associated shift in cultural values was beginning to take hold. The legacies of involution that haunt post-colonial Indonesia, Geertz contends, are the lack of accumulated capital, the encumbering over-population of its wet-rice heartland and its cultural hyper-traditionalism.[7]

Geertz' analysis falls victim to the unstated premises adopted from positivist sociology and neo-classical economics welded together in modernization theory. Predictably, his work has been criticized on the two counts mentioned previously.[8] First, it relies on a stereotyped static and functionalist conception of traditional society. Second, it directs our attention to the stultifying consequences of the persistence of traditionalism rather than the structural causes of contemporary underdevelopment. For Geertz, the tragedy of the cultivation system introduced by the Dutch was that it put the traditional tendencies of Javanese society into 'overdrive'.

Pre-capitalist social structure: revisionist debates

Considerable attention has been devoted by radical critics in recent years to defining the nature of the class structure before, during and after the colonial period in Southeast Asia, in order to rectify the culturalist bias of modernization theory in general and the Geertzian paradigm in particular. For pre-colonial society, the difficulties in both theoretical and empirical terms are enormous. Not the least of these is the distortion of the official accounts of the nature of indigenous social relations. Onghokham, for example, argues that the traditional Javanese 'communal village' salvaged by twentieth-century Dutch scholars seeking to resurrect and preserve traditional *adat*-law, was a convenient figment of their imaginations, in fact recording the nineteenth-century situation created by the colonial administration itself.[9]

Current debates centre on questions concerning the extent of communal ownership of land and collective production techniques, whether rights to land or labour were the crucial factors differentiating pre-colonial societies in the region and consequently whether their structures are best approximated by a Feudal or an Asiatic Mode of Production model. There is general consensus that access to land was not a significant problem throughout Southeast Asia until the nineteenth century[10] and that control over labour was most important in defining the nature of pre-capitalist relations of production.[11] A complex variety of tributary relations prevailed in the region, ranging from collective services and tribute paid by corporate villages to personal patron-client arrangements between landowner and dependents or landholder and state, in which cases duties were individual responsibilities. At either extreme, however, evidence suggests that much greater flexibility existed and that the degree of surplus extraction was considerably less severe in pre-colonial times. Relative enclosure and self-control of villages in some parts of Southeast Asia inhibited too much state intervention and enabled manipulation of tax rolls, etc., where collective tributary arrangements prevailed.[12] Patron-client and other relations of exploitation based on personal service of dependency obligations were ameliorated to some degree by the relative shortage of labour and opportunities for opting out by attaching oneself to a different patron or opening up new land.[13] In the final analysis the picture that emerges from regional historical studies portrays societal relations which were neither classless nor static, and in which community values and practices arose from practical productive strategies.

If rigid cultural determinism and stereotyped notions of 'tradition' have been undercut by recent research, we should not go to the extreme of denying the existence[14] of social mechanisms which enabled resources to be shared and placed some constraint on exploitation within peasant communities. Inequalities in power, wealth and status existed in all of the pre-capitalist states of Southeast Asia which we must certainly define as class societies. But the notion of a 'moral economy'[15] within the peasant community is not entirely incompatible with relations of production implied in the Marxist model of the Asiatic Mode. In this admittedly abstract and problematic conceptual type the centralized state is superimposed on relatively self-contained agricultural village communities which provide tribute in labour and kind.[16] Exploitative pressures from outside may reinforce communal orientation and the importance of a 'social rationality'[17] as the basis of productive relations to ensure survival. In other words, cultural (moral and symbolic) expressions and social relations have rational bases in the logic of the system of production.

Capitalist penetration during the colonial period created social formations which grafted the new mode of production onto forms and relations characterizing prior modes. The new class structures that emerged varied across the region according to the amalgam of pre-existing indigenous structure and the nature of state and economy in the colonizing society itself. So that in the Philippines, for example, Spanish restructuring created a peasantry in a private estate system combining feudal and capitalist relations. Full private ownership replaced usufruct rights, while landlord-tenant arrangements retained some of the features of clientage and personal dependency of the indigenous pattern.[18]

In Java, the cultivation system partially reinforced, some say it actually created, a form of Asiatic Mode[19] by reversing the balance between individual and communal landholding patterns. Dutch development of the sugar plantation system was facilitated by strengthening communal land rights. Only after the demise of the cultivation system in 1870 did capitalist penetration seriously undermine village self-sufficiency and access to land. According to Gordon it was not until the 1960s that share-cropping may have become the dominant form of relations of production in Java, and even then in a highly fragmented form, circumscribed by 'various group and communal practices . . . which constrain the free disposal of land and its produce'.[20] Elements of a pre-capitalist social rationality, though asymmetrical, persisted even in landlord-tenant relationships so long as the economic security and political and social status of the landholder had determinants within the village itself. The relative 'enclosure' of the village community, the degree of internal integration and independence from outside political and economic forces, is generally regarded as having a considerable influence on the effectiveness of village-level social sanctions and the implementation of reciprocal and redistributive obligations oriented to subsistence. The full-scale development of capitalist relations of production necessarily depended on the creation of a 'free' labour force, the loss of direct access to the means of production and the corresponding dissolution of ties of communal and personal dependence.[21]

Rural capitalism in Southeast Asia

As Higgott and Robison suggest in their introductory chapter to this book, there is growing concurrence between orthodox theorists and Marxists that the development of capitalism in Southeast Asia is today proceeding apace. The growth of landlessness and wage-labour appear to represent the final transition from communal or patron-client based productive relations to capitalist ones. The incidence of share-cropping with reasonably secure tenure is on the decline and may be considered 'comparatively marginal and privileged'[22] in contrast to wage-labour and seasonal contracts on increasingly unfavourable terms which are supplanting it. In the accumulation process, even minor differences in strategic access to land have been ramified by the penetration of capitalist relations in the last decade.

Again, the paradigmatic case is Java, where so much attention has been devoted in recent years to the micro-level impact of rural development programmes and, notoriously, the effects of the Green Revolution on village social structure and living standards.

The Green Revolution epitomized the classic modernization formula for development – a kind of alchemy of inputs. New Technology in the form of High Yielding Varieties (HYV) of rice, plus capital in the form of foreign aid and investment were to raise agricultural productivity dramatically. This in turn would have the multiple effects of enabling food production to outstrip population growth – the surplus providing a base for indigenous capital accumulation and supporting the relocation of labour from agriculture to industry. At the same time, a rise in farm income and new consumption needs would stimulate individual incentive and wean the peasant from a subsistence to a profit-oriented production mentality.

Geertz himself was pessimistic about the outcome of this 'last trump' in the hand of the rural economy, fearing it would be frittered away in the political and cultural climate of post-independence Indonesia.[23] Indeed, much of the early literature on the Green Revolution focuses exclusively on inefficiency and corruption at the top and peasant conservatism at the bottom. The failure to take account of the effects of class structures at the local and international levels is a reflection of the culturalist bias of modernization theory, and allowed policy-makers in the initial stages to ignore the implications of capitalist development in which output grows while access to its benefits constricts.

The argument that social values inhibited peasant response to Green Revolution opportunities and that they account for its failure in Java is taken to extraordinary lengths in an article by Seavoy.[24] More than enough evidence from village studies in recent years make such assertions at this late date inexcusable. Where high yielding rice strains and the rest of the Green Revolution package have been rejected or discarded, it has clearly been for good economic reasons. The high yielding varieties, pesticides, herbicides, fertilizers and improved irrigation they require were never simply 'inputs'. These were part of a package with strings attached. And all-peasants-not-being-equal, they had differential access to the cash, credit and infrastructural requirements necessary to make the new HYVs work. Those with large holdings usually had better land, more immediate access to credit facilities, a smaller margin of risks and could afford to withhold grain until prices reached optimum levels. This group did not hesitate to adopt the package.

Marginal landholders (in Java, those owning about 0.5 of a hectare) were, of course, much more vulnerable to the vagaries of nature and prices. But where credit and extention services operated to their advantage[25] HYVs did offer potential increases in surplus production. Other farmers on the subsistence margin could not afford to make optimum use of fertilizer and pesticides and consequently did not generally have maximum potential yield increases when using the HYVs. Over several years cumulative successes or failures have tended to polarize farmers in this category, allowing some to increase their holdings through purchase or lease of land belonging to those who could not meet their debts and who were in turn reduced to wage-labour.

The peasant with a very small holding usually had no access to the new technologies at all. In Java and Bali it is estimated that more than half of rural families are unable to subsist on the output from their own fields.[26] It is they who have been most adversely affected by the capitalization of agriculture having relied heavily in the past on village redistributive practices and customary labour rights for access to the surpluses of better-off neighbours. These included gifts or extra shares of padi which were expected by close friends and relatives after a successful harvest, and work-sharing practices such as the open-field harvesting system (*bawon*) which allowed anyone to participate in a harvest for a fixed proportion (ranging from 1/5 to 1/8 in different regions) of the grain cut.[27]

While the extent and character of village redistributive systems remains the subject of contention, their demise in the last two decades is incontestable. It is now conventional to talk about 'deGeertzification' and the 'end of involution' in Java.[28] Most observers note the dramatic shift to an overtly commercial basis in production decisions, as large and middle landholders adopted the HYVs and became subject to the necessity of weighing direct cost against benefit in monetary terms.[29] A concomitant is the effect of the credit system and its links with bank and government agencies outside the village on the 'enclosure' of the community and control over its numbers. Where social and political status and long-term economic security may previously have been defined within the village, the landowner is now hooked into a set of relations with banks and government agencies which transcend local sanctions.

One popularly cited symptom of the shift from 'social' to 'economic' rationality and the capacity of landowners to ignore any traditionally prescribed obligations to provide employment opportunities to fellow villagers has been the ascendency of the system of *tebasan*, most acutely felt in the areas of intensified production.[30] This is the practice of selling rice just before harvest to a contractor from outside the community who is therefore not bound by customary obligations.

The contractor is able to bring in a smaller team of itinerant agricultural labourers (again from outside the village) who will accept labour-reducing methods such as the use of the sickle instead of the traditional labour-spreading *ani-ani* knife which cuts padi panacles individually. They invariably work for a smaller proportion of the harvest, with shares commonly falling as low as 1/12 to 1/20.[31]

The Green Revolution had been expected to increase rural employment opportunities by extending double cropping. The net effect appears on balance to have accelerated unemployment levels, through organizational changes in labour use and mechanization encouraged by government credit policies. The labour displacing effects of mechanical rice hullers and tractor-tillers is well documented. According to Sinaga,

> one tractor in normal use . . . replaces 2,210 man-days of human labour per year if replacing cultivation by hoe, or 650 man-days per year if replacing a combination of plough and hoe. This represents a potential shift of more than Rp. 1 million per tractor per year away from the pockets of labourers . . . [32]

Collier estimates that the introduction of mechanical rice-hullers eliminated 125 million days of wage-labour previously open to women on Java. At the average rate of payment of 2 kilos of rice per day, this represents 250 million kilos of rice income lost annually[33] by rural Javanese families. The consequences of the modernization of agriculture have been deleterious for the poorest sectors of the rural populace despite the fact that the growth rates in agricultural productivity have been outstripping population increases.[34]

Current debate concerns whether statistical evidence conclusively demonstrates growing income disparities, and whether it actually indicates an increase in absolute poverty. As Booth and Sundrum point out, differing interpretations tend to depend upon the measures used.[35] Sundrum, relying on household expenditure data from a series of national surveys, expresses the tentative opinion that rural income distributions in Indonesia may have become more equal because expenditure in the lower income groups between 1970 and 1976 has risen at a greater rate than in the higher groups.[36]

Serious methodological problems plague the use of these statistics, however. The tendency of upper income groups to under-report expenditure and of lower income groups to over-report, as well as the difficulty of correcting for the differential impact of inflation on various income groups, has been noted.[37] Counter-conclusions arise from village level research and from the same macro-data when comparisons are based on poverty lines calculated in calorie consumption terms. Sajogyo found consumption in rice equivalents to have stayed the same or fallen for the three poorest sectors of the rural population by his calculations. His work indicates a rise in the percentage of the population in rural Java falling below the poverty line from 52 per cent in 1969 to 61 per cent in 1976.[38]

Contrasting interpretations of rural underdevelopment are further complicated by the population issue, which has long been something of a scapegoat for modernization strategists. Robert McNamara, President of the World Bank, gives it unqualified priority, 'the greatest single obstacle to the economic and social advancement of the majority of peoples in the under-developed world is population growth'.[39] The rural poverty literature has been predictably divided along theoretical lines on the extent to which causal weight is attributed to population growth in explaining evidence of eroding living standards. Interpretations from the political economy perspective analyse regressive change in terms of the process of class formation and the nature of capitalist development. Those operating from within a modernization framework, still in the tradition of the involution account, concentrate heavily on population growth.[40] Nevertheless, greater recognition of the problems of structural distortion by some writers in the latter tradition does reflect the convergence suggested by Higgott and Robison.[41]

Certainly the same patterns of increasing concentration of wealth, dispossession and labour displacement are emerging across Southeast Asia. Especially interesting are the cases of Malaysia and Thailand where the population problem could not be considered a major factor impeding development. A 1978 World Bank special report on Thailand produced devastating evidence of impoverishment and land alienation in the countryside. The bank mission estimated tenancy rates at a conservative 40 per cent in the rich rice-growing Central Plains. The number of landless and land-poor agricultural labourers is expanding by 8 per cent annually compared to the general rural population increase of about 1 per cent and now constitutes nearly a third of the rural work force.[42] Eighty per cent of farming families are seriously indebted,[43] foreshadowing no doubt the acceleration of land concentration.

In the Malaysian case, despite dramatic success in the intensification of rice production and consistently high national economic growth rates, there has been little or no improvement in living conditions for the rural poor. Three-quarters of all farms under five acres are worked by tenant farmers and increases in rent have risen tenfold over the twenty-year period to 1973.[44] Here too, credit facilities are disproportionately available to the large landholder and the advantages of adopting mechanized means of ploughing and harvesting have resulted in a disregard of previous conventions stressing the priority of the subsistence rights of landless and poor neighbours.[45]

In his paper Brian Fegan outlined the impact of harvest increasing technology in the last decade in Central Luzon, Philippines. Agricultural labour there has been replaced at every stage of the rice cycle: land-preparation, transplanting, weeding and threshing are now handled by a combination of machinery and chemicals, the result being to redistribute income 'from landless poor to the farmers, and from both the lenders and owners of capital.'[46]

Discussion of the commercialization of Southeast Asian agriculture would not be complete without some reference to the activities of transnational corporations. One widely publicized example is the introduction of plant patenting legislation in several Western countries which has been described by one author as the second stage in the Green Revolution.[47] Seed companies, progressively falling under the control of conglomerates with large holdings in fuel and chemicals, are pressing for exclusive control of genetic material used in the new hybrids. Given the inevitability that these will be bred for their responsiveness to chemical inputs, monopolization will further erode the position of independent farmers.

Notable also is the expansion of transnational agribusiness in the region on an unprecedented scale. Aside from the stranglehold that vertical integration of processing and marketing has over the small producer and the very low wages that prevail in the plantation sector, the expansion of food production for export diverts food resources from local needs and escalates the cost of basic subsistence commodities.[48] The prices of fish, tropical fruits, as well as the traditional basic staple rice, are already beyond the reach of the local consumer in many parts of the region.[49]

Conclusion

The traumatic effects of agricultural change have been a salutary lesson in the paradox of capitalist development. They reveal the critical weakness of the involution account of rural underdevelopment which did not call attention to the continuity of international structural distortions in the post-colonial period pinpointed by dependency theorists, or to the existence and transformation of indigenous class-structures emphasized more recently by the Marxists.

If capital 'did not exploit enough' to create the conditions for the full internal emergence of capitalist relations of production in Southeast Asia during the colonial period, the evidence suggests it is doing so now. To this extent, the pattern of change in rural Southeast Asia is indeed following in the path of early capitalist development in Europe in which peasants were thrown off the land as the 'so-called primitive accumulation of capital' was accomplished.[50]

The process of rural transformation is not unilineal, however, and the contradictions inherent in the change process are reflected also in debates over its longer term implications for theory and strategy. These debates no longer concern whether capitalism has arrived for the rural masses but what the eventual consequences of its debut are to be: for the modernization theorists, whether and how productivity increases will be translated into distributive advances; for the Marxists, whether and how structural change will be translated into effective class consciousness.

The negative distributive effects and potential destabilizing impact of capitalist development policies have weakened some of the evolutionary optimism of growth theorists and led to revisions in policy proposals. Renewed attention to land reform and the popularity of the Basic Needs concept indicate recognition that trickle down is not necessarily a by-product of economic growth. New proposals are concerned to reconcile growth with greater distributional equity through state intervention. Recommendations include expanding access to land through redistribution of large holdings, accelerated transmigration and settlement scheme projects, greater provision of education and credit facilities to increase opportunities for self-help and mobility for the poor, and promotion of labour-absorbing economic policies.[51] But real distributive equity contradicts the logic of private capital accumulation and the interests of those classes who hold power. The failure of land reform attempts in the recent past should be some indication of the likely outcome of the new policy approaches.

In Indonesia limits on the maximum size of holdings established by Land Reform acts have been circumvented by larger farmers who continue to expand by leasing land from those who are forced into debt or whose holdings are too small to support them. Paradoxically, legal controls on harvest shares or rentals in such cases may adversely affect the poor.[52] In the Philippines, Wurfel reports large-scale conversion to export crops in order to avoid land reform stipulations. These conversions, as well as displacement of tenants or owner-occupiers by government grant, purchase or lease of lands for corporate farming, have more than offset gains by the small number of tenants who have benefited from land reform provisions to date.[53] Redistribution of land through transmigration and settlement schemes do not offer bright prospects either. They are extremely expensive (M$47,000 per family in the case of the Federal Land Development Authority (FELDA) Settlement Scheme in Malaysia), transgress land rights of tribal minorities and often reproduce the same patterns of land concentration and disenfranchisement developing outside the pioneer areas.[54]

There is no doubt, however, that despite less sanguine projections of the advantages of development for the majority of the peoples of Southeast Asia, the modernization approach based on profit motive and private investment continues to underpin the development policies propagated in the West and adopted by most governments of the region.[55] While structural considerations seem to be making their way into the modernization literature on problems of rural underdevelopment, solutions are rarely tackled at this fundamental level. Referring to the World Bank Mission Report on Thailand which noted the dangers of the 'widening disparity of welfare among population groups' but repeated the prescription that 'development must still be based mainly on private initiative', Ho Kwon Ping comments caustically: 'Whether this was a tenet of faith, a veiled threat to those who might have contrary ideas, or wishful thinking, is difficult to know, since no reasons were given for the bank's assertion.'[56]

Redistributive reform proposals have been the main response to perceived contradictions in the development process for orthodox development theories. Ironically the new approaches might be interpreted as attempts to patch over the fissures with a revised traditionalism. The Basic Needs Model looks very much like a reinstitution of the subsistence ethic at the national level. In practice it depends on promotion of the same values of communal and household self-sufficiency mutual obligation and restrained expectations[57] previously held to inhibit development.

For political economists the determinate character of emerging class alignments is a matter of serious contention. Gordon, Hinkson and others are unqualified in asserting the impending predominance of a rural proletariat. But, while pre-capitalist relations of production are being superseded in one respect, wage-labour opportunities in both urban and rural sectors have not been sufficient to absorb the population freed from the land.

Growers' contracts in commercial livestock rearing and agricul-

History and society

ture, piece-work in manufacture, lease-rent in the urban informal sector and a range of debt-labour arrangements replicating elements of pre-capitalist patron-client relations offer advantages over wage-labour for surplus extraction in some cases. Whether these will prove to be merely transitional articulations or less transient labour forms arising from the peculiar nexus of various kinds of peripheral capitalism remains contentious.[58] One consequence of internecine debate in the radical camp has been recognition of a far greater complexity in the character of productive relations in underdeveloped social formations and consequently of the need for a more sophisticated analysis of the points at which organization and consciousness become effective possibilities. In recent years both ends of the theoretical spectrum have been forced to confront the perverse unevenness of the change process and the absurdity of tidily dichotomizing traditional and modern or capitalist and non-capitalist relations if we genuinely seek to understand it.

Notes

1 Weber, M., *The Theory of Social and Economic Organization*, (New York, Free Press, 1964).
2 Foster, G., 'Peasant Society and the Image of Limited Good', *American Anthropologist*, 67, 1965; Wolf, E., 'Closed Corporate Peasant Communities in Meso-America and Central Java', *Southwest Journal of Anthropology*, 13, 1957. See also Rambo, T., 'Closed Corporate and Open Peasant Communities: Reopening a Hastily Shut Case', *Comparative Studies in Society and History*, 19, 1978.
3 See Rostow, W.W., *The Stages of Economic Growth*, (Cambridge University Press, 1960), but also his more recent book, *How it All Began: Origins of the Modern Economy*, (New York, McGraw Hill, 1975), pp.29-32 where he specifies cultural and mental attitudes as the basis for modern economic growth; McClelland, D., *The Achieving Society*, (N.Y., Van Nostrand, 1962); Lerner, D., *The Passing of Traditional Society: Modernizing the Middle East*, (Illinois, Glencoe Press, 1958).
4 The cultivation system used compulsory peasant labour to plant and process sugar and maintain road and irrigation systems. At the same time it was designed to enable the Javanese peasantry to maintain themselves within the subsistence sector. In *Agricultural Involution*, (Berkeley, University of California Press, 1963) Geertz argues that the complementarity of sugar and wet-rice cultivation on the same fields, using the same labour, had the paradoxical effect of increasing production in both the export and subsistence sectors, while reinforcing the divide between the capital-intensive character of the former and the labour-intensity of the latter. Excellent case studies of the impact of the cultivation system on the Madiun and Pasuruan regions of Java by Elson and Onghokham provide valuable contributions qualifying Geertz'

conclusions. Elson, R.E., 'The Cultivation System and Agricultural Involution', Monash Centre of Southeast Asian Studies, Working Paper No.14, and Onghokham, 'The Residency of Madiun: Priyayi and Peasant in the Nineteenth Century', Ph.D. Dissertation, Yale University, 1975.

5 Geertz, *op. cit.*, p.79.

6 *Ibid.*, p.100.

7 Geertz uses the term 'post-traditionalism' to describe the rigidifying consequences of involution on the Javanese social and economic structure. Rostow, on the other hand, uses the term in its more logical sense to denote alterations in the characteristics of traditional society 'which permit regular growth'. (Rostow, *op. cit.*, p.6.) In that the weight of Geertz' argument concerns a failure to transcend the subsistence orientation, 'post' is less appropriate perhaps then 'hyper'-traditionalism, which better indicates the laboured 'virtuosity', formal elaboration and 'tenacity of basic pattern' he proposes to have taken place. Geertz, *op. cit.*, pp.82ff.

8 See, for example, Utrecht, E., 'American Sociologists on Indonesia', *Journal of Contemporary Asia*, 3, 1973; and Hinkson, J., 'Rural Development and Class Contradictions on Java', *Journal of Contemporary Asia*, 5, 1975.

9 'For the levelling effects of transforming individual land into communal land was in the interest of the [colonial] state . . .', Onghokham, *op. cit.*, p.212. Boeke's dual economy thesis particularly influenced Geertz. But Boeke stressed to a much greater extent the cultural basis of Javanese economic stagnation. 'Boeke argued that the great differences in economic development between Indonesians and foreigners in Indonesia was cultural and racial in nature.' *Ibid.*, p.210.

10 Even what are today among the most densely populated areas of the region are reported to have had no severe land shortages until well into the nineteenth century. See Larkin, J., 'The Causes of an Involuted Society: A Theoretical Approach to Rural Southeast Asian History', *Journal of Asian Studies*, 30, 1971, p.788 on Pampanga Province in the Central Luzon Plain of the Philippines. In Java new lands were still being opened up for expansion before appropriation of 'waste' land by colonial authorities in the early nineteenth century. Onghokham, *op. cit.*, pp.175, 188 and White, B., 'Demand for Labor and Population Growth in Colonial Java', *Human Ecology* 1(3), 1973, pp.217-44.

11 Onghokham, *ibid.*; McLennan, M., 'Land and Tenancy in the Central Luzon Plain', *Philippine Studies*, 17(4) 1969, p.657.

12 Paul Mus describes the deeply rooted autonomy of Vietnamese villages whose relative enclosure and solidarity enabled them to check intervention of external political authority. Mus, P., 'Mandate of Heaven and Politics as Seen from the Vietnamese Village', in J. McAlister (ed.), *Southeast Asia: The Politics of National Integration*, (New York, Random House, 1973), pp.297-310.

13 Onghokham, *op. cit.*, p.175.

14 As, for example, Utrecht, *op. cit.*, does in his interesting but somewhat over-zealous attack on the work of American Indonesianists.

15 Scott, J.C., *The Moral Economy of the Peasant*, (New Haven, Yale University Press, 1976).

16 Lichtheim, G., 'Marx and the Asiatic Mode of Production', *St Anthony's Papers*, No.14, 1963; Krader, L., *The Asiatic Mode of Production*, (Assen, Netherlands, 1975); Godelier, M., 'The Concept of the Asiatic Mode of Production and Marxist Models of Social Evolution' in D. Seddon, *Relations of Production*, (London, Cass, 1978).

17 I prefer the term 'social rationality' to 'moral economy' in discussing security oriented peasant relations because it recognizes the logic of analysing peasant strategies in terms of economic security without implying that they are averse to individualist risk-taking behaviour or that communal activity is grounded in a basically egalitarian ethic. It is the particular social structure which generates norms and often contradictory values, and it is the individual's position in that structure that predisposes, constrains or enables him or her to respond in certain ways and that determines the compatibility or otherwise of individually and collectively 'rational' interests. See Popkin, S., *The Rational Peasant*, (Berkeley, University of California, 1979), for a critique of the idealistic and functionalist tendencies of the moral economy approach.

18 McLennan, *op. cit.*

19 Taylor, Hill and Gordon accept the applicability of the AMP concept to pre-colonial states in Southeast Asia because of the importance of communal land and the fact that the villages remained largely self-supporting, giving tribute in produce and services on the basis of theoretical proprietary rights of the state. Taylor, J., 'Pre-Capitalist Modes of Production', *Critique of Anthropology*, Autumn 1979, pp.127-55; Hill, H., 'Class Relations within Neo-Colonialism in Southeast Asia' in K. McLeod and E. Utrecht, *The ASEAN Papers*, Queensland, Transnational Corp., 1978; Gordon, *op. cit.*; Onghokham does not accept this designation, possibly because of too rigid an approach associated with the Wittfogel 'Oriental Despotism' version of the AMP. He points out that individual ownership and patron-client relations did exist under the aegis of the Javanese State. He suggests, however, that the colonial state comes very close indeed to this model in the growth of state power and functions which had the effect of destroying private ownership and reinforcing communalism. Onghokham, *op. cit.*, pp.152-213 and 336-7.

20 Gordon, A., 'Stages in the Development of Java's Socio-Economic Formations 1700-1979', *Journal of Contemporary Asia*, 7(2), 1979, p.136.

21 Marx, K., *Capital*, Vol.1. London, Penguin, 1976, p.910 and *Grundrisse*, Harmondsworth, Penguin, 1973, pp.163-4.

22 Franke, R.W., 'The Green Revolution in a Javanese Village', Ph.D. Thesis, Harvard University, 1972, cited in R.M. Sundrum and A. Booth, 'Income Distribution in Indonesia: Trends and Determinants', in R. Garnaut and P. McCawley, *Indonesia: Dualism, Growth and Poverty*, Canberra, Australian National University, 1980.

Husken's research in a central Javanese village contradicts the conclusion that wage-labour is necessarily replacing sharecropping. His data shows that the number of sharecroppers too is expanding. These arrangements, however, are of a contractual type that is more advantageous to the landowner and provides only seasonal security to the sharecropper whose terms of rent are inevitably adversely affected by the supply of a cheap labour force. Husken, F., 'Landlords, Sharecroppers and Agricultural Labourers; Changing Labour Relations in Rural Java', *Journal of Contemporary Asia*, 8(2), 1979. See also Franke, R.W., 'Miracle Rice and Shattered Dreams in Java', *Journal of Contemporary Asia*, 4, 1974.

23 Geertz, *op. cit.*, p.146.
24 Seavoy, R., 'Social Restraints on Food Production in Indonesian Subsistence Culture', *Journal of Southeast Asian Studies*, 8, 1977.
25 This possibility was not uncommonly forestalled by political pressures exercized by village elites in their own economic interest. See Franke, R.W., 'Miracle Rice and Shattered Dreams in Java', *Journal of Contemporary Asia*, 4, 1974, pp.387-8.
26 *Kompas*, November 20 1976, cited in Collier, W., 'Food Problems, Unemployment and the Green Revolution in Rural Java', *Prisma*, No.9, March 1978, p.38.
27 Boedhisantoso, 'Rice Harvesting in the Krawang Region (West Java) in Relation to High Yielding Varieties', Monash University Centre of Southeast Asian Studies, Working Paper No. 6, n.d.
28 Hinkson, J., 'Rural Development and Class Contradictions on Java', *Journal of Contemporary Asia*, 5(3), 1975, p.328; Krinks, S., 'Rural Changes in Java: An End to Involution', *Geography*, 63(1), 1978, pp.31-6.
29 Sundrum and Booth, *op. cit.*, p.471; Husken, *op. cit.*, p.145.
30 Boedhisantoso, *op. cit.*; Husken, *op. cit.*; Singarimbun, M., 'Sriharjo Revisited', *Bulletin of Indonesian Economic Studies*, 12(2), 1976; Collier, W., 'Tebasan System, High Yielding Varieties and Rural Change', *Prisma*, 1(1), 1975; Hayami, Y. and Hafid, A., 'Rice Harvesting and Welfare in Rural Java', *Bulletin of Indonesian Economic Studies*, 15(2), 1979.
31 See Hayami and Hafid, *op. cit.*, p.107 for comparative statistics on distribution of harvesters' shares under *bawon* and *tebasan* systems in forty-eight west and central Javanese villages. Similar figures are given in Boedhisantoso, *op. cit.*, p.17; and Singarimbun, *op. cit.*, p.123. In Bali, Astika also reports a decline in the communal character of harvest labour. Astika, K.S., 'Social and Economic Effects of the New Rice Technology: the Case of Abiansemal, Bali', *Prisma*, 10 (1978), pp.51-2.
32 Sinaga, R.S., 'Implications of Agricultural Mechanization for Employ-ment and Income Distribution', *Bulletin of Indonesian Economic Studies*, 14(2), 1978, p.104.
33 Collier, W., 'Choice of Technique in Rice Milling', *BIES*, 10(1), 1974, p.120.
34 In 1980 the record rice crop represented an increase of 13 per cent over the previous year, while the 1980 census revealed a 2.3 per cent annual increase in population. Daroesman, R., 'Survey of Recent Developments', *BIES*, 17(2), 1981; *Tempo*, 24 January 1981.

35 Sundrum and Booth, *op. cit.*, pp.461-2.
36 Sundrum, R.M., 'Income Distribution, 1979-76', *BIES*, 15(1), 1979, p.171. Dapice criticizes Sundrum's choice of statistical data and discusses other evidence suggesting deteriorating income distribution, Dapice, D., 'Income Distribution 1970-77: A Comment', *BIES*, 16(1), 1980.
37 White, B., 'Political Aspects of Poverty, Income Distribution and their Measurement: Some Examples from Rural Java', *Development and Change*, 10, 1979.
38 Sajogyo's work is discussed in White, *ibid.* See also Arief, S., *Indonesia: Growth, Income Disparity and Mass Poverty*, (Sritua Arief Associates 1977). Booth and Sundrum, *op. cit.* provide a critical discussion of the limitations of both methods of assessing income disparities.
39 *New Internationalist*, No.15, 1974, p.11. For an elaboration of this position see the sections on population growth in Asian Development Bank, *Southeast Asia's Economy in the 1970s*, (New York, Praeger, 1971) and Myint, H., *Southeast Asia's Economy: Development Policies in the 1970s*, (New York, Praeger, 1971). Marxists argue that 'over-population' is not an objectively measurable phenomenon since it is relative to the stage of development of a society. Samir Amin contends that focus on the population issue obscures the real causes of underdevelopment which rest instead with national and international class divisions. See Amin, S., 'Population and Development', *Socialist Review*, 6, 1976.
40 The two positions are represented best by the material published in the *Journal of Contemporary Asia* and *Bulletin of Indonesian Economic Studies* whose editorial policies tend to be political economy and economic growth oriented, respectively.
41 The Booth and Sundrum discussion, *op. cit.*, is one example.
42 Ho Kwon Ping, 'Thailand's Broken Ricebowl', *Far Eastern Economic Review*, December 1 1978, pp.40-6.
43 Turton, A., 'The Current Situation in the Thai Countryside', *Journal of Contemporary Asia*, 8, 1978, p.13.
44 Peacock, F., 'The Failure of Rural Development in Peninsular Malaysia', in J. Jackson and M. Rudner, *Issues in Malaysian Development* (Kuala Lumpur, Heinemann, 1979), pp.380-3.
45 See, for example, Barnard, R., 'The Modernization of Agriculture in a Kedah Village 1967-1978', *RIMA: Review of Indonesian and Malayan Affairs*, 13(2), 1979.
46 Fegan, B., 'The Grim Reaper: A Decade of Harvest Increasing and Income Redistributing Changes in Central Luzon', unpublished manuscript, 1981.
47 Byres, T.J., 'The Green Revolution's Second Phase: Review of *Seeds of the Earth – A Private or Public Resource?*' by P.R. Mooney, *Journal of Peasant Studies*, 7(2), 1980.
48 Ho Kwon Ping, 'Profits and Poverty in the Plantations', *Far Eastern Economic Review*, July 11 1980.
49 Throughout Southeast Asia a substantial proportion of the rural population now depend upon cassava or maize rather than rice for the

bulk of their diet. The relative cost of these once cheap sources of carbohydrates has risen substantially in recent years because of their export value as stock feed. At the same time, average *per capita* calorie consumption in Indonesia, the Philippines and Thailand is estimated to be below the minimum daily requirement set by the FAO. See Slamet Sudarmadji, 'Food Consumption Patterns and the ASEAN Food Dilemma', *Contemporary Southeast Asia*, 1(1), 1979 and Dixon, J., 'Production and Consumption of Cassava in Indonesia', *Bulletin of Indonesian Economic Studies*, 15(3), 1979.

50 Marx' reference to the forcible destruction of feudal relations which had previously assured the European peasant access to land. The expropriation of the agricultural population, Marx argued, constituted the real process of primary capital accumulation in setting labour free from the means of production and forcing it into the general slavery of wage-labour. *Capital*, Vol.I., Penguin, 1976, pp.873-942.

51 Soedjatmoko, 'National Policy Implications of the Basic Needs Model', *Prisma*, 9, 1978; Thee, Kian Wie, 'From Growth to Basic Needs', Jakarta, Leknas-Lipi, 1980.

52 Hinkson, *op. cit.*, p.332; Utrecht, E., 'Land Reform in Indonesia', *Bulletin of Indonesian Economic Studies*, 5(3), 1969.

53 Wurfel, D., 'Philippine Agrarian Policy Today: Implementation and Political Impact', Singapore, Institute of Southeast Asian Studies, Occasional Paper No.46, 1977, pp.28-32.

54 See Peacock, *op. cit.*; Suratman and Guinness, P., 'The Changing Focus of Transmigration', *Bulletin of Indonesian Economic Studies*, 8(2), 1977; Fachurrozie, S.A. and MacAndrews, C., 'Buying Time: Forty Years of Transmigration in Belitang', *Bulletin of Indonesian Economic Studies*, 14(3), 1978.

55 A really thorough comparative analysis of the impact of contrasting approaches to development awaits parallel research on the economic and social transformation of the socialist nations of Southeast Asia – Kampuchea, Laos and Vietnam – as well as Burma which has been least committed to developmentalism in its policies to date.

56 Ho Kwon Ping, 'Thailand's Broken Ricebowl', *op. cit.*, pp.41 and 45.

57 Soedjatmoko, *op. cit.* See also Turton, *op. cit.*, p.119 on a 1977 scheme in Thailand to develop rural infrastructure using 'a kind of semi-feudal method of requisitioning unpaid labour'.

58 See Scott, C.D., 'Peasants, Proletarianization and the Articulation of Modes of Production: the Case of Sugar Cane Cutters in North Peru, 1940-69', *Journal of Peasant Studies*, 3, 1976; Husken, *op. cit.*; and Fegan, B., 'Rent capitalism in the Philippines', Working Paper No.25, Third World Studies, University of the Philippines, 1981, for differing views on the nature and tenacity of these labour relations in the Third World.

PART III   *Development strategies and the global economic order*

5 Reformist capitalist development and the New International Division of Labour

RICHARD LEAVER – *Flinders University*

The study of underdevelopment, and of the policies that contribute to it or might alleviate it, is almost entirely a post-war phenomenon.[1] As the editors have already outlined, there have been a number of phases in the intellectual evolution of 'development studies'. The most important theoretical cleavage occurred about a decade ago, when a melange of radical and Marxist scholars forcefully attacked the hitherto dominant evolutionist framework with an argument cast in a structural, totalizing logic.[2] This neo-Marxist 'revolution' struck at a point in time when liberal theorists were in low spirits after the apparent failure of the first development decade. Their arguments about the inevitability of underdevelopment within the world capitalist system were influential upon some liberals who came out of this experience highly critical of their earlier techno-cratic assumptions as champions of 'reformist capitalist development', 'basic needs development', etc.[3] The debate thus continues about whether or not the development of capitalism in the periphery can be channelled into a reformist mould that might reverse the long-run historical trend towards the worsening of mass poverty.

This chapter looks at the prospects of reformist capitalist development in the periphery in the light of existing, historically given conditions and processes. The framework employed here owes a good deal to the neo-Marxist vision of a 'world capitalist system' which was correct in establishing that the prospects for national development are never given solely by national conditions. Yet neo-Marxist analysis ultimately flounders on the reef of its own making. If, like Frank and many of his followers, we invest this totalizing world capitalist system with organic properties, then we have created a system that is a prison from within which there is no possibility of reform save total escape. The failure of all structural analysis is its total inability to recognize social change when it is staring it in the face. This is as true today of structural neo-Marxism as it was fifty years ago of structural anthropology. Reform is seen as adaptive and integrative and therefore, by nature, reform strengthens the system as a whole.[4]

The culture of structural method promoted by neo-Marxists, whereby we are constantly invited to relate everything to its broader capitalist context, has many undesirable theoretical effects. Only one of these deserves special mention here – its effect on the theory of the state. At its extreme, this structural method divests the peripheral state of all autonomy over domestic and international policy and turns it into an outpost of 'the imperial state'. One sees this in Frank's concepts of 'the lumpenbourgeoisie'[5] and of a comprador bourgeoisie and, more recently, in the writings of Petras.[6] Even when neo-Marxists retreat from this extreme, they generally end up embracing a position akin to that of Lenin in his classical analysis of imperialism – a position which sees the peripheral state as the captive of its national capitalist class. Either way, the instrumental theory of the state is unescapable, and one can only debate which class, or combination of classes, has this repressive weapon in their possession. Such debate may produce amusing recantations,[7] but on the whole it is particularly sterile.

For even in the less offensive Leninist mould, the neo-Marxist tradition assumes something that really ought to be proved – that the nationality of capital matters.[8] In this chapter it will be argued that it does not. We therefore begin with a theory of the state which does not concede this possibility *ab initio* as does the classical Bolshevik view. We start from the assumption that the state in the periphery is, by its nature, concerned both with the accumulation of capital within its boundaries – for the existence of a healthy stream of profit is in its own interest as a revenue collector and as a producer – and with the social legitimation of this accumulation process. This is not an endorsement of traditionalist theories of the state which see it as the purveyor of some common good in its internal or external policies. It is, rather, relatively autonomous from any and all 'fractions' of capital and at least partially concerned with a range of social functions that are beyond the ken of capital which, by its nature, is inherently individualistic and competitive. The degree of this relative autonomy cannot be given *a priori*, but must be established by and through concrete historical analysis.

The state is, then, more than the conduit binding external and internal interests, as neo-Marxists posit. It is an interface rather than a transmission belt, and its policies cannot be explained solely in terms of the interests of any one class, either internal or external. This is not to say that class interests are irrelevant to the form of state policy, but rather that they create a field of feasible choices rather than a single choice. In the analysis that follows, I hope to demonstrate the potency of this framework of analysis of the post-war development experience of the periphery, and that evolutionary trends within the global economy over the last decade have placed reformist strategies of capitalist development within this field of possible state policies. Neo-Marxists, because of their adherence to structural methodology, are unable to give these evolutionary trends the importance they deserve – if indeed they can see them at all.

Accumulation under import substitution

The post-war development of the periphery was, until the last decade, almost universally guided by the policy of import substitution industrialization. The general rationale for this state strategy is well known. It was originally conceived during the depression and years of the Second World War as a means of promoting the national production of industrial goods which had previously been imported but which were no longer entering world trade.[9] These physical shortages persisted into the immediate post-war years, but the policy was buttressed by the arguments of Prebisch[10] in criticism of neo-classical theories of comparative advantage. For the 'new states' of the periphery just set to emerge from the colonial shroud, these arguments were particularly convincing for colonial rule had failed to endow the colonies with any significant industrial sector.[11] Import substitution sought to remedy this handicap.

It sought to do so by using the national market as an inducement to increased levels of investment.[12] The flow of modern imports was cut off by a combination of tariff and non-tariff barriers to trade, and the captive demand for 'modern' consumption and production goods acted as a magnet to investment. Though initial investments were often modest, the theory suggested that a creeping process of backward integration would eventually turn these 'assembly plants' into fully fledged industrial complexes. Development in the periphery would be freed from the one-sided primary emphasis that had arisen under the influence of the colonial division of labour and placed on a more rounded basis not dependent on the vicissitudes of international trade for its dynamic.

Internal state policy followed the trail laid down by the state's vigilance over imports and exchange rates. Investors were favoured with cheap access to local capital markets and offered inducements such as tax holidays and favourable price structures. All 'traditional' forms of production were, by comparison, discriminated against. As in secondary industry, so in the primary sector state preference was bestowed upon the 'big farmer' in the name of progress towards modernity. Feeding the cities with low-priced consumption grains was the functional necessity clamped upon the agrarian economy. This goal, it was argued, required preference for the surplus producing big farmer using modern inputs; small farmers were starved of credit and land in an attempt to make their rural life much less attractive than that of the industrial proletariat.[13] Bias in favour of modernity therefore became endemic within the peripheral economy once the rationale for import substitution was accepted.

With hindsight, it is apparent that import substitution policies have proven an abject failure. Their fundamental goal – of easing the pressure applied by the foreign exchange constraint upon the rate of development – has not been met. There has been a change in the form of imports, but not necessarily in their overall level; indeed one can argue that these policies increase foreign exchange deficits.[14] 'Assembly plant' industries have failed to grow into mature industries as (even within free trade areas) expansion would quickly saturate the small market for 'modern' products. The choice of technique in industry adapted to small markets, with the result that these incipient industries proved uncompetitive on world markets where the superior techniques and economies of scale of industry in Western democracies ruled supreme. Import substitution policies were, therefore, congenitally incapable of altering the composition of the periphery's exports, and the distortion towards primary exports was reinforced rather than eroded.[15]

Thus the external indebtedness of the periphery escalated rapidly – from about US$27 billion in 1965 to a figure approaching US$400 billion some fifteen years later.[16] True enough, OPEC figured largely in this escalation of debt, but the failure of agricultural modernization was equally significant. Aggregate levels of food production in the periphery have barely kept ahead of population growth rates; in many countries they have slipped behind and the necessity to import food grains has been widely felt across the periphery.[17] The picture is even worse when income distribution is taken into account. Impeccably conservative econometric studies sponsored by the World Bank are showing that the welfare of the poorest 40 per cent of the periphery's population is declining absolutely as well as relatively.[18] Big farmers, as with industrialists, have not lived up to the norm of the frugal bourgeois that they were supposed to aspire to. Their profit levels are determined mainly by state incentives and disbursements, and their reinvestment patterns reveal a tendency towards speculative activities in the burgeoning tertiary sector. Such unexpected behavioural traits, it should be stressed, are not distortions but rather reflections of the social structure which modernity was supposed to wrench into the main course of modern history. Even the state, that apogee of rational calculation in bourgeois theory, is not immune to these 'distortions'.[19]

One cannot deny the facts of increasing mass poverty in spite of (perhaps because of) sometimes impressive growth rates. To neo-Marxists, this is evidence of 'the development of underdevelopment' and of the persistence of the structural form and exploitative functions of the world capitalist system. They are in no doubt that the strategy of import substitution is an adaptation to metropolitan interests, and that it is evidence of the comprador nature of the national bourgeoisie in the periphery. As Frank put the case,

> such import substitution . . . when undertaken within the framework and structure of the capitalist system, cannot afford the advertised [national] salvation, but must instead be but another step into greater dependence on the metropolis and deeper structural underdevelopment.[20]

Evidence for this position is found in the fact that import substitution generated an increase in the level of foreign investment which, in turn, ultimately leads to the excess of profit remittances over capital inflow. Import substitution both denationalizes and decapitalizes the periphery.

Elsewhere I have questioned some of the evidence marshalled in support of this conclusion. Mack and I, using figures provided by radical theorists and making assumptions favourable to their case, have argued that though there may be decapitalization occurring, this net outflow of profits does not offer a potent explanation for the perpetuation of underdevelopment.[21] The point taken up here is a different but complementary one – can we say that the peripheral state policy of import substitution is in the interests of metropolitan capital because it leads to an increase in foreign investment?

Neo-Marxists have often tried to show that foreign investment in the periphery attracts a higher rate of profit than does equivalent investment at the centre, and that the root of this 'super-profit' lies in the cheapness of wage labour in the periphery. This high profit may well be true for some foreign investment in high grade natural resources, such as oil, but in these cases labour costs are irrelevant by comparison with the chance factor of natural endowments. But for foreign investment in manufacturing under import substitution regimes, 'natural' profitability is difficult to determine. Given the possibility for transfer pricing and over-invoicing available to large corporate investors, and given the low rates of corporate taxation in the periphery *vis-à-vis* the centre, it is logical for the foreign investor to try to aggregate a large slice of his total corporate profit in the periphery. But let us be clear that in this instance it is political rather than economic factors that determine declared rates of profit.

The argument that import substitution regimes created a climate that served the economic interests of foreign investors must counter several objections. Firstly, there is the fundamental point that import substitution policies increase, rather than cheapen, the cost of peripheral labour. The institutional biases within the capital markets of the periphery in favour of 'modern' investments led to the undervaluation of capital to the modern entrepreneur and the undervaluation of labour to the 'traditional' producer. In addition, it is clear that modern investors generally paid wage rates that were well above market rates. If, therefore, one wished to argue that cheap labour constituted the economic reason for foreign investment, it would be impossible to say that import substitution policies were tailored to the interests of the foreign investor.

Secondly, the neo-Marxist argument fails to assess the opportunity costs of foreign investment behind import substitution barriers. As is now recognized, assembly plants exhibited low levels of technical efficiency. They often showed endemic underutilization of capacity in spite of their 'old' technological mix, and the stop-go characteristics of the importing process often added to those problems that were ultimately rooted in the small markets available to their products. There is now widespread evidence that import substitution industries subtracted from, rather than added to, the value-added calculations which make up aggregate indices of national accounting such as GNP.[22] To say that foreign investors had an economic interest in setting up plants that destroyed value is to stretch the credibility of analysis. Had the new states of the periphery followed a more 'open' policy package of free trade, these assembly plants would never have been born – for there is no economic justification for them. The markets of the periphery would have been serviced through imports rather than foreign investors, with the added advantage that economies of scale in industries at the centre would have increased.[23] Free trade policies in the periphery could more plausibly be said to represent the interests of advanced foreign investors than could the restrictive policies of import substitution.

To put these arguments in their bluntest form, we would argue that the phenomenon under discussion – foreign investment in the periphery behind import substitution barriers – is moulded by state policies in the periphery, and that it is not an expression of the pure logic of capitalist development, the logic of accumulation. Indeed, the policy of the peripheral state (import substitution) seems to detract from, to be in opposition to, the pure logic of accumulation. The implication is that the phenomenal post-war growth of the multi-national corporation is to be explained by reference to political forces and policies rather than economic interests. This is not to suggest that the politically ordained growth of the multinational corporation has done other than exacerbate the problem of mass poverty in the periphery, but it should be recognized that insofar as it has intensified this poverty, these consequences cannot be explained by asserting that the peripheral state was a 'captive' of the economic interests of foreign capital. If anything, the reverse seems more nearly true.

Reformulating the framework

The instrumental theory of the state is thus a barrier to the understanding of this situation. We cannot understand the rationality of import substitution in terms of a simple calculus of class interest. In this section, I hope to show that a conception of the peripheral state as relatively autonomous from all class forces (or economic interests), yet whose policy choices are limited by the structure of class interests within and beyond its domain, offers a more cogent explanation of the rationality of import substitution policies than does the theory of the comprador bourgeoisie, or indeed any variant of the instrumental theory of the state. I will start by outlining relevant features of the international system as it existed at the time when most of the new states of the periphery achieved independence, and show how, in the context of the domestic class interests within the new states, import substitution represented an optimal policy choice for the state, being concerned as it is with both the furtherance and the legitimation of accumulation within its sphere of sovereignty.

The fundamental fact of the international system in the immediate post-war years was the bipolar distribution of power within it – or, to put it slightly differently, the hegemonic position of each superpower within its sphere of influence.[24] The economic power of the United States over the 'free world' profoundly influenced the avenues in which capital could be accumulated and the ways in which national governments could tap into this process. This influence was indirectly expressed in the nature of the international institutions set up at Bretton Woods in 1944 under American guidance, and more directly expressed in the policies of the most developed forms of capital within this framework. For most of the periphery, formal independence was still some way off; when it was achieved, the framework of Bretton Woods confronted them as a 'given'.

The Bretton Woods system is commonly described as a liberal or open system. More properly, these adjectives should be used sparingly; the system was liberal in tendency but not in fact, and not even liberal in tendency so far as centre-periphery relationships were concerned.[25] The high point of post-war liberalism – the Kennedy Round of tariff reductions – was noticeable for its exclusion of the periphery and the question of primary commodities. Protectionist loopholes were built into the institutions of Bretton Woods, since neither of the main protagonists of this conference – the United States and the United Kingdom – was willing to compromise the domestic achievement of full employment policies in the name of liberal internationalism. The failure of the ITO charter reflected this transitive ordering of priorities within the Western democracies, for this was the most thoroughly liberal of the institutions proposed at Bretton Woods.[26] The General Agreement on Tariffs and Trade (GATT), the fallback position to the ITO, enshrined the right to protection at the heart of its charter. 'Escalator' tariffs imposed by Western powers restricted the degree of primary commodity processing undertaken within the periphery, and effectively buttressed the colonial division of labour within which the embryonic new states of the periphery had been conceived. The IMF did not possess the credit-creating capability to deal with long-term deficits in the balance of payments, and the sanctioning of the accumulation of trade surpluses (against the advice of Keynes), in combination with protectionist loopholes, implied that the corresponding deficits would mainly be experienced in the periphery. Conservative lending policies within the IBRD fitted into this mercantilist logic so far as north-south relations were concerned.

These institutions, and the generally restrictive thrust of their policies, were both well established by the time that 'the winds of change' signalled the rapid demise of colonialism. The already independent states of Latin America did voice their discontent at the structure established by these institutions, but their view was a minority one backed up by little bargaining power. The result was that these institutions were set on a policy course that precluded the possibility of a totally 'open' economy in the periphery; protectionism at the centre implied protectionism at the periphery. To have opened up the peripheral economy to the forces of free trade while the centre was able to block off imports from the periphery would have undermined the delicate state of social stability in the periphery. The periphery would exist only as a market for advanced consumption goods, since export of capital from the centre to the periphery would be limited to the production of primary commodities and high grade raw materials. Investment in manufacturing and processing would be strangled at birth by the protectionist loopholes available to Western democracies in defence of full employment. Overall productivity in the peripheral economy would remain low with output essentially non-industrial in composition; employment levels would remain static through lack of investment; multiplier effects would be experienced in the centre rather than the periphery, and technological capacity would remain retarded. While the bourgeoisie in the periphery could have adapted to these 'open' policies by assuming a mercantile character in importing, exporting and local distribution, such a policy mix could only generate mass discontent at declining living standards. The spectre of revolution would constantly confront the state, whose functionaries had assumed power on the promise of overcoming the defects of the colonial experience. To now reinforce those defects would be political suicide.

In the given historical conditions, then, an open economy in the periphery would have traded off too much social legitimacy for not enough fruits of the accumulation process. This implied a degree of closure for the peripheral state, yet total closure of the economy was an option ruled out for the opposite reason – that it would compromise state access to the social surplus in the name of political legitimacy. Let us see why this is so.

The extreme of a totally closed economy in the periphery would have implied the total re-ordering of production and consumption patterns. Export-earning cash crops would have to be consumed locally – which was probably impossible – or replaced by products catering to mass demands. Production would tend to take the form of petty commodity production, with the small producer owning and controlling his means of production as well as his product, and exchanging it through barter mechanisms rather than market mechanisms. From the point of view of the peripheral state, which had historically grown into a dirigiste mould, this devolution of control over production would deprive it of access to the productive processes and the streams of profit that they generated. The state could not justify an economic role for itself; it would be essentially redundant and parasitic. Attempts to crystallize and concentrate a social surplus around the state so as to further the process of accumulation could only provoke forms of populist discontent targeted at the encroachments of a parasitic state. Closure would underwrite domestic stability, but at the cost of slowing down the process of accumulation.

Seen in the light of these alternatives, import substitution policies avoided the excesses of both the open and closed strategies. Deprived of access to the deep market structures of the metropolis, these policies made possible some limited accumulation of capital in the periphery without totally compromising the delicate ideological bond that linked nationalist state functionaries to their domestic underclasses. Given that the option of utilizing cheap peripheral labour to provision markets in Western democracies was pre-empted by the mercantilist logic of the Bretton Woods system, import substitution was a defensive policy that protected the peripheral state from the full force of this protectionist tendency. Accumulation could and did proceed within the ambit of the peripheral state, and the state itself, by virtue of its orchestration of this accumulation, was simultaneously able to preserve some pretence of nationalist ideology. Yet the brunt of this accumulation process had to be borne by the underclasses within the periphery, since it was clear that peripheral accumulation was to be confined to the periphery. The heavy tax burden, depressed price structure for 'traditional' products and producers, and the state bias in favour of modernity and propertied classes in general – these are the means by which import substitution policies channelled the accumulation of capital in the periphery.[27] Seen in the broader context of the international system, these policies are the proximal cause of the perpetuation of mass poverty in the periphery in the post-war era.

The evolution of constraints on state policy

Import substitution was once a rational policy for the peripheral state under the given domestic and international conditions. It allowed some accumulation of capital within the periphery, and guaranteed the state a central role in this process. But the conditions which underwrote the rationality of this policy package twenty years ago were not fixed for all time. It is the evolution of these constraining conditions upon state policy in the periphery that will be investigated in this section. This forms a backdrop to an assessment of the rationality of strategies of reformist development in the present day and age.

It is worthwhile observing that the evolutionary trends sketched out here have little to do with calls from the periphery for a New International Economic Order. It is true that ever since 1944, the diplomacy of the periphery has shown disapproval at the Bretton Woods system, and that there have been successive attempts by peripheral states to aggregate their grievances. This perceived common interest, which transcends the diverse ideological positions held by different states, first found expression in the distinctive peripheral foreign policy of non-alignment. The more shrewd practitioners of this policy saw it as a means of attracting development funds to the periphery by engaging the superpowers in a bidding contest. More recently there are the 'trade union' activities of UNCTAD. Yet the continuity of such opposition is as marked as its failure. With the single exception of OPEC, the periphery has failed in any bids for unilateral initiative or reasoned compromise.

Proposals for reform of the international order will only be reflected in the formation of international institutions when their conditions of existence are already in being. It is the evolution of political and economic structures of the international order that interests us here.

The Bretton Woods system expressed norms of conduct that are not relevant today. Firstly, the general constraint of bipolarity – or superpower hegemony within their spheres of interest – is long gone,[28] in spite of recent talk of 'a new cold war'. American hegemony over the free world came to a decisive end a decade ago, and was signalled militarily in the Tet offensive of 1968, politically in the Guam doctrine of 1969 and economically in President Nixon's unilateral abrogation of dollar convertibility in 1971. This final crisis is the one most relevant here. The institutionalization of the dollar as a reserve international currency at Bretton Woods was the basis of American power over the free world; when this basis eroded, differences between the major Western democracies became more apparent and assumed a more political character. This lack of cohesion amongst the developed countries has given the periphery a greater degree of freedom, and one can see the significance of this in, for instance, the success of OPEC. There was no unified Western response to OPEC, while the Third World, which bore the economic brunt of oil price rises, stood behind OPEC and refused to break ranks.

Secondly, the forms of political alliances which gave expression and substance to the post-war popularity of Keynesian policies in Western democracies have collapsed.[29] These alliances between organized labour and capital depended upon the willingness and ability of the state to provide sufficient levels of employment and underwrite adequate levels of profit simultaneously. These goals implied the regulation of competition amongst capitals through state policy. Insofar as deficit spending was required to meet these onerous objectives, Keynesian policies gave rise to inflation which, in turn, undermined the very basis of Keynesian class alliances between labour and capital. The last decade has therefore witnessed an intensification of inter-capitalist competition both within Western democracies and as a result of trade, and the ballooning out of unemployment levels to heights that were unthinkable in the years of the long boom. The potentiality for trade wars amongst the major Western powers has been ever-present, and the tendency towards protectionism in north-north trade has gathered momentum, so reversing the tendency towards greater degrees of liberalism that was the hallmark of the Bretton Woods system.

Thirdly, and as a direct offshoot of the decline of Keynesian class alliances, the patterns of investment of the most developed forms of capital – the multinational corporation – have begun to alter in significant ways. These changing investment patterns are one index of the intensification of inter-capitalist rivalry that, in a sense, no one wants but no one can prevent. For the first time in the history of the post-war era, save for the reconstruction of the Axis powers, whole industries are being re-tooled with an eye to reducing labour costs and increasing productivity. This process has some important international dimensions which are of fundamental significance to the form of state policy in the periphery and, through this, to levels of mass welfare in the periphery.

The most important of these changes in global investment patterns has been referred to as the dedomiciling of capital.[30] This refers to the tendency for industrial capital to move into selected locations in the periphery, so combining cheap labour with the most modern forms of industrial technology, with the aim of producing for the markets of the Western democracies. This form of investment is not to be confused with foreign investment behind import substitution barriers, where technology was not modern and the aim was merely to supply domestic markets. The dedomiciling of capital, by its very nature, amounts to a radical attack upon the international division of labour that was hitherto enforced by the mercantilist tendencies of the Bretton Woods system. Wage differentials between centre and periphery of the order of 10:1 are the proximal cause of this relocation of capital, but the reduction of bulk transport costs and the ability to reduce the process of manufacture to a series of elemental steps are facilitating conditions.[31] One consequence of this movement of capital into the periphery is a radical shift in the composition of the exports of the periphery in conjunction with an abrupt upward movement in the level of exports.[32] Under the Bretton Woods system, the periphery's aggregate contributions to world trade suffered a long-run relative decline, while its qualitative contribution to world trade was restricted to primary products. The dedomiciling of capital has the potentiality to reverse both of these features.

Fourthly, the dedomiciling of industrial capital is a process that is complementary to the shifting strategies of accumulation in the extractive industries. The case of the oil industry is the best example of this, and though there are many features of this case that must be explained in terms of the peculiar characteristics of petroleum as a use-value,[33] there are lessons to be learned from OPEC that are of general relevance to extractive industries across the world.[34] The most important of these is the evolution of a common interest between producer states and oil companies in the regulation of the global market. This can lead to an effective alliance between corporate interests in accumulation and state interests in the balance of payments at the expense of consumer nations. The possibilities which this raises for the patterns of capitalist development in the periphery are of historic significance.

A short digression is in order here to clarify the issue of the lessons to be learned from oil. The industry is a classic example of the workings of monopoly capital, and it figured prominently in Lenin's analysis of imperialism. A high degree of vertical integration and a high level of concentration of ownership characterize the industry – at its zenith, 80 per cent of the world's oil was handled by the seven 'majors'. The tendency towards cartel formation has been a constant preoccupation of the majors as a glut of oil that would send its price through the floor is the last thing that they would want.[35] The various consortia that were established to tap the rich fields of the Middle East show substantial evidence of restraint upon the total output. At times the majors worked closely with their home governments just as Lenin and neo-Leninists would predict.[36] But during the 1960s, their political allegiances began to shift towards a closer relationship with their host governments. The reason for this shift was that the majors were losing control over the supply of oil as new producing states and independent companies moved into the market, creating some measure of price competition.[37] The companies and their home governments were powerless to put an end to this competition, but OPEC states were not. Though OPEC has never been able to achieve unanimity on production quotas for members, their common interest in stabilizing the market for oil gave them a bargaining point for negotiations with the majors. Immediately prior to the spectacular price rises of 1973 – rises that are probably unique to the case of oil – the oil majors and producer states had thrashed out, at the Teheran and Tripoli negotiations, arrangements that traded off market instability for moderate, programmed price rises.[38] These negotiations exposed a common ground between producer states and oil majors in market stability, and it is here that there are lessons for other producers and host states.

In this case, as with the dedomiciling of capital, it is clear that neo-Marxist analyses which begin with the Leninist assumption that capital is inherently national, and that it works hand in hand with its 'home' state, are simply obscuring the processes at work. These assumptions may be warranted at certain points in the passage of historical time, but they are not universally valid. British capital is still very productive in its overseas activities, but this is of little benefit to the overall state of development of the British economy – indeed, many would argue that the British post-war crisis is partly the result of the overseas strength of British capital. The United

States, as a 'young' capitalist country, may just now be facing the prospect of a similar process of degeneration in the dedomiciling of capital.

Yet the state in advanced Western democracies is unable to put an end to this dedomiciling even though it would like to.[39] The fact that industries, or the labour-intensive parts of industries, are being physically wrenched out of the metropolis and grafted on to the periphery implies a lower growth rate, reduction in levels of employment and adverse effects upon the balance of payments for the metropolis. The process will encounter union hostility and electoral disapproval, yet such forms of popular opposition will prove ineffectual. The state will offer sops to domestic opposition while covertly supporting and facilitating the outward drift of capital, for when the most advanced forms of capital are forced to relocate in search of a competitive edge, the long-run cost of not facilitating this relocation is a strike of capital. Protectionist lobbies that once worked will prove ineffective without the support of the multi-national corporations. Insofar as the state can offset the real and adverse effects of this capital export, it will attempt more aggressive exporting policies into the markets of other advanced democracies. Thus the liberalization of north-south linkages will tend to be accompanied by rising mercantilization of north-north linkages. The result may tend towards what Evans once called the 'super-bloc'[40] – a condominium of an 'advanced' region with several offshore 'satellites'. The EEC's African policy is the exemplar of this tendency.

Implications for peripheral development

The question that remains to be answered is this: what will the easing of these international constraints upon the process of accumulation imply for the form of state policy in the periphery? If this implies new policies from the peripheral state, will these policies be able to lift the burden of peripheral accumulation from the underclasses in the periphery? I shall argue here that, under these new evolving conditions of the international order, reformist policies in the periphery are not only made possible but also have decided advantages.

These are rather different questions than those that are commonly asked of reformist strategies in that they focus upon the inter-relationship between domestic policy and international order. More usually, discussion of reformist strategies has been confined to a purely national framework, and the reformist impulse has consequently been rooted in a conception of enlightened self-interest amongst dominant classes. Within this framework, neo-Marxists are entirely correct to argue that reformist strategies are naive and idealistic in thinking that enlightenment is a sufficient cause for reform.[41] Dominant classes cannot be expected to favour policies that would redistribute against their interests. But the questions that we are asking do not have this 'zero-sum' flavour since we have inserted domestic policy in the periphery within the dynamic context of the changing international division of labour. Given the changes in this division of labour that have been discussed, and in particular the lifting of the foreign exchange constraint upon the rate of peripheral development, domestic policy in the periphery has been transformed into a 'positive-sum' game. It is, therefore, not solely a question of one class benefiting at the expense of another, but of reform whereby all peripheral classes benefit at the expense of the metropolis. Such possibilities lack the naivete that has traditionally surrounded discussion of reform in the periphery.

The crucial question in determining the fact of reformist strategies concerns the ways in which the peripheral state disposes of the increments of foreign exchange that it will inherit from the multinational corporations which are in the process of relocating in the periphery. There are several ways in which these increments can be squandered. Firstly, foreign exchange surpluses can be re-exported to the metropolis and invested there. This can be seen in the OAPEC states, and on this basis some commentators have argued that there is an insuperable problem of surplus 'absorption' for the periphery.[42] Insofar as this is a problem – for the level of OAPEC absorption has been rising[43] – it is primarily a political one. OAPEC states, especially the more conservative ones, have applied brakes to the rate of development in the name of preserving Islamic culture – and the quasifeudal political structure. There is little economic imperative to recycling in this manner, as OAPEC investments have been channelled into 'soft' forms within the metropolis where the rates of return are not exceptionally high. There is nothing necessary in this placement of surpluses.

Secondly, these surpluses can be disbursed as subsidies to the multinational corporations whose activities are responsible for their creation. This is certainly happening in Southeast Asia today, where the export-oriented regimes have instituted a process of outbidding one another in attracting foreign investment to their free export zones.[44] But let us be clear that such subsidies are not the cause of the relocation of capital in the periphery – the cause is the intensification of capitalist competition in the aftermath of the Keynesian era. Such subsidies are, at best, a marginal influence upon the choice of location. They are politically dangerous in that they may appear in Western democracies as a new method of promoting 'dumping' – subsidies may therefore invite mercantile restrictions against peripheral exports, so slowing down the formation of the new international division of labour. It is likely that the practice will in time prove to be a temporary phenomenon characteristic of the formative years of the new international division of labour. As the dedomiciling of capital gathers momentum over the coming decades, there will be less need to attract it to the periphery. This form of capital export is a 'push' rather than a 'pull' phenomenon.

Thirdly, and perhaps most wastefully, export surpluses can be used to bolster the tottering industrial structure created by import substitution strategies. Free export zones often appear as no more than an appendage, an enclave, to the peripheral economy which remains unaffected by the zones save for the employment of labour and the earning of foreign exchange. The foreign exchange surpluses can be made to pay for more imports, more production subsidies and more profits for domestic producers, but this is rather like disposing of these exchange surpluses in a bottomless pit. The basic inefficiencies of import substitution economies would remain un-altered, and this usage of exchange surpluses would be a stop-gap solution to a structural problem.

The one thing common to all of these methods of disposing of export surpluses is that they are defensive reactions to the rather novel conditions offered by the evolution of the international order. By defensive, we mean that they continue to isolate the domestic economy of the periphery from impulses emanating in the inter-national economy. This tendency to isolation was entirely appropriate thirty years ago when the prevailing norms of the Bretton Woods system prevented the periphery from benefiting by integrating its domestic economy into the global market in an open fashion. But in the coming decades, with the likelihood of significant liberalization of north-south linkages, the field of possible domestic policies is much wider than it has previously been. To be content with inegalitarian policies as restrictive and inefficient as import substi-tution in these more liberal times is to pass these opportunities by.

The opportunity which these defensive or conservative uses of export surpluses avoid can be expressed in many ways. Perhaps the clearest is to say that these strategies do not confront the structural incompatibility between an export sector based on market principles and a domestic economy that is profoundly anti-market. One sign of this incompatibility would be that the domestic economy fails to provide the export sector with the one factor of production which motivates it – cheap labour. Of course all peripheral labour is cheap compared to labour costs in the metropolis, and it is likely to remain so given the ability of metropolitan trade unions to peg wage levels to inflation. But import substitution strategies overvalue the price of peripheral labour and undervalue the price of capital within the 'modern' sector. To this extent, the continued adherence by peripheral regimes to import substitution strategies will act as a brake on the process of the dedomiciling of capital.

There are other indices of this incompatibility. From the point of view of dedomiciled capital, the dirigiste character of import substitution policies is a constant threat to the market principles that guide their operation. Labour supply is not as cheap as it could be, and labour tends to be undernourished, underproductive and defiant of training. Political life appears uncertain, administration is usually corrupt, and the long-run security of investment remains problematical. All of these incompatibilities feed into a general uneasiness which can be seen in the frequent relocations of dedomiciled capital within the periphery (the suitcase factory). Solution of these incompatibilities would strengthen the pact of the multinationals with the periphery, but they are inherently insoluble so long as import substitution policies continue to guide internal capitalist development in the periphery.

Reformist policies which reversed the predatory aspects of import substitution strategies could help ease these incompatibilities. At the same time, these policies are more feasible than they have ever been before, for the increment of surplus that is needed to prime domestic reformism is available to peripheral states not as a deduction from the welfare of domestic elites but rather as a deduction from the aggregate welfare of the metropolis. Let us look more closely at elements of this argument.

Basic needs strategies take their point of departure from the interrelation between the choice of technique, the distribution of income and the distribution of political power. Though there are a variety of strategies of this ilk,[45] they do have some common threads. One of these is seen in their 'rediscovery' of the informal economy within the periphery[46] – the economy of the small producer and mass consumption goods, the economy actively discriminated against by the state in the name of erasing 'traditionalism'. It is argued quite plausibly that the small producer, in industry and in agriculture, is inherently more efficient, more labour-intensive and producing a range of products that are not confined to elite tastes and levels of effective demand. Growth in the periphery could proceed more equitably and probably more quickly if the state would give the small entrepreneur reasonable terms of access to the capital market – access that is denied by the discriminatory state biases of import substitution regimes. As the International Labour Office has argued, the informal sector is not a survival of traditionalism but rather a product of contemporary state policy.[47]

Many of the theorists of basic needs strategies write within the neo-classical traditions, and almost all are essentially saying that the forms of production within the periphery should bear a closer resemblance to the periphery's 'natural' endowment of productive factors – especially cheap labour. It is this market orientation of basic needs strategies that offends many radicals and which leads them to reject such reformist strategies. But the free market, or a policy package tending towards the free market, is not by definition alone the worst of all possible worlds, and distortions from the free market ideal are not progressive or egalitarian at all time. To starve the small producer of capital, as happened under import substitution, is to bring about an economic structure that is grossly inegalitarian and inefficient for the vast majority of the peripheral population. Ideological predilections aside, any movement from such a position back towards a free market, insofar as it eased this oppressive yoke, must be assessed as progressive.

We believe that such market-oriented reforms are possible within the periphery given that the dedomiciling of capital is likely to bestow moderate balance of payments surpluses upon peripheral regimes, and that such reforms would not contradict the primary functions of the state – i.e., the promotion of accumulation and social legitimacy. No one would deny that such reforms of state policy could not help but improve the ailing stocks of legitimacy of the peripheral state. The widespread tendency for authoritarian forms of political rule in the periphery over the last two decades is the most obvious index of this decline of legitimacy. But how would the accumulation of capital proceed within the periphery under such reforms?

We have seen some of the unproductive and conservative ways in which surpluses on the external account could be squandered. What we are suggesting here is that these surpluses could provide the basis for increased capital funding to 'the informal economy' of the periphery.[48] Such a redistributive arrangement would not entail sacrifices from the bourgeoisie in the periphery, since these surpluses are essentially levied against the metropolis. The peripheral bourgeoisie that import substitution strategies created could be encouraged to enter equity arrangements with multinational capital, and state policies in favour of participation agreements would assist in the achievement of this end. Reform of the institutional structure of the state to phase out import substitution policies could be timed to coincide with the efficient expansion of the informal economy and the spread of cooperative agreements with dedomiciled multinational capital. Such movement towards a liberalized internal market would be congruent with the tendencies towards liberalization of north-south linkages in the international economy. So far as mass welfare standards are concerned, the achievement of higher levels of efficiency would go hand in hand with, rather than in opposition to, the achievement of greater equity.

Problems of adjustment to a more liberal internal policy are likely to be most acute in the agrarian sector. Unlike their former industrial class allies, the 'big' farmers have no recourse to alternative modes of accumulation under reformist strategies unless their investment portfolio had previously been diversified to take in industrial assets. State policies encouraging the leasing of land would be necessary but perhaps not sufficient to break up large estates. At the extreme, mass mobilizations might be required. A second agrarian problem would be to ensure that rural smallholders do market enough of their expanded output to provision urban populations with consumption grains. A more favourable pricing policy for these grains, and a tough state policy to enforce the payment of interest on capital advanced, would provide adequate incentives to prevent over-consumption of grains by small farmers and their families.

One can see evidence for the plausibility of these arguments in the two states that have, to date, been at the forefront of the 'newly industrialized countries' – Taiwan and South Korea.[49] In both cases, agrarian structures and state institutions have a much more egalitarian flavour than is common for the periphery. Agrarian reforms here were largely the result of 'historical accidents' – the colonization of Taiwan by mainlanders in 1949, the annihilation of the feudal landed classes in Korea during the Korean war, and the legacy of Japanese colonization. Distribution of income in these states is more even here than in other peripheral countries, and their export performance has been stunningly successful. Neo-Marxist accounts of these states and their performances rarely draw out these relevant comparisons – instead they tend to be fixated upon their authoritarian political forms and their alleged 'technological dependence'. The latter argument is unconvincing – how many countries today have a technological capability that is independent of the investment decisions of multinationals? The former argument is not clearly relevant to the problem at hand.

Our argument, in summary, is that reformist development within the periphery is possible within the evolving new international division of labour, and that such internal reforms in turn feed into and reinforce the evolution of that division of labour. The problem for the periphery is much less rooted in its integration into the world capitalist system than the terms of that integration. Clearly our argument would integrate the periphery into this 'system' more completely than it has been, for reformist strategies are premissed upon the generalization of capitalist norms throughout the periphery. But insofar as this unshackles the hitherto repressed informal economy, and guides its growth under a rationality of increasing productivity, output and equity, it is hard to deny that such reformist strategies would have positive welfare effects for the broad base of the population. This goal is, presumably, something that we can all agree is long overdue.

Notes

1 For a useful discussion of the pre-war precursors of development economics, see H.W. Arndt, 'Development Planning Before 1945' in J. Bhagwati and R.S. Eckaus (eds), *Development and Planning* (London: Allen & Unwin, 1972), pp.13-29.

2 The distinction between structur*al* and structural*ist* analysis is carefully drawn out by M. Glucksmann, *Structuralist Analysis in Contemporary Social Thought* (London: Routledge & Kegan Paul, 1974), Chapter 2.

3 The best example of this is the later work of M.ul Haq, *The Poverty Curtain* (New York: Columbia University Press, 1976).

4 As Gunder Frank once argued, 'bourgeois reform . . . reforms for the bourgeoisie', *Capitalism and Underdevelopment in Latin America* (Harmondsworth: Penguin, 1969), p.296.

5 See A.G. Frank, *Lumpenbourgeoisie: Lumpendevelopment* (New York: Monthly Review Press, 1972).

6 J. Petras, 'New Perspectives on Imperialism and Social Classes in the Periphery', *Journal of Contemporary Asia*, 5, 1975, pp.291-308, and (with M.H. Morley), 'The U.S. Imperial State', *Review*, 4, 1980, pp.171-222.

7 See the radically different analyses of the Kenyan case offered by C. Leys in the space of a few years. *Underdevelopment in Kenya* (London: Heinemann, 1975) and 'Capital Accumulation, Class Formation and Dependency – The Significance of the Kenyan Case', *The Socialist Register*, 1978, pp.241-66.

8 See the highly influential analysis of the multinational corporation by P. Sweezy and H. Magdoff, 'Notes on the Multinational Corporation' in their *The Dynamics of U.S. Capitalism* (New York: Monthly Review Press, 1972), pp.88-112.

9 These formative years are discussed in detailed fashion by L. Bianchi, 'Notes on the Theory of Latin American Economic Development', *Social and Economic Studies*, 22, 1973, pp.96-121.

10 R. Prebisch, *The Economic Development of Latin America and its Principal Problems* (New York: United Nations, Department of Economic Affairs, 1950) and 'Commercial Policy in the Underdeveloped Countries',

American Economic Review, Papers and Proceedings, 44, 1959, pp.251-73.

11 For evidence of the degree of industrial development engendered under colonialism, see P. Kilby, 'Manufacturing in Colonial Africa', in P. Duignan and L.H. Gann (eds), *Colonialism in Africa 1870-1960*, Vol.4 (Cambridge: Cambridge University Press, 1975), pp.470-520.

12 A clear outline of the philosophy underlying import substitution policies is found in R.B. Sutcliffe, *Industry and Underdevelopment* (London: Addison-Wesley, 1971), pp.249-60.

13 The importance of enticing/forcing labour out of the subsistence sector was stressed, amongst others, by W.A. Lewis in his classical article, 'Economic Development with Unlimited Supplies of Labour', *The Manchester School of Economic and Social Studies*, May, 1954, pp.139-91.

14 An elegant argument demonstrating this is provided by G. Lee, 'An Assimilating Imperialism', *Journal of Contemporary Asia*, 2, 1972, pp.345-60.

15 A thorough analysis of the periphery's export performance is provided by K. Morton and P. Tulloch, *Trade and Developing Countries* (London: Croom Helm, 1977).

16 A succinct break-down of debt trends within the periphery is found in H. Hughes, 'The External Debt of the Developing Countries', *Finance and Development*, 14(4), 1977, pp.22-5. See also R.M. Bird, 'Debt and the Developing Countries', *Co-existence*, 13, 1976, pp.17-33.

17 See the annual reports of the Food and Agriculture Organization of the United Nations, *The State of Food and Agriculture*.

18 See I. Adelman and C.T. Morris, *Economic Growth and Social Equity in Developing Countries* (Stanford: Stanford University Press, 1973).

19 OPEC recycling of export surpluses to the developed countries is the best example of this.

20 Frank, Capitalism and Underdevelopment . . . , *op. cit.*, p.233.

21 A. Mack and R. Leaver, 'Radical Theories of Development: An Assessment' in A. Mack, D. Plant and U. Doyle (eds), *Imperialism, Intervention and Development* (London: Croom Helm, 1979), pp.257-85.

22 This point is made firmly in the neo-classical analysis of I. Little, T. Scitovsky and M. Scott, *Industry and Trade in Some Developing Countries* (London: Oxford University Press, 1970).

23 Such an argument, based on the product-cycle theory of direct foreign investment, is drawn out at length by T. Moran, 'Foreign Expansion as an "Institutional Necessity" for US Corporate Capitalism: The Search for a Radical Model', *World Politics*, 25, 1973, pp.369-86.

24 The best interpretation of cold war history from this point of view is R. Aron, *The Imperial Republic*, tran. F. Jellinek (London: Weidenfeld & Nicolson, 1974).

25 An excellent introduction to this topic is J.E. Spero, *The Politics of International Economic Relations* (London: Allen & Unwin, 1977). See also F.L. Block, *The Origins of International Economic Disorder* (Berkeley: University of California Press, 1977).

26 On this, see W. Diebold Jr, 'The End of the ITO', *Essays in International Finance*, 16, October 1952, pp.1-37.

27 Evidence from the Indian case reveals these biases against the 'traditional' sector; see A. Mitra, *Terms of Trade and Class Relations* (London: Cass, 1977), esp. Chapter 10.

28 This theme is ably discussed by A. Buchan, *The End of the Post War Era* (London: Weidenfeld & Nicolson, 1974).

29 A detailed argument on this topic is provided by D.A. Gold, 'The Rise and Decline of the Keynesian Coalition', *Kapitalistate*, 6, 1977, pp.129-61.

30 See G. Adam, 'New Trends in International Business: Worldwide Sourcing and De-domiciling', *Acta Oeconomica*, 7, 1971, pp.349-67. For other discussion, see M. Sharpston, 'International Subcontracting', *Oxford Economic Papers*, New Series, 27, 1975, pp.94-135; H. Plaschke, 'International Subcontracting', *Instant Research on Peace and Violence*, 2/1975, pp.88-97 and G. Adam, 'Some Implications and Concomitants of Worldwide Sourcing', *Acta Oeconomica*, 8, 1972, pp.309-23.

31 These various factors are analysed in F. Frobel, J. Heinrichs and O. Kreye, 'The New International Division of Labour', *Social Science Information*, 17, 1978, pp.123-42.

32 Some evidence of such shifts is provided by G.K. Helleiner, 'Manufactured Exports from Less Developed Countries and Multinational Firms', *The Economic Journal*, 33, 1973, pp.21-47.

33 This argument is most forcefully made by S. Krasner, 'Oil is the Exception', *Foreign Policy*, 14, 1974, pp.68-84.

34 Some attempt to discuss the relevance of OPEC for other commodity groupings is found in I. Smart, 'Uniqueness and Generality', *Daedalus*, 104(4), 1975, pp.259-81. See also Z. Mikdashi, *The International Politics of Natural Resources* (Ithaca: Cornell University Press, 1976).

35 This theme is best analysed by J.M. Blair, *The Control of Oil* (London: Macmillan, 1976).

36 The vicissitudes of the political affiliations of the oil majors can be gleaned from D. Morano, 'Multinationals and Nation-States: The Case of Aramco', *Orbis*, 23(2), 1979, pp.447-68.

37 See A. Sampson, *The Seven Sisters* (London: Hodder & Stoughton, 1975), Chapter 7, and L. Turner, *Oil Companies in the International System* (London: Allen & Unwin, 1978), Chapters 3 and 4.

38 The importance of these negotiations was lost in the crisis of 1973, but they served as the basis for the important analysis of J.E. Akins, 'The Oil Crisis: This Time the Wolf is here,' *Foreign Affairs*, 51(3), 1973, pp.462-90.

39 Aspects of American policy on tariffs towards the dedomiciling of capital are discussed in G.K. Helleiner, *op. cit.*, pp.32-8.

40 D. Evans, *The Politics of Trade: The Evolution of the Superbloc* (London: Macmillan, 1974).

41 For such a critique of reformist strategies, see C. Leys, 'Interpreting African Underdevelopment: Reflections on the ILO Report on Employment, Incomes and Equality in Kenya', *African Affairs*, 72, 1973, pp.419-29.

42 The best example of this argument is A. Carlo, 'The Oil Crisis and the Iron Law of Underdevelopment', *Telos*, 31, 1977, pp.5-34.
43 Deeper analysis and projections of the absorptive capacity of the oil states is provided by T.H. Moran, *Oil Prices and the future of OPEC* (Washington, D.C.: Resources for the Future, 1978), esp. Chapter 2.
44 These Asian trends are well analysed in the special issue of *Ampo*, 8(4) and 9(1-2), 1977, on the topic of 'Free Trade Zones and Industrialization in Asia'.
45 See, for example, E. Owens and R. Shaw, *Development Reconsidered* (Lexington, Mass.: D.C. Heath & Co., 1972); J.W. Mellor, *The New Economics of Growth* (Ithaca: Cornell University Press, 1976); H. Chenery *et al.*, *Redistribution with Growth* (London: Oxford University Press, 1974); ILO, *Employment, Incomes and Equality: A Strategy for Increasing Productive Employment in Kenya* (Geneva: ILO, 1972) and M. Lipton, *Why Poor People Stay Poor* (London:Temple Smith, 1977).
46 One of the first to point to the significance of the informal economy was K. Hart, 'Small Scale Entrepreneurs in Ghana and Development Planning', *Journal of Development Studies*, 6, 1970, pp.104-20 and 'Informal Income Opportunities and Urban Employment in Ghana', *Journal of Modern African Studies*, 11, 1973, pp.61-89.
47 ILO, *op. cit.*, Chapter 13.
48 Lipton argues that only 20 per cent of the periphery's development resources find their way to the bottom 80 per cent of the population; *op. cit.*, p.16.
49 A brief but pertinent discussion of state policy in these countries is found in B. Balassa, 'Industrial Policy in Taiwan and Korea', *Weltwirtschafliches Archiv*, 106, 1971, pp.55-77.

6 Industrialisation and the Singapore state in the context of the New International Division of Labour

GARRY RODAN – *Murdoch University*

The debate over how to promote the economic development of the less developed countries (LDCs) has passed through distinct stages.[1] Of late, however, there has been a clear return to orthodox growth theory from various policy-makers, lobby groups and academics. The contemporary form in which this theory is expressed is the export-oriented industrialisation (EOI) strategy, effected through free trade. The inspiration for this revival comes largely from the experiences of the rapidly industrialising countries of East and Southeast Asia.[2] One of the most concise and ominous reaffirmations of free trade and EOI came in the 1981 World Bank Development Report, marking an official dispensing of the Basic Needs approach which had coloured the Bank's thinking in the 1970s.[3] Drawing on the successful and dramatic industrialisation programmes of the newly industrialising countries (NICs) of East and Southeast Asia, it is argued in the Report that structural adjustment in the advanced countries can facilitate a general emulation of these models by LDCs.[4] Trade liberalisation is promoted as the means for bringing about this structural adjustment.

Structural adjustment, in the context of trade liberalisation, amounts to an increased international specialisation in production. Understandably, import-substitution industrialisation (ISI) policies are under renewed attack for inhibiting such specialisation. The argument goes that by protection from international market forces, ISI policies have encouraged an inefficient utilisation of domestic resources (or an inefficient allocation of factors of production). Put another way, continued protection has prevented countries from specialising in areas in which a comparative advantage in international trade exists. The comparative advantage of LDCs, so goes the argument, lies in the abundance of cheap labour, therefore it makes sense for these countries to specialise in labour-intensive production. Conversely, those countries which cannot remain competitive with the manufactured exports of LDCs or NICs should shift emphasis in production towards their own peculiar comparative advantages, rather than increase trade barriers.[5] The logical extension of this is an international hierarchy in which there are varying degrees of technological sophistication in different countries' specialisations. Of course in some cases this would theoretically involve a shift, structural adjustment, away from the manufacturing sector altogether and into the service sector, for example. It is all quite rational a hierarchy, nonetheless, based on technical considerations of factor endowment, i.e. comparative advantage.

Though the above represents the general line of reasoning characterising arguments in favour of EOI strategies, there are nevertheless some important distinctions to be made about different free trade positions. First, there are those free traders of the Milton Friedman variety who advocate a totally laissez-faire economy, seeing any government intervention as necessarily negative. Government intervention simply distorts a country's comparative advantage and therefore contradicts economic rationality. Theorists of this position point to the NICs as conclusive proof that less government equates with greater economic growth.[6] For these writers, not only is a free market practically possible it is also ideologically preferable. In contrast to this position, there is also the view that trade liberalisation is compatible with the government playing positive, although essentially secondary, social and technical roles in the distribution of income and resources and provision of infrastructure. Thus, free trade theory is perfectly compatible with social democratic theory,[7] as well as some acknowledgment of the states of the various East and Southeast Asian NICs playing a part in industrialisation.[8] It remains, however, that even where economists have attempted to attribute some significance to the state in the industrialisation of the NICs, the analysis has usually been unsatisfactory. This is the consequence of both the restrictive nature of economics itself as a method of inquiry, avoiding serious political and social questions, as well as the analytical preoccupation with market forces and comparative advantage as explanatory concepts.[9] As a result, we find that the different free trade positions, in effect, tend to urge the realisation of a new international division of labour, guided by the rationality of comparative advantage.

The discussion to follow is by no means an attempt to counter the argument in favour of EOI with support for ISI. On the contrary, the purpose is to offer a quite different understanding of the rapid industrialisation of East and Southeast Asia, drawing on the case of Singapore. Whilst recognising that the industrialisation of Singapore need not be indicative of such processes in NICs generally, the point is to raise arguments of a fundamental theoretical nature which have serious implications for the analysis of industrialisation generally. It is attempted in these arguments to show that the industrialisation of Singapore is by no means a confirmation of the technical superiority of free trade or minimal government. In the following discussion, three points are concentrated on which address these misconceptions: the role of the state; the specific historical conditions in which NICs have grown; and the theoretical utility of comparative advantage as a guide for policy. Some brief elaboration on these points might be helpful from the outset so that readers are aware of exactly what is being attempted in the discussion to follow.

First, the association between successful EOI and a passive or minimalist state is not supported by close analysis of the relationship between state and capital, or state and labour, in East or Southeast Asia. Instead of posing the question of how the state in Australia can withdraw from the economy to enable uninhibited expression of comparative advantage, as free marketeers are currently disposed to, we should be drawing quite a different insight from the economic growth of these NICs. Recognising that the state has played an integral and positive role in the industrialisation of these countries, it is more appropriate to ask questions about how the state might better facilitate industrialisation in Australia. This implies something quite different from emulating models. Close attention must be paid to the political question of whose interests would be served by different forms of state intervention, at whatever level.

Second, the industrialisation of NICs has, by no coincidence, occurred at an historically unique phase in the development of international capital accumulation. The flowering of EOI policies followed closely the birth of transnational corporations in the 1960s. These corporations had developed a new perspective on the organisation of production as a result of having extended their interests worldwide. It became apparent that production could be organised internationally, transcending the nation-state as the unit of analysis, at a considerable cost advantage. Technical advancements in communications and transportation, the decomposition of production processes in a number of industries, a large pool of unemployed labour in LDCs, and an intense struggle amongst international capital for market dominance all gave rise to what Fröbel *et al.*[10] call a 'new logic' in international capital accumulation. Fröbel *et al.* have contended that this logic has been responsible for what is at this stage the embryo of a new international division of labour. It is this division of labour which free trade advocates wish to see ushered in. It is argued in the following, however, that greater analytical attention should be paid to comprehending this specific historical form of accumulation and the implications of participation in such a new international division of labour.

Finally, advocates of submission to the logic of this new international division of labour have so far been able to work comfortably with the assumption that comparative advantage is objective, almost self-evident with the implication that correct government policy is that which eliminates the distortion of this objective condition. Comparative advantage, however, is not the objective, almost self-evident entity implied by this approach, and policies rooted in this belief might have disastrous consequences – especially since the prognosis of such policies depends vitally on the actors in the economy universally recognising this comparative advantage. It is also questionable whether such an abstract level of conceptualisation constitutes a useful guide to policy.

Importance of the state

The mistaken idea of the free marketeers that successful EOI is inseparable from minimal state intervention in the economy is most clearly contradicted by the experiences of South Korea, Taiwan and Japan. In these cases, state assistance to industry and protective use of trade and non-trade barriers went hand in hand.[11] Investment incentives, infrastructural provisions, effective labour management policies, productive investments and the provision of loan capital all contributed to shape the investment climate in countries which have successfully adopted export-oriented industrialisation. The proliferation of free trade zones in Southeast Asia, with all the associated privileges, is a naked manifestation of the state's importance to these programmes.[12]

Taking the case of Singapore for illustrative purposes, it can be seen that the state's role has been anything but incidental to the success of EOI. Rather, it is very doubtful whether any EOI strategy in the mid- to late 1960s could have been contemplated had not steps already been taken by the People's Action Party (PAP)[13] to substantially improve power and water supplies, sewerage, transportation and communication networks, port facilities and technical training. The creation of the statutory body, the Economic Development Board (EDB), in 1961 to, amongst other things, develop industrial estates in which all of the above facilities were centralised (save technical training) was an initiative beyond the inclination or capacity of private investors.[14] By the end of May 1968, the original cost-value of the fixed assets (in the form of industrial estate development) reached S$136 million.[15] So rapid had become the expansion of these estates and so important their function that in

1968 the Jurong Town Corporation (JTC) was formed to specialise in responsibility for industrial estates, leaving the EDB greater specialisation in research and promotional work. As the pace of foreign investment picked up, so too did the investments of the JTC. It invested $161 million in fixed assets in 1974 alone.[16] Singapore was actually the first country in Southeast Asia to develop industrial estates. They were intended to provide the necessary attraction to capital to compensate for the relatively late start to industrialisation – especially given the competition Singapore faced for investment in the region.[17]

The PAP's development of housing estates through the Housing Development Board (HDB) in conjunction with industrial estates has also played its part in increasing Singapore's attractiveness as an investment site.[18] These industrial estates have been divided into different zones: park, recreational, business, residential, light, medium and heavy industrial. The government's provision and dispersion of social and economic infrastructure has involved a degree of planning and foresight which should not be taken for granted.

The PAP's provision of infrastructure has been enacted through the state monopolies of the Public Utilities Board (PUB), Telecommunications Authority of Singapore (TAS), Port of Singapore Authority (PSA) and the HDB. Urban renewal and property development have also been carried out by the state Urban Redevelopment Authority (URA). Apart from these interests, the state has a monopoly over radio and television, the Singapore Broadcasting Commission (SBC); an airline, Singapore Airlines (SIA);[19] a trading company (INTRACO);[20] an industrial research institute (SISIR); a shipping company, Nepture Orient Lines (NOL); two state joint-venture shipyards, Keppel and Sembawang Shipyards; and numerous other wholly and partly state-owned productive enterprises.

The pattern of government investment has been to expand and diversify over time. Keppel Shipyard Limited,[21] for example, has diversified in recent years into property-owning and financial service. In December 1981, the state Monetary Authority of Singapore (MAS) granted a full operating license to one of Keppel's subsidiaries, Shing Loong Credit (Pte) Limited, to provide various financial services.[22] Keppel's expansion and diversification dates back to the early 1970s. Today it has a total of thirty-four subsidiaries and twenty associated companies.[23]

The government's direct participation in the financial sector has been sizeable and of importance to its ability to provide infrastructure. Through the Central Provident Fund (CPF), a compulsory employee superannuation scheme, and the Post Office Savings Bank, the government appropriates the major share of domestic savings. Monetary policy itself is also fundamentally the domain of the MAS. The Development Bank of Singapore (DBS), a public company with a majority government ownership, bears special significance to Singapore's export programme in that it was established in 1968 ostensibly to provide finance for industry at relatively low interest rates. Interestingly, the DBS too has expanded its interests over time.

The recent establishment of the Government of Singapore Investment Corporation (GSIC) to manage foreign reserves also constitutes an interesting move towards more specialised direct involvement. Up until 1980, this was the responsibility of MAS. MAS came under fire for allowing surplus foreign reserves to accumulate beyond that necessary to meet its legal obligations. So gigantic are these foreign reserves – officially declared at S$15.84 billion at cost value[24] – and so important is the opportunity to maximise their investment potential, that a separate body has been deemed appropriate to handle these reserves. The GSIC is chaired by Lee Kuan Yew himself, with Goh Keng Swee, the First Deputy Prime Minister, the Director. The government is busily scouting for investment opportunities abroad, having identified the US, Japan and Australia as the prime targets.[25] With the state's increasing financial commitments to industrial restructuring, the use of these reserves assumes new importance.

The government has also shown a preparedness to take a lead, where necessary, in the so-called 'Second Industrial Revolution'. In the aerospace industry, for example, the establishment of the Singapore Aerospace Maintenance Company (SAMCO)[26] has been intended, amongst other things, to provide the stimulus to private companies. In this preferred area of investment, SAMCO has announced plans to diversify into the manufacture of aircraft parts and components – the priority for this industry's long-term development.[27]

The association with EOI and a minimalist state is indeed incorrect in Singapore's case. The recent adoption of policies intended to assist in restructuring the economy will only enhance the government's already considerable stake in direct productive investments and finance. About this Goh Chok Tong[28] is in no doubt when clarifying the government's role to critics:

> We will continue to go in for big business where the private sector finds it difficult to go into. We will also go into business where the market is international like a shipping line, or airline. If it's

international why should we worry about the government taking part? What we meant by reviewing our role was that we would divest ourselves of some shares in companies in which we no longer see important roles for ourselves. We may even sell off 100%.

But that does not mean we will not invest in new companies. In fact my recent remarks about a new venture company (to be set up by the government and to finance promising but high-risk ventures) indicated that we would invest in more companies. But once these companies succeed, we should in fact divest ourselves of their shares . . . they (private businessmen) come in and they take over . . . and we'll move into something else, my own view is that we'll grow bigger and bigger.

Whether or not the Singapore government will divest its interests in profitable concerns or continue 'to see important roles' in such concerns is an interesting question. To this point there is little precedent to support the proposition that the profitability of government concerns leads to divestment. More likely it leads to expansion and diversification. However, with the increasing import-ance of finance to Singapore's industrial restructuring, Goh's vision of a proliferation of government companies is no doubt insightful and informed.[29]

The government's importance to the success of capital restruc-turing is underlined by its own estimates which show that gross domestic fixed capital formation will need to grow by 11 per cent per annum between 1979 and 1984. This is 3 per cent higher than the average of 8 per cent for the period 1970-8. The government has thus set about boosting its budgetary spending on development from 1980, most of which goes into fixed capital formation, to supplement that from the private sector. In the financial year 1980 there was a 41.3 per cent increase in development expenditure to S$3.6 billion, raising its share of total expenditure from 43 per cent to 47 per cent. For the financial year 1981, development expenditure increased to S$5.04 billion, representing 52 per cent of total expenditure and exceeding recurrent expenditure for the first time ever. Apart from the enormous outlays in physical infrastructure and finance, the government is playing a crucial role in expanding tertiary and technical education and providing attractive training subsidies.[30]

Apart from the government's involvement through the provision of infrastructure, and an assortment of productive and financial interests, a host of investment incentives, subsidies and tax exemptions have been provided to manufacturers. The 1967 Economic Expansion Incentives (Relief from Income Tax) Act marked the first comprehensive provision of such inducement for export production. Subsequent modifications to this act have taken place to reflect the changing priorities in investment.[31]

The government's influence over the economy has been considerable in its control of organised labour. Through the Employment Act (1968) and the Industrial Relations Act (1968) employees' benefits were reduced, working hours increased and the bargaining power of unions severely curtailed. The government's suppression of labour has been systematically institutionalised, since unions may only be formed under very restrictive rules and can lose their registration at the discretion of the Labour Minister – without it being incumbent upon the Minister to justify this decision. The government-controlled National Trade Union Congress (NTUC) accounts for 90 per cent of total union membership which, in any case, amounts to only about 30 per cent of the workforce. Instead of unions exerting pressure on behalf of their members for improved conditions and remuneration, Singapore unions are an instrument of the government's social and economic management.[32] Suppression of wages in the early 1970s thus generated a favourable basis for investment and the overall control of labour provided the stability for long-term commitment by capital.

The adoption by the PAP of the 'corrective' wages policy certainly does not connote a change in the nature of the government's attitude towards labour. The substantive wage increases over the years 1979-81 were rationalised by the government as technically necessary rather than socially desirable.[33] These increases have been required to deter labour-intensive production and promote an increase in the organic composition of capital through the adoption of labour-saving production techniques. It has been argued that the policy has been necessary to restore wages to their market value. The very notion of a 'corrective' wages policy is an indictment on the freedom of labour as a factor of production. It is an open admission of the government's control over a key aspect of the economy. For this reason alone, it is hard to accept uncritically the notion of a comparative advantage in labour costs as having any meaning in isolation from account of the state's role in helping to define these costs. The 'advantage' is thus anything but natural or given.

The case of Singapore serves to highlight the important ways in which the state has shaped the allocation of resources. In various ways the state has acted to cut the costs of production to private, notably international, capital.[34] Singapore, however, is not unique in this regard. An active role by the state in helping to cut production costs is inseparable from EOI programmes in East and Southeast Asia. The competition for capital, in a context of growing capital mobility, suggests little likelihood of the state's role diminishing. The question of whether or not the state adopts or continues EOI is, however, dependent upon the domestic classes. The importance of internal class composition to the relations between the state and international capital cannot, of course, be admitted by an analysis which downplays the significance of the state. The point, however, is that the viability of EOI is closely related to the capacity of the state to support international capital. The nature of the state, and the determinants of this nature, must be inseparable from the analysis of EOI. Analyses which conclude that free trade or trade orientation per se account for the rapid industrialisation of the 'Asian Miracles' have only been possible by ignoring the integral role of the state in the industrialisation process. Growth is thus mystified, not explained.

Historical specificity

The free market proponents of EOI have tended to hypothesise the universal superiority of this strategy. The successful industrialisation of East and Southeast Asian countries can be duplicated anywhere so long as resources are allocated efficiently in an open market. Starting from the simple and systematically moving up the ladder into increasingly complex production is the normative evolution of countries adopting EOI. Such an hypothesis is, of course, grounded in a structural systems theory approach. In attempting to understand the experiences of the East and Southeast Asian NICs, however, particularly for the purposes of policy formation in other LDCs, such an ahistorical and reductionist approach provides little account of the logic which has underpinned the massive infusion of capital in the NICs. The evolutionary notion of a country's changing position in the international division of labour which accompanies this approach can only be supported in disregard of this logic.

As was briefly touched on in the introduction, the wave of investment in East and Southeast Asia occurred at a time of intense competition amongst international capital following World War II, notably between Japanese, European and US-based firms to capture markets[35] – both in LDCs and developed capitalist countries (DCCs). Undercutting the competitiveness of rivals by taking advantage of low-cost labour brought about an intense inertia of investment in LDCs as a necessary measure to remain in business in DCCs. This movement of capital to LDCs reflected the increased dissatisfaction of capital with the militance and cost of unionised labour as well as the perceived gains from the lower labour costs in LDCs.

Given the historically unprecedented rivalry between capital for markets, the option of moving to LDCs to remain competitive was itself only possible due to historically specific changes in the social and technical division of labour – notably the decomposition of the production process. Decomposition has always been an objective of capital.[36] It has now reached such a point, however, that previously complex production processes are separated into a series of simple units of production. This had made it possible to locate those aspects or processes of production which are labour-intensive at sites where labour is cheap and abundant.[37] Thus the production of skill-intensive products is no longer the exclusive domain of DCCs. This is particularly true of the electronics industry where labour-intensive assembly operations and component manufacture have been carried out for sophisticated products such as microprocessors. The electronics industry has featured heavily in the EOI of East and Southeast Asia. It is, for example, Singapore's largest industry in terms of employment and value-added and second largest to petroleum in output value, with 90 per cent of output value directly exported.[38]

The point being emphasised is that the successful adoption of EOI cannot be separated from specific historical conditions. Amongst the works of EOI advocates, however, there is a dearth of explanation for the timing of these programmes, with emphasis rather on the appearance of 'take-off'. The delay in this 'take-off' is presumably due to the delay in adopting EOI. As argued before, though, EOI for LDCs was not a possible strategy until a certain stage in the development of the accumulation process and technology, as well as in the relations of production in LDCs. EOI is not a technical process which can be transposed anywhere at anytime but requires objective prerequisites which are historically and socially specific.

Belief in the universal validity of EOI derives from a preoccupation with quantitative measures of industrialisation. This preoccupation in part explains the tendency to interpret the rapid industrialisation of NICs as 'on course' in duplicating the growth patterns of the DCCs. However, a qualitative analysis of industrialisation leads to a questioning of theories which portray evolutionary product development, from simple to complex. The basis of the assumption of an evolution from labour-intensive production towards capital-intensive production is that rising incomes and labour scarcity force this changing specialisation. However, incorporation into an international division of labour in the assembly process need not lead to the eventual manufacture of that entire product nor even to a newfound comparative advantage in some other area of production.[39]

In the case of Singapore, there has clearly been an increase in higher value-added production as wages and labour scarcities have risen. However, the heavy involvement of the state in training the workforce and providing the necessary infrastructure for this investment shift have been important. It is not possible to move into sophisticated technology without adequate technicians – in fact, the shortage of skilled technicians is such that it slows an otherwise even more rapid movement into higher value-added production in Singapore. Therefore, it is not the cost of labour or the scarcity of it per se which determines the degree to which specialisation changes in favour of higher value-added production.

The long-term prospects of Singapore evolving its product specialisation towards higher value-added production is problematic because of the decreasing importance of labour, at a cost, to higher value-added production. For companies exporting their products to the markets in the US or Europe, Singapore's attraction in the areas considered of higher value-added still remains that of 'cheap labour'. The labour may not be absolutely cheap but it is still cheaper, in most cases, than labour in comparable industries in the US or Europe. The decision to invest in Singapore or closer to the market may thus continue to rest on labour costs in spite of their diminishing contribution to overall production costs.[40] The indifferent response of Japanese-based firms to the Singapore government's attempt to move industry upstream, in spite of these labour costs, underlines the precariousness of mobility in the international division of labour. This 'tight-rope' which is being walked can be countered only by a strong growth in Southeast Asia for the demand of higher value-added goods. This, of course, is not guaranteed. It is not out of the question for the state to find itself increasingly pressured to keep the clamp on wages again to ensure a successful export-orientation.

The structural constraints associated with the prospects of changing specialisation have, of course, been mentioned by previous writers.[41] Clearly not all positions in the international division are equally attractive, differing in the degree of value-added and the nature of work. More than this, should Singapore, for example, complete a successful transition towards higher value-added production this could limit the scope for Malaysia doing the same. An appropriately expanding market would be required to prevent such a constraint.

Taking into account the historical circumstances associated with the industrialisation of the 'Asian Miracles' and the structural constraints on the number of entrants possible at any one level of industrialisation for export, it is clearly dangerous to advocate a general adoption of EOI – for LDCs or DCCs alike. Argentina's experiment[42] with this strategy might, in part, serve as an illustration of the perils of placing ideological faith in market forces at the expense of a few historical and structural considerations. Indeed, the conditions under which successful EOI have occurred need to be better articulated, with less faith in the orientation of trade as an explanatory tool and greater effort to specify how any given country's programme fits into the logic of international capital accumulation (itself not static).

Comparative advantage

To economists of the twentieth century it was evident that the classical trade theory of comparative advantage required modifying. The free trade model, associated with Ricardo and Stuart Mill, was seen as in need of revision primarily because it depicted labour costs as the sole determinant of comparative advantage. The neo-classical revision was intended to provide a more sophisticated analysis, accounting not just for the differential factors omitted, which help to determine comparative advantage but also the effect of economic growth on trade patterns over time. Factor endowment theory, championed by Heckscher and Ohlin,[43] thus emerged with emphasis on the different factor supplies of land, labour and capital between countries and the differential mix of such factors required for particular product specialisation. Thus it follows that countries with abundant labour, for example, should specialise in labour-intensive production and capital-abundant countries should concentrate on capital-intensive production.

One of the assumptions made by Hecksher and Ohlin was that there would be a free passage of goods between countries and that people of different countries shared equally in a pool of technical knowledge about production. As was argued by Posner,[44] however, technological innovation and the transfer of technology greatly affect comparative advantage precisely because of its uneven distribution. Vernon addressed this problem in his theory of the 'product cycle'.[45] Johnson has also pointed out that government-imposed trade barriers serve to halt the process whereby lower-income countries specialise in labour-intensive production.[46] The debate goes on as economists attempt to refine the method of analysing the comparative advantage of a country. The assumption, derived from classical theory, remains that free trade maximises world output and that all participants in this trade stand to gain. Refinement in method is simply required to identify this comparative advantage. Once identified, countries exploiting comparative advantage will consequently experience growth, with countries transcending their own limited production possibilities by securing capital and consumption goods from other countries. As shall be argued below, however, this preoccupation with establishing a country's comparative advantage has actually obscured the realities of international capital accumulation. Government policies based on analysis which do not grasp the logic of international capital accumulation are a poor basis for industrial restructuring policies.

The level of abstraction of analyses of comparative advantage by trade theorists has made it possible to ignore the structures and complexities of multinational corporations and the extent to which this complexity might influence the shape of world trade. Trade theory has not catered for the fact that investment decisions are based not on abstract notions of comparative advantage but detailed, concrete assessments of how best (in the case of multinationals) to disperse resources globally. This assessment amounts to qualitatively more than a collectivity of individual national assessments. The actors in the international economy are incorporated into this economy in a variety of ways – in part the results of regional and historic circumstances. The structures and interests which they develop, being so diverse, negate a common comparative advantage for manufacturers in a particular line of production in any one country. Though models of comparative advantage can abstractly identify areas in which a country should specialise its production it would be naive to expect investors to draw the same conclusions.

That comparative advantage is not universal in its meaning is evident by the different ways in which firms respond to changes in the allocation of resources. Broad structural differences in the placement of companies in the international economy have influenced the response of capital to the measures adopted to encourage higher value-added production in Singapore, for example. US-based firms have been at the fore in the upgrading of generations (i.e., the introduction of more technically sophisticated operations), and the adoption of labour-saving techniques of production.[47] US capital investment in the manufacturing sector in Singapore rose by an estimated US$1.5 billion from 1978 to 1980. A survey conducted by the US embassy in Singapore in 1980 of nearly all major manufacturing firms (with 10 per cent or more US equity) discovered a significant gain of 48.9 per cent average investment per firm in 1980 over the results of the 1978 survey.[48] In contrast, Japanese companies have been rather cool towards the hikes in wage costs initiated in 1979. There was a drop in the level of Japanese investments from 1979 to 1980 of 55 per cent, from a record US$151 million to US$69 million.[49] The Japanese commercial attaché to Singapore, Hideo Nagashima,[50] interpreted this slowdown as evidence of a general reassessment of Singapore by Japanese capital:

There is little prospect of more sophisticated ventures being established in Singapore . . . Japanese firms keep their business in Japan until they lose their competitiveness. Then, they move out to take advantage of lower wages or to establish export markets abroad.

Nagashima singled out the wage rises as the prime reason for the slowdown in Japanese investments. The observation of Nagashima is borne out by the fact that Japanese investments have traditionally and continually been located in relatively low value-added (per worker) production.[51] Rather than do as US capital has, and move into higher value-added production in Singapore, Japanese capitalists have tended to invest in more capital-intensive production in Europe and the US.[52] This measure has been intended to ensure access to markets.[53] Thus, for Japanese capital, whilst Singapore is losing its status as a low-cost production centre, it is not inevitable that it becomes attractive as a site for higher value-added production. Thus, what makes sense for a US company need not for a Japanese company in the same line of production. Their different capacities to penetrate export markets from Singapore need to be taken into account. The Singapore government has been disappointed at the lack of response from Japanese investors to its call for higher value-added investments and in 1981 sent two EDB promotion missions to Japan to attempt to identify the specific needs of Japanese capital. No doubt the Singapore government will have subsequently recognised that investment decisions can be based on a complex of considerations. Rising wages and labour shortages do not inexorably lead capital in general into higher value-added production.

The circumstances which can influence the ways in which capital responds to changing factors of production, including trade liberalisation, can be infinitely more complex than demonstrated above. The operations of companies which belong to an international group may appear irrational on the surface but may make perfect sense within the global context of that group's investments. This needs to be comprehended by policy makers in LDCs and DCCs alike.

In the context of Australia's industrial future, for example, any hope of an export-oriented manufacturing sector rests to a large extent on the initiative of multinational affiliates based in Australia. Australian manufacturing industry is about 40 per cent controlled by foreign interests with the tendency of foreign ownership on the rise.[54] The overwhelming motivation for these investments has been to enjoy the benefits of tariff protection to produce for the Australian market.[55] So clearly distinguished is the purpose of production in

Australia for companies belonging to international groups that, in cases, there must be doubt about the extent to which Australian-based multinational companies can or would export to, or produce in, Southeast Asia. For some companies their operations in Australia are circumscribed by the overall group strategy for the region or they have restrictive export franchises. Rheem Australia Limited, for example, has had its activities in Southeast Asia confined because of an agreement with Rheem International, Incorporated, which is itself a subsidiary of the City Investing Company of the USA. The City Investing Company of the USA has plants operating in nineteen countries, several of which are in Southeast Asia. No studies have been carried out to identify in what ways and to what extent companies are hamstrung in the operations which they can carry out in Australia and Southeast Asia beyond immediate cost questions. Just how interested is international capital in using Australia as an export base? For those companies with the capacity it might make more sense to expand production at their Southeast Asian sites and service Australia through imports. There might be many more profitable or 'rational' options other than responding in the way predicted by models of comparative advantage.

The likelihood of capital being moved out of labour-intensive production and into the more competitive areas of capital-intensive production as a result of trade liberalisation is thus problematic. It is not incumbent upon capitalists to reinvest their capital in the same country. Thus, although models of comparative advantage may suggest Australian specialisation in metal engineering, for example, displaced capital from labour-intensive areas of production may be reinvested in another area of production outside Australia. It is beyond the analytical power of trade theory to accommodate this possibility precisely because the level of abstraction is the nation. It is not just the international mobility of capital which poses problems for this theory but, more than this, the historically unique structure within which capital transfers occur, the multinationl corporation.

The question we are left with in the end is: to what extent do the actors in the economy decide their investments according to the comparative advantage model of trade theory? Whilst some argue that the model necessarily operates on unreal assumptions, they also argue that the prescriptive power of the model is still important to devising policies for economic growth. In response, however, it can be argued that the prescriptive value of analysis must rest on its measure of concrete reality.

The reification of comparative advantage has served a definite political function in the debate over industrial strategies. By giving it the appearance of an entity waiting to be discovered by abolishing the distortions concealing it, notably trade barriers, free trade advocates have managed to define a specific role for the state in this process. The state's role becomes that of facilitator of international capital, only intervening in the economy to smash down the barriers to its full realisation. The outlay of resources by the state in this role is not made explicit. By analytically concealing the role of the state in quite deliberately shaping comparative advantage and industrialisation, however, the full range of policy options for governments is not exploited. As we have seen in the case of Singapore, for example, the government has consciously set about to promote a new position in the international division of labour by increasing wages and heavily investing in social infrastructure (particularly that pertaining to raising productivity levels). There are degrees to which the state can intervene to change position in the international division of labour. Of course, the state could be much more active than the Singapore example (a greater direct participation in production to shape the direction of industry, as well as publically appropriate the rewards of the government's subsidisation of industry, being more active roles). Once we start to speculate about these forms of state involvement, however, it raises questions about what sort of industry is preferable and how it can be ensured that economic growth serves social needs. For some theorists it would be more comfortable to disregard such questions.

The policy implications of the above are quite serious. I have emphasised that abstract analyses of comparative advantage do not take into account complex international structures of multinational corporations. It is thus an act of faith to eliminate trade barriers in the expectation that growth will obediently follow. It may be necessary to see policies on trade barriers as inseparable from those on investment if governments seek to promote a particular position in the international division of labour.

Conclusion

In the discussion above I have argued that export-oriented industrialisation in East and Southeast Asia has occurred in quite specific historical circumstances. I have also argued that the state has played a central role in this industrialisation. Using the example of Singapore I have shown that this role is ongoing and, if anything, becomes increasingly important in subsidising and financing capital as industry becomes more capital-intensive.

In examining the notion of comparative advantage, I have tried to demonstrate that there are certain problems associated with such models. The peculiarities of international corporate structures and the differential constraints and needs of international capital invalidate any general meaning of comparative advantage. The danger of basing policies for restructuring industry solely on models of comparative advantage must be clear. Since I have shown that the state has played an important and, analytically, inseparable role in EOI, it may be pertinent to consider the various alternative forms of intervention which the government could exercise. Once we put comparative advantage into a less mystifying context, as something which can be shaped by selective resource allocation, it becomes clear that there is no pre-ordained role for a country in the international division of labour. There are conditions which limit the options but, within these limitations, decisions should not be made about a country's industrial future in such a way as to conceal the interests served.

The real worry about industrial strategies based on trade liberalisation is that it is assumed that international capital or the domestic industrial bourgeoisie is likely everywhere to respond positively to the challenge. Seeing as these EOI advocates do not prescribe a role for the state in productive investments, such a strategy ultimately rests on faith. It would be a bitter reality, however, if private capital were found not to share the view expressed in abstract models of comparative advantage.

Policy-makers must recognise that the question being put is not necessarily that of protectionism or free trade. The question might rather be at what level should an economy become integrated into any international division of labour? Having once decided this, and within certain constraints, governments can set about to shape and influence this integration. The options start to appear wider once the process of industrial growth is demystified and the role of the state is no longer seen as neutral or secondary.

Notes

1   At the academic level, this debate is critically surveyed by Henry Bernstein, 'Sociology of Underdevelopment vs Sociology of Development?', in David Lehman (ed.), (1979), *Development Theory. Four Critical Studies*, London: Frank Cass, pp.77-106.

   At the policy level, the United Nations Economic Commission for Asia and the Pacific has also undergone various distinct shifts in position. For a detailed comprehension of these shifts see the Yearly Economic Surveys in *Economic Bulletin for Asia and the Pacific* (formerly *Economic Bulletin for Asia and the Far East*), Bangkok: United Nations. These shifts can be traced from 1950 onwards.

2   See Bela Balassa (1982), 'Structural Adjustment Policies in Developing Economies', *World Development*, 10(1), pp.23-8 for a recent succinct

argument in favour of EOI through trade liberalisation which draws on the experiences of East and Southeast Asia. For one of the earliest and more influential statements of the EOI position, see Donald B. Keesing (1967), 'Outward-Looking Policies and Economic Development', *The Economic Journal*, June, pp.303-20.

It is possible to promote EOI through protective policies also but currently the dominant wisdom is that protection is counter-productive for export programmes. For an argument in favour of EOI through protection see Clive Edwards (1978), 'Restructuring Australian Manufacturing Industry – Is Free Trade the Only Answer?', Institute of Southeast Asian Studies, Occasional Paper, No.51, April.

It should also be kept in mind that EOI and ISI are not mutually exclusive programmes, though obviously there are certain contradictions between them.

3   For an explanation of this approach see Hollis Chinery *et al.* (1974), *Redistribution With Growth*, London: Oxford University Press.

4   For data on the increase of the export of manufactured goods by LDCs see Donald B. Keesing (1979), 'World Trade and Output of Manufacturers: Structural Trends and Developing Countries' Exports', *World Bank*, Staff Working Paper No.316, January; Also D. Nayyar (1978), 'Transnational Corporations and Manufactured Exports From Poor Countries', *The Economic Journal*, March, pp.59-84.

5   See Bela Balassa (1979), 'The Changing International Division of Labor in Manufactured Goods', *Banca Nazionale del Lavoro Quarterly Review*, No.130, Sept., pp.243-85.

6   See Milton Friedman (1981), *The Invisible Hand in Economics and Politics*, Singapore: Institute of Southeast Asian Studies.

7   For a statement on the relationship between free trade and social democratic theory see Ross Garnaut (1981), 'Australian Protection, Structural Adjustment and International Development', paper presented to Fifth National Conference of Labor Economists, Adelaide, 20-22 November.

8   For some general economics works which analyse industrialisation and make some limited observations about the state see I. Little, T. Scitovsky and M. Scott (1970), *Industry and Trade in Some Developing Economies: A Comparative Study*, London: Oxford University Press; and Hla Myint (1972), *Southeast Asia's Economy: Development Policies in the 1970's*, Harmondsworth: Penguin.

9   From the point of view of economics as a discipline this is an understandable weakness, since economists do not presume to deal with these questions. The point is, however, that they do think the analytical separation is valid. Obviously, sociologists can make some contribution here but the answer lies not in combining the works belonging to different disciplines. Rather, what is required is a political economy which simultaneously investigates both sorts of questions.

10   See Fröbel, F., Heinrichs, J., and Kreye, O. (1977), *The New International Division of Labour*, Cambridge: Cambridge University Press. It should be remembered too that Fröbel *et al.* are examining a tendency in

international production and capital accumulation. The overwhelming majority of investment by international capital in LDCs remains ISI. Further, MNCs are ultimately directed by but one 'logic', i.e., the drive to increase surplus-value. The methods of achieving this, however, have been transformed by the prerequisites referred to by Fröbel *et al.*

11 See Clive Edwards, *op. cit.*

12 Free trade zones are usually physically distinct areas, enclaves, set aside for the location of plants engaged in manufacture for export. Special provisions and conditions apply in these zones which enhance maximum utilisation of low-cost labour. For details on the extent and nature of free trade zones see N. Vittal (1977), *Export Processing Zones in Asia: Some Dimensions*, Hong Kong: Nordica International Limited.

13 The heavy involvement of the state in the upgrading of infrastructure in the State Development Plan 1961-4 gave Singapore a good footing for the export-orientation which was decided in 1965. For details of the State Development Plan 1961-4 see Lee Soo Ann (1973), *Industrialization in Singapore*, Camberwell: Longman, pp.35-46.

14 The establishment of industrial estates was advocated in the United Nations Industrial Survey Mission report to the PAP soon after it took office.

15 Kunio Yoshihara (1976), *Foreign Investment and Domestic Response*, Singapore: Eastern Universities Press, p.22.

16 See JTC (1974), *Annual Report*, pp.49-61 for details on the allocation of this sum.

17 Plans for extensions to the industrial estates include a 559 hectare estate at Sembawang which will cost an estimated S$800 million (US$383). See S. Karene Witcher (1980), 'Singapore Firms Up Plans to Make More Sites Available for Industry', *Asian Wall Street Journal*, 26 November. In the 1981 financial year budget, S$202 million was outlayed to the Jurong Town Corporation for industrial estates.

18 In 1974 the JTC Act was substantially amended to allow JTC greater control over the sale of flats under the Home Ownership for People Scheme. One of the aims of this scheme was to establish a more permanent population in Jurong Town to provide a steadier workforce. As labour shortages become more widespread in the Singapore economy, the PAP continues to see the need for industrial estates being related to housing development: 'One of the most effective ways to get more women to work is to site factories in or close to HDB housing estates . . .', Goh Chok Tong, 'Towards Higher Achievement', Budget Speech 1981, Singapore Ministry of Culture, p.34.

19 Ninety-two per cent of SIA's stocks are owned by the Singapore government through a state company, Temasek Holdings (Pte) Ltd. SIA has come under attack from its American competitors who have charged that SIA's competitiveness is enhanced by state subsidisation. SIA has denied the charge but in March 1982 SIA requested that Temasek subscribe a minimum of S$368 million of a S$400 million new share-offering deal aimed at reducing the airline's debt. This, of course, has done little to allay the suspicions which have been formally registered

with the Civil Aeronautics Board. See Eduardo Lachica (1982), 'SIA Trying to Counter US Claims of Unfair Competition', *Asian Wall Street Journal*, 29 March.

20 INTRACO Ltd was set up soon after the DBS was formed (and included DBS equity participation) with the following objectives: developing export markets for domestic manufactures; enhancing the bargaining position of Singapore merchants in their trade with state monopolies (particularly of the socialist trading partners); and participation in the anticipated national shipping line (Neptune) on an equity basis.

21 Keppel Shipyard Limited is 71 per cent owned by the Singapore government through its wholly-owned holding company, Temasek Holdings Pte Ltd.

22 The company is now called Shing Loong Finance Limited.

23 The Keppel group's revenue in 1981 amounted to 34 per cent of the marine industry's overall total of S$2.4 billion, and profit for the year (after taxes and minority interests) was at a healthy S$87.2 million – up 17.5 per cent on 1980. See Ian Gill (1982), 'Singapore's Keppel may Diversify Further', *Asian Wall Street Journal*, 4 June.

24 It has been estimated that the actual market value of these reserves could be anything up to S$40 billion. See Susumu Awanohara (1981), 'A Storm in Singapore', *Far Eastern Economic Review*, March 6, p.51; see also 'Official Foreign Reserves of Singapore Rise by 0.8%', *Asian Wall Street Journal*, 27 May 1982.

25 See Michael Richardson (1982), 'Goh Gets Set to Slice his Cake', *Far Eastern Economic Review*, 15 January, pp.36-7; Michael Richardson (1982), 'Singapore $ millions Likely for Australia', *Age*, 9 January; Chris Pritchard (1982), 'Singapore Government Planning Large Investment in Australia', *Asian Wall Street Journal*, 13 January. It was reported in the *Age* that a sum equivalent to $A6,300 million has been set aside for overseas investment.

26 A subsidiary of the Sheng Li Group of government-owned companies.

27 *Business Times* (Singapore), 24 September 1982.

28 'Singapore Inc's Boss on the Republic's Future', *Far Eastern Economic Review*, 10 August 1979, p.44.

29 Goh Chok Tong said in his 1981 Budget speech: 'As we want to restructure and upgrade our economy quickly, the state must resume its role as an entrepreneur, not to supplant private enterprise but to encourage and assist entrepreneurs to venture their capital on new machinery with labour-saving devices . . .'

30 Special training centres, financial assistance (loans) and several industrial training schemes operate to assist manufacturers in the qualifying industries. Government Joint Training Centres with international companies Tata (India) and Philips (Netherlands), engaged respectively in machine tools and electronics, involve significant costs which include the sophisticated equipment used in the training. These costs are covered by the government.

31 Special encouragement and incentives currently apply to the following selected industries: automotive components, machine tools and machin-

ery, medical and surgical instruments, computer hardware, computer peripheral equipment and electronic instrumentation, optical instruments, precision engineering, advanced electronic components, speciality chemicals, pharmaceuticals, aerospace components and service and computer software.

32 This is exemplified by the recent reconstitution of the two major unions, the Singapore Industrial Labour Organisation and the Pioneer Industries Employees' Union, into nine industry-based unions. This move is designed to administer more effectively the technical changes to the labour force necessary for successful capital restructuring. Not unrelatedly, the move will also ensure even tighter control over union affairs by the government through constitutional provisions to increase the PAP's monitoring influence in the nine executive councils of the new unions. See Patrick Smith (1982), 'The Union Engineers', *Far Eastern Economic Review*, 25 June, pp.57-62.

33 The following statement by Goh Keng Swee in his 1981 Budget Speech summarises the government's thinking:

> Our wages must be related to the labour market. In a full employment economy, low wages will lead to an overtight labour market. Inefficient businesses, which have no place in a fully-employed economy, will continue to hoard labour which should be more productively employed by more efficient firms.

34 Based on the national average wage, labour costs to employers should have risen between 65 per cent and 70 per cent over this period if the National Wage Council's (NWC) recommendations have been adopted (nearly 94 per cent of companies recently surveyed by the National Trade Union Council indicated that they accept the NWC recommendations). Of these increases, not all pertain to wages. Increases in employer and employee contributions to superannuation (Central Provident Fund) and employers' contributions to the Skills Development Fund are included in this increase. The cumulative increase of 65 per cent to 70 per cent should be interpreted as a cost to employers rather than an outright gain to employees in wages. This is precisely how the policy is intended to be felt, inducing employers to replace labour wherever possible.

Although the government has introduced the Small Industries Finance Scheme (SIFS), it remains that the nature of the industries pursued by the government generally exclude local capital. Their lack of expertise and resources in highly internationalised production make it difficult to compete on an equal footing with large international companies without considerable state assistance. The capacity of domestic capital to absorb the costs of the wage rises and to automate and upgrade is disproportionate to that of international capital. See Chua Swee Kiat (1979), 'Caught Short', *Singapore Business*, 3(10), pp.34-5.

35 With the rapid reconstruction of Western Europe and Japan after World War II and the subsequent development of those economies, the

technological gap between Japan and Western Europe on the one hand, and the United States on the other, began to close. The increased competitiveness of these countries' products began to show. The economies of West Germany and Japan, in particular, enjoyed the advantages over the US of relatively cheap labour, more government assistance and more modern plants and equipment (see M. Landsberg (1979), 'Export-led Industrialization in the Third World: Manufacturing Imperialism', *The Review of Radical Political Economy*, 11(4), pp.50-63). The improved position of European and Japanese-based capital in the world market in the 1960s started to cost US-based capital overseas markets. At this time US-based capital even began to experience challenges to its domestic market from its foreign competitors.

36 See Harry Braverman (1974), *Labour and Monopoly Capital*, New York: Monthly Review Press.

37 The abundant supply of cheap labour was often brought about by the disruptive effects of LDC agricultural production being oriented towards the requirements of DCC markets. The introduction of capitalist production techniques released peasants to the urban areas where these unskilled masses sought work. Of course, the transition to wage labour relations was smoother in those societies not dominated by enforced agricultural relations.

38 Source: *Census of Industrial Production*, Department of Statistics Industry Codes: 38211-2, 38321, 38329.

39 This may be particularly relevant to Australia. Wages may be too high in Australia to allow manufacturers to compete internationally in labour-intensive technology but it does not mean that Australian manufacturers can be internationally competitive in relatively capital-intensive technology.

40 One of the problems with increasing automation is that payback periods tend to be longer. With rising wage costs coupled with this factor, such considerations as nearness to market start to assume greater significance in the overall decision of where to invest. See Andie McCue (1980), 'Firm's Plan to Assemble Semi-Conductors in U.S. Could Threaten Asian Producers', *Asian Wall Street Journal*, 7 June.

41 See Ignacy Sachs, 'Outward-Looking Strategies: A Dangerous Illusion?' in Paul Streeten (ed.) (1973), *Trade Strategies for Development*, London: Macmillan, pp.51-61.

42 See *Business Times* (Singapore), 16 June 1981.

43 See Bertil Ohlin (1933), *Interregional Trade and International Trade*, Cambridge, Mass.: Harvard University Press, revised 1967; Eli Heckscher (1919), 'The Effect of Foreign Trade on the Distribution of Income', *Ekonomisk Tidskrift*, Vol.xxi, pp.497-512.

44 See M.V. Posner (1961), 'International Trade and Technical Change', *Oxford Economic Papers*, Vol.XXXI, pp.323-41.

45 See Raymond Vernon (1966), 'International Investment and International Trade in the Product Cycle', *Quarterly Journal of Economics*, Cambridge, Mass., Vol.LXXX, pp.190-207.

46 See Harry G. Johnson (1968), *Comparative Costs and Commercial Policy*

for a Developing World Economy, Stockholm: Almqvist and Wiskell; and (1971), *Aspects of the Theory of Tariffs*, London: Allen & Unwin.

47   This upgrading, or restructuring, predates the NWC decision to recommend substantial wage increases. Government measures have made it increasingly possible and attractive to upgrade and automate.

48   Source: US Department of State, Airgram: Singapore A-045, 'Biannual Embassy Survey of American Investment in Singapore', September 1981.

49   See Ian Gill, (1981) 'Industrial Nations' Investment in Singapore Rises by 53%', *Asian Wall Street Journal*, 3 November.

50   See Freida Koh, (1981) 'Singapore Policy on Wages is seen Discouraging Investors from Japan', *Asian Wall Street Journal*, 17 March.

51   See Singapore Department of Statistics, *Report on Census of Industrial Production 1978*, Tables 11 and 6, pp.19 and 15.

52   See Alan L. Otten (1982), 'Japan Firms Are Expanding Their Investments in Europe', *Asian Wall Street Journal*, 21 April; Akhiro Sato (1980), 'Production of Autos in Europe Offers Way for Nissan to Circumvent Trade Barriers', *Asian Wall Street Journal*, 8 March; Atsuko Chiba (1979), 'Direct Japanese Investment in the UK Likely to Accelerate, Nikko Study Suggests', *Asian Wall Street Journal*, 12 June; Gene Gregory (1974), 'Japan Finding a Toehold in Europe', *Far Eastern Economic Review*, 6 Dec., pp.67-70.

53   This has not been the only motivation but a major and thematic one.

54   See David Hickie (1981), 'How Much Industry Can We Call Our Own?', *The National Times*, 28 June to 4 July, pp.24-34.

55   See Donald T. Brash (1966), *American Investment in Australian Industry*, Canberra: Australian National University Press.

7 Imperialism, dependency and peripheral industrialization: the case of Japan in Indonesia *

WAYNE ROBINSON – *University of Waikato*

Introduction

This chapter is an empirical contribution to the now celebrated debate between Bill Warren and James Petras concerning under-development.[1] Specifically it seeks, by a case study of Japanese-Indonesian relations to explore the relevance of their thinking on the relationship between imperialism, capitalism and Third World industrialization. The Warren thesis first advanced in 1973 has attracted widespread attention for its attempt to defend from a Marxist position the optimistic 'liberal' prognosis for Third World industrialization. In sharp contrast to Petras, who has laid particular stress on the international determinants of this process, Warren has asserted the primacy of domestic factors. Petras readily acknowledges the formidable nature of the post-colonial state for it must dominate all aspects of society in order to assure long-term security to foreign capital. But he rejects Warren's view that the internal politics upon which the state is based are autonomous from imperialist forces. Thus:

> The emergence of neo-fascism in third world countries of disparate historical backgrounds and internal social structures suggests that there is a common external factor which is operating along with internal processes to produce the common phenomenon we know by the generic term 'neo-fascism'.[2]

This 'common external factor' Petras identifies as close integration with 'the growth of the accumulation of capital on a world scale'.[3] Reactionary dictatorships and their policies are not products of internal evolution but responses to specific demands originating primarily on a global level.

---

* This chapter was originally given as a paper at Asian Studies Association of Australia, Fourth National Conference, Monash University, 10-14 May 1982.

Against this Warren argues that imperialism, far from hampering development has been the 'pioneer' of modern capitalism's transfer into the Third World. He argues that, with the spread of political independence, imperialism has been compelled to act increasingly as its own gravedigger by creating 'national capitalisms'. To prove that imperialism has functioned in this manner Warren amasses impressive aggregate statistics to show that industrialization has indeed become widespread in the Third World. Warren thus abandons the classical Leninist assocation of imperialism with predatory attempts by monopoly capital to stave off declining profitability. Here his position has been strongly criticized for its failure to connect specific crises of accumulation in the capitalist core with expansion abroad. This failure obscures what is distinctively imperialist, namely the targeting of particular countries, irrespective of their own developmental needs, to the total neglect of some others.[4] Thus, the high degree of selectiveness shown by Western industrial capital in responding to the demand for a New International Economic Order after 1970 is not brought out. This selectiveness, however, stands in sharp conflict with the picture of an increasingly even global distribution of capitalism's productive forces, painted by Warren.

While asserting the sovereignty of internal over external factors in Third World development Warren nevertheless recognizes the continued importance of inter-capitalist tensions. These tensions borne of uneven development arising from 'realignments within the structure of global productive capabilities and investment patterns'[5] flared once more in the 1970s. In their efforts to maintain international competitiveness the powers were forced to relocate modern industries to the Third World to exploit cheaper factors of production. Intense jostling for privileged bilateral access to underdeveloped countries resulted, disrupting the coordination of international Keynesian welfarist measures by the Western aid agencies. It will be argued here that this happened in the early 1970s when Japan sought to challenge the dominance exercized over Indonesia's economy by Euro-American capital. Warren argues that from such a conjuncture, linking internal and external forces, new 'openings' arose for Third World groups wishing to accelerate industrialization. In the Indonesian case important Japanese interests turned to collaboration with powerful bureaucratic nationalist leaders, Chinese and marginalized petty-bourgeois elements hostile to the 'liberal' Western strategy, seeing in them a privileged means of access to the country. The objective of these groups was not the complete severing of links with international capital but the subordination of such links to a programme of accelerated state-capitalist industrialization. To achieve this end the anti-mainstream forces turned to Japan, seeking by informal political contact and command of Indonesia's energy resources to draw Japan into a special partnership.

Warren rejects the view that such attempts are internally flawed and doomed to fail. He argues that the achievement of capitalist industrialization need not be associated with a particular ruling class. It may be initiated and directed by a variety of classes and combinations, ranging from semi-feudal ruling groups to bureaucratic military elites or petty-bourgeois professional elements. Underlying this optimism is a distinction by Warren between the forces he sees merely 'leading industrialization' and those social forces actually 'compelling' it. While therefore holding that the post-colonial state is the author of its own actions, Warren clearly envisages that the real impulse for development will come from outside it. It will be argued here that in the case of Indonesia those seeking the special relationship with Japan constituted the social forces Warren sees compelling industrialization.

Petras has recently given theoretical attention to the potentiality of the 'Indonesian type' counter-current phenomenon.[6] Within the context of over-arching subordination to international capital:

> centralization of state power, the command of the state over international resources and the growth of state forms produces a 'nationalist' component within the neo-fascist regime which conflicts with foreign capital on a series of issues within their common economic development project. Absolute political control creates, in some factions of the neo-fascist regime, a desire to extend the power of the state into the economic sphere, competing and displacing foreign capital. This national-fascist element is held back by the long-term dependence established within civil society and the state and by the fact that it has little independent basis outside of the military and within the neo-fascist institutional arrangement.[7]

It will be argued that Japan, by its links with Indonesia's national bureaucratic forces in the 1972-6 period, greatly enhanced its economic position in Indonesia *vis-à-vis* the United States and Western Europe. However, the attempt at accelerated national industrialization by Indonesia's counter-strategists, though initially successful, was ultimately emasculated by supervening world capitalist dynamics. While Indonesia's national bureaucratic forces were successful in using the country's oil income for industrial projects, they proved less able to regulate Japan's economic priorities. Further, during 1975-6 resolution of difficulties facing the 'nationalist' attempt became subordinated to the solution of crises facing American and Japanese interests. While correct in emphasizing the importance of inter-capitalist rivalry for nationalist factions, Warren fails to see that as conjunctural phenomena they remain highly vulnerable to imperialism in its more collusive phases.

The anti-communist putsch by the Indonesian Army, following the coup attempt of 1 October 1965, came at a time when Japan was rapidly re-establishing close relations with its former colonies, Taiwan and (South) Korea. The military takeover, not wholly unexpected in Tokyo, presented the possibility that Jakarta also might be incorporated into the newly emerging Tokyo-Taipei-Seoul axis. Behind this hope lay a recognition in Tokyo of Indonesia's long-term strategic importance to Japan as a source of raw materials and energy.

The new political structure that quickly emerged in Indonesia ended the era of mass politics. In its place was put a finely graded system of consultation, co-optation, patronage and repression which drastically curtailed the numbers able to engage in politics. This in no sense reflected Japan's role, but rather the counter-revolutionary strategy of the Suharto regime itself and the political requirements imposed by adherence to the terms of the Western-backed economic stabilization plan.

Japanese policy towards the Suharto regime was guided by acceptance of overall US dominance. Japan, with US encouragement, assumed an active role in the affairs of the newly constituted creditor consortium, the Intergovernmental Group for Indonesia (IGGI), channelling fresh aid to Jakarta and writing off old debts. Nevertheless, there were pressures that worked against Japan's remaining exclusively within the IGGI framework in its relations with Indonesia. Among these was Japanese resentment over the speed with which US interests had staked their claim to Indonesia's natural resources. This was notably true of oil.[8] There was also tension within the IGGI over Japan's preference that direct private investment – including joint venture capital – form part of its official IGGI aid.[9] This caused considerable consternation particularly among European members who saw it as a manoeuvre allowing Japan to classify as aid, funds lent to its own companies.[10] A further source of friction was Tokyo's wish to determine its infrastructure loans in Tokyo in order, it was alleged, that Japan could coordinate them with the interests of its own companies. For the technocratic group, and the World Bank, which sought to determine these priorities, this represented an important conflict of principle. The United States sided strongly with the Bappenas IMF-IBRD group on these matters within the IGGI.[11] In part the United States backing reflected its wish for a collective approach, over which it could itself exercise decisive control. Partly it reflected a desire to preserve the authority of the technocratic group in Jakarta.

For the large Japanese suppliers and contractors with a long history of successful tendering for contracts from Japan's soft loan agency, the Overseas Economic Cooperation Fund, and with strong political connections in Jakarta, the limitations imposed by these pressures were negligible. To a substantial degree the specific projects Japan selected for funding at annual IGGI meetings were reflective of understandings these companies had already reached with authorities in Jakarta. For new Japanese companies, however, with few inside connections, that crowded Jakarta after 1969 seeking to promote the export of manufacturing plant and machinery, steel, glass, cement and chemical equipment, etc., the situation was more difficult. It seemed to these companies that their objectives in Indonesia could not be achieved via an expansion of state loans within the IGGI. The response of these companies was to turn to investment capital, funds being channelled to affiliates in Indonesia set up for the purpose of promoting exports. Essentially a mercantilist strategy, it rested on exceptionally heavy borrowing, a fact which appears to account, in part, for the dramatic scale of Japan's subsequent private investment in Indonesia. This response by business considerably weakened any incentive Japan had to contribute more than its 'fare share' to the IGGI.

On the strategic plane of control over natural resources, there was a further implication for Japan's continued adherence to the IGGI. Japan's ability to wield control over its oil deliveries from Indonesia was limited, due principally to the dominating position of the Americans. While the world energy situation had remained favourable for Japan, this was little cause for concern. With the intense international rivalry that developed over energy during 1972, Japan's resource nationalists had good reason to be wary of submitting initiatives in Indonesia to detailed scrutiny by the IGGI forum, for it could have sparked preemptive moves by international oil and gas interests.

By the early 1970s Japan thus found itself forced to grapple with new ways of reconciling its political support for the Suharto regime through the IGGI, with the creation of business opportunities for its companies. Tokyo's influence in Jakarta, however, was no longer what it had been earlier, in the 1960s, at the high point of War Reparations payments. Japan also played little part in planning Indonesia's future. Decisions on major priorities that affected Japanese interests were in the hands of technocratic and World Bank personnel not closely attuned to thinking in Tokyo. During 1971-2 as the tight credit policy and foreign penetration generated public anger in Indonesia, Japan's 'one-legged economic imperialism' seemed far less tenable than the multi-legged economic, political, military, cultural and communicative variety of its major competitors.[12] Ironically, because of this, Japan found itself peculiarly vulnerable to public criticisms of a stabilization programme it had had little part in determining. Finally, Japan was exposed, through association, to the increasingly vitriolic attacks directed at Chinese groups receiving preferment from the government in the granting of credit, import licences and joint-venture opportunities. Japan's position in Indonesia by 1972 was thus an ambiguous one. It remained closely identified with the IGGI-IMF-IBRD complex but distrusted it. At the same time Japan was linked with interests in Indonesia subject to growing domestic attack. Japan's need was for an effective political bridgehead in Jakarta, able to withstand pressure from international capitalist competitors, the Western Aid Agencies, and Indonesian critics of the Suharto regime.

By 1972 a significant level of extractive and manufacturing investment fuelled by Japanese, American and Chinese capital was occurring in Indonesia. This proto-industrialization was conducted under the general supervision of the technocratic planners. Its social leadership, however, appeared to come from those who, by their own strength, their client-comprador status, or control of politico-bureaucratic resources had withstood internationalization of Indonesia's economy after 1966. From the standpoint of important groups who had supported the military takeover in 1966 two serious difficulties accompanied the inflow of foreign capital. These were the exclusion of large segments of the middle class and the relative lack of state power over the priorities and operational decisions of foreign capital. During 1971-2 the outlines of an indigenous reaction to these difficulties began to appear. At the head of those calling for an alternative approach were General Sutowo, president of the state oil company, Pertamina, and two pro-Japanese generals in Suharto's kitchen cabinet, Ali Murtopo and Sudjono Humardhani. Underlying their attitude was a recognition of the close connection between foreign economic penetration and failure to achieve a more consolidated, bourgeois, form of state.

Sutowo's continued commitment to a nationalist position is well brought out in a little noted but revealing speech made during 1967. In this Sutowo alluded to the 'imperialist cunning' of international oil companies and their propensity to replace nationalist regimes with puppets amenable to their wishes.[13] He argued that despite the scrapping in 1963 of the 'concession system' that had given Caltex, Shell and Stanvac virtual sovereignty over Indonesia's oil, little had changed. Sutowo pointed with obvious approval to attempts by other oil producers, notably Iran, Iraq and Ceylon to nationalize their assets and the retaliation it engendered:

> Ceylon nationalized oil refineries – not the fields – but this step was immediately countered by the Americans through the stopping of credits, so that it caused difficulties in Ceylon's economic relations. Finally, Ceylon had to give in to the American counter measure by cancelling its brave step of nationalizing the refineries of the foreign oil companies.[14]

Sutowo was forced to concede that the Indonesian Communist Party (PKI) had instigated similar moves to nationalize foreign companies in Indonesia: 'Personally I don't deny that I fully agree with the operation of oil by ourselves . . . but I strongly oppose the way used by the PKI.'[15]

Sutowo further sought to distinguish his position from that of the PKI by criticizing its 'unilateral and arbitrary' methods in pursuit of nationalization. He contended that the Party had only supported nationalization to 'isolate Indonesia and destroy her good relations . . . especially with the Western countries, in the hope of dragging Indonesia into the orbit of Communist China.'[16] Given Sutowo's concern to ensure his own political survival this somewhat convoluted reasoning is explicable. In the context of Indonesia's wholesale reversions to laissez-faire capitalist principles Sutowo's words struck a discordant note. In essence they reflected a strong commitment to the Sukarnoist ideal of economic sovereignty publicly excoriated by the regime.

Implicit in Sutowo's view was the belief that modern technology offered a more effective means to secure a transfer of economic surplus within the international division of labour than the agriculture-orientated policies favoured by the IMF-IBRD group. Such advance could not be secured through reliance upon the goodwill of the IGGI and foreign investors, but only by using the country's oil wealth. Here Sutowo and those supporting him had solid ground under them. In 1969-70, in the order of 19.7 per cent of the government's revenue came from oil, whereas 27 per cent came as aid from the IGGI. By 1972, however, 30.8 per cent of government revenue was coming from oil while the IGGI contribution as a proportion had slipped to 21.1 per cent.

The backing received by Pertamina, as Warren's thesis suggests, was heterogeneous. Its major political support came from Ali Murtopo and 'OPSUS', the politico-strategic think-tank which he headed. For Murtopo, and Humardhani the appeal of the strategy was its contribution to 'national resilience' defined as preservation of existing socio-political hierarchy. Socially the support appeared to comprise petty bourgeois elements, including petty commodity producers supplying inputs that largely capitalist enterprises were unable to offer, such as cheap food and consumer goods. Salaried managers, independent entrepreneurs performing a variety of services and some intellectuals, notably among the Chinese, were drawn in also. Far from being a traditional, isolated or self-contained group it occupied a contradictory, highly unstable position in Indonesia's capitalist nexus. Because of this its members shared a strong desire to win protected market and status opportunities. These were seen to flow from the kind of national economic ownership advocated by Sutowo.

By using Indonesia's oil wealth as collateral to attract further international capital, a way forward was available that did not seriously divert oil from its political role within the military clientage network, a step that could have threatened Suharto's own position. At the same time repayment of the additional debt could be met from the anticipated rises in oil earnings. Such a strategy potentially posed a major challenge to the IGGI for it would allow Jakarta to escape from the tight credit control which IGGI consensus had been intended to ensure, and a redirection of the country's energy income away from debt repayments, IGGI imports and financial regularization. From the standpoint of the IGGI consortium, which saw provision of aid as conditional upon how the petro dollars were to be used, these aspirations of Indonesia's petty bourgeois nationalists constituted an inadmissible claim upon the country's energy wealth. Politically the question it posed was whether the Suharto government could steer a course that did not result in a lessening of IGGI aid, but which allowed sufficient internal autonomy for Indonesia's oil income to serve as collateral for special projects.

The catalyst drawing Japan and Indonesia's national bureaucratic forces together, affording Tokyo the political bridgehead it urgently needed and Indonesia the ability to steer its new course, was the United States' decision to recognize China. The immediate effect of this shift in US policy was to erode support by Japanese big business for a continuance of close links with Taiwan, accelerating further popular disenchantment that was already widespread with the leadership of Sato Eisaku and the Taiwan-South Korea lobby.[17] For the Suharto regime, the Nixon Administration's entente cordiale with Peking, and its decision to withdraw American military forces from mainland Southeast Asia, appeared to threaten political isolation and a weakening of 'national resilience'. The new realities also gave rise to fears in the Sato faction that the Suharto regime's position had seriously weakened. It resulted in urgent steps by both sides to strengthen the Suharto regime before the Sato faction's probable loss of power.

It was with these considerations in mind that Suharto visited Tokyo in May 1972. The key questions discussed during this five-day meeting were the Nixon visit to Peking and the changing military balance in Indo-China.[18] Suharto stressed to the Japanese side the urgency of proceeding with the giant Asahan hydro-electricity and aluminium smelter project at Lake Toba in North Sumatra. Despite Sato's willingness to accommodate Indonesia the Japanese government was faced with opposition from interested companies resentful over pressure from the Ministry of International Trade and Industry (MITI) for collective tendering. There was, however, an agreement that Indonesia would provide Japan with an additional 58 million kilolitres of oil 'in excess of the supply through existing commercial channels'.[19] In return for this Japan granted Indonesia an untied project loan of 62 billion yen (US$234 million). Additionally, as part of the oil deal, but not mentioned in the communiqué, was a further $100 million from Toyota Motor Sales. The manoeuvre was an extremely complex one involving not only the interests of the Sato-Kishi faction and Toyota, but contention for the presidency of the ruling Liberal Democratic Party between Fukuda Takeo and Tanaka Kakuei. Fundamentally, however, it reflected the skill of the ex-bureaucrat political leaders Sato and Kishi in securing for the Suharto government a large, soft public loan outside the IGGI, that allowed the Indonesian side maximum manoeuvrability.[20]

The Suharto visit to Tokyo in May 1972 brought an appreciable quickening of economic contact between the two countries. In mid-November Marubeni announced it was sending a 'development team' to Indonesia. A large Mitsubishi mission led by Fujino Chujiro, the Chairman of Mitsubishi Corporation, was announced, with renewed interest being expressed in the Asahan smelter project.[21] Mitsui's President Wakasugi Sueyuki, indicated that his company, too, would send a delegation at the same time. Further, in January 1973 a twenty-man delegation went to Jakarta in connection with Japan's $300 million oil loan. The timing of the new capital push into Indonesia was thus in part related to the 'oil loan' and the protective canopy it had created over Japanese interests in Indonesia. But it also reflected part of a generalized movement in no sense directed specifically at Indonesia, having its roots rather in Zaibatsu resurgence, major world currency realignments and expansionist policies by the new Tanaka government.[22] Japan's enhanced international economic capacity significantly altered its relations with a weakened US, leading rapidly to a more aggressive American posture towards Japan in their rivalry for Asian business.

In this wider contest to internationalize, Japan lagged far behind its American and European rivals within the IGGI. Palloix shows that by 1971 the book value of Japan's international investments was a modest US$4,480 million. By comparison the US figure stood at $86,198 million, the British at $24,020 million, the French at $9,540 million and West Germany's at $7,270 million.[23] Despite this low base the huge capital surpluses Japan now commanded gave it unrivalled flexibility in the credit terms its banks could offer resource-rich countries like Indonesia.

Japan, in the 1972-6 period, scored a remarkable success *vis-à-vis* US and European capital in the transfer of direct private investment to Indonesia. Up to the end of 1976 a total of $2,340 million had been invested under the New Order government. Of this figure Japan accounted for 44 per cent or $1,030 million making it far the largest investor.[24] The United States, the European members and Japan each provided a third of total official IGGI aid to Indonesia. No formal link existed between this formula and their investment shares. Nevertheless, when Japan's investment in Indonesia is compared with that of the Europeans and the Americans, Japan's achievement bears little relation to the IGGI contribution. This can be seen in Table 7.1.

Table 7.1 *Investment in Indonesia by Japan and other IGGI members: 1967-76* (US$000)

Country	Amount	No. of Projects
Britain (excl. HK)	36,725.4	31
West Germany	28,744	14
Japan	1,030,424	162
Canada	96,203	4
Netherlands	77,412	28
New Zealand	70	1
France	11,959	4
Belgium	77,854	15
United States	147,695	45
Australia	64,794	23
TOTALS	1,571,880.4	327

Source: BKPM – Realized basis.
Notes: 1 Excludes oil, banking and insurance.
      2 The totals given represent the total of (1) capital supplied by the foreign investor, (2) contribution from the Indonesian side in case of joint ventures, and (3) investors' outside borrowings.

The question of the extent to which this Japanese investment converged, ultimately, on sectors controlled by national bureaucratic forces will be examined at a later point. Taken overall, however, the tempo of the investment reflected more closely the dynamics of Japan's global capital push than factors specific to Indonesia. By 1973 Japan's cumulative stock of overseas investment capital had risen to US$10.27 billion[25] – an increase of nearly $6 billion in less than two years. Japan's realized investment in Indonesia went from a modest $58,504 million in 1972 to $236,269 million in 1973 rising still further to $241,058 million for 1974.[26] By 1974 severe official restrictions had been imposed on Japan's capital export drive to deal with the rise in cost of crude oil imports which increased to $21.6 billion from $6.72 billion a year earlier.[27] The huge investment realized in Indonesia for 1974 was thus a 'spill over' from the momentum generated in 1973. By 1975 Japan's global stock of investment had risen only $2.4 billion in two years to $12.66 billion. In Indonesia, Japan's realized investment for 1975 dropped precipitously to $61,344 million. Between 1975 and 1976, however, a vigorous export drive by Japan had again boosted capital exports, cumulative global investment climbing sharply to $15.94 billion.[28] Reflecting this, Japan's investment in Indonesia also rose reaching a substantial $152,314 million.[29]

Japan, the IMF-IGGI and the United States

Tension over Tokyo's more assertive role, the oil loan and Pertamina's greatly enhanced ability to raise funds for Indonesia outside the IGGI heightened considerably in the latter part of 1972. The Fund was particularly angered to discover that in the course of 1972 Pertamina had borrowed over US$3,000 million abroad, much of it on short or medium term.[30] This violated the conditions of an IMF 'standby loan' facility that had been extended to the Suharto government in March 1972. As the principle guarantor of the IMF and its philosophy the United States was compelled to act, suspending official aid to Indonesia.[31] Two commercial credits to Pertamina, one for $120 million from the US Export-Import Bank and the other for $200 million from an American consortium led by the First National City Bank (FNCB) were also stopped.[32]

Between 7 and 9 February 1973 the United States' Vice-President, Spiro Agnew visited Jakarta and held talks on Pertamina's borrowing.[33] Suharto was reported to have delivered a vigorous defence of Pertamina, informing Agnew that the oil company undertook a number of government projects on direct presidential orders for which there was no special budget allocation.[34] Agnew also held talks with Ibnu Sutowo which were said to 'have gone well'.[35]

Shortly after Agnew's departure US aid to Indonesia was resumed. No public reason was given for the United States' abrupt turn about. Publicly also, Indonesia had conceded little. A significant detail of the US policy change, little noted at the time, concerned funding for a new oil refinery by the US Export-Import Bank. A credit of $120 million by the Bank had now been cleared to Pertamina for its Cilacap refinery in South Central Java but not the $200 million FNCB loan. Cilacap was intended to refine Middle East crude oil for local use, releasing Indonesia's higher priced low-sulphur crude oil for international sale. A consortium of Japanese companies comprising Mitsui, Tomen, C. Itoh and Nippon Steel had been widely reported to be the engineering contractors for this project.[36] The official US loan for Cilacap appeared to be in breach of the IMF credit ceiling on Pertamina, but no official US or IMF statement was forthcoming on this matter. Nor was it explained why the FNCB loan remained suspended.

Behind the scenes the US position in support of the IMF had in fact become entangled with its pursuit of concrete commercial interests involving Indonesia's oil and gas. Between late 1972 and mid-1973, as the world energy picture radically changed, Stanvac (Mobil Oil) and US Banking interests fought to win control of Indonesia's newly discovered natural gas. Mobil Oil sought to claim ownership of the gas that was found in its exploration block. This, however, was blocked by the Indonesian government, forcing Mobil to acquiesce to contractor status.[37] At the same time Pertamina opened talks with Nissho-Iwai, a medium-sized Japanese trading company having close connections with Japan's new Prime Minister Tanaka Kakuei, concerning finance and marketing of the gas in Japan. The decision was taken by Suharto and Sutowo that, for reasons of national prestige, the two liquefaction plants needed would be owned by Indonesia herself despite objections in technocratic quarters that ownership was unnecessary.[38]

By early 1973 it was clear that around one billion dollars (US) would be needed to construct the liquefaction plants and attendant facilities. Finance became the key issue. American banks were anxious to lend but the US government's policy of support to the IMF made it difficult for the US Export-Import Bank to provide guarantees for such large sums. Japanese banks, notably the Industrial Bank of Japan supported by Nissho-Iwai, lobbied strongly to win from the Japanese government a large-scale official loan to Indonesia. There was opposition to the proposal from Japan's Foreign and Finance Ministries, both of which felt that the massive loans, coming so soon after the 'oil loan' of $300 million would be strongly resented by the other IGGI members and the IMF-IBRD.

The Ministry of International Trade and Industry, however, was strongly in favour of a Japanese bid for Indonesia's liquefied natural gas (LNG).

Behind this determination within MITI was the strategic objective of gaining control of an 'intermediate range' energy substitution for oil, that was not dominated by foreign companies. Tokyo was acutely aware of US sensitivity concerning independent Japanese oil initiatives; with the assertion of Indonesian sovereignty over its natural gas, however, a Japanese thrust appeared to run little risk of serious conflict with US oil interests. Faced with the tightening world energy picture the Tanaka cabinet decided in May 1973 to implement the course advocated by the energy nationalists, authorizing an offer of $898 million in loans for the Indonesian gas project.[39]

Little was revealed publicly of Tokyo's decision. However, further information about Indonesia's energy projects became available at the end of July, this time concerning Cilacap refinery. It was announced that Pertamina would receive $54 million from the US Export-Import Bank for the project. A further $54 million, to be guaranteed by the Bank was to come from a consortium headed by the FNCB.[40] Most significantly, an American company, Fluor Engineering of Los Angeles, was now to build Cilacap at a cost of $161 million. Of the Mitsui-led consortium that, until April, had been the probable contractor, there was no word.

From circumstantial evidence and information which subsequently became available, we are able to reconstruct what had transpired. The Suharto government, in defence of national bureaucratic objectives, had at the time of Agnew's visit made concessions to American energy interests in return for a resumption of US aid. Though not giving ground on Pertamina's autonomy nor the new bilateral relationship with Tokyo, the Suharto government made concessions that involved sacrificing the Japanese refinery consortium to US interests. Cilacap thus became the responsibility of the US Export-Import Bank and Fluor Engineering. The United States, however, was forced in turn to recognize the reality of the strengthened Jakarta-Tokyo axis and Japan's pre-eminence over Indonesia's natural gas.

This interpretation is supported by the testimony of Erland Heginbotham, a State Department officer, before a Senate subcommittee investigating the role of US banks abroad.[41] According to Heginbotham, in the course of 1973 the IMF and the United States government had been urging Indonesia to accept a change from general funding to project-specific loans that were more readily monitored. In the course of this attempt, however, it became evident to the parties that 'the United States had a special interest in Indonesia and that Japan did as well . . .'.[42] These special interests, according to Heginbotham, were the Cilacap oil refinery and the liquefied natural gas project, both of which were being funded by the US and Japan outside the IMF guidelines. In this testimony Heginbotham noted:

> these two projects became subjects for discussion between the Indonesian Government, the IMF, the US Government, the Japanese Government, and others, to consider how these projects might be melded in with responsible policies and the credit ceiling arrangement. In a period of about 2 or 3 months, as I recall it, an agreement was reached under which these projects were considered to be compatible with the IMF-accepted ceilings.[43]

What Heginbotham's testimony strongly suggests is that the US and Japan had colluded, with Jakarta's active encouragement, to frustrate IMF attempts to limit Indonesia's bilateral international borrowing. The manoeuvering this entailed appears to explain the failure of the US to give its reason for resuming aid despite the breach it involved of the IMF ceiling. Consistent with the Warren thesis, Cilacap and the gas project had become linked in a process of horse-trading between Washington and Tokyo, the outcome of which seriously undercut the prestige of the IMF in Indonesia. The US government's inclusion of FNCB in the Export-Import Bank loan for Cilacap, but continued blocking of the larger FNCB loan of $200 million to Pertamina, seemed intended to mollify IMF feelings over the deliberate breach that had occurred.

The new Japanese-American equilibrium in Indonesia resting on redrawn boundaries of influence left US petroleum investments intact. It also assured Mobil, Bechtel and other US companies of a secure place in the construction of the Japanese-funded gas project. Appearing to confirm its acceptance of continued US dominion over Indonesia's oil, Japan swung markedly away from Indonesian crude to similar, low-sulphur Chinese oil during 1974. Whereas 71.4 per cent of Indonesia's crude oil exports went to Japan in 1973, by 1976 this figure had dropped to 43.4 per cent with the US becoming Indonesia's biggest customer.[44]

The effect of the realignment was to soften United States' pressure on Jakarta to conform with the IMF-IBRD requirements. This opened wider the breach already created by Tokyo's partial move outside the IGGI. The strengthened framework of Indonesian-Japanese energy cooperation – consecrated by the visit of Tanaka Kakuei to Jakarta in January 1974 – thus constituted a major political triumph for the national bureaucratic forces. The Japanese government's commitment of the huge sums necessary for the physical installations of Indonesia was irrevocable. While guarantees could be demanded, ultimately the security of the investment involved a major act of faith in the survival of the Suharto leadership. Coming little more than a year after Suharto's abortive attempt to win Japanese backing for the Asahan hydro and aluminium project, the LNG venture became a substitute showpiece for the regime, demonstrating its international standing and commitment to the nationalist cause.

According to a senior Pertamina official, national ownership of the liquefaction facilities, which the Japanese loans had assured, became of major importance in enabling the company to raise further loans on world capital markets.[45] Confirmation of this view came in February 1974 when Pertamina was given presidential authorization to raise $500 million abroad for Indonesia's nationally owned 'Krakatau Steel' project. During March the first part of Japan's official gas loans, cumulatively standing at $1,085 million, was made available to Indonesia.[46] A further indication of weakened technocratic control came in April when the government exempted Pertamina from a new 30 per cent non-interest bearing deposit requirement on all government borrowing abroad, introduced at the behest of the IMF.[47] Also, later in 1974, Pertamina received presidential authorization to withhold approximately $800 million in oil taxes from Bank Indonesia to sustain the momentum of the special projects. These moves, while not undermining the flow of oil finance into the military clientage network, accentuated further IGGI-IMF hostility towards Suharto's state capitalist attempt.

The Suharto government's decision to undertake massive new international obligations, this time in the energy sector, could be interpreted as a response to a favourable world market situation. But in domestic political terms, it could be seen as reflecting the dead end facing attempts by Operasi Khusus (OPSUS) (Special Operations) to bridge the widening rift during 1973 between Chinese business interests and marginalized indigenous groups angry at their neglect by the government. Paralysed in the face of these pressures by its internal contradictoriness, the OPSUS leadership had turned its hopes from guided investment to international loan finance. In doing this the original 'class integrating' rationale of the national bureaucratic projects became subordinated to their use as a 'trickle down' mechanism. Seen in the light of the 'floating mass' doctrine, the brainchild of Ali Murtopo, the de-activation of the Suharto regime's own party, Golkar, official emasculation of opposition parties and serious socio-political tensions that exploded in January 1974, the energy gambit represented less a spur to industrialization but the extension of political demobilization to national capitalist groups. While ostensibly in pursuit of national bureaucratic objectives the national bureaucratic projects seemed increasingly calculated to head off a more serious challenge by the strategy's supporters to the whole policy of closer integration with international capital.

The authoritarian stability that had been achieved by mid-1974 was shortlived. By late 1974 the national bureaucratic strategy had run into serious difficulties. In the context of global capitalist recession, Pertamina's heavy debt burden, associated with its policy of short-term borrowing at high rates of interest, was exceeding the company's capacity to pay. Further, extravagant time-chartering of foreign oil tankers to exploit the world oil boom faced the company with massive long-term commitments that could not be recouped. Caught between falling oil sales and the inflated cost of Western technology imports, Pertamina faced the spectre of large uncompleted projects for which it could no longer raise funds.

For the Suharto clique whose claim to leadership had rested heavily on its developmental capacity, the obvious parallel this suggested with that the Sukarno era posed a potential threat to its authority. To stave off a loss of credibility, notably with international financial circles, the Indonesian government sought massive new stabilization loans from the IGGI, seriously weakening Pertamina's independence from technocratic control by this step. Domestically there appeared little resistance to this retreat from groups wedded to the defence of the national bureaucratic domain. The failure of a counter-response reflected dramatically the lack of encouragement by the Suharto regime for the creation earlier of consultative/ mobilizing structures.

The response of Indonesia's creditors to the crises was prompt. At its 17th meeting in Amsterdam in May 1975, the IGGI granted aid totalling approximately $2 billion for fiscal year 1975-6. In June, as part of the new stabilization package, a West European, American and Canadian consortium provided $425 million. This was followed in October by a further Morgan-led consortium loan of $425 million. Attached to these loans was a cross-default provision that gave Morgan the right to call in the loans at any time should Indonesia unilaterally raise similar loans elsewhere. This was essentially a falling into line by the private banks with the IMF's tight credit control which the IGGI consensus had failed to achieve earlier, due in part to the actions of the US itself. Japan, for its part, contributed on a bilateral basis two emergency loans totalling $200 million.

By early 1976 the full dimensions of Pertamina's external indebtedness were becoming evident, with a figure as high as $10 billion being officially acknowledged as likely. On 3 March 1976, the

President-Director of Pertamina, Ibnu Sutowo was dismissed 'with honour' from his position by Suharto.[48] The dismissal of Sutowo brought a positive response from the IGGI. Drs. J.P. Pronk, the Dutch Minister for Development Cooperation and Chairman of the IGGI, on his arrival in Jakarta in April expressed pleasure that Indonesia had 'obtained a single government', avoiding the issue of Suharto's personal role.[49] Pronk said he was convinced that the steps taken to 'finalize' Pertamina's problems would obtain a positive response at the May meeting of the IGGI in Amsterdam.

Sutowo's fall, though precipitated by personal tensions with Suharto, reflected more fundamentally in acceptance by the Suharto clique that the national bureaucratic strategy could no longer be sustained outside the supervision of Indonesia's creditors, the IMF-IBRD[50] and Bappenas. At the May 1976 meeting of the IGGI, Indonesia was guaranteed a massive $2,400 million in aid for 1976-7. A mood of cynicism, however, appeared to pervade proceedings, with little attempt to disguise bilateral interests. Thus the probability of an additional $1 billion in emergency finance to cover cost-overruns on projects involving West Germany, the United States and Japan was discussed and approved within the IGGI. West German banks marshalled an additional $475 million to complete the Krakatau Steel plant. The United States hinted that it, too, would lend a further $50 million to cover the increased cost of the Cilacap refinery.[51] A new attitude by Jakarta towards Japan also became apparent, reflecting the revived influence of the technocratic group. Tokyo was informed that unless additional finance in the vicinity of $500 million was forthcoming, there was no guarantee of when the gas project might reach completion.[52]

With these developments the wheel appeared to have turned full circle against Japan's position in Indonesia. How effective, therefore, was Japan during the 1975-6 crisis period in holding the ground it had won against its capitalist rivals in Indonesia?

A look at the renegotiation in 1976 of the terms for natural gas cooperation, originally agreed to between Indonesia and Japan in 1973, provides the clearest insight into the first question. By the latter half of 1975 Japan had become aware of manoeuvres to raise the cartage charge it would have to pay for deliveries of the LNG. Originally, Japan itself had chosen not to take responsibility for transportation of the gas. The task had duly been contracted out to a British company, Burmah Shipping, which had in turn ordered five LNG tankers from General Dynamics of the United States. By mid-1975, however, there was considerable doubt that Burmah would be able to pay for the ships. Further, General Dynamics had seriously underestimated the construction costs involved and stood to lose heavily unless it could become an equity participant in the gas trade. Behind the move then to raise the cartage charge to Japan was General Dynamics' attempt to stave off a major financial crisis. Were it to be successful it would threaten to wreck the entire cost structure calculations upon which Japanese final users had decided to proceed in 1973.

It was in the midst of this wrangle – in September 1975 – that Indonesia approached Japan for approximately $500 million in loans to complete construction of the liquefaction plants. To the Japanese side it appeared that Indonesia was exploiting the uncertainty created by General Dynamics' threat not to cooperate with Burmah as a means of extracting unneeded funds. By May 1976 an impasse existed. Little progress had been made in talks between Tokyo and Jakarta on the overrun question. Also American interests continued to press for a direct transportation contract with Pertamina that would have enabled them to force up the gas cartage payable by Japan.

In June 1976 Komoto Toshio, the Minister for MITI in the new Miki cabinet, impatient with further delay, intervened. Komoto applied pressure on Burmah to withdraw part of its tanker order from General Dynamics, linking this demand to the provision of the extra funds to meet the cost overrun. Jakarta in turn came under pressure from the American side to prevent such a withdrawal. Any move to do this, however, exposed Indonesia to the risk that the Japanese side would refuse to participate further in the cost-overrun talks. A new escalation now followed with a threat by Komoto to repudiate Japan's transport contract with Burmah entirely, and to give the responsibility to Japanese shipping interests.[53] This move raised doubts concerning the viability of General Dynamics. Alarmed at the turn of events Philip Habib, the US Undersecretary of State, authorized a cable to the Japanese government protesting at the threatened action.[54]

With the US intervention Tokyo appeared to adopt a more conciliatory position. Behind the change appeared to lie, in part, a fear in Tokyo that to have pressed harder may have rendered Suharto's own position untenable. Japan now agreed at this stage to lend Indonesia an additional $416.9 million raising its total investment in the LNG project to $1,547 million.[55] It agreed also to a 20 per cent increase in the cartage charge and to drop the demand that the tankers be supplied by Japan. These concessions saved Burmah's position and resulted also in guarantees of financial aid to General Dynamics by the US government.

For the Indonesian side, however, the cost was heavy. The price of the gas was partly unpegged from that of oil, a linkage which had been agreed to by an anxious Japan in 1973.[56] Japan also gained greater flexibility over the volume of gas it had to take. More significant, the 1973 LNG loan agreement had given legal title of the two liquefaction plants to Indonesia in accordance with national bureaucratic aspirations. Under the revised terms negotiated by Komoto's officials Indonesia was forced to concede to Japan *de facto* ownership of the plants as collateral for the additional funds. Indonesia was also required to assign to the Japanese side her rights in the insurance policies and monies payable to Pertamina under any agreement relating to construction of the plants.[57] Japan thus gained an unbreakable lien on the gas revenue and how it was to be used.

The Tokyo-Jakarta deal concluded in some secrecy, breached the cross-default provisions of the 1975 Morgan Guaranty loans. Its effect was to place Morgan Guaranty – and by implication the IGGI – in a subordinate position to Japanese interests as a claimant on Indonesia's energy assets and revenues. The expected gas revenue was very large in gross terms, being calculated at $2,177 million for the first two years.[58] Behind Japan's actions, therefore, lay a determination to ensure that the future gas income would not be seized to underwrite debts incurred by Indonesia to US or European banks for activities unrelated to gas or Japanese interests. Suharto's preparedness to override commitments made to the IGGI, to meet Japanese wishes, reflected how closely his personal position had become bound-up with the successful outcome of the LNG project.

If the consortium loans – totalling $850 million – were to be 'called in' in retaliation, there was the high probability that Indonesia would default. The result of this could be unwillingness on the part of IGGI members to lend further. Such an eventuality invited Indonesia's repudiation of her external debt and the collapse of the capitalist structure rebuilt after 1966. In the specific case of US interests also any disruption of the additional Japanese funds for the LNG project threatened both Mobil Oil and Bechtels, the main contractors. With these concerns in view the United States government committed itself to preventing activation of the cross-default provisions. Morgan Guaranty, acting under State Department influence, called for a vote of confidence in Indonesia asking its partners not to call in the loans. Behind the scenes firm guarantees of indemnification against risk appear to have been given to the banks by the US government. On the basis of this understanding the request was heeded.[59] By December 1976 Japan, against IMF and IGGI opposition, had successfully reasserted its claim to the energy sphere it had won in 1973. Its success in achieving this owed little to the national bureaucratic forces or any other bridgehead within Indonesia.

By the end of 1976 Japan's loan finance debt-stake in Indonesia was huge. Commercial lending by other IGGI members for the 1972-6 period is not accurately known. It can safely be said, however, that, while important, US and West German bank lending did not attain the level of Japanese transfers. The official figures presented in Table 7.2 are from Japan's Export-Import Bank, far the single largest Japanese lender to Indonesia. What is striking about the lending is its rapid build-up from 1972, its scale, and sustained pattern throughout.

Table 7.2 *Lending to Indonesia by Export-Import Bank of Japan, 1972-1976 (Disbursement basis)*

Year	Amount ¥ billion	US dollars equivalent
1972	21	72,114,000
1973	43	148,276,000
1974	92	317,241,000
1975	143	493,103,000
1976	135	465,517,000
Total	434	1,496,251,000

Source: Export-Import Bank of Japan.[60]
N.B. Original data in yen. Rate used for conversion to US dollars, ¥290 = $1.

The loan total shown in Table 7.2 exceeds, by a wide margin, Japan's cumulative IGGI aid pledges for 1972-6 totalling 287.26 billion yen (approximately US$991 million). This figure constituted 66.2 per cent of actual Export-Import Bank disbursement.[61]

The Export-Import Bank total is particularly impressive for it does not include the loans for the Asahan aluminium/hydro-electricity project which began to flow only after 1976. Asahan, agreed to finally by the Miki government in 1975, was the Suharto regime's crowning achievement. Coming at a time when world aluminium prices were seriously depressed and Pertamina faced bankruptcy, Tokyo's decision seemed explicable only in terms of the special relationship consecrated in 1972.

The Japanese decision, however, to go ahead rested on more substantial grounds. As in the case of the LNG project, MITI was the real driving force. Its central consideration was that electricity constituted 40 per cent of the cost of producing aluminium. Given the dependence of Japan on oil-fired electricity generation this factor had become of critical importance in the wake of the 1973 oil price rises. In June 1975 MITI let it be known that the power cost at Asahan could be held to less than three yen/KWH.[62] According to

Hasegawa Noroshige, the President of Sumitomo Chemical, 'considering that the power cost, which used to be about three yen/KWH, is now nearly eight yen/KWH, the Asahan project is very appealing'.[63] The MITI's support, at such an unpropitious time for Suharto, was in reality motivated by a concern to bring the electricity cost for Japan's aluminium producers back to its earlier level. Thus Asahan reflected less the special relationship with Tokyo than Jakarta's desperate attempt to shift public attention from the Pertamina debacle. By gaining for the consortium a thirty-year electricity supply agreement and low interest official loans for 85 per cent of the $617 million required, MITI for its part successfully enhanced Japan's international competitiveness.[64]

Pertamina finally received $522,783,000 or 35 per cent of the total Export-Import Bank funds flowing to Indonesia in the 1972-6 period.[65] These funds paid for a wide range of Japanese export items as well as engineering and construction services. The remainder of direct lending by the Export-Import Bank, however, flowed almost exclusively to Indonesia's LNG project. Two direct loans were made for gas, one of $700 million in 1973, the other for $231 million in 1976. These loans, totalling $1,453,783,000, thus comprised virtually the Bank's entire lending (see Table 7.3). If the 1972 'oil loan' of $234 million, $198 million guaranteed by the Bank for LNG in 1973, an OECD loan of $187 million and further guarantees for $230.9 million in 1976 are added, the grand total of official energy-related loan finance transfers comes to $2,303,683,000. This is nearly one and a half times total realized foreign investment in Indonesia for the whole post-1966 period and more than twice Japan's direct investment (see Table 7.3). It is clear then that Japan's finance capital was bureaucratically steered towards extraction of resources of high strategic importance to Japan. Further, there is little evidence that the transfers were used for Indonesia-orientated projects beyond those in which Japanese export items were immediately involved. The one, perhaps perverse, exception to this was the 1972 oil loan which, as already noted, had a large political component.

Such was the extent of fusion between Japanese loan finance and national bureaucratic objectives. A final judgement, nevertheless, on how effective the national bureaucratic forces were, ultimately calls for an assessment of the influence they were able to exert over Japan's direct private investors. Table 7.3 gives a clear view of Japanese investment priorities up to 1976.

Five sectors dominate the picture: textiles, chemicals, cement and glass, metal manufactures, and assembly. Together these amounted to $826,870,000 or 80.2 per cent of Japan's total private investment.

Table 7.3 *Sectoral composition of Japan's cumulative investment in Indonesia (US$000)*

Sector	Local Share Capital	Japan's Capital Investment	Borrowing	Total
Agriculture	1,056	3,756	6,807	11,619
Fishing	3,737	14,751	22,461	40,949
Timber	6,233	17,957	13,096	37,286
Food	1,493	3,183	809	6,985
Textile	26,420	136,969	332,417	524,839
Wood	1,516	4,052	9,307	14,875
Paper	864	1,542	—	2,406
Chemicals	4,728	19,371	45,450	72,049
Cement/Glass	7,108	16,132	94,847	118,087
Metal Mnfg.	4,360	11,240	36,140	51,740
Assembly	6,147	24,315	29,693	60,155
Construction	1,842	7,594	3,900	13,336
Trade	992	952	6,000	7,944
Hotel	1,090	3,410	24,950	29,450
Transportation	1,103	2,547	13,606	17,256
Real Estate/Lease	1,800	2,200	8,190	12,190
Mining	—	500	8,758	9,258
TOTALS	70,489	270,471	656,431	1,030,424

Source: Compiled from BMPM-PMA. Includes joint ventures.

By 1976 textiles had absorbed just over half of the entire Japanese investment, some $525 million going into twenty-seven ventures. By contrast, Pertamina had only a single investment in this sector, a $2 million equity share in P.T. Canvas Indonesia, a joint venture with Toyo Menka.[66] Much of Japan's textile investment in Indonesia was in place prior to the OPEC oil price increases. For this reason it cannot be regarded as having been markedly influenced by Pertamina's guiding hand. Further, the second surge of textile investment in 1973-4 received its impetus from Japan's liquidity boom, though rising mass consumer demand in Indonesia was also important.

By 1974 Pertamina was mounting a large-scale assault on Japan's dominant position in Indonesia's synthetic textiles. A plant, capable of producing 20,000 tons of polypropylene resin annually, had been built at Pladju in South Sumatra. A vertically integrated second stage to spin the polypropylene into fibres, costing $26 million, was also planned as a joint venture with Teijin and Tomen. Combining the use of local gas as feedstock with 70 per cent domestic ownership, it constituted, with the Pladju plant, a major challenge to Japan's textile hegemony. During 1974, however, it was postponed until 1980 'due to market trends and Pertamina's difficulties'.[67] The same fate befell a joint venture between Pertamina, Nippon Petro-Chemical, Asahi-Chemical Industries and Toyo Menka for production of 300,000 tons of ethylene using North Sumatra gas. Japanese companies thus showed little inclination to proceed once Pertamina's financial position weakened. Perhaps the one major linkage of Japanese capital with Pertamina in this sector was Bridgestone Tyre, which during 1973 established a $32 million plant at Bekasi near Jakarta to service Indonesia's vehicle industry. Here too, however, Indonesian equity was minimal, reaching only 3.75 per cent by 1976.

By 1976 Japan had invested $72 million in chemicals production.[68] However, what stands out overall is the proliferation of small-sized Japanese chemical and pharmaceutical investments. Ozawa notes that by the end of 1975, 41.8 per cent of Japan's parent firms involved abroad in manufacturing were small or medium-sized firms with a capital of less than 100 million yen and fewer than 300 employees.[69] In Indonesia's case the affiliates of such companies concentrated heavily on the production of printing ink, paint, soda, plastic goods and pharmaceutical preparations. Ogawa observes that they 'had been driven overseas by the scarcity of production factors at home and the growing environmental constraints on further industrialization of their economy, rather than by the growth of their individual internal capacities to operate on a global scale.'[70] Pertamina here too had little direct role to play.

In cement and glass, by 1976, Japan had invested just over $118 million. Surprisingly, despite Pertamina's heavy involvement with construction projects, it had few direct links with Japan in this sector. The giant Semen Nusantara, capitalized at $100 million and owned jointly by Onoda and Mitsui, operated at Cilacap, the site of the new Pertamina oil refinery. The venture however, had a 30 per cent shareholding by the Suharto family and appeared to fall outside Ibnu Sutowo's domain.[71]

It was in metal manufacture and vehicle assembly that the strongest convergence between Pertamina and Japanese interests occurred. These were major areas of Pertamina's direct investment outside oil and gas exploration. They were also, in terms of sales turnover, vital for Japan's overall economic position in Indonesia.

By 1976 there were some twenty Japanese iron and steel ventures in Indonesia producing mainly bars, wire, rods and ingots, and capitalized at between $2 and $3 million. There were also, however, two big joint ventures beween Pertamina and Japanese interests. Marubeni, together with Nippon Kokan K.K. and Toshin Steel, collaborated with Pertamina in P.T. Budhidharma Jakarta, capitalized at $30.5 million.[72] Originally Pertamina was to have held 30 per cent of the shares, but by early 1977 this figure had only reached 6.9 per cent.[73] The other joint venture, P.T. Baja Indonesia, was capitalized at $16 million and also involved Marubeni as the leading Japanese partner.[74] By 1976 P.T. Baja Indonesia was still at an early stage of physical development. The only other sizeable Japanese steel venture, P.T. Kyoei Steel Works, capitalized at $12.5 million, appears to have had no links with Pertamina. Much of Japan's iron and steel investment was thus outside Pertamina's direct sphere of control. It was ultimately left to a trading company, Marubeni, to spearhead the fusion with Pertamina in this field. Nippon Steel, Japan's largest steel maker, mysteriously failed to enter into direct local production. As in the case of chemicals, we again find that Pertamina guided the two largest Japanese ventures.

It is in motor vehicle assembly, however, that the strongest link between Japanese interests and Pertamina is evident. Until 1970 Indonesia imported most of its vehicles fully assembled, principally from American and European makers. Beginning in 1970 a rapid shift to local assembly of Japanese vehicles occurred. Although ranking only fifth in the amount of private capital deployed in Indonesia by Japan, by 1973-4 this sector was of particular importance owing to highly successful market penetration and sales turnover. According to Okada, by early 1974 no less than 84.8 per cent of Indonesia's vehicle imports came from Japan.[75] Industry figures show that whereas in 1970 Indonesia imported 4,093 trucks from the USA – the largest supplier in that year – by 1975 this figure had fallen to 430.[76] Over the same period Japan's exports rose from 3,836 to 39,604 units.

Ibnu Sutowo, via his personal business interests and through Pertamina, played a powerful role in facilitating Japan's dominant position. Through share-holding, and directorships held by himself or his nominees, and through Pertamina's vehicle purchases, Sutowo was able to influence the relative market shares of competing Japanese companies and to have a major say over who was to benefit locally from Japan's presence. Most Japanese vehicle manufacturers were represented in Indonesia by 1972-3. The most successful, however, in terms of local sales and investment, were two ventures directly connected with Sutowo and OPSUS. The first, P.T. Toyota-Astra Motor, owned and operated by the Chinese businessman William Suryajaja, enjoyed strong political sponsorship from General

Ali Murtopo and Ibnu Sutowo. This company also received backing from Adam Malik, the Indonesian foreign minister, a figure having strong war-time as well as post-war connections with Japan.[77]

Until 1971-2 Toyota-Astra held the dominant sales position among Japanese makers in Indonesia. In 1971 Mitsubishi Krama Yudha, a wholly Indonesian enterprise, was established, a partnership between Ibnu Sutowo and Haji Sjarnabi, an Indonesian business survivor from the State Capitalist period. The company quickly established dominance in the commercial vehicle field. By 1974, out of a total of 35,105 commercial vehicles assembled, 17,385 or 49.5 per cent were Mitsubishi's. During 1975 the company produced 25,133 vehicles representing 52 per cent of the commercial market.[78] During 1976 assembly of commercial vehicles continued to increase in Indonesia with a total of 51,282 units being produced. However, Mitsubishi's share fell off severely, dropping to 22,355 units or 43.6 per cent reflecting Sutowo's diminished influence. The strong momentum of Japan's advance in this sub-sector right up to 1976, despite Pertamina's difficulties, suggests that Sutowo's influence throughout may have been less important than the vigour of Japanese companies themselves in promoting local demand.

It is useful, finally, to ask whether Pertamina was able to draw Japanese companies, with which it collaborated, exclusively into its own domain and away from other, presumably less urgent, fields? Here we can take most active Japanese companies, the sōgō shosha. Marubeni had three joint ventures with Pertamina including the major ones already noted in steel. However, Marubeni was involved in nine other, non-Pertamina ventures that included steel, livestock, fish and forestry. Sumitomo Shoji had seventeen ventures by 1976, but only two of these, both relatively minor in nature, were with Pertamina. Toyo Menka Kaisha was involved in eleven investments, but only two of them were with Pertamina. Mitsui, although the most extensively committed Japanese company in Indonesia by 1976, with participation in thirty-four activities, appears to have had no joint ventures with Pertamina. Mitsubishi, ranking second to Mitsui with sixteen investments, had only one modest joint venture with Pertamina. In the case of Itoh-Chu, again we find that despite a total of fourteen investments, only one of them, P.T. Stanvac Indonesia, also involved Pertamina. Finally, there is Nissho-Iwai, the shosha that had played a key role in persuading the Tanaka government to finance Indonesia's natural gas development. By 1976 this aggressive trader had become involved in ten ventures in Indonesia. Like Marubeni and Itoh-Chu, Nissho-Iwai evinced a strong interest in the iron and steel sector, having a total of three investments there – its largest commitment. Surprisingly, however, it was only linked with the state oil company through a single import-construction venture, P.T. Toyo Kanetsu Indonesia.

In the iron and steel sector we see again the familiar pattern of Pertamina promoting the largest ventures. How far the strong commitment by the three Japanese traders to this sector can be read, however, as reflecting Pertamina's influence behind the scenes, is problematical. Only in the case of Marubeni were two of its projects in this field linked directly with Pertamina. Given Sutowo's strong promotion of steel, however, and the lack of interest shown by the larger companies, e.g. Mitsui, Mitsubishi, Sumitomo and Nippon Steel, it appears that Pertamina may have successfully exploited rivalry among middle-rank traders to its advantage here.

Overall the evidence suggests, therefore, that Pertamina did not enjoy a monopoly over joint ventures with Japanese companies. There was a clear ability on the part of Japanese companies associated with Pertamina to range widely across the whole economic spectrum.

Conclusions

Several conclusions emerge from this case study. Japan's cooperation with Indonesia's national bureaucratic forces proved highly effective *vis-à-vis* Western monopoly capital in gaining privileged access to Indonesia. Ultimately, however, while the national bureaucratic forces increased their dependence on Japan, Japan decreased its dependence upon them. The national bureaucratic strategy, though having strong historical and structural roots outside the Indonesian state, was dependent for its activation upon inter-imperial rivalry.

Warren, as noted at the beginning of this chapter, sees the basis of inter-imperialist rivalry in realignments 'within the structure of global capabilities and investment patterns'. Curiously, however, he views centre-periphery interaction, where unevenness in the level and dynamics of production and trade structures is even sharper, as being non-antagonistic. However, as von Braunmühl notes:

> In the violent process by which the structure of the international division of labour was established, the trade and productive structures of the colonies were formed so as to suit the requirements of manufacturing and industrial capital, and thus achieve the accumulation necessary to secure the capital expenditure needed for the success and prosperity of the capitalist mode of production in the metropolitan regions.[79]

Warren's voluntarist theory of post-colonial international relations allows him to see, as outcomes of choices taken at the periphery, strengthened bonds with the metropolis that have their basis in imperialist logic. Thus, the frequent journeys to Tokyo by Suharto, Ibnu Sutowo, Ali Murtopo and Sudjono Humardhani, pleading first for accelerated state sector industrialization then finance capital, were prompted by socio-political contradictions inherent in internationalization that the Suharto regime was powerless to contain by any other means. Further, Warren's preoccupation with the kind of struggle described earlier between Japan, the IMF-IBRD and the US obscures the fact that it was over the assets of a third party, not present at the table. Warren's thesis fails to show how a country like Indonesia can be forced to bear the burden of crises in accumulation at the core. Japan's acceptance of a higher freight charge saved the viability of General Dynamics and Burmah Shipping. The price, however, was the Japanese demand that Indonesia forfeit effective control over its highly prized LNG facilities and revenues.

Warren's theoretical approach does not envisage the possibility of direct integration of peripheral productive structures with those of the metropolis, or the subordination of their dynamics to core requirements. What is evident, however, from the study of Japan's role in Indonesia is that such a process of integration and subordination did occur. It is significant that the national bureaucratic forces became most closely identified with Japanese state loan finance rather than the private Japanese investment capital they had sought to guide. Pertamina clearly made strong efforts in several fields to achieve, with Japanese cooperation, a capital goods capacity, but its success in this was limited. It was at the level of international loan capital that the petty bourgeois aspiration for national ownership was most completely fulfilled, rather than at the level of productive relationships. Yet it was at this second level, i.e. of Indonesia's productive forces, where Japan's potential impact was presumably greatest, that the national bureaucratic forces were, contrary to the Warren thesis, ultimately least effective. During 1972-6 the national bureaucratic forces did attract considerable attention from large private Japanese investors, notably in chemical, iron and steel, and vehicle assembly. However, this direct private investment moved broadly in accordance with pressures emanating from Japan and only to a limited extent in response to local Indonesian dynamics. This must be said even in the case of the large national bureaucratic monuments funded by the Japanese state. Thus, with the exception of the Pertamina export credits, Japan's entire official lending was directed to Indonesia's gas, and its extraction for use in Japan. Von Braunmühl notes that the structure of international relationships is the expression of a particular division of labour, altering in accordance with it.[80] Thus the high concentration of Japan's concessional aid on Indonesia and its energy can be said to have reflected the incorporation of Indonesia's natural gas as an integral sphere of Japan's own productive structure.[81]

Notes

1   See Warren W., 'Myths of Under-development', *New Left Review*, No. 81, September-October 1973 and *Imperialism Pioneer of Capitalism*, New Left Books, London, 1980. For Petras *et al.* see 'Imperialism and the Contradictions of Development', *New Left Review*, No. 85, May-June 1974.

2   Petras, James, 'Neo-Fascism: Capital Accumulation and Class Struggle in the Third World', *Journal of Contemporary Asia*, Vol.10, No.1/2, 1980, p.124.

3   *Ibid.*

4   See O'Leary, G. and McEachern, D., 'Capitalist Recession and Industrialization in the Third World: Reflections on the Warren Thesis', *Journal of Australian Political Economy*, No.7, April 1980, pp.86-104.

5   *Ibid.*, p.87.

6   Petras, J., 'Neo-Fascism . . .', *op. cit.*, p.124.

7   *Ibid.*, p.121.

8   Japan in 1961-2 had advanced Indonesia US$53 million for oil development and by 1966 had built up a modest stake in Indonesia's oil sector.

9   Verified in interviews with several Japanese officials who were close to IGGI negotiations at the time.

10 Weinstien, F.B., *Indonesian Foreign Policy and the Dilemma of Dependence from Sukarno to Suharto*, Cornell University Press, 1976, p.235.

11 *Ibid.*, p.235.

12 Galtung, Johan, 'Japan and Future World Politics', *Journal of Peace Research*, No.10, 1973, p.365.

13 Source: Fabrikant, R., *The Indonesian Petroleum Industry: Miscellaneous Source Materials*, Institute of Southeast Asian Studies, Singapore, 1973.

14 *Ibid.*

15 *Ibid.*

16 *Ibid.*

17 See Ogata S., 'The Business Community and Japanese Foreign Policy: Normalization of Relations with the People's Republic of China' in Scalapino, R.A. (ed.), *Foreign Policy of Modern Japan*, Berkeley, University of California Press, 1977, pp.175-203.

18 Communiqué, Japanese Foreign Office, Tokyo.

19 *Ibid.* Approximately 365,000 barrels of oil.

20 Including an unusual provision allowing nearly half of the loan to be used for 'local costs'.

21 *Japan Times*, 24.11.72.

22 Tanaka Kakuei replaced Sato as Prime Minister in July 1972. Following

Nixon's decision to take the US off the gold standard in August 1971 the yen's value rose from 360 to 308 to one dollar. As the result of revaluations and hot money flowing into Japan, the country's foreign exchange reserves which stood at US$6.2 billion in December 1971 had by December 1972 climbed to $18.36 billion. Source: Sōgō Shōsa, *Year Book 1977*, Tokyo Economic Information Service, p.36.

23 Palloix, C., 'The Self-Expansion of Capital on a World Scale', *Review of Radical Political Economy*, Vol.9, No.2, 1977, p.9.

24 Figures calculated from Penanaman Modal Asing (PMA – Foreign Investment), Badan Koordinasi Penanaman Modal (BKPM – Investment Coordination Board), Jakarta, March 1977 (BKPM).

25 Source: Japan External Trade Research Organisation (JETRO).

26 Calendar basis investment figures calculated from PMA-BKPM. Several cases where no project date could be ascertained have been omitted – understating the realized investment slightly for some years.

27 Wu, Y.L., *Japan's Search for Oil: A Case Study on Economic Nationalism and International Security*, Hoover Institute Press, 1977, p.35.

28 Ozawa, T., 'Japan's Multi-National Enterprise: The Political Economy of Outward Dependence', *World Politics*, Vol.XXX, No.4, p.521.

29 BKPM.

30 This did not include the Japanese oil loan.

31 See McDonald, H., *Suharto's Indonesia*, Fontana, 1980, p.155.

32 *Ibid.*

33 Kraar, L., 'Oil and Nationalism Mix Beautifully in Indonesia', *Fortune*, July 1973, pp.99-156.

34 *Ibid.*

35 *Ibid.*

36 See *Japan Economic Journal*, 12.9.72, and *Petroleum News*, April 1973.

37 See *Nihon Keizai Shimbun*, 20.12.72.

38 Interview with senior Pertamina official, Jakarta, 6.2.78.

39 Source: Organization of Economic Cooperation and Development (OECD), Tokyo.

40 *Petroleum News*, Vol.4, August 1973, p.16.

41 Erland Heginbotham, Deputy Assistant Secretary, Bureau of East Asian and Pacific Affairs, Department of State, 6 October 1977. Source: *The Witteveen Facility* and the OPEC Financial Surpluses Hearings Before the Sub-Committee on Foreign Economic Policy of the Committee on Foreign Relations, United States Senate. Ninety-Fifth Congress, First Session, September-October 1977, Washington US Government Printing Office, 1978, pp.83-112.

42 *Ibid.*, p.94.

43 *Ibid.*, p.94.

44 Adimir Adin, 'Peranan Minyak Dalam Pembangunan', *Prisma*, No.4, p.6, May 1976; and 'Indonesia's Petroleum Sector 1977', US Embassy, Jakarta, p.28.

45 Source: legal aide to Ibnu Sutowo, 6.2.78.

46 Before the final terms of the gas contract were settled in December 1973

Japan found it necessary to commit a further $187 million on soft terms via the OECD to ensure the project would proceed. Eighty per cent of the larger loan of $898 million, i.e. $700 million, was to come directly from Japan's Export-Import Bank at an interest rate of 5 per cent over fifteen years. The other $198 million was guaranteed by the Bank. In all, official lending thus totalled $1,085 million at this stage. In return for Japanese loans, Indonesia undertook to supply 7.5 million tons of gas per annum for twenty years. (See *Petroleum News*, Vol.4, December 1973. This is equivalent to 180,000 barrels of crude oil per day.) A major concession by Japan was its agreement to link the price of gas to that of crude oil.

47 See Arndt, H.W., 'Survey of Recent Developments', *Bulletin of Indonesia Economic Studies*, Vol.X, No.2, July 1974.

48 Glassburner, B., 'In the Wake of General Ibnu: Crisis in the Indonesian Oil Industry', *Asian Survey*, Vol.XVI, No.12, December 1976, p.1099.

49 *Sinar Harapan*, 26.4.76.

50 Whether further IGGI aid was made conditional upon Sutowo's dismissal has never been made clear.

51 See *Far Eastern Economic Review*, 2.7.76, 'Indonesia: The Debt Pile Rises Further', pp.62-3.

52 Source: senior Indonesian energy official. This was in large part bluff for the Indonesian's had no cards left to play.

53 Senior Official Migas, Jakarta, 10.3.78.

54 Pertamina Official, Jakarta, 13.3.78.

55 Source: OECD, Tokyo.

56 See *Indonesia Times*, 23.12.77.

57 There is no public evidence to substantiate these concessions but from confidential material to which the writer has been given access there are strong grounds for believing that this was the arrangement finally reached.

58 For the 'Morgan Telex' informing its partners of the breach see News Supplement, *Petroleum News*, January 1977.

59 See the *Asian Wall Street Journal*, 17.11.77.

60 It is the Bank's policy not to make public its cumulative lending, country by country, due to the politically sensitive nature of such information. The disbursement figures above were provided by a senior official of the Bank and may be taken as authoritative.

61 Calculated from *Economic Cooperation of Japan*, 1976, Table 67, p.73, and actual disbursement figures for some years supplied by OECD, Tokyo.

62 *Toyo Keizai*, 28.6.75.

63 *Keidanren Monthly Bulletin*, September 1975.

64 It is interesting that the MITI was the ministry from which Kishi came.

65 Calculated from data supplied by Far East Oil Trading Co., Pertamina's marketing partner and negotiator with Japanese banks, in Tokyo. To this amount going to Pertamina, would have to be added approximately half the 1972 'oil loan' of US$234 million channelled via the OECD.

66 Much of the data for the following analysis is drawn from BKPM

The case of Japan in Indonesia

Penamanan Modal Asing, *op. cit.*; 'Appendix: List of Japanese Enterprises in Indonesia' published in *AMPO, Japan-Asia Quarterly Review*, Vol.12, No.4, 1980, a special issue devoted to Japanese Transnational Enterprises in Indonesia, pp.50-91, and from *'Pertamina' Reference Book*, second edn, Inter Asean Consultants, Singapore, 1974.

67 Source: Editor, *Heavy and Petro-Chemical News*, Tokyo.
68 BKPM.
69 Ozawa, T., *op. cit.*
70 *Ibid.*, p.525.
71 See Robison, R., 'Capitalism and the Bureaucratic State in Indonesia 1965-1975', Ph.D. Thesis, Appendix B, p.xvii.
72 BKPM.
73 *Ibid.*
74 *Ibid.*
75 'Ekspansi Ekonomi Jepang ke Asia Tenggara: Tinjauan Perdagangan Jepang dan Asean', *Prisma*, No.11, 1979, p.91.
76 Source: Gaakindo – Vehicle Assemblers Association of Indonesia, Jakarta.
77 *Ibid.*
78 Source: Gaakindo 'Car Assembly Industry', *ICN*, No.89, November 1977, p.30.
79 von Braunmühl, C., 'On the Analysis of the Bourgeois Nation State within the World Market Context', in Holloway, J. and Picciotto, S. (eds), *State and Capital: A Marxist Debate*, Arnold, 1978, pp.170-1.
80 von Braunmühl, *op. cit.*, p.171.
81 The extent of Japan's 'targeting' is remarkable. Cumulative lending to Indonesia between 1968 and 1976, by Japan's Overseas Economic Cooperation Fund, reached 52.1 per cent of the Fund's total aid in the Asian region, making Indonesia far the largest recipient of Japanese soft aid. Calculated from *Japanese Contribution to Economic Development of Indonesia Through OECD Loans*, Tokyo, 1981.

8 The debate on the 'political economy' of Australian-ASEAN relations

ROBYN LIM – *University of New South Wales*

The debate on the 'political economy' of Australia's relations with the ASEAN (Association of Southeast Asian Nations) countries is an infant industry. Writers such as Jamie Mackie[1] and Tom Millar[2] have addressed themselves to the political and strategic aspects of Australia's relations with Southeast Asia, but have eschewed discussion of the economic issues. On the other hand, economists such as Ross Garnaut[3] and Clive Edwards[4] have examined the question of the consequences to Australia of the industrialisation of Asia, but have not touched on the political questions involved. The separation of economics and politics in academic studies in Australia is obviously a luxury we can no longer afford.[5] The only attempts at a 'political economy' approach to the study of Australian-ASEAN relations have been the Harries Report and the work of what might loosely be called the 'repressive-development' school of writers. This chapter discusses the implications of these contending approaches, and suggests some areas which call for a re-examination of theoretical assumptions and for further empirical investigation.

The Harries Report

The Harries Report[6] does not deal specifically with Australian-ASEAN relations, but is a report to government on Australian relations with the Third World generally. It does, nevertheless, have a good deal to say about Australia's interactions with Southeast Asia. Discussion of the Report is made difficult by some internal inconsistencies, which are to be expected in a document compiled by ten people in a short time. The economic sections of the Report reflect the traditional themes of Treasury doctrine. While this is not the place for a recital of familiar critiques of neo-classical economic theory, two aspects of the Treasury approach are noteworthy. These are the uncritical approach to Transnational Corporations (TNCs), and the conviction that the obstacles to 'development' in the Third

World are mainly internal. As will be indicated, these are assumptions under heavy fire from *dependistas*.

The more overtly political sections of the Report appear to reflect the views of some sections of the Foreign Affairs Department, to which Professor Harries had been seconded for some time prior to his appointment as Ambassador to UNESCO. The underlying theme of this part of the Report is the kind of neo-conservatism to be found in the American journals *Commentary* and *The Public Interest*. The message is that the Developed Countries (DCs) should realise that stubborn resistance to the more moderate demands for a New International Economic Order is not in the DCs best interests. Co-option is a better tactic. It has been put perhaps in its bluntest form by Farer, who urges the DCs to remember the way in which class conflict in the West was mitigated by the creaming off and co-option of the natural elite of the working class.[7] This policy of *embour-geoisement* has its parallel in the strategy of inviting some of the Newly Industrialising Countries (NICs) to share in the benefits of an essentially unchanged international economic system. The tenor of much of the Harries Report reflects this kind of approach.

In relation to the ASEAN countries, the Report argues that they are moderate members of the Third World, and that unless some of their more reasonable requests are met, more radical demands may follow. Unless for example, Australia further reduces its protective barriers against labour-intensive imports from ASEAN countries, they may become more critical of us. The Report says that the ASEAN states 'have it within their means to widen an issue by airing it in Third World forums, drawing on Third World support and solidarity, and attempting to link it with central Third World preoccupations'. This is an apparent reference to the 1979 dispute over civil aviation policy.[8]

Whether this neo-conservative ideology is a realistic reflection of Australian-ASEAN relations is questionable. One central issue is the extent to which the ASEAN stand on 'North-South' questions is to be taken seriously. If Singapore's economic success is emulated by other members of the Association, and they also graduate to the ranks of the NICs, their support for 'southern' issues will be mostly rhetorical. For the moment, however, it is a mistake to underestimate the strength of anti-colonial sentiment, especially in Indonesia and Malaysia. The vehemence with which the Mahathir government in Malaysia is attacking the vestiges of colonialism has led to a downgrading of the importance which Malaysia places on the Commonwealth connection; this is one factor in the termination of past close and comfortable relations between Malaysia and Australia.

While underestimating the strength of anti-colonial feeling in

ASEAN, the Harries Report exaggerates the extent to which anti-communism is a shared concern between Australia and ASEAN. In the 1950s and 1960s, Australian governments entertained morbid fears of China which fed on deep-seated fears of Asia generally; since the Fraser government came to power in 1975, Australia has responded to changes in the regional power balance by asserting that the Soviet Union is now the predominate threat to regional stability. However, anti-communist they may be in internal policies, the ASEAN states do not see the situation in such simplistic terms. The Soviet-supported Vietnamese invasion of Cambodia, combined with the Soviet incursion into Afghanistan, have clearly raised apprehension about Soviet policy. Yet Indonesia and Malaysia in particular remain more concerned about China's long-term intentions. Australia's tendency to look towards its 'great and powerful allies' has also led to an underestimation of the extent to which the ASEAN states wish to keep great power rivalries from feeding on and exacerbating existing regional rivalries. The Harries Report, for example, does not place enough significance on the ZOPFAN (Zone of Peace, Freedom and Neutrality) concept, however difficult that may be to achieve in the short term.[9]

The Harries Report does draw attention to the problems that Australia has had, and can expect to have, in dealing with the authoritarian governments of the ASEAN states. It does not, however, address the issue of the relationship between authoritarianism and the economic development strategy being pursued by those states. This is a question to which the 'repressive developmentalist' school has devoted much attention.

The 'repressive developmentalist' approach

If the reader cares to think back to the central elements of the dependency perspective outlined in Chapter 1 by Higgott and Robison then it would appear hardly surprising that it gained a following among Australian observers of Southeast Asia. Those who opposed American hegemony and Australia's involvement in the Vietnam War found the *dependencia* perspective to be a theoretical underpinning far superior to both neo-classical economics or 'structural-functional' analysis in political science. The attack on such orthodoxies was often explicit. *Dependistas* argued that in countries such as Indonesia and the Philippines, the only beneficiaries of 'development' were corrupt and repressive elites with close ties to America and Japan. The price of development was paid by the majority of the population which was subjected to 'marginalization' and 'immiseration'. Dependent countries, it was argued, could not achieve 'real' development under the conditions imposed by 'peripheral capitalism'.[10]

In the late 1960s and early 1970s, some ASEAN countries began to follow the example of South Korea and Taiwan in setting up Free Trade Zones. Rather than concentrate on import substitution, which was leading to stagnation, governments decided to attempt export-led industrialisation, concentrating on labour-intensive production. Incentives were offered to foreign firms to begin production for export in the Free Trade Zones. The adoption of this new strategy seemed to coincide, in the Philippines for example, with the appearance of much more repressive political forms. *Dependistas* argued that the new strategy of export-led industrialisation *required* an authoritarian form of government.[11] Different concepts were used – 'repressive-developmentalist';[12] 'bureaucratic-authoritarian';[13] 'bureaucratic-Bonapartist';[14] 'corporatist'.[15] The terminology may have been inelegant, but the central idea was that the logic of export-led industrialisation in the Third World leads to repression. In the early stages of industrialisation, governments need to be authoritarian in order to keep wages low and strikes illegal. Only thus can they attract foreign investment, and utilise their 'initial comparative advantage' (the term favoured by orthodox economists) of cheap, abundant labour. The 'repressive-developmentalist' concept assigned to the national bourgeoisie a much more important role than did Frank's version of dependency theory. As Herb Feith put it,

> Repressive-developmentalist regimes are strong-state regimes engaged in facilitating fast capitalist growth, some of it industrialisation, in the era of the transnational corporation. Warmly hospitable to transnational business, and dependent on it in many ways, they nevertheless avoid becoming its comprador vassals.[16]

The 'repressive-developmentalist' idea also had some implications for the debate on Australian-ASEAN relations. By the mid-1970s, the consequences to Australia of the industrialisation of Asia were attracting attention. The Whitlam government's 25 per cent across-the-board tariff cut of 1973, combined with revaluations and other factors, led to the imposition by the following year of restrictions on the import of 'sensitive goods' such as clothing, footwear and textiles. East Asian exporters were the targets of the restrictions, but when Australian importers turned instead to ASEAN suppliers, the government imposed restrictions on imports from Malaysia, Thailand and the Philippines.[17] The fact that Australia was the first country to restrict imports of labour-intensive goods from ASEAN countries led to a barrage of criticism from those governments. Australia was seen as hypocritical in that it claimed to be sympathetic towards ASEAN, yet discriminated against their goods.

The view of most Australian economists was that Australia should slowly dismantle protective barriers against labour-intensive manufacturers, and concentrate on its most competitive industries, such as agricultural foodstuffs, raw materials and some manufactures. It would then be able to take advantage of the industrialisation of Asia, rather than perceive it as a threat.[18] If, on the other hand, Australia declined to set about restructuring its industries, extraordinarily high levels of protection would be needed. Political costs would also be incurred. 'Such attempts to avoid major contraction of labour-intensive industries in the medium term would be certain to generate friction in relations between Australia and developing countries. It would come to dominate Australia's relations with countries in the region.'[19] As has been indicated, similar views are expressed in the Harries Report.

Very different conclusions were drawn by writers influenced by the 'repressive-developmentalist' concept. An explicit criticism of the economists' arguments was made by Philip Eldridge, who claimed that 'if the Australian economy is to be planned to become complementary to that of ASEAN, then logically the respective political systems must sooner or later be "harmonised"'.[20] He argued that the 'official doctrine of "asymmetry"' which 'has prevailed for the past decade or so in our relations with Indonesia and with ASEAN as a whole' means that Australia is 'far more dependent on and has far more incentive and obligation to adapt herself to the needs and policies of the ASEAN countries than they to her'. He concluded:

> A strong nationalistic assertion by Australia of equality in her relations with ASEAN countries, if linked to policies of reducing dependence on the USA, might well prove politically acceptable to them. This is especially true of Indonesia, in the light of her own national independence struggle. However, while such an approach would establish a more healthy environment for the conduct of relations at the official level, it is important to recognise that once the process of 'integrating' Australia with ASEAN begins it cannot be confined to government dealings or even remain within the framework of government control. Demands for liberalisation of trade may prove incompatible, even in a purely economic context, with plans for harmonising official policies. Logically, they will lead also to free trade in the political sphere.[21]

This linking of economic and political factors is not very convincing. Australia's economic relationship with ASEAN, although expanding in recent years,[22] is not nearly as significant as its economic ties with Northeast Asia. Even if it were, it is not at all clear why the Australian political system should be 'contaminated' by ASEAN authoritarianism. Why should it be beyond its wit to conduct worthwhile economic relationships with governments of different political complexions? The Australia-Japan trade flow is now the fifth largest in the world; the boom in the Australian economy in the late 1960s and early 1970s was predicated on Japanese imports of minerals. Yet it would be hard to find evidence of any 'Japanising' of the Australian political system. Eldridge's fears are the obverse of the concern expressed in the Harries Report that if the ASEAN countries became communist Australia would not be able to conduct worthwhile economic relationships with them.[23]

The weakness of Eldridge's argument is related to some fundamental problems with the 'repressive-developmentalist' approach. It provides some useful insights, but is much too close to a monocausal analysis. One can, for instance, hardly discuss authoritarianism in South Korea without reference to that country's almost unbroken authoritarian political tradition. The situation in each country needs to be carefully considered. The efficient, austere and didactic kind of authoritarianism found in Singapore is *not* the same as the 'conspicuous-consumption' and corrupt political system of the Philippines. The theory that export-led industrialisation *per se* is responsible for authoritarianism needs examination. What of the communist states such as China which have opted for such a strategy? Does the 'repressive-developmentalist' concept apply to non-capitalist states?

Nor does the concept appear able to explain changes in the political systems of capitalist Third World states as they move beyond the initial stages of export-led industrialisation. Feith acknowledges that

> there is a contrast ... between situations in which labour shortages have begun to exert upward pressure, at least for particular groups of workers – Singapore, South Korea and to a lesser extent Iran in the years of the Shah – and Indonesia and the Philippines where large reserve armies of workers have prevented urban real wages from rising significantly.[24]

But he offers no explanation why this should be so. Should we expect government to become less repressive when they no longer need to keep wages low? In Singapore, for example, economic success has led to substantial rises in real wages and the elimination of the 'reserve army of the unemployed'. Whether the government has become less authoritarian, or simply more subtle in its methods, is a moot point. One would not want to make too much of the alleged 'mellowing' of

Lee Kuan Yew. Eldridge also seems to imply that ASEAN governments may become less repressive. ' "Bureaucratic" or "feudal-capitalist" leaders of the Suharto and Marcos type will become redundant if Southeast Asian economies move to a more "liberal-capitalist" phase.'[25] Again, no explanation is offered why this should be so.

The 'repressive-developmentalist' concept is also weak when it comes to the question of alternatives. How else, for example, can the Philippines hope to employ its present and future workforce without some kind of industrialisation? Even the most thorough-going land reform would not provide enough jobs. Vague notions about 'opting out' of the world capitalist system are not very convincing. Vietnam's recent experiences would not appear to be encouraging. The inescapable conclusion is that the 'repressive-developmentalist' concept has been much more valuable as a critique of both neo-classical economics and 'modernisation' theory in political science than as an alternative framework on which empirical work can be based.

Conceptual problems with both approaches

Neither the neo-classical economic doctrines underlying the Harries Report nor the 'repressive-developmentalist' concept has a convincing explanation for what might be called the 'NICs phenomenon' – the economic success of the Newly Industrialising Countries of Asia, namely South Korea, Taiwan, Hong Kong and Singapore. South Korea, for example, is often cited by those who preach the doctrine of the 'magic of the market' as a country which has graduated from the ranks of the poor by following 'classic' free trade doctrines. Other observers are more cautious. Larry Westphal of the World Bank put it thus:

> While a variety of factors have contributed to Korea's successful development, the key fact none the less remains that economic policies have made a large contribution to fostering what appears to be a reasonably efficient and equitable process of industrialisation. In short, given Korea's poor natural resource endowment and assuming that its comparative advantage lies in labour-intensive activities, Korea provides an almost classical case of an economy following its comparative advantage and reaping the gains predicted by conventional economic theory.
>
> The most important lessons from Korea's experience appear to be that exports respond to incentives while efficiency in the resource allocation can be assured by operating close to a free trade regime. Both of these conclusions require further scrutiny.[26]

This caveat has been followed up by other economists such as Clive Edwards, who has agreed with the view that South Korea has utilised its comparative advantage in labour-intensive activities, but has challenged the notion that the country has operated close to a 'free trade regime'. In a critique which raises the whole question of the applicability of Western economic thought to the Korean Case, he argues that market interventions have been numerous, complex and significant.[27] It seems likely that detailed studies of the Korean model will indicate that the role of the state in Korea's economic development surpasses even that of Japan in the early stages of industrialisation.

The so-called Asian 'gang of four' also pose problems for analyses based on dependency theory precisely because they are so deeply embedded in the world capitalist system. Hong Kong and Singapore might be brushed aside because they are city states, but South Korea and Taiwan are not so easily dismissed, although they too might be conceded to be 'atypical' in some ways since they are both political oddities[28] and former colonies of a non-Western country. Within the dependency perspective, an important attempt to deal with the 'NICs problem' has been made by Cardoso.[29] The rapid industrialisation of some areas of the 'periphery' had revived an ancient debate among Marxists about the feasibility and necessity of capitalist industrialisation in 'backward countries'.[30] Reformulations by Cardoso and (with some differences of emphasis) by Amin[31] within the dependency school admitted that rapid industrialisation, instigated by TNCs, had taken place in some countries of the periphery. But it was still not 'real' development. In Brazil, for instance, it was argued that rapid industrialisation was accompanied by rising inequality and escalating national debt. Similar criticisms were made of South Korea.[32] Yet even writers influenced by Cardoso's thinking conceded the significant 'deepening' of South Korea's industrial structure by the late 1970s.[33] Once the possibility that South Korea might become 'another Japan' is conceded, the dependency perspective becomes shaky indeed.

Whether other Asian countries, for example Malaysia, will soon graduate to the NIC ranks is an important question in the ideological debate. Most Australian economists argue that they will. Peter McCawley has gone so far as to argue that Australia should emulate some of Malaysia's successful policies.[34] Those influenced by the dependency perspective, on the other hand, will presumably continue to argue that the success of the 'gang of four' was based on a peculiarly propitious set of factors, and that they 'hardly offer a model to be duplicated *ad infinitum* elsewhere in the Third World (except, with modifications, in Israel)'.[35] It is apparent that neither of the contending approaches discussed in this chapter has an entirely convincing explanation for the 'NICs phenomenon'. Nor has either approach grappled with the very complicated cultural factors which appear to be involved.[36]

Coming to terms with Australia's history

The two approaches under discussion are both fundamentally ahistorical. No attempt has been made to place the 'political economy' of current Australian-ASEAN relations in the context of Australia's past relationships with Southeast Asia. A striking aspect of the Harries Report is the continuing tendency to look mainly at the great power relationship in the region and to argue that Australia's interests lie with our 'great and powerful allies'. The ASEAN states tend to be treated as if they are only pawns in the great power game, seen primarily in terms of *their* utility to *us* as buffers against communism. This tendency to 'look over their heads' in a fashion reminiscent of the colonial past is precisely what the ASEAN states complained of during the civil aviation dispute in 1979. As has been indicated, the Harries Report fails to recognise that one of ASEAN's fundamental aspirations is to avoid being used as a pawn in great power rivalry.

The same patronising tendencies are to be found in the contending conceptual approach. There is an inclination to exaggerate Australia's economic role in the region, despite the fact that our aid and investment is miniscule compared with that of Japan and the US. The picture of Australia's aid programmes 'propping up' repressive ASEAN regimes is a fantasy. Unless very carefully handled, the 'repressive-developmentalist' approach can also slot into traditional Australian fears of Asia. The fact that Japan's *per capita* income has recently overtaken ours has not been widely noticed, but would probably arouse little concern if it were; we are, after all, to a large extent dependent on Japanese economic success. The success of ASEAN industrialisation, if it comes about, is much more likely to be perceived as a threat. Those influenced by the 'repressive-developmentalist' approach are inclined to argue, for example, that Australia is being 'de-industrialised' as TNCs move out to lower-wage countries where the labour movements are suppressed. This claim is frequently asserted but remains unproved. It can easily, unfortunately, pander to traditional Australian fears of unfair competition from 'cheap Asian labour'.

Australians of all political persuasions have become accustomed to thinking of our 'Asian neighbours' as worthy of our charity, pity and, at times, indignation. Yet if their *per capita* income begins to overtake Australia's, as Singapore's is expected to do within this century, Australians are going to find it difficult to come to terms with the fact that their relative economic and political power in the region will be substantially reduced. If academics are to have any useful role in the discussion of these issues, a re-examination of fundamental conceptual issues needs to be combined with careful research, and the artificial distinction between economics and politics overcome.

Notes

1 See in particular 'Australia and Southeast Asia', in Coral Bell (ed.), *Agenda for the Eighties*, Australian National University Press, 1980.

2 See, for example, T.B. Millar, *Australia in Peace and War*, Australian National University Press, 1978.

3 See R. Garnaut, 'Industrialisation of Southeast and East Asia and some Implications for Australia', in W. Kasper and T. Parry (eds), *Growth, Trade and Structural Change in an Open Australian Economy*, Australian National University and University of New South Wales, 1978.

4 See C.T. Edwards, 'The Impact of Economic Change in Asia on Australia', Conference of Labor Economists, May 1979.

5 S. Harris, 'The Separation of Economics and Politics: A luxury we can no longer afford?', in Coral Bell (ed.), *Academic Studies and International Politics*, Department of International Relations, Australian National University, 1982.

6 *Australia and the Third World: Report of the Committee on Australia's Relations with the Third World*, Australian Government Publishing Service, 1979. Subsequently cited as 'the Harries Report'. For critiques, see Hedley Bull, 'The Harries Report and the Third World', *Quadrant*, July 1980; Preston King, 'On Developing an Interest in the Right Policy', *Quadrant*, August 1980; Peter King and Martin Indyk, 'Australia's Relations with the Third World: a Review of the Harries Report', *Current Affairs Bulletin*, 56, 12 May 1980; reviews by J.D.B. Miller, Harold Crouch and Stuart Harris in *Australian Outlook*, 34 1 April 1980. Owen Harries has replied to critics in *Current Affairs Bulletin*, May 1980, and *Australian Outlook*, 34, 2 August 1980.

7 T. Farer, 'The United States and the Third World', *Foreign Affairs*, 54, Ocober 1975, p.91.

8 See Frank Frost, 'Australian-ASEAN Relations', *Asia Pacific Community*, 7, Winter 1980; Robyn Lim, 'Current Australian-ASEAN Relations', *Southeast Asian Affairs* (Singapore), 1980.

9 See Mackie, *op. cit.*, pp.129-34.

10 See Rex Mortimer, 'From Ball to Arndt: the Liberal Impasse in Australian Scholarship on Southeast Asia', in R. Mortimer (ed.), *Showcase State: the Illusion of Indonesia's 'Accelerated Modernisation'*, Angus & Robertson, 1973.

11 See *AMPO, Japan-Asia Quarterly Review*, Special Issue, 'Free Trade Zones and Industrialization of Asia', 1977.

12 Herb Feith, 'Repressive-Developmentalist Regimes in Asia: Old Strengths, New Vulnerabilities', Conference on Indonesian Class Formation, Monash University, August 1979.

13 See G. O'Donnell, *Modernization and Bureaucratic-Authoritarianism: Studies in South American Politics*, University of California, Berkeley, 1973.

14 P. Evans, 'Industrialization and Imperialism: Growth and Stagnation on the Periphery', *Berkeley Journal of Sociology*, 20, 1975-6.

15 See R. Stauffer, 'Philippine Corporatism: A Note on the "New Society"', *Asian Survey*, XVII, 4, 1977.

16 Feith, *op. cit.*, p.3.

17 See Frost, *op. cit.*

18 See Bureau of Industry Economics, Research Report 1, *Industrialisation in Asia – Some Implications for Australian Industry*, Australian Government Publishing Service, Canberra, 1978.

19 Garnaut, *op. cit.*, p.39.

20 Philip Eldridge, 'Emerging Issues in Australia-ASEAN Relations', Asian Studies Association of Australia, Second National Conference, May 1978.

21 *Ibid.*, p.1.

22 Australia's exports to ASEAN countries have increased from 6.5 per cent of total exports in 1977 to 8 per cent in 1980. Australia's imports from ASEAN have increased from 4.8 per cent of total imports in 1977 to 6.8 per cent in 1980. Department of Trade and Resources, Central Statistics Section, *ASEAN 1980*.

23 Harries Report, *op. cit.*, p.112.

24 Feith, *op. cit.*, p.15.

25 Eldridge, *op. cit.*, p.16.

26 L. Westphal, 'The Republic of Korea's Experience with Export-Led Industrial Development', *World Development*, 7, 3, 1978, p.375.

27 C. Edwards, 'South Korea's Industrial Development Strategy: Implications for Australia', Eighth Conference of Economists, Economic Society of Australia and New Zealand, August 1979, p.7.

28 In the sense that Korea is a divided country and that Taiwan's political status is in limbo.

29 See F. Cardoso, 'Associated-Dependent Development: Theoretical and Political Implications', in A. Stepan (ed.), *Authoritarian Brazil*, New Haven, Yale University Press, 1973.

30 See G. Palma, 'Dependency: A Formal Theory of Underdevelopment or a Methodology for the Analysis of Concrete Situations of Underdevelopment?', *World Development*, 6, 1978.

31 See S. Amin, *Unequal Development: An Essay on the Social Formations of Peripheral Capitalism*, Harvester, 1976.

32 G. McCormack, 'The South Korean Phenomenon', *Australian Outlook*, 32, 3 December 1978.

33 B. Cummings, 'Industrialising States and Human Rights: the Case of

South Korea', mimeo, University of Washington, 1978.
34 Peter McCawley, 'The Challenge from Asia', *The National Times*, 27 June to 3 July 1982.
35 Andre Gunder Frank, 'Asia's Exclusive Models', *Far Eastern Economic Review*, 25 June 1982.
36 Some observers, for example, attribute the success of the 'gang of four' primarily to alleged Confucian values. (See W. Sharpe, 'The Outlook for Asia's Star Performers', *Asian Wall Street Journal*, 14 February 1980.) The current 'neo-Confucian' revival in Singapore and Malaysia's 'look East' policy raises these sorts of issues. Yet cultural factors must be treated with great caution. See, for example, Syed Hussein Alatas, *The Myth of the Lazy Native: A Study of the Image of the Malays, Filipinos and Javanese from the 16th to the 20th Century and its Function in the Ideology of Colonial Capitalism*, Frank Cass, London, 1977.

PART IV **_Politics, the state and economic development in Southeast Asia: selected cases_**

9 The Philippine political economy: (dependent) state capitalism in the corporatist mode

ROBERT B. STAUFFER – *University of Hawaii*

The 'New Society' – the phrase comes from President Marcos[1] – is now more than ten years old, has survived the cosmetic transformation from a martial law base to a more civilian form of authoritarianism, and has, as a result of recent elections, been assured another six years of leadership from its chief architect.[2] While the apolitical vacuity of the defining term 'New Society' gives little clue as to the direction in which the Philippines was to be pushed, pushed it has been since 1972, and massively. And although Ferdinand E. Marcos has been instrumental as a decision-maker and as a center through and around which the forces pushing for change work, the vast struggle over the future of the Philippine political economy that has been raging in that nation over the past several decades can certainly not be explained by examining his idiosyncratic behaviour, however great his public relations people make him out to be. Rather than focusing on individual leaders, this chapter will attempt to explain the wrenching transformations that are being imposed on the Philippines by examining changes in the way the Philippines is integrated into the capitalist world economy, changes in class structures and alliances, new uses of state power, and the search for a new political formula.

The processes that have produced these changes have left a visual impact. Any 'old Philippine hand' returning today to Manila for the first time since the beginning of the New Society will be struck by all the evident physical signs of modernity: Manila has a modern skyline for the first time, new freeways, impressive new public buildings, elegant hotels, elite condominiums, world-class shopping centers, etc. It is partially ringed by sleek branch plants of the world's transnational corporations (TNCs). Makati, its suburban finance and corporate-headquarters center, is a high-rise hymn of faith to the type of future promised by the New Society.

Comparable physical changes can be seen throughout the countryside. High-power transmission lines march across the land;

241

huge dams impound mountain rivers; arching bridges connect segments of the newly constructed north-south national highway; new export crop plantations employ elements of capital intensive technology (e.g., crop dusting airplanes, large earth moving machines); and many provincial cities begin to display more of the physical characteristics of Manila's modernity.[3]

These impressionistic indications of successful modernization need to be brought into balance. Not only has the New Society never achieved sufficiently high growth rates to qualify for membership in the 'miracle economy' club, but it has in recent years fallen considerably short of projected growth goals,[4] has faced mounting inflation and, in general, has presented such a picture of economic crisis and political decay as to trigger fears among foreign investors and their governments of impending political instability.[5] But long before the sharp downturn at the end of the decade other indicators challenged the shallow optimism of the government's development claims. While GNP *per capita* may have more than doubled (to above US$600 by 1980) during martial law years, prices went up nearly three times during the same period while skilled workers' wages fell to 67.2 per cent of their 1972 level, and for unskilled workers, to 57.4 per cent.[6] Rural conditions, if anything, have been more oppressive judging from the steady flood of migrants from the countryside to the squalid squatter slums of Manila.

It does not take a flight of imagination to sense that the development policies of the New Society are producing the all too familiar pattern of a small, increasingly affluent Western-style 'middle' class at the top while the great mass of Filipinos are forced to endure mounting pressures to survive at the bottom: as a recent World Bank report indicates, poverty is widespread in the Philippines (and with it, malnutrition, endemic major health problems, etc.) and its incidence, as measured by the percentage falling below the poverty line, is increasing.[7]

Beneath the facade of patriotic public festivals the New Society's political costs have been high. Although the number of political prisoners has been reduced to the low hundreds today, tens of thousands have been held for varying lengths of time in the detention centers: many have been tortured.[8] Elections have been turned into plebiscites and attempts made – none too successfully – to build a single-party system. The national legislative body can only call to mind the reference made to Hitler's *Reichstag* that it was the highest paid male choir in the world. The usual paraphernalia of authoritarianism have been put in place: the large army, the centralized police force, the many clans of the 'intelligence community,' the growing number and size of paramilitary forces, etc.

And above it all reigns President Marcos, with his younger, dynamic and politically ambitious wife Imelda waiting in the wings to take over. It seems extremely unlikely that those who organized the destruction of politics in the Philippines will be permitted to remain in power long enough for that to happen. Before looking more carefully at the immediate present, however, it is necessary to probe, if only briefly, the legacy of the past.

The Philippine political economy: pre-martial law era

The scattered political communities of Malays who were later to become Filipinos were linked to world trade and cultural movements long before the arrival of European colonialists: Islamic traders and proselytizers provided an expanding network of relationships moving up from the south, and merchant ships, primarily from China but also from India and Japan, tied Manila and probably other island entrepot centers to Asia. Whatever potential for the independent development of the Philippines that these beginnings had was cut short by Spanish conquest and the imposition of a colonial political economy over the islands.

Spain's long (1561-1898) control over the Philippines provided the setting within which a 'classical' colonial economy grew and in which a corresponding class structure emerged. The particularities of Spain's world position gave a variety of special contours to the final result. Spain's lack of a direct trade route to the Philippines for the first two centuries of colonial rule provided a logistical reason for keeping the Philippines from producing goods for world trade, and keeping it a mere transshipment station for the China-Mexico-Spain flow of high-cost/low-bulk products. Moreover, keeping the Philippines relatively undeveloped accorded with the higher priority Spain gave to spreading Christianity throughout the islands and to fighting Islam.

By the end of the eighteenth century Spain began to move away from its policy of keeping the Philippines largely outside world trade and economically oriented towards its own market. Direct shipping routes were opened and export agriculture was started. It was not, however, until the official opening of Manila to foreign trade in 1834 that agricultural production for the world market became a driving force in the development of the Philippines and by that time Spain was in no position either to prevent its occurrence or to profit by its happening. What Spain had done was to provide the centralized political and administrative structures under which rapid economic change could take place, the legal codes to protect the large landowners, a population largely socialized into a common belief system as a result of the work of the Church, and a class structure that could increasingly produce sufficient products for an expanding export trade. Spain, however, lacked the entrepreneurial, administrative, and financial resources to capitalize on the rapidly growing Philippine economy. Consequently, other nations – especially the United Kingdom – moved in to reap the benefits. As two scholars have concluded, by the 'decade of the 1880s British economic hegemony was so complete that, certainly in an economic sense, the Philippines was a *de facto* British colony'.[9] The United States was not far behind the UK in penetrating the Philippine economy. The same authors paraphrased an aphorism used earlier to describe relationships with Latin America: 'Spain kept the cow while Britain and the United States drank the milk.'[10]

Spanish policies repeatedly produced strong opposition from Filipinos. There were many peasant revolts, occasional examples of defiance by indigenous individuals grieved by Spanish exclusionist policies and, most importantly, a revolution. The latter, begun in the mid-1890s under the leadership of an urban-based movement headed largely by individuals representing the petty bourgeoisie (government workers, employees of foreign merchant houses, etc.) in alliance with representatives from the higher bourgeoisie (landowners, professions, etc.), established an independent republic of the Philippines and had largely defeated Spanish military forces when the United States intervened and, at enormous cost to Filipinos, defeated the republican forces to establish a new colonial era in the islands.[11]

If the Philippines developed a classic colonial economy largely despite Spanish policies, the Americans moved resolutely to rationalize that condition and deepen the integration of the Philippines into the capitalist world economy via the United States on the basis of colonial specialization in producing primary products. The key became sugar which was given a special and subsidized quota in the American market thereby guaranteeing a continuation of the Philippine political economy with its heavy reliance on the sugar plantation landowning class. The Americans largely edged out the British and moved in to organize the processing and export of other major agricultural crops, and into mining and other raw materials. While some small-scale manufacturing was done during the American period – much by Americans who remained after completing a military or administrative tour – American educational policy pushed the most talented into one of the professions, usually with a position in government as the career goal. Others with talent and drive were encouraged to engage in politics since the US saw the legitimacy-generating power of local and eventually national elections early on. With laws that gave Americans equal rights with Filipinos to exploit the resources and the markets of the Philippines, and considering the greater resources that the former could usually command, it is not surprising that the basic outlines of the Philippine economy remained so maldeveloped by the outbreak of World War II. Americans and their Filipino allies sold a vast array of imported products, especially in the urban areas of the Philippines by that time: the Philippines exported an ever increasing quantity of agricultural export crops and minerals, with much of the profit from those transactions taken by the Americans. Filipinos had, however, developed a highly successful independence movement, one that worked through reformist channels with American approval. Commonwealth status had already been achieved, with independence promised by 1946. The US, apparently, felt secure in promising independence since it held such a dominant role over the economy.

The Japanese occupation, aside from the brutal hardships imposed on Filipinos by a military administration relentlessly bent on extracting resources for the Japanese war effort, did little to change the colonial political economy. It did, however, provide the occasion for the second American military conquest of the Philippines, this time against Japanese defenders. The consequences were massively destructive, leaving the economy in shambles, the major cities largely flattened and much of the industry wiped out.[12]

After Japan's defeat the United States proceeded with its promise to grant the Philippines independence, although extension of aid for reconstruction of the massive damage caused by liberation was withheld until the Filipinos changed their constitution to permit Americans to continue to enjoy the special privilege of equal rights with Philippine citizens to exploit its land and natural resources. In return, the US continued the sugar quota system, with its landlord-class supports for the sugar barons.

The political economy of neo-colonialism

At the time when formal power was transferred from the United States to the Republic of the Philippines (4 July 1946), the same hegemonic class alliance was in power that had struck the bargain with the US in the mid-1930s for 'Commonwealth' status and promised independence. The export-crop landlord class, the bourgeoisie in commerce and manufacturing, and their closely allied professionals, many of whom were elected politicians or high civil servants, remained united and firmly committed to capitalism, to a conservative nationalism that did not challenge the Philippine role in the world division of labor, and to 'special relations' with the

United States that amounted to acceptance of neo-colonialism.

Ruling class unity – despite a great deal of petty factionalism expressed during electoral campaigns and throughout legislative sessions – rested at the time of independence on the relative weakening of the export-crop class due to the enormous damage inflicted by the war, on its ties to the commercial and manufacturing sectors of the bourgeoisie, and on the patent dependence all sections of the ruling class had on the United States. This dependence sprang from short-term situations such as the American decision not to push the prosecution of those in the Philippine elite who had collaborated with the Japanese during the occupation. Since a large proportion of the elected officials had done so, this amounted to creating heavy debts of obligation to the United States.[13] Moreover, all property-owning groups must have been apprehensive over the mounting threat from guerrilla forces created during the war, some of whom were beginning to make common cause with the hard-pressed peasants of central Luzon to demand radical changes in the system. The obvious weakness of the Philippine state and its military forces[14] left little choice but reliance on the United States. Finally, the enormous cost of rebuilding the war-damaged economy gave the United States tremendous leverage: not only did the US tie the release of reconstruction funds to the granting of legal 'parity' rights for Americans, as already noted, but it assured that the vast bulk of those funds would be spent for imported American manufactured products by demanding free trade between the two countries for eight years, thereby further re-establishing consumer product preference patterns and marketing networks, both broken down by the war, and reassuring all sectors of the ruling class of continuing prosperity under neo-colonial ties with the United States.

These relationships were soon put to the test. Immediate post-liberation repression by American and Filipino forces of the Hukbalahap guerrillas and their peasant allies failed to stop their demands for major agrarian reforms. With Communist party support, the peasant/Huk alliance developed into a full-scale peasant rebellion, which, at its peak in 1949-51, constituted a major threat to the survival of the government.[15] The United States responded with massive flows of arms and an array of military and psychological-warfare technicians to back up the Armed Forces of the Philippines and to guide its strategic responses to the Huks.[16] The anti-Huk campaign was a 'success,' thereby postponing any but a repressive response to the legitimate demands of the peasants (the 1955 Land Reform Act constituted primarily a symbolic act) and providing reaffirmation of dependency ties with the United States.

Other challenges were mounted simultaneously or were to follow shortly. Labor, newly united in the Congress of Labor Organization (CLO) after liberation, represented a threat (largely potential) to the ruling class. The CLO federation had ties with the Huks and with several other peasant organizations and contained a number of radical industrial unions, a sufficiently threatening package to lead to government intervention. The CLO leaders were rounded up and the federation shattered in 1950. In place of the CLO 'class-based, politically-oriented movement' the government pushed to restructure labor on 'conservatively economistic' lines through co-optation of its leaders.[17]

In addition to these real and potential threats to the hegemonic position of the allied property classes, new intra-class tensions were soon generated. While American rehabilitation support provided windfall profits to all sectors of the ruling class, this support (amounting to approximately 50 per cent of the 1946 Philippine GNP) was a one-shot arrangement. Lacking continued large-scale American financial support (the military and the sugar exporters being the exceptions), class fractions began to push, through the political institutions they controlled (the Congress, for example), for new uses of the state in ways that would directly and immediately benefit them. The campaign to redefine the role of the state began with a generalized attempt to redefine nationalism, to step away from the bland, conservative nationalism of the independence movement and to demand that Philippine nationalism must rest on a 'Filipino First' base. Leaders such as Senator Claro M. Recto provided the impetus for this first post-independence attempt at redirecting the Philippine political economy.

The immediate consequences of the new nationalism were twofold, with both overlapping in time. One emerged in the form of a piece of anti-Chinese legislation. Historically the Chinese in the Philippines developed a strong position in merchandizing and commerce, a growing strength in light industry, and a dominant control over the handling of two of the main agricultural crops – rice and corn. The Retail Trade Nationalization Act, passed in 1954, was designed to force the Chinese out of that trade so that it would be returned to Filipino hands thereby strengthening the ethnic Filipinos against the still largely 'alien' Chinese.[18] Although the United States was able to secure assurances that the act was not aimed at Americans involved in other areas of retail trade, it was manifestly clear from the congressional debates that the 1954 'nationalization' drive, while limited to the Chinese at the moment, was only the beginning if the nationalists had their way. They did not, of course, but they did add to the strengthening of the state's interventionist role in the economy. And their concrete anti-Chinese contribution did much to push Chinese resources out of rural commerce and into urban manufacturing.

The second consequence of the heightened nationalism of the late 1940s, and early 1950s was the drive to use the state to promote industrialization. A complex set of tax incentive laws and foreign exchange controls was erected both through legislative enactments and administrative fiats that successfully carried the Philippines through the 'import-substitution' phase of industrialization. The share of the Philippine labor force engaged in 'manufacturing' rose from 6.6 per cent in 1952 to a pre-martial law high of 11.6 per cent in 1964 and the total in 'Industry' (= manufacturing plus mining and construction) rose from 9.3 per cent in 1952 to 15.2 per cent in 1964.[19] The success of the attempt, however, was marred by the usual leveling off of the growth curve and the subsequent stagnation of the economy. Further, because of the special position Americans held in the economy, they gained many of the incentives extended by the state to new industries.

Already by the early 1960s an additional consequence of the import-substitution industrialization strategy had appeared: balance of payments problems and an overvalued Philippine currency. The US and its International Monetary Fund-World Bank allies stepped in and forced devaluation – in 1962 – and the elimination of internal currency controls.[20] The results of devaluation were severe, leading to sharp price rises for consumer goods.

The combined impact of rising prices, an increasingly stagnant economy, and an increased presence of foreign (largely American) assembly plants in the manufacturing sector of the economy led to a new type of nationalist movement. By 1964 massive student demonstrations were being held before the American embassy protesting against American imperialism in the Philippines. From then, intermittently, until the imposition of martial law in September 1972 a broadening coalition insistently demanded a fundamental change in what the state was doing. Beginning with demonstrations aimed at the symbol of American dominance, the movement soon gathered strength and expanded to bring mass protest to the doors of the Philippine Congress, the presidential palace, and selected administrative buildings (e.g., a summer-long mass camp in front of the Department of Agriculture building to protest agrarian conditions).

The nationalist coalition drew support from a variety of groups. Segments of the bourgeoisie, chaffing over the subordinant position they saw themselves in relative to foreign corporations, provided financial support and some respected leaders; the increasingly radicalized student movement – especially in Manila – provided masses of protesters for the large-scale confrontations with authority, a large number of energetic, imaginative leaders, and effective mobilizing networks; existing worker and peasant unions took on a new ideological perspective along with heightened demands; and many intellectual, artistic, and professional groups either formed new caucuses within their old organizations or participated in one or other of the larger nationalist organizations. The most important of these was *Makabansang Adhikaang Nagkakaisa* – Movement for the Advancement of Nationalism (MAN).

Marxists participated in all phases of the nationalist struggle over the state prior to martial law, and gave the movement as a whole some of its major themes, e.g., the rallying slogan of a thousand demonstrations: 'Down with Imperialism, Feudalism and Fascism!' In 1968 a group of young Marxists formed a new party – the Communist Party of the Philippines – to take the place of the old and discredited communist party, and soon created the New People's Army to give the struggle for the state a guerrilla arm. But despite the great success of the Marxists in providing the nationalist movement with a critical perspective for interpreting the causes of Philippine maldevelopment, they were unable to establish a hegemonic position among those planning for the future. Even though the nationalist movement was to grow in intensity and size, its major components were never able to resolve their ideological and programmatic differences. As a consequence the movement remained divided internally over the type of political economy to be built once the struggle had been won. The unity achieved under the banner of nationalism hid basic differences between those committed to a socialist transformation of the Philippines and those who would use the state to protect and advance a Philippine economy that would remain basically capitalist and provide for a more just distribution of the benefits deriving from that economy. These basic differences increased the movement's vulnerability, as was sadly demonstrated when martial law was imposed.

Ferdinand E. Marcos held the office of President of the Philippines during the greater part of the period just described. Elected in November 1965 in the midst of the early anti-American demonstrations, he, nonetheless, later sent Philippine troops to Vietnam to honor a commitment he had made to President Johnson, and immediately upon assuming the presidency embarked on a campaign to entice more American (and also Japanese) private foreign investment into the Philippines. Before the end of his first four-year term he was to demonstrate full support for the new export-oriented/export processing zone development schemes proffered by the US/World Bank technocrats. In sum, Marcos proclaimed his allegiance to orthodox forms of dependent development, firmly imbedded in continued acceptance of US guidance and support, early on. By doing so he placed himself in full confrontation with the forces constituting the nationalist movement. His aggressive moves to push the Philippine political economy in directions opposite to those advocated by the leaders of the nationalist movement did much to polarize Philippine politics by the end of the 1960s.

Having consciously pushed for confrontation, Marcos prepared well for the seizure of power. He worked to concentrate power in the president's office and to create new administrative agencies directly responsible to him, relying in large part on financing supplied from the US for 'development'. He accepted American technical assistance and funding for upgrading the anti-guerrilla capabilities of the Philippine armed forces, for modernizing Manila's police, for building a new communications network for the military, for improving the intelligence community, etc. He built his inner circle of development planners and key cabinet members about those with the closest ties to American agencies currently working in the Philippines and/or with a firm commitment to American models of 'nation-building' and 'development.' The result was a Marcos-led coalition of technocrats (civil and military), with close support ties from various American public and private agencies, that was ready to push the confrontation with the nationalist coalition to a showdown. As nationalist pressures mounted in the year and a half before martial law, as nationalist victories were scored,[21] and as strong counter-pressures were brought to bear on the Marcos coalition to 'restore stability,' Marcos moved. Armed forces, beginning on 21 September 1972, rapidly rounded up and imprisoned hundreds of people identified with the nationalist movement. A few – including the leadership of the Communist Party of the Philippines (CPP) – had already gone underground and escaped.[22]

The New Society: creating apolitical politics

The immediate political tasks facing the new martial law regime were those of destruction and creation. The former was easy, the latter infinitely difficult. Destruction entailed two interrelated processes: (1) destroying the nationalist movement; and (2) eliminating the major institutions through which politics was normally carried on. The task of creation has involved a search for forms of participation that are purely symbolic and carry no threat that demands will be made on those in power, and ideologies that sound appropriately 'national' while hiding the opposite or that sound bravely equalitarian while obscuring the widening gulf between classes. Both the destructive and the creative acts of the martial law regime were aimed at the larger problem, namely finding a formula to assure 'stability,' to provide a setting of 'law and order' within which technocrats could go about their business of attracting private foreign investment and domestic capital to accelerate capitalist economic growth. That setting, of course, is the apolitical climate of authoritarianism.[23]

As suggested, destroying – for the short term – the nationalist movement, based largely in Manila and a few other large cities, was relatively easy.[24] Detention of leaders, destruction of the mass media and the creation of a controlled press, radio and television, limited use of torture and occasional resort to government murder, and rapid expansion of the surveillance community made this possible.[25] The second act of destruction was carried out swiftly, involving as it did the elimination of Congress primarily. The old system of politics rested on the ability of congressmen and senators to develop local bases of electoral power only nominally attached to one or other of the two pragmatic national political parties, and to use that power to wrest very particularistic concessions from the national government. The overall result was a highly politicized national administration, a congressional setting uncongenial to the rationalizing policies of the developmentalists in the Marcos administration, and a forum for a small handful of outstanding spokesmen for the nationalist movement. By eliminating Congress and the whole political subsystem that it represented, Marcos removed the only mass-based, institutionalized center of power that would have continued to oppose the types of economic development strategies being advocated for the Philippines and that could have been expected to oppose his draconian political tactics.[26]

These acts of destruction effectively depoliticized the Philippines and, simultaneously, created a dangerous vacuum. If the martial law regime did not intend to rule by force alone and if it did not intend to turn the newly created political space over to the rapidly growing underground opposition,[27] it had to find a new ideology that would provide legitimation to its policies, and new mass-based political institutions that would assure central control over those 'participating' in politics and yet provide some illusion that participation was taking place. Admittedly, these tasks constitute the heart of the political problematic and are not unique to a specific period of time in the Philippines. But, having destroyed existing political formulae and their supporting institutional base, Marcos was constrained to try to create new answers specific to the type of political economy he was attempting to build.

One of the more dramatic failures of the Marcos era has been its near total inability to articulate a new political formula that could fit into place the various parts of what, together, would constitute the 'New Society.' Although repeated attempts have been made, beginning with the original justification for the New Society a year before martial law,[28] the New Society remains, ideologically, a mélange of ideas drawn from Western political theory, from the American school of 'nation-building,' from Catholic theories of justice, and even from the Marxists. Greater political equality is promised along with some limitations on wealth (while hastening to reassure the rich that economic equality is *not* a goal), greater discipline urged, pre-colonial local communities – *barangays* – held up as models of communal democracy to be emulated, authoritarianism praised because the New Society represents its *constitutional* form, etc. Nationalism – energetically promoted in all the New Society's many public pageants – remains a low-key, underdeveloped theme in the political tracts of the regime.[29] This is understandable since the basic economic development model of the regime is one demanding much greater integration into the capitalist world economy, with ever more penetration of the Philippines by outsiders and the constant need for new assurances of cooperation (asymmetrical) in the development of the Philippines.

Despite the creation of a variety of corporatist institutions – to be discussed below – the theorists of the New Society never drew on corporatism[30] for inspiration, or at least never admitted doing so, which is understandable since they were arguing that martial law was democratic in nature while corporatism remains tainted by its historic association with fascism. A few political scientists did attempt to bolster the theoretical basis of the New Society, especially during the early years. One argued against the highly individualistic definition of human rights and freedom found in the West with its upper class bias (O.D. Corpuz), and another for a quite literal organic view of the state and politics as historically in tune with Philippine values (Remigio E. Agpalo). Despite these gestures, the search for 'new mentalities'[31] – for a new political ideology that would express but also guide the building of a new society – failed.

The New Society: creating corporatist institutions

Even if the spokesmen for the New Society have not articulated a corporatist ideology,[32] they have proceeded, almost from the opening days of the martial law era, to create corporatist political and social institutions through which to organize forms of tightly controlled participation and establish central controls over corporate and associational forms of life hitherto relatively free from government regulation. Within three months Marcos had ordered the creation of 'Citizen's Assemblies' – later renamed 'Barangay Assemblies' – in each of the nation's 40,000 barrios (local administrative units). By that time he had already transformed the locally elected barrio officials into administrative personnel under the central control of the agency that later became the Ministry of Local Governments and Community Development. With centralized controls in place, limited mobilization at the local level was safe enough and promised some limited legitimacy-creating benefits. From the beginning the Barangay Assemblies provided for sectoral representation – of youth groups and other barrio associations – a feature central to corporatist ideas on 'representative' assemblies.

In time a hierarchy of these assemblies was created stretching to the national level, with each repeating the sectoral ideal (but with the higher levels accommodating representatives from the professional, the 'capital,' the industrial labor, and the agricultural labor sectors).[33] In addition, a separate hierarchy of youth assemblies was created, along with elaborate training programs designed to instill commitment to the ideas of the New Society in the minds of those selected as youth leaders.

Although there were some preliminary moves made towards creating an appropriate 'party' to serve the New Society – the 'Mabuhayang Pilipino Movement' in the early days of martial law comes to mind – it was not until national elections for the Interim National Assembly were planned in 1978 that a national political party was formed. Typically, corporatist regimes rely on a single 'movement' party to guide and control the forms of political participation. The Philippine parallel was created by former elected officials, strongly pro-Marcos, who, with the support of the administration, proceeded to form a party to field candidates and to organize the campaign. The party – 'Kilusan ng Bagong Lipunan' (KBL) or 'New Society Movement' – ran unopposed in most of the nation's constituencies, although in Manila it was faced by a rival slate as it was in several southern districts. It naturally won an overwhelming official victory (a handful of mild oppositionists won seats) but at a high cost: its Manila 'victory' was won only through what is widely believed to have been massive fraud on the part of the government.[34]

The regime's drive to rationalize society extends into many sectors other than politics. Labor was forced to create a single overarching organization – the Trade Union Congress of the Philippines – and, through it, bargain in a tripartite congress with business and government over wages. Strikes are illegal in 'essential' industries and virtually so in others (which has not eliminated occasional strikes, however) due to the tight controls exercized through compulsory arbitration. As noted earlier, the system has worked poorly for labor: wage levels under the New Society have dropped from 30 to 40 per cent.

From the earliest days of the New Society attempts were made to build business and industrial associations that would be interlocked with their government parallel organizations as a way of bringing about harmony and more effective planning. This drive has continued, producing, in 1978, the designation of a relatively new Philippine Chamber of Commerce and Industry (PCCI) as the official representative of private business, a chamber that combined all 'business' sectors into a single 'community' and that was organized through government intervention from previously independent rival chambers. Since that time the government has designated some twelve business groups as its chosen instruments to promote Philippine exports, and has promised very close cooperation and support.[35] Each of the twelve represents a separate sector and can be expected, if the plan works out successfully, to enforce discipline over the other producers in its sector and to provide the strength that comes from size and government backing to compete more aggressively in the global economy. Each will be helped by an industrial association (underneath the umbrella PCCI), also linked to government agencies, to rationalize its sector. Comparable corporatist organizations exist in agriculture and especially for each of the major export crops. Finally, similar pressures have been brought to bear on the professionals to force rival associations to merge into single bodies and, where appropriate, to create new national peak organizations to provide the linkage mechanisms for government supervision.

Against the backdrop of the historical predisposition of Filipinos to factionalism,[36] the probability that all these elaborate corporatist structures would provide the unity and harmony that is promised is slim. They do, however, constitute the regime's attempt to build new institutions appropriate to the interests of the coalition in command of the New Society.

The New Society: creating (dependent) state capitalism

At one time or other the term 'state capitalism' has been applied to selected capitalist industrial nations, to the Soviet Union, and various nations in the Third World, and consequently viewed by some to have lost all meaning.[37] Despite this, the term is widely used in discussions of Third World political economy, and because it calls attention to the centrality of the state in these political economies, seems worthy of continued use.[38] In view of the rapidly expanding involvement of the Philippine state in economic development, the term seems appropriate under which to organize analysis of certain of the main trends.

As previously discussed, the Philippine state, prior to martial law, performed a limited number of economic development functions. These included, in addition to the earlier use of tax incentives and foreign exchange controls, a new package of inducements for private foreign investment as well as an increasing number of government corporations. But since many of the latter were involved in welfare activities (the Rice and Corn Administration's grain distribution program, for example) and some others were undercut by protectionist codes, the cumulative effect was limited.

The Marcos coalition with its close ties to American and World Bank sources of support made clear its commitment to the type of development model they were advocating and its willingness to use the Philippine state to push through the necessary changes in the political economy.[39] Primarily, in the beginning years of martial law these changes entailed expanding the range of enticements for private foreign investment, radically altering the business 'climate' in the direction favoring foreign corporations, opening the Philippines to a flood of bilateral and international aid to promote infrastructure projects, accepting successive waves of 'development' experts in every field from public administration to population control, expanding the 'planning' functions of the government, creating new development agencies and pushing through previously planned projects such as the export processing zone, opening up the economy to greater penetration by foreign banks, etc. Further, the Philippine state increasingly pushed its own private entrepreneurs to rationalize production in certain sectors, to venture into others, to accept joint ventureships with foreign TNCs, etc. Simultaneously the state steadily increased the number of economic activities in which it was directly involved as manager and, in the process, gradually shifted the focus away from service and welfare type roles to functions demanding entrepreneurship within a production-oriented framework.[40]

Two trends should be noted. The first is the role of the government in transforming agriculture. From the beginning, the New Society has placed its greatest emphasis on agriculture, from the highly rhetorical 'land reform' program, to its total cooperation with all the US 'rural development' programs and the steady tempo of World Bank rural infrastructure projects – irrigation dams, roads, etc. The government has pushed hard to extend the Green Revolution, cooperating fully with TNC petrochemical corporations in devising advertising and 'delivery' programs to reach the farmers.

The government has used its power to clear people off land needed for new banana plantations, and for the more recent joint-venture oil palm plantations. It has invited foreign agribusiness to come into the Philippines to participate in expanding export agriculture through joint ventures, with the Philippine government using its National Development Company to secure needed land, and in quantities of any size despite constitutional limits on foreign holdings of 1,024 hectares. Finally, the government has moved aggressively to take over the marketing functions as well as some of the processing in sugar and coconut oil, and in so doing has captured some of the wealth that had traditionally gone to the owners and to foreign-owned corporations. It remains to be seen how this wealth will be used, although preliminary evidence suggests that it has largely been concentrated in the hands of the heads of the agencies and used to support the close allies of the Marcos coalition.[41]

In the industrial sector, most of the New Society's strategies have already been touched on: reliance on TNCs and foreign loans for building an infrastructure supportive of capitalist development; pressure – both positive and negative – to force the pace of local entrepreneurial activity; strong enticements to go into labor-intensive manufacturing for export; etc. In the late 1970s, however, the government has moved to begin building the basis for heavy industry. The plans were outlined in the government's announcement in late 1979 that it would seek foreign financial backing, both public and private, to carry through eleven major industrial projects. It appears as if the Marcos regime is willing to accept approximately one-third foreign ownership in these industrial projects, with the other two-thirds divided between private Filipino capital and the Philippine government.[42] Moreover, the government is going along with tariff reductions pushed by the World Bank despite vehement protests from those sectors of the local manufacturing community likely to be adversely affected. And as if to suggest their proper role, the government is encouraging small and middle sized manufacturing companies to enter into joint-ventures with foreign corporations.[43]

The pattern that emerges from all these trends is of a government that is rapidly expanding its role in the major sectors of the economy in ways to expand and diversify greatly the capitalist economy while simultaneously reproducing past patterns of dependency-creating relationships with nations, foreign corporations and international financial institutions.[44] The trends mark the emergence of a type of state capitalism in the Philippines, but a state capitalism uniquely hobbled by its acceptance of what might well be termed a joint-ventureship between the Philippines and the representative institutions of the center nations and international organizations. How rapidly this dependent form of state capitalism will be changed hinges on the dynamics of the internal class struggle and on the longer-term consequences of the current 'crisis' of the capitalist world economy,[45] and, most importantly, the interactions between the two.

To date, under the policies of the New Society, the interactions have largely led to the elimination of what might be called the national bourgeoisie through its incorporation in TNC-linked activities. Some sectors of the old landlord class were weakened while most were pushed to participate in a general deepening of capitalist development in both agriculture (through joint-venture agribusiness arrangements) and industry. The widely discussed rise of the new 'oligarchs' in the 1970s (the Marcos-centred clique of public/private industrialists mentioned in note 41), is also deeply tied to the operations of transnational capital. The overall conclusion is that the most dynamic sectors of the Philippine bourgeoisie have been closely integrated as participants in the institutions of the global economy becoming in the process what can be termed a transnationalized bourgeoisie.[46]

Facing them is a working class that is expanding as a consequence of the greater degree of labor-intensive manufacturing in the Philippines and that is willing to challenge the government's strong restrictions against strikes. Further, the massive demonstrations that have been held recently (on May Day, 1981, for example) suggest that the urban working class, despite all the corporatist controls the government has attempted to impose over it, can mount large-scale organized actions in opposition to the regime.

Similarly, the organizing of the peasants – who are increasingly forced into becoming agricultural laborers under the accelerating capitalist pressures in the countryside – has made progress despite the government's attempts to institute its own forms of organization. Much of this organization results from the work of the Christian 'left' as well as from the expanding network of rural New People's Army (NPA) support groups.

At this juncture it is apparent that the Marcos alliance of transnationalized bourgeoisie and its bureaucratic technocrats in the government and military remains relatively firmly in command. This is the case despite the ability of practically every opposition group in the Philippines to come together for the first time in a solid political coalition opposing Marcos's 1981 campaign for the presidency. Feeling certain, however, that Marcos would never permit an honest election to be conducted,[47] the coalition agreed to an election boycott, as mentioned earlier (c.f. note 34). The immediate results of the boycott were a failure since, as one editorialist wrote immediately before the election, Marcos 'is capable of controlling the size of his own landslide.'[48] The longer-term consequences, while problematic, nevertheless point in the direction of the possibility of cooperation among the quite disparate opposition groups. Unity seems to be based on a rebirth of nationalism, long hidden under the Center-serving political obfuscation of the New Society, and on the demand for a development strategy that would not confer nearly all the benefits of economic progress on the transnationalized bourgeoisie and the costs on the workers and peasants. The latter area of agreement remains but slightly beyond populism: as the coalition is tested, the outlines of a new Philippine political economy might be hammered out.

Conclusions

Powerful forces are engaged in a struggle over the future of the Philippines. Since gaining national independence, those sections of the bourgeoisie seeking state protection to build a Philippine version of capitalism have found some political and administrative support in their battle against the entrenched American business community and its local Filipino allies. After initial skirmishes in the 1950s, the divisions took on an element of confrontation as Marcos, beginning with his first term as president, pushed for a type of development demanding a depoliticized, anational populace at the very time a multi-class nationalist coalition was gaining strength on the basis of its demands for a *national* development strategy that would work for the direct benefit of Filipinos. Marcos resolved the confrontation by imposing martial law, calling on the forces of repression to provide the type of apolitical climate needed by his American-trained technocrats.

The number and scope of institutional changes made in the Philippine political economy have been great. Cumulatively, they have brought the Philippines into closer integration with the capitalist world economy than at any other time in its history, and have done so through the close working relationships of the Philippine transnationalized bourgeoisie and its counterparts in the industrialized nations of the north and their supportive international institutions. Most recently the state has been used increasingly to take a direct entrepreneurial role in the economy, but to do so in close cooperation with local and foreign bourgeoisie via joint ventures. An embryonic state capitalism exists but in a form that reproduces historic dependency-creating patterns.[49]

The very success of these policies has, however, because of their enormous costs to the majority of Filipinos, led to a growing opposition united around a populist nationalist ideology that would reject the Marcos development strategies and attempt to build an alternative future based on a more independent development of the Philippines for the benefit of Filipinos. As the most widely read Philippine nationalist writer has recently argued:

> Economic independence should be a crusade, not merely the subject of scholarly discussion. It should be a call for militant action, one that will involve in principled unity oppressed labor, exploited peasantry, Filipino capitalists, frustrated professionals, and suffering consumers all striving for a just society.[50]

Notes

1 President Marcos first talked about the need to build a 'New Society' in the Philippines in a book published a year before he – with military backing – imposed martial law on the nation (21 September 1972). Martial law was lifted in a formal sense in January 1981, although all the major tools for controlling people remain in place. The book in which he outlined his plans for a 'New Society' was *Today's Revolution: Democracy* (Manila: no publisher, 1971). Also in January 1981, Marcos added 'New Republic' to the political vocabulary to refer to his authoritarian era.

2 He was elected to a new six-year presidential term in elections held in June 1981 in which the major opposition political parties refused to run candidates. Marcos was first elected president (for a four-year term) in 1965.

3 The essence of such eulogies is captured in an elegant 'coffee table book' published by the government. *The Marcos Revolution: A Progress Report on the New Society of the Philippines*, a folio size pictorial, presents the regime's case on several hundred pages of color prints accompanied by a minimal, but consistently upbeat, text (Manila: National Media Production Center, 1980).

4 *The Five-Year Philippine Development Plan, 1978-1982*, called for an average growth in GNP of 8.0 per cent during that period (Manila: Government of the Philippines, 1977), p.25. At the end of 1980 the Minister of Economic Planning, Gerardo Sicat, stated that the government accepted a lowered goal of 'over 5 per cent' and that he was sharply critical of a private Philippine research organization – Communication Research Center – for providing the foreign press with data to support the prediction that the GNP growth rate for 1980 would be as low as 3 per cent. See 'Businessmen's Conference,' *Business Journal* (November 1980), p.2. Communication Research Center is a highly respected business-oriented organization employing well-trained economists and linked with the Opus Dei movement.

5 See Larry A. Niksch and Marjorie Niehaus, *The Internal Situation in the*

Philippines: Current Trends and Future Prospects (Washington, D.C.: Congressional Research Service, Library of Congress, 1981) and W. Ascher, 'Political and Administrative Bases for Economic Policy in the Philippines,' draft paper (Washington, D.C.: World Bank, 6 November 1980) as illustrations.

6 *1980 Philippine Statistical Yearbook* (Manila: Republic of the Philippines, National Economic and Development Authority, 1980), p.14.

7 *Aspects of Poverty in the Philippines: A Review and An Assessment* (Washington D.C.: World Bank, 1980, two vols). See also Philip Bowring, 'The Poverty Puzzle,' *Far Eastern Economic Review* 27 March 1981), pp.125-31.

8 The government admits that more than 60,000 have been detained. See International Commission of Jurists, *The Decline of Democracy in the Philippines* (Geneva: 1977), p.32. Also *Report of an Amnesty International Mission to the Republic of the Philippines* (London: Amnesty International, 1976). The government has repeatedly been charged with murdering individuals engaged in organizing opposition groups. A recent case was Fr. Godofredo Alingal, a critic of the Philippine military, killed in his convent by five armed men. The Task Force on Detainees of the Philippines reported to Amnesty International 303 substantiated cases of 'salvaging' – the Philippine term for government murder – for the period 1975-80. *Ang Katipunan*, 16-31 May 1981, p.5.

9 Jonathan Fast and Jim Richardson, *Roots of Dependency. Political and Economic Revolution in 19th Century Philippines* (Quezon City, Philippines: Foundation for Nationalist Studies, 1979), p.10.

10 *Ibid.*

11 Various estimates of the American slaughter of Filipinos range up to 1,000,000 out of the then population of 6,000,000. American forces simply used burn and destroy tactics and the most modern weapons available against an unarmed civilian population charged with 'cooperating with the enemy' and against very poorly armed Philippine forces. This explains the incredible gap in kill ratios: only 883 Americans died in battle, another 3,349 deaths resulted from other causes, primarily disease. For an overview of the conquest see Luzviminda Francisco, 'The First Vietnam,' in *The Philippines. End of an Illusion* (London: Association for Radical East Asian Studies, 1973).

12 Many have been highly critical of General Douglas McArthur for his decision to 'return' to the Philippines as its 'liberator.' They argue that he could have followed his own highly successful 'island hopping' strategy and left the Japanese forces in the Philippines there to sit out the war since by the time of the American invasion of Leyte, the Japanese had already lost the ability to defend supply lines to their forces. McArthur's strong emotional (he was the commander of the Philippine Armed Forces at the time they were overrun by the Japanese) and financial (owner of shore-front land on Manila Bay) ties with the Philippines seem to have affected the decision.

13 General McArthur personally intervened to 'clear' one of his friends – General Manual Roxas – who had been captured by the Japanese and

later worked for them in a high position in the puppet government. McArthur subsequently backed Roxas for the Philippine presidency, a position he won in the 1946 elections.

14 This analysis runs against the 'strong state' thesis advanced by Hamza Alavi for new Third World nations, as does the argument of a relatively united, hegemonic class alliance in the Philippines. Reasons have been given for the ruling class unity. State weakness at the time was largely the consequence of the Japanese occupation (destruction of the Philippine armed forces; creation of guerrilla forces; curtailment of state functions, etc.) and liberation (when many state functions were taken over by the American armed forces). This was a temporary situation, however. The main argument in the following analysis will be the struggle over how the rapidly strengthened state was to be used. For the Alavi position see 'The State in Post-Colonial Societies: Pakistan and Bangladesh,' *New Left Review*, 74 (July-August 1972). Also see W. Ziemann and M. Lanzendörfer, 'The State in Peripheral Societies,' *The Socialist Register 1977*; Bharat Patankar and Gail Omvedt, 'The Bourgeois State in Post-Colonial Formations,' *Insurgent Sociologist*, 9 (Spring 1980); Atilio Boron, 'New Forms of Capitalist State in Latin America: An Exploration,' *Race & Class*, 20:3 (1979); and Raymond D. Duvall and John R. Freeman, 'The State and Dependent Capitalism,' *International Studies Quarterly*, 25:1 (March 1981).

15 See Benedict J. Kerkvliet, *The Huk Rebellion, A Study of Peasant Revolt in the Philippines* (Berkeley, Calif.: University of California Press, 1977) for the most thorough study of this rebellion.

16 The crucial role played by the US in this is documented by a participant in Edward G. Lansdale, *In the Midst of Wars* (New York: Harper and Row, 1972). This interpretation is supported from the Filipino side in Jose V. Abueva, *Ramon Magsaysay. A Political Biography* (Manila: Solidaridad Publishing House, 1971).

17 Elias T. Ramos, *Philippine Labor Movement in Transition* (Quezon City, Philippines: New Day Publishers, 1976), p.33.

18 Even though born in the Philippines (and to parents also born in the Philippines), normally the Chinese were legally considered aliens. Only very few could gain citizenship, unless totally assimilated through long inter-marriage. Under martial law, Marcos issued decrees to encourage the rapid inclusion of the Chinese as citizens. On the 1954 law see Remigio E. Agpalo, *The Political Process and the Nationalization of the Retail Trade in the Philippines* (Quezon City, Philippines: University of the Philippines, 1962).

19 Vincente B. Valdepeñas, Jr, *The Protection and Development of Philippine Manufacturing* (Manila: Ateneo de Manila University, 1970), p.14. Interestingly, the 1964 levels of labor in manufacturing and in industry have not been equalled since. The current five-year plan proposes that by 1982 labor in manufacturing will reach the level of 10.6 per cent, and in industry 15.1 per cent. The figures for 1987 are: 11.8 and 17.5 per cent respectively. *Five-Year Philippine Development Plan, 1978-1982, op. cit.*, p.43.

20 See Edberto M. Villegas, 'The Philippines and the IMF-World Bank Conglomerate,' Third World Studies, University of the Philippines, Series No.17, May 1979.

21 In the summer of 1972 the Philippine Supreme Court handed down several decisions challenging the rights and prerogatives of foreign corporations.

22 Some months earlier the government plan for carrying out martial law had fallen into the hands of the nationalists. It was widely discussed in Congress and in the media. Nevertheless, the leaders seemed incapable of devising a defense for the movement.

23 Whereas, historically, capitalism had long been associated with the development of parliamentary and democratic political systems, it seems obvious that at the present conjuncture of the capitalist world system the key instruments of capitalist penetration into the Third World gravitate towards those polities offering the most repressive political environments.

24 The separate task of dealing with the NPA fell to the armed forces which proceeded to mount large-scale assaults on their few guerrilla strongholds. These failed to destroy the NPA. Today the NPA has bases in nearly all areas of the Philippines. Similarly, the threat from the Moro National Liberation Front (MNLF) in the south was treated largely as a military problem, although with more willingness to combine political strategies with the regime's response.

25 Effective at the beginning of martial law, these tools have not prevented the growth of a wide-based, anti-martial law movement, not transformed into an anti-Marcos coalition. As in the pre-martial law era, basic differences weaken this coalition.

26 For a more complete analysis see Robert B. Stauffer, *The Philippine Congress: Causes of Structural Change*, Sage Research Papers in the Social Sciences, vol.3, Series No. 90-024 (Beverly Hills: Sage Publications, 1975).

27 Almost immediately various groups in the old nationalist coalition began underground publications and organizational work, despite the loss of many of their leaders. Additionally, segments of the Catholic Church, increasingly radicalized into the Christian 'Left' tradition, stepped in to provide a national communications network relatively safe from the government, and leadership in opposing the policies of the authoritarian regime.

28 Ferdinand E. Marcos, *Today's Revolution: Democracy* (Manila: 1971). Numerous books bearing his name have come off the press since that time, most continuing the argument that the regime represents a democratic revolution, (*Revolution from the Center* (Hong Kong: Raya Books, 1978); *Notes on the New Society of the Philippines* (Manila: 1973). The regime also attempts to stand as a leader of the Third World. Several books by Marcos state this position, e.g. *The Third World in an Age of Crisis* (Manila: 1980).

29 The government is, however, publishing a multi-volume history of the Philippines, again 'written' by Ferdinand E. Marcos. Furthermore, the

many publications of the Department of Public Information and the other public relations arms of the government all advance a national image of progress, modernity, effective government planning, etc.

30 Contemporary theorists of corporatism argue that corporatism is the typical form that Third World authoritarianism takes in the search for an institutional framework for 'managing' the pressures of development and for organizing those societies to greater efforts. See the work of Philippe C. Schmitter, and especially 'Still the Century of Corporatism?' in Frederick B. Pike and Thomas Stritch (eds), *The New Corporatism. Social-Political Structures in the Iberian World* (Notre Dame, Ind.: University of Notre Dame Press, 1974). See also Robert B. Stauffer, 'Philippine Corporatism: A Note on the "New Society",' *Asian Survey* 27:4 (April 1977) for a discussion of corporatism, a review of the literature, and a description of Philippine examples. Frederic C. Deyo has recently used corporatist theory to guide his study of another Southeast Asian nation, Singapore. *Dependent Development and Industrial Order. An Asian Case Study* (New York: Praeger, 1981).

31 To use corporatist terminology. Schmitter found that the Brazilian technocrats, despite their early success with the economy, also failed to solve the problem of creating a set of 'compliant "mentalities"' consonant with the needs of the regime among the people. 'The "Portugalization" of Brazil?' in Alfred Stepan (ed.), *Authoritarian Brazil* (New Haven, Conn.: Yale University Press, 1973), p.229. For an application of the corporatist approach to a communist Eastern European state see Daniel Chirot, 'The Corporatist Model and Socialism. Notes on Romanian Development,' *Theory and Society* 9:2 (March 1980).

32 Marcos and his top spokesmen have, however, consistently used the central cluster of corporatist values in their speeches: e.g., a strong belief in discipline, hierarchy, in the need for sacrifice, in harmony of classes, in unity and against the divisiveness of 'politics,' for great respect for the nation-building role of the military, etc.

33 For a fuller discussion of these assemblies see Stauffer, 'Philippine Corporatism,' *op. cit.*, pp.402-6.

34 While political 'campaigns' of unopposed 'movements' can, under well-orchestrated conditions, provide some of the 'feel' of elections, they can also become an embarrassment, especially when viewed from the outside. In the June 1981 national election for president, the major opposition groups formed a coalition titled the United Democratic Oppositon (UNIDO) and agreed *not* to run a candidate against Marcos and, further, not to urge the voters to boycott the election (in the face of decrees making it a crime not to vote). Marcos was faced with the prospect of staging a full-scale national election for an office for which he was the only candidate. He finally found a friendly candidate to stand against him (some other political unknowns also ran, including one standing for American Statehood). Needless to add, Marcos won his new six-year term as president.

35 Announced in a speech by President Marcos to a national business conference, 7 December 1978. *Official Gazette*, 5 February 1979, p.1095.

36 I dislike this type of statement since Filipinos are probably no more nor less given to factionalism than other nationalities. The characterization is commonly made, however, both by outsiders and by Filipinos.

37 Alex Dupuy and Barry Truchil argue that the term should be discarded because of this confusion. See 'Problems in the Theory of State Capitalism,' *Theory and Society* 8:1 (1979).

38 A more restricted usage – limiting the term only to those Third World states that are actively using state power to break away from externally dominated industrialization – is developed by James Petras in 'State Capitalism and the Third World,' in *Critical Perspectives on Imperialism and Social Class in the Third World* (NY: Monthly Review Press, 1978). See also Berch Berberoglu, 'Toward a Theory of State Capitalist Development in the Third World,' *International Review of Sociology* 9:1 (January-June 1979). Since the rapid expansion of the role of the Philippine state in the economy has only belatedly touched the institutions of foreign domination, and since the regime still actively promotes continued reliance on TNCs, foreign-supplied technology, foreign infrastructure funding and, in general, massive foreign support, I have added the additional adjective (in parentheses) 'dependent' to the term, illogical as that may at first appear.

39 This is discussed in detail in Robert B. Stauffer, 'The Philippine Development Model: Global Contradictions, Crises, and Costs,' *Philippine Journal of Public Administration* (forthcoming).

40 There has been nearly a doubling in the number of state-owned enterprises since 1972 – the number is now more than 100 – and probably many times that in size; the post-1972 additions include the government corporations or agencies in oil, sugar marketing, coconut processing and marketing, to name the larger additions. Further, power generation has been taken over by the government, even if 'ownership' remains obscure: Marcos forced the Lopez family to turn ownership of the Manila power plants over to the 'Marcos Foundation.'

41 See Gary Hawes, 'The State, Transnational Corporations and Agricultural Development,' Third World Studies Program, University of the Philippines, 1981. The most complete study of the extreme concentration of wealth in the hands of a very small circle of relatives and close friends centering on Marcos is Reuben R. Canoy, *The Counterfeit Revolution, Martial Law in Philippines* (Manila: Philippine Editions Publishing, 1980). There is clearly an element of what Richard Robison calls bureaucratic capitalism – raising funds through public corporations to 'sustain existing politico-bureaucratic power structures' present. 'Toward a Class Analysis of the Indonesian Military Bureaucratic State,' *Indonesia*, 25 (April 1978), p.27.

42 The eleven are: a copper smelter; a phosphate fertilizer plant; an aluminum smelter; diesel engine manufacturing; expansion of the cement industry; an integrated pulp and paper mill; additions to the petrochemical complex; beginning of a heavy engineering industry; an integrated steel mill; and an alcogas program. For a discussion and comments by the Minister – Roberto V. Ongpin – responsible, see 'Basic

Industrial Projects,' *Business Journal* (October 1980). In the case of the aluminum smelter, the split will be fifty-fifty between the Philippine government and Reynolds Aluminum Co., and will rely on the cheap power generated by a dam built with World Bank Funds.

43 See the discussion in Gary Hawes, 'The Theory of the Third World State and Capitalist Development in the Philippines,' paper delivered at the 2nd International Philippine Studies Conference, Honolulu, Hawaii, 1981.

44 See Robert B. Stauffer, 'The Philippine Development Model,' *op. cit.*, for a fuller discussion of this point. The new relationships are described as producing 'transnationalized dependent development.'

45 Arguments that the capitalist economy is undergoing a long-term cyclical downturn (of the Kondratieff wave type) that produce a condition of 'crisis' for some participants have been advanced for some time. For the basic argument see André Gunder Frank, *Crisis: In the Third World*, and *Crisis: In the World Economy* (NY: Holmes and Meier, 1980); S. Amin, G. Arrighi, A.G. Frank and I. Wallerstein, *Crisis, Which Crisis?* (forthcoming, 1981); and Raul Prebish, 'Crisis of Advanced Capitalism,' *Mainstream* (2 May 1981).

46 The payoff for this is, of course, extremely rewarding. The Minister of Industry mentioned earlier – Roberto V. Ongpin – at the time of his appointment in 1979 reportedly earned US$400,000 a year in the accounting firm that does most of the work for TNCs in the Philippines. That figure represents approximately 660 times the annual average GNP *per capita*. A comparable ratio between a high corporate salary and *per capita* income in the US would run between one fifth and one sixth that spread.

47 The one potential candidate around whom many of the groups might well have rallied – Benigno Aquino – was denied the chance to run by an amendment to the constitution that Marcos had approved (among others) in a plebiscite held in April 1981. The amendment raised the minimum age for the Philippine president to fifty, some two years older than Aquino at the time.

48 *Honolulu Sunday Advertiser*, 14 June 1981, p.B2.

49 David Wurfel, after examining the empirical evidence for a particular set of relationships, comes to the same conclusion. See 'Philippine-American Relations since 1972: The Rise or Fall of Dependency?' paper presented at the First International Conference on Philippine Studies, Kalamazoo, Michigan, 1980. See also Robyn Lim, 'The Philippines and the "Dependency Debate": A Preliminary Case Study,' *Journal of Contemporary Asia* 8:2 (1978).

50 Renato Constantino, 'Economic Independence,' *We*, 13-19 December 1980, p.5.

10 The state and capitalist development in Thailand

KEVIN J. HEWISON – *Murdoch University*

1 Introduction

While they do not deal explicitly with the state as a specific unit of analysis, the most influential English-language texts discussing Thai politics do exhibit an implicit conception of the state and its role.[1]

At the most basic level, Wilson, Siffin and Riggs, in common with other writers who adopt the perspective of structural-functional theory, believe that a developed polity will approximate the Western democratic system. For them, a modern political system is based upon inputs from its political environment, where all people have more or less equal power. The state or government (political system) is seen to be responsive to these inputs, so that in the last instance, everyone's best interests are served; the state is viewed as being a neutral aggregator of interests, discerning society's general will and acting for the general good.

However, in the Thai case, Wilson, Siffin and Riggs came to the conclusion that there were very few inputs into the political system. Political parties, trade unions, and various interest groups which were believed to provide the inputs in the Western system did not seem to perform the same functions in the case of Thailand. The vast mass of the Thai people were thus considered to be unconcerned and apolitical individuals dominated by an elite of civil and military bureaucrats. The elite, separated from the social and economic environment, became the focus of these studies of Thai politics. The 'bureaucratic polity', as it came to be known, was seen to be static and unresponsive, serving its own best interests. Such a system was considered to be characteristic of a society which had failed to fully modernise its polity.[2]

Writers influenced by dependency theory considered these structural-functional approaches to Thai politics to be inadequate.[3] With respect to the state, dependency theorists argued that studies focusing on the Thai elite and the behaviour of individuals within the elite obscured the international context of politics and economics. Dependency theorists argue that the civil and military elite and local capitalists are basically compradors who facilitate the exploitation of Thai peasants and workers by international capital. The state is seen to implement policies which are favourable to metropolitan investors and their local agents, but which tend to be to the detriment of the small, local bourgeoisie. Because of this, Thailand is said to exhibit all of the essential features of underdevelopment, and the possibility of local capitalist development is seen as negligible unless Thailand can extract itself from the world capitalist system.

While a focus on the role of international capital and its impact within the Thai socio-economic structure is not without utility, recent Marxist discussions of the role of the state in capitalist development in the Third World have indicated that the state and local bourgeois classes can cooperate to enhance domestic capitalism, often in competition with international capital.[4] This research has suggested that dependency theorists have, by their focus on imperialism, tended to obscure the total process of class formation and reproduction, and the continuing accumulation of capital in the Third World.

As has been indicated in the introductory chapter of this book, at different stages of the accumulation process, the capitalist state will perform different functions, but will usually attempt to secure the general conditions necessary for the capitalist mode of production. Contrary to the tenets of dependency theory, it is quite clear that some Third World states are not acting in the interests of international capital alone. Domestic bourgeoisies have been able to manipulate the state to provide the conditions they require for expanded accumulation (e.g. industrial promotion policies, credit facilities, tariff protection). It is thus important to delineate the strengths of the domestic bourgeoisie if a clear picture of the state's relationship with the bourgeoisie is to be determined. It must, however, be emphasised that the

> social character of a regime is not defined by the class origin of those who occupy the state apparatus but by the nature of state policy .... [A] bourgeois state ... is a state which provides the economic conditions for capital accumulation and the political protection for the bourgeoisie in the process of class conflict.[5]

In this chapter I will attempt to show that the general conception of the state in capitalist development, outlined in the introduction to this book, holds true in the Thai case. I will argue that a domestic bourgeoisie, capable of acting as an independent class within the international capitalist system, has emerged in Thailand, and that the state has played a substantial role in securing and expanding this class's accumulative base in finance and industry. In completing this task it is necessary to: (i) briefly outline the international context of Thailand's capitalist economic development; (ii) delineate the Thai bourgeoisie; and (iii) discuss the role of the state in determining the course of capitalist development.

2 Thailand

(i)   The international context of Thai economic development

From the mid-nineteenth century to the 1960s Thailand's role in the world capitalist system was to supply primary commodities for the world market. Throughout the period, rice, teak, rubber and tin accounted for between 50 and 90 per cent of all Thai exports.[6] Thailand's small industrial sector was of no international significance until recent times.

Prior to World War II, Britain and its colonial empire had been Thailand's major trading partner, but the war, and rising national-ism throughout Asia, weakened Britain's imperial grip, and the US emerged from the war as the major power in the region. The American perception of Thailand was, at the time, basically similar to that of the British. The Allies considered Thailand to be an essential source of vital raw materials and primary commodities, and they wanted these back on the market to supply a war-ravaged world.[7] Towards the end of the 1940s, however, the Americans began to place more stress on strategic considerations. As one US government agency explained the situation.

> [S]outh of the ominous mass that is Red China, Thailand, along with her embattled but still free neighbors, shares a peninsula. The Communists want it. They covet its riches: rubber, tin, rice and teak. They consider it a prize base, for like an oriental scimitar, the peninsula's tip is pointed at the throat of Indonesia .... In Malaya, Burma and Indo-China, Communist-led rebels plunder, kill and burn. Thailand is surrounded by these countries, each a smouldering bomb .... The fuses are short.[8]

Strategic and business concerns were inextricably intertwined, and an anti-business Asian government was considered pro-communist or, at best, dangerously neutral – a 'free' Asia meant an Asia open to free enterprise.

From the beginning of the 1950s, Thailand's foreign policy

became unequivocably pro-American,[9] and various Thai military leaders soon learnt that the US government would nurture its friends. From 1951 to 1969 Thailand received more than $900 million in aid and loans from the US, while in the 1960-70 period US military expenditures in Thailand exceeded $1,100 million.[10] The Americans reaped a bountiful harvest from this alliance also, and in addition to gaining a base on the Southeast Asian mainland became, in the 1950s, Thailand's major trading partner.[11] While the Japanese soon replaced the Americans in this position, the ability of the Japanese to expand was, in many respects, a legacy of US policy in the region.

In addition, Thailand's position as an exporter of primary products was reinforced by the Bretton Woods agreements, which locked Third World countries into a system of trade and finance designed by and for the advanced capitalist nations.[12]

Since 1960, however, Thailand's trading position has become less dependent on the export of primary commodities, and this has coincided with a more footloose period for international capital. Transnational corporations have become increasingly interested in taking advantage of such benefits as cheap labour, generous tax concessions, bans on organised labour, and growing domestic markets in Third World countries when considering the relocation of industrial investments becoming less profitable in the advanced industrial countries. This restructuring of international capital has also provided new opportunities for the expansion of accumulation by domestic capitalists in the Third World. In Thailand, the manufacturing sector has seen remarkable growth since 1960,[13] with manufactured exports having expanded from just 1 per cent of total exports in that year, to 27 per cent in 1979.[14] The trend towards increased industrial activity can be seen in Table 10.1.

While the majority of the Thai people continue to work in the agricultural sector, and while agriculture remains the single most important sector of the economy, Table 10.1 clearly indicates the increasing importance of the manufacturing sector. There can be little doubt that it will continue to grow in the future, particularly as the interdependence of international and national capitals increases, and as the Thai state determinedly maintains the country as a haven for capitalist enterprise, providing 'abundant natural resources' and 'plentiful, inexpensive and dextrous labour'.[15]

(ii) The development of the Thai bourgeoisie

The origins of the capitalist class in Thailand can be traced to the middle of the nineteenth century. From this time we can begin to

Table 10.1 *GDP by industrial origin, selected years (%)*

Industrial Origin	1951	1960	1971	1979
Agriculture	50.1	39.8	29.8	25.5
Mining and Quarrying	1.9	1.1	1.5	1.7
Manufacturing	10.3	12.6	17.5	20.8
Construction	2.9	4.6	5.5	5.4
Electricity and Water Supply	0.1	0.4	1.8	1.8
Transport and Communications	3.1	7.5	6.7	7.3
Wholesale and Retail Trade	18.0	15.2	17.1	16.6
Banking, Insurance and Real Estate	0.4	1.9	4.2	5.4
Ownership of Dwellings	3.7	2.8	1.9	1.5
Public Administration and Defence	2.8	4.6	4.3	3.8
Services	6.7	9.6	9.7	10.2

N.B. The 1979 figures are provisional.
Sources: 1951 and 1960 figures are from Ingram, *op. cit.*, p.234, while the figures for 1971 and 1979 are from Bank of Thailand, *Annual Economic Report*, 1974 and 1979 issues.

discern the emergence of private ownership of the means of production, the development of generalised commodity production, the beginnings of wage-labour, the gradual separation of economic and political power, and the first indications of the movement of capital from the sphere of circulation into the sphere of production.

Perhaps the most distinctive feature of this emerging class was its compromised position in relation to the traditional, *sakdina* ruling class, which held rights to the agricultural and trading surpluses through taxation and trade monopolies. Rather than emerging as an openly antagonistic class, the bourgeoisie found it necessary to accumulate much of its initial wealth by cooperation with the *sakdina* class.[16] This class's functionaries, who were often Chinese merchants involved in monopoly trading, tax-farming and administration, were able to amass large personal fortunes. With the development of commodity production in sugar, rice, pepper, tin, teak and rubber, some of these merchant-functionaries were able to invest their wealth in productive enterprises such as sugar, rice and timber mills, often jointly financed with royal money.[17] Others took advantage of the expansion of European business within Thailand, acting as compradors, and providing the essential link between the foreigners and the local economy. This also facilitated the compradors' own enterprises, for their own firms were usually the distributors of foreign imports and the collectors of Thai exports.[18] At the same time the *sakdina* class had begun to invest heavily in land, and within a short time, managed to monopolise much of the best, newly-opened rice lands and most of the valuable urban land, thus augmenting their accumulated fortunes with rent and land sales.[19]

It was from this group of Chinese merchant-functionaries and compradors, and from the upper ranks of the *sakdina* class, brought together in a symbiotic relationship, investing in land, industry, commerce and banking, that the Thai bourgeoisie emerged.

Milling became an important area of accumulation for the developing Chinese and Thai capitalists, especially as they controlled the vast majority of mills.[20] While the first banks in Thailand were foreign-owned, it is significant that there soon developed a number of local banks, all supported with capital subscribed by Chinese millers and merchants.[21] The most successful of these banks was the Siam Commercial Bank, officially opened in 1906, and capitalised with a combination of royal, noble, Chinese merchant and foreign funds (the latter being very much in the minority).[22]

Milling, trading and banking and finance (including pawnshops and Chinese remittance agencies) remained the principal sources of accumulation for the small bourgeoisie until about 1926, when Thailand's trade treaties with Western powers were revised. These revisions allowed the Thai government to increase its import duties from 3 per cent (set in 1855) to a general level of 5 per cent. Coupled with the temporary retreat of European capital during the depression years, higher tariffs stimulated a minor resurgence in the sugar industry, and encouraged a movement into, and expansion of, manufacturing industries.[23]

In 1932 the absolute monarchy was overthrown, and the new, constitutional regime developed a more nationalistic approach to economic development. Previously, there had been increasing concern in some circles (especially amongst foreign-educated civil servants) about the lack of domestic industrial development, and the fact that the economy seemed to be dominated by alien Chinese and Westerners.[24] The coup of 1932 was aimed primarily at eliminating royal privilege,[25] but some members of the coup group, representing the commoner elements of the civil service and commissioned military officers, considered that 'foreigners' (and this included alien Chinese) were not particularly affected by the economic crisis of the time.[26] The economic nationalism of the next two to three decades was a reflection of this perception.[27] The new regime sought to move the small industrial sector into 'Thai' (ethnic Thai and Sino-Thai citizens') hands, and to initiate industrial development from this base, in an early attempt at import substitution industrialisation. Statistically, the achievements of this policy, prior to 1942, were not impressive. However, they did provide some valuable experience for domestic managers and entrepreneurs, and allowed for some increased accumulation as a number of small, private firms and some larger, government-backed enterprises were established.[28]

The impact of World War II upon domestic patterns of accumulation requires considerable emphasis, for it allowed Thai capitalist enterprise to expand quite considerably. While foreign investment does not seem to have ever exceeded Thai and Chinese investment,[29] the Japanese occupation of 1942-5 meant that all British and Allied business activities were suspended, and local firms had to develop and expand in an attempt to fill the gap, especially in the production of previously imported consumer goods.

In banking, the eclipse of the foreign banks, wartime inflation (the Bangkok cost-of-living increased 100-fold between 1941 and early 1945[30]), and minimal interference by the Japanese, provided fertile ground for the consolidation of the five locally-capitalised banks which were established.[31] The money behind these banks was predominantly Sino-Thai, having been accumulated in trading and merchandising, and also in the manufacturing sector during the 1930s.[32] Manufacturing itself received a wartime boost, as both private and state enterprises expanded in an effort to overcome shortages in sugar, paper, textiles and other manufactures, with the newly-established Ministry of Industry actively encouraging private investment.[33]

Following the war, however, industrial expansion was hampered by war-damaged infrastructure (particularly power generation), and the influx of foreign-made goods. The export of primary commodities remained dominant, partly because the government could not meet the costs of infrastructural reconstruction and expansion, and partly because export was particularly profitable, for both the government and traders, at a time when world demand was exceptionally high. But an important development occurred within this trading sector. Whereas in earlier decades Thailand's foreign trade had been in the hands of Western and Chinese trading companies, with profits either leaving the country or remaining in the sphere of circulation, local banks now took on a new and increasingly important role, and were able to divert some of their profits from financing Thai trade into the productive sphere.[34] At the same time, deposits in commercial banks grew from about 800 million *baht* in 1946 to over 5,000 million *baht* in 1961, while loans and overdrafts totalled 4,300 million *baht* in 1961.[35]

Despite this expansion, significant fractions of Thai capital, including the financial fraction, believed that far more investment capital was required if Thailand was to develop, and if they were to expand their base for accumulation. They felt that it was imperative that the government curtail its investments in production and divert them into infrastructural development. While the government of Plaek Phibunsongkram (hereafter, Phibun) moved hesitantly in this direction towards the end of its time in office, it was not until after 20 October 1958, when General Sarit Thanarat took full power, that new investment promotion and infrastructural development policies were implemented, together with the active encouragement of foreign aid and investment (these points are discussed more fully in the following section).

Whereas the inflow of foreign investment had been low after the War – the Bank of Thailand estimated a total of 800 million *baht* in 1954 (excluding the assets of foreign banks), and net direct investment in the 1955-60 period of just 70 million *baht* – after 1960 this grew rapidly, with almost 2,700 million *baht* entering the country in 1974 alone.[36] Thai capitalists were not, however, swamped by these inflows, which amounted to between 1.2 and 6.2 per cent of total capital formation in the 1955-79 period.[37] For example, if we examine only the loans and overdrafts granted by commercial banks in 1979 we find that they totalled almost 129,000 million *baht*, while deposits reached 170,000 million *baht*.[38]

Certainly the Thai economy received tremendous stimulation from foreign aid and investment, and from US military spending,[39] but joint-venture arrangements have allowed Thai capitalists to gain access to capital, experience and skills in areas they had previously been unable or unwilling to expand into. In order to expand their enterprises, some Thai capitalists were willing to pay the price of subordinate integration into the international capitalist system - eventual net overflows of capital, trade dependence, etc.

Nevertheless, although the available statistical evidence is by no means complete, it would seem that the contemporary Thai economy is dominated by domestic capital. In industries promoted by the Board of Investment (BoI), Thai capital accounts for over 75 per cent of total registered capital.[40] In the important financial sector, Thai capital is overwhelmingly predominant, as shown in Table 10.2.

While the data for the financial sector are reasonably accurate, those presented in Table 10.3 give but a very rough indication of the extent of foreign ownership and control in the sectors indicated. Real ownership and control is often submerged in a complex web of interlocking directorships and shareholdings. For example, in the textile industry, which is generally considered to be foreign-dominated, ownership of registered capital seems to be evenly split between foreigners (mainly Japanese and Taiwan-based Chinese) and Thais. However, registered capital does not necessarily reflect

Table 10.2 *Foreign ownership of the Thai financial sector, 1979*

Financial Activity	No. of foreign companies	Assets (in millions of baht	% of market controlled
1 Commercial Banks	14	18,106	6.15
2 Life Insurance Cos	3	1,282	32.10
3 Non-Life Insurance Cos	9	447	16.15
4 Investment and Securities Cos (a)	15	13,797	27.58

Note: (a) Includes joint-ventures and foreign-owned companies registered in Thailand.
Source: Krirkkiat Phipatseritham, *Wikhro laksana kan pen chaokhong thurakit khanat yai nai prathet thai*, Bangkok: Thai Khadi Research Institute, 1981, p.258.

Table 10.3 *Ownership of various sectors of Thai industry*

Sector	% Foreign-owned	%Thai-owned
1 Auto industry	55.5	44.5 (a)
2 Textiles	54.7	45.3 (b)
3 Petroleum	96.0	4.0 (c)
4 Cement	neg.	100.0 (c)
5 Sugar	2.0-10.0	90.0-98.0 (c)
6 Tin	90.0	10.0 (c)
7 Steel	20.0	80.0 (c)
8 Milk	60.0-70.0	30.0-40.0 (c)
9 Soap products	65.0	35.0 (c)

Sources: (a) *Business in Thailand*, May (1980), pp.112-13, calculations made on the basis of registered capital; (b) *Business in Thailand*, August (1976), pp.61-4, calculations made on the basis of registered capital; (c) Krirkkiat, *op. cit.*, pp.147-243, calculations made on the basis of total assets of companies in 1978-9.

the real ownership and control situation, as capital investments will usually be far in excess of the registered capital figure.[41] This is certainly the case in the textile industry. But it should equally be noticed that the textile companies have raised most of their investment capital in Thailand, with industry sources estimating that the Bangkok Bank alone finances 70 per cent of the industry.[42] In general, the data presented here suggest that while foreign companies are a major force within the Thai economic structure, Thais remain dominant in certain key sectors, most notably finance, and retain significant control in many other important areas. Table

10.3 also hints at an aspect of the development of the Thai bourgeoisie which cannot be pursued in this chapter, the fractional-isation of the class into financial capital, industrial capital, with groups representing royal capital (e.g. cement), joint-venture capital (e.g. auto and textile industries), and comprador capital (e.g. tin and petroleum industries). Certainly, in 1979, the largest and most profitable companies in Thailand were, to a very large extent, Thai-owned.[43]

It seems likely that the power of the Thai bourgeoisie will increase as the secondary and tertiary sectors of the economy continue to grow. Its power is enhanced by the close business and familial ties it has both within itself, between the various fractions of capital, and with influential functionaries of the Thai state, particularly the military hierarchy. Additionally, connections between elements within the Thai bourgeoisie and similar groups, both regionally and internationally, are enhancing the domestic power of this class.[44]

With this background in mind it is now appropriate to examine the role of the Thai state in the process of capitalist development outlined above. As it is not possible in this chapter to examine the whole period discussed in the previous sections, I have chosen to emphasise three aspects of the state's activities, and to concentrate on the post-1958 period. The areas to be discussed are:

a) the adoption of investment promotion policies and the strategy of import substitution industrialisation;
b) the provision of credit for capitalist development;
c) state policies towards the working class and organised labour.

(iii) The Thai state and capitalist development

The period from 1947, when a coup brought Phibun back to power, until he was overthrown by another coup in 1957 (followed by the Sarit 'revolution' in 1958) can perhaps best be described as an era of haphazard, state-led development. In a seemingly confused and disorganised manner Phibun's administration had implemented programmes which were aimed at the Thai-ification of economic activity. Anti-Chinese policies were promulgated in an effort to force Chinese to assimilate, to become 'Thai'. Also, some petty trading and service sector activities were reserved for Thai nationals, and various Western companies, such as Shell Oil, were threatened with closure, government competition, and/or non-renewable contracts.[45] More significantly though, the government began establishing semigovernmental monopolies in various enterprises including brewing, plywood, paper, sugar-refining, and gunny bags. There does not seem to have been any pattern to these investments, although all ventures were in the import substituting area, and there appears to have been a vague desire to reduce Thailand's dependence on foreign imports, with the hope that these enterprises would be a 'pioneering effort and set an example for the private sector'.[46]

It is usually asserted that governmental intervention in the private sector during Phibun's time represented an attempt by the 'bureaucratic elite' to tap 'Chinese financial resources and managerial expertise to provide funds for Thai political activities'.[47] While this is true, it is not the complete picture. It needs to be emphasised that most of the government's economic activities at this time were carried out in partnership with influential Chinese business people who also derived considerable benefit from the partnership. Business cooperation with powerful political figures meant that one's business could be carried out without fear of competition and, as was the case with the National Economic Development Corporation Limited (NEDCOL), finance became only a relatively minor consideration when the Thai government was one's guarantor. Thus, the influential businessmen involved in the NEDCOL project could obtain overseas loans and begin the operation of a corporation with external contract obligations of more than 600 million *baht* when only three million *baht* of its authorised 50 million *baht* capital had been paid up.[48]

Thus, even though Phibun's policies tended to disadvantage many Chinese business people, some obtained tremendous benefits from them, and like the Sophonpanich family (of the Bangkok Bank), their businesses expanded rapidly.[49]

The problem with such government policies was that they were haphazard. For most business people the investment climate was uncertain, especially as the government, while encouraging private investment in public statements, always added a codicil which reserved for itself the right to intervene in any area of the economy it deemed to be of national importance, or those industries where private enterprise was unable to operate due to shortages of capital, skill or initiative.[50] Potential investors were continually concerned that if they established a profitable enterprise it might well be nationalised, especially if they did not have the support of important members of the military hierarchy.

Despite the fact that some local capitalists were benefiting from this situation, the business community was generally unhappy with it, for business was placed in an unpredictable position. Important business groups urged a more limited role for the state, with the Bangkok Chamber of Commerce arguing that

Free private enterprise would still be the best course for Thailand . . . This does not mean that the State should not enter the field of business . . . nor [are public and private enterprise] incompatible. . . . On the contrary, if public authorities are extended into the orthodox areas such as the procurement of goods and services for the [Armed] Forces, the supply of water, electricity and light, bus or rail transport, harbours, and so on, private enterprise can certainly live happily together with public monopolies.[51]

Sarit's policies, implemented from 1958, gave the domestic and foreign capitalists the guarantees they felt they needed. Sarit was determined to bring stability and progress to a Thailand he considered to be corrupted by mock-Westernism, and his policies on economic development, education, stringent law and order, the abrogation of the constitution, monarchism, and his pro-American foreign policy can all be related to his desire for order, stability, and 'civilised' progress.[52] While Sarit might well have had other motives in mind, there is no doubt that his policies towards business and economic development were generally well received by both domestic and foreign investors, after some initial hesitation.

It appears that the pressure for a change of policies came from a larger number of sources. As noted above, domestic capitalists were in the forefront of this movement. At the same time, foreign investors, and particularly Americans, were actively encouraging changes. The confrontation between US oil companies and the Ministry of Defence in 1957-8 became a focal point of private versus state enterprise strategies, as the Ministry attempted to take over some sectors of the oil industry. Backed by threats of the removal of aid funds, the US companies attempted to force the Thai government to be more positive towards foreign investment and private enterprise. Indeed, aid was seen by many American business people and officials as a means to encourage 'healthy' attitudes towards private enterprise, and Thai officials who exhibited such attitudes were encouraged.[53] Additionally, various international agencies were urging a more limited, infrastructural development role for the state.[54] In many ways though, the reports of the missions of these agencies merely reflected changes which were already underway within the Thai bureaucracy itself. Sarit came to power while the IBRD mission was in Thailand, and at a time when the full impact of the NEDCOL crash was being felt, leaving the government with a huge debt. Sarit, who at first tried to save NEDCOL, came to see its failure as being indicative of the failure of this type of state enterprise; a view shared by many rising administrators. Nevertheless, the fall from favour of state enterprise also had political implications. As Silcock explains,

> Sarit was well disposed towards the condemnation of government enterprise. Unlike Phibun he did not base his power ... within the system of government enterprise, but had extensive private interests in which he used his political power to help his friends, mainly outside the system of formal government control.[55]

Echoing a common sentiment amongst young, mainly foreign-educated, technocrats of the time, Amnuay Virawan later explained that he had come to feel that state enterprises were inefficient and discouraged private investment; 'the only way to promote a sustained economic growth is to encourage economic expansion both in production and investment in the private sector with a minimum of governmental interference.'[56] Together, all of these factors set the stage for the changes of policy which Sarit refered to as his 'revolution'.

*(a) Investment promotion policies and Import Substitution Industri-
       alisation*

From the moment he came to power, Sarit made it clear that economic development was to be emphasised in his crusade to modernise Thailand. In early 1959 he stated:

> The national economy is beset with difficulties, it is, therefore, time that something was done to save the beloved country from this plight and to lead it on the path of welfare and prosperity ... [T]he Revolutionary Party ... cannot brook anything lying athwart the path of progress. All obstacles ... have, therefore, to be swept away.[57]

It was the IBRD report that mapped out the 'path of progress' for Thailand. The World Bank mission reported that it was essential that the 'relative importance of manufacturing activity ... be increased', and that this should be achieved through 'private initiative, both domestic and foreign'. They urged that the government 'restore the confidence of private businessmen and ... assist them in expanding industry ...' by granting special promotional privileges, streamlining laws relating to business, improving credit, providing infrastructure, encouraging import substitution industrialisation (ISI), and by implementing rational development planning.[58] The initial phase of Thailand's first national development plan followed these recommendations almost to the letter.

With the assistance of the United States Operations Mission (USOM) the government withdrew the 1954 Investment Promotion

Act which had been criticised in the IBRD report, and replaced it with the Promotion of Investment Act B.E. 2503 (1960), and established the BoI.[59] Section 18 of the new Act contained two specific guarantees for private enterprise, stating that the government would neither compete with nor nationalise any private industrial activity. It also allowed for the conditional repatriation of profits, the right to land ownership, some import duty exemptions, a two-year income tax holiday, and additional benefits which could be granted by the BoI in specific cases.[60] This Act did not, however, immediately convince many investors that a fundamental change in government policy was taking place[61] and in 1962 a revised Act was promulgated, designed to 'provide more privileges and benefits to investors and to expedite the process of granting such promotional assistance'.[62] Remaining in force for almost a decade (with some minor changes), this Act provided for duty and business tax exemptions on all imported capital goods and raw materials, a five-year tax holiday, wider opportunities for profit repatriations, and gave wider discretionary powers to the BoI. The Act had the desired effect, as an increasing number of companies applied for promotional privileges.[63]

While the government was keen to attract foreign investment, it must be remembered that promotional privileges were designed as much for domestic investors as for foreigners. As one Minister for National Development explained his conception of industrialisation,

> Thailand's industrial growth . . . must be based upon a built-in private enterprise system with minimum government interference. By this I mean that the government must take it as its responsibility to ensure that there always exists an economic environment conducive for the growth of private investment, both foreign and local. The government must not in any way obstruct the path of private industrial growth.[64]

While there were some local investors who were opposed to foreign investment, the big, domestic capitalists, and particularly the banks and their industrial allies, were very much in favour of increased foreign investment, and it was this latter group which had most political influence.[65]

At the time the big capitalists gave, essentially, two reasons for 'needing' foreign capital: (i) insufficient supplies of local capital, and (ii) lack of local managerial and technical skills.[66] While there is some truth in both of these claims, it could also be said that the promotion of foreign investment, particularly in the form of joint-ventures, provided a sound political basis for the rapid expansion of domestic business. In the first place, many of the promotional privileges provided local capitalists with significant benefits, and in particular, the right to own land, a right which had often been denied to alien Chinese business people in the past. Second, the threat of nationalisation of a joint-venture firm, or the harassment of Sino-Thai partners in these ventures was all the more unlikely if Westerners and Japanese were involved, especially at a time when a staunchly pro-American foreign policy was being followed. Indeed, it was only the big capitalist who could enjoy promotional privileges as it was necessary for the applicant to prove that a project could be adequately capitalised. Thus, between 1959 and 1965, the average investment of promoted firms was in excess of 23 million *baht*.[67]

The majority of capital invested with promotional privileges went into import substituting industries. While many of the industries established in the 1930s and 1940s had also been import substituting, they had generally been on a small scale, and had not been a part of any overall governmental plan. Despite the fact that many of these industries had only met with limited success, World War II had convinced many Thais that ISI was the only sure path to industrial development:

> The bitter lesson learnt from the wartime shortage of goods and services was that Thailand must be industrialized, at least to the point of self-sufficiency in a number of essential items in order to avoid a repetition of such economic hardships.[68]

Thus, when the World Bank report suggested that ISI should be encouraged, the Thai government was enthusiastic, as were local manufacturers and potential investors.[69]

Even though the first National Economic Development Plan placed most emphasis on increasing agricultural production, the policy for industry was unequivocally ISI.[70] This policy continued to be followed until 1972 when growing financial problems forced the government to look more towards export promotion as a means of rectifying trade deficits, with the third Plan (1972-6) emphasising both ISI and export-oriented industrialisation.[71] The growth rate of manufacturing industry averaged 11 per cent per annum (at constant 1962 prices) during the 1960s, and its contribution to GDP has grown from 10.3 per cent in 1951 to 20.8 per cent in 1979 (see Table 10.1).[72]

Those who have most benefited from this growth have been the big financial and industrial capitalists. For example, the Bangkok Bank has grown to become the largest bank in Southeast Asia, with assets of almost 105,000 million *baht* in 1979 (about 40 per cent of total commercial bank assets in Thailand), and has control over more than 40 per cent of all bank borrowing and lending in

Thailand. The Bank's declared profit in 1978 was 825.5 million *baht*, the largest profit declared by any Thai-registered company in that year.[73] The Bangkok Bank and its principals, the Sophonpanich family, have, since the late 1950s, invested heavily in manufacturing, and together with other large banking and industrial families, have attained monopolistic control over the Thai economy.[74] Their debt to Sarit's determination to develop the economy is indeed great. At the time of Sarit's death, the Bangkok Bank referred to him as the 'greatest prime minister ... since the 1932 Revolution', attributing his stature to his ability to provide 'political stability', and to his efforts in the field of development.[75]

Whether Sarit and the officials of the Thai state considered monopolistic control of the economy to be the likely outcome of their policies, and whether the Thai bourgeoisie can take some credit for having moved state policy in this direction, are points which cannot be adequately discussed in this chapter. What is significant, however, is that the state implemented policies in the areas of investment promotion and ISI which advanced the process of accumulation from petty commodity and enclave commodity production to a higher level, ISI. Such policies were of immense benefit to the powerful fractions of the bourgeoisie, in that it consolidated their accumulative base. However, there was a price to be paid – the stagnation of the smaller, less powerful capitalist sector, and the loss of a certain amount of capital as profits to foreign investors. From 1966 to 1978 reported outward remittances totalled almost 27,000 million *baht*.[76] But, as one official explained,

> We fully realize that, by leaving the economy wide open ... we run certain risks of being exploited; in certain circumstances, we may even appear to compromise certain aspects of our sovereignty. But we firmly believe that the ... nation can meet this challenge ... [for we] are short of capital, technical know-how, and managerial ability ....[77]

Obviously the price was one that both officials and big capitalists felt Thailand could afford.

(b) Provision of credit for capitalist development

The World Bank report, echoing the sentiments of local capitalists, made it clear that there would be a need for the development of industrial credit facilities in Thailand, and supported the establishment of an Industrial Finance Corporation. In addition the Bank urged a more active lending role for domestic commercial banks, to be financed by increased deposits; the banks had to be more attractive for depositors.[78]

The provision of credit assumed an important position in the first Plan, with the Industrial Finance Corporation of Thailand (IFCT) being accorded special significance.[79] The IFCT had been established in 1959 with two objectives: (i) to assist in the establishment, expansion or modernisation of private industrial enterprise; and (ii) to encourage the participation of both domestic and foreign capital in these ventures.[80] These objectives were to be achieved through the provision of medium- and long-term loans to worthwhile private projects. Although intended to be a private company, the IFCT was established by the government with interest-free and low-interest loans. Over the years the government has given considerable support to the IFCT, providing a number of additional loans on soft terms, with the aim of rationalising industrial financing and allowing the development of modern business enterprises, without the need for the IFCT to make large profits on its lending programme. The IFCT has worked closely with the BoI and the Department of Industrial Promotion, and has clearly been an instrument of state policy, even though the largest shareholders are now local and foreign banks. Some 53 per cent of the IFCT's shares are owned by Thais, and Thai bankers hold the majority of directorships. Names like Lamsam (Thai Farmers Bank), Sophonpanich (Bangkok Bank), Cholvijarn (Union Bank of Bangkok), the Boonsoong (Laemthong Bank) have consistently appeared amongst the directors of the company.[81] Given that these names are also associated with some of the largest industrial enterprises in the country, it is not surprising to discover that the IFCT has given considerable aid to the large and powerful fractions of the bourgeoisie. The World Bank mission apparently believed that the IFCT would finance small entrepreneurs,[82] but small capitalists have seldom been able to take advantage of IFCT credits. In 1960 the average loan was 1.4 million *baht*, rising to 4.45 million by 1964, with very few loans of less than one million *baht* being made since then. In 1978 the average size of outstanding loans was 9.8 million *baht*.[83]

The role of the IFCT has been to finance projects associated with big capitalists, who, while having capital available, prefer to utilise the IFCT's state-guaranteed reputation for stability to acquire low-interest, foreign-currency loans from international sources.[84] The state has accepted and promoted this situation and various governments have continually used the authority of the state to promote the IFCT both within Thailand and overseas. Its efforts in this area are in contrast to its measures ostensibly designed to aid small entrepreneurs.

In the second phase of the first Plan the government noted that some assistance was required for small-scale industries 'in which category falls by far the majority of Thailand's total industrial establishments'.[85] Accordingly, 20 million *baht* was set aside for loans not exceeding 500,000 *baht* each.[86] While many small entrepreneurs applied for such loans, unlike the IFCT, the government did not substantially increase its commitment in this area From 1964 to 1976, applications for loans totalling 759 million *baht* were received, but only 294 million was lent to 941 applicants. This performance should be measured against a 1976 survey which showed that the real demand for capital by small- and medium-scale firms, for expansion alone, was 900-1,000 million *baht* per year.[87] The state has chosen to neglect small industry in favour of consolidating and expanding the position of large capital.

A strikingly similar pattern of state intervention in favour of big capital can be seen in the commercial banking sector. This sector had received little legislative attention after 1945, but in 1962 the new Commercial Banking Act was promulgated. The basic aim of this Act was to increase public confidence in the banks, so as to attract increased deposits (as suggested by the IBRD mission). As far as the government was concerned, banking had become an essential element of the economic system:

> Operations of commercial banks in which the main resources of the country are concentrated ... have an important bearing on the economic development policy of the country. Thus, at this take-off stage ... it is vital that measures be taken to build up a firm foundation for a sound banking system.[88]

Whilst some commercial bankers expressed reservations about the new Act, the results over the long term were evidential. Between 1961 and 1965, deposits grew by 240 per cent from 5,000 million *baht* to 12,000 million, and by a further 1,400 per cent to 170,000 million at the end of 1979.[89] There is little doubt that depositors, who were not taxed on interest earned on deposits, found commercial banks attractive, stable and secure, qualities which seemed to be lacking in the 1950s.

Soon after the 1962 Act came into force legislation was also created to control the small, 'irrational', financial sector. The Pawnshop Act (1962) was an attempt by the government to limit the role of these shops, and to take capital out of their hands and place it in the commercial banking sector.[90] Pawnshops were effectively limited to the poor who did not have investible cash assets.

Certainly, the unorganised capital market still exists, but its role has diminished over the years, while commercial banks have grown ever stronger, becoming more interested in banking proper rather than the financing of trade. The result of this state-initiated reorganisation of the capital market has already been noted: the financial bourgeoisie is the dominant fraction of the contemporary Thai bourgeoisie.

(c) State policy towards the urban working class and organised labour

Within the general context of its concern with providing the condition for accumulation, the state has consistently taken the side of capital in its disputes with labour, and has severely curtailed the rights of workers to organise themselves. The result has been that workers' struggles have been most prominent when the state itself has been divided by internal rivalry (e.g. 1956-8 and 1973-6).

Phibun, in his attempts to outmanoeuver his political rivals, Sarit and Police-General Phao Sriyanon, had legalised unions in 1956. No doubt Phibun hoped that he could control the unions to his own advantage, but many of the newly-formed unions organised strikes, demanding better wages and conditions for their members.[91]

When Sarit assumed full control of the government unions were again banned, and some 200 labour leaders were arrested.[92] Sarit announced that he would 'eliminate all behaviour which caused disunity . . . ', and unions clearly fell into this category.[93] Sarit's 'Thai-style democracy', where the government knew what was best for all, became the order of the day. Strikes were absolutely forbidden, and although some workers risked imprisonment to demand their rights, the government reported only eighty-two strikes between 1958 and 1968.[94] Both local and international capital were generally satisfied with this situation as it allowed them to keep wages extremely low without too much fear of retaliation from labour. Certainly the big capitalists actively encouraged state policy in this area, and concurred with the state's reasoning on the need to ban strikes and unions. The Bangkok Bank explained that:

> We have found from past experience that whenever trade unions are allowed . . . they fall into the hands of undesirable elements who use the trade unions as a tool to subvert the democratic working of Government. Therefore, for security reasons, it has been found necessary to prevent the functioning of any trade union.

As far as the Bank was concerned, the problems between workers and capitalists could best be resolved by the government itself acting as a 'safeguard to prevent any employer from indulging in any malpractices . . . [It] will be in a position to take appropriate measures to prevent any employer from exploiting his workers.'[95]

Now unexpectedly, the government, having abolished the (inadequate) labour legislation of 1957, did not see any need for such legislation, and it was not until 1969 that another law was drafted, to be promulgated in 1972, but again in an inadequate form.[96] So, from 1958 to 1972, the only legal 'protection' a worker had was a 1965 Act on dispute settlement, designed more for the employer than the employee.

By 1971 reports of gross exploitation of workers had become commonplace. Some 500,000 factory workers were receiving wages of only 7-10 *baht* per day, which was barely adequate for food alone, and thousands were forced to sleep at their workplace. There was little or no compensation for overtime, holidays, accidents or sickness; there was no guarantee of employment; working conditions were often unsafe and unhealthy; and child labour was not uncommon.[97] While workers paid dearly with their labour, health and lives, capitalists continued to accumulate. Table 10.4 gives an indication of the surplus-value extracted by industrial capitalists.

Table 10.4 *Average profits per employee, Bangkok industrial sector, 1972*

Size of firm	No. of firms	Average profit/employee
1-5 employees	9,134	11,300 *baht*
6-9	6,761	7,600
10-49	1,775	9,900
50-99	374	34,100
100-249	184	31,800
250-500	71	61,400
500-1000	24	19,700
more than 1000	17	46,300

Source: adapted from N.K. Sarkar, *Industrial Structure of Greater Bangkok*. (Bangkok, United Nations Asian Institute for Economic Development and Planning, 1974), p.31.

Exploitation of the level indicated in Table 10.4 was compounded in 1971-3 by a domestic slump and inflation, and strikes began to occur with regularity. From 1969 to 1972 there were 108 officially recorded strikes, involving more than 21,000 workers. However, as the demise of the military regime grew more likely, strikes mushroomed, with 501 occurring in 1973. From 1973 to 1976, when workers had far more freedom to organise following the overthrow of the dictatorship, there were a further 716 strikes, involving over 261,000 workers.[98]

Initially capitalists were not too concerned about this increased activity as they were able to resist workers' demands or make but small concessions. However, as the strikes multiplied, the first warnings by capitalists to workers were issued, when Major-General Pramarn Adireksarn, then president of the Association of Thai Industries, and a leading political figure, stated that strikes were still technically illegal, and that there would be serious economic problems if strikes did not cease.[99] Not long after there were declines in both domestic and foreign investment levels, and coupled with the defeat of the US in Indochina, wealthy Thais began to channel their money overseas.[100] Thai capitalists and state officials became increasingly determined to defeat the workers, and the government repeatedly used the state's repressive powers (augmented with privately-hired thugs and assassins) to break strikes. For example, in one instance 100 anti-riot police were used to smash picket-lines established by women textile workers, and in another, about 200 Red Gaur thugs were hired by the management of the Dusit Thani Hotel to break a strike there in 1975.[101]

Nevertheless, in the 1973-6 period unions did manage to double the minimum wage paid in Bangkok. However, the Thai bourgeoisie, foreign investors, and factions within the military had decided that a situation where labour was becoming more militant and where the business and political climate was becoming increasing unstable could not continue. Thus, in October 1976 the military returned to power following a bloody massacre of students at Thammasat University in Bangkok. The new administration quickly sought to rectify the situation for business, allowing previously delayed projects to begin immediately with BoI incentives.[102] Local capitalists felt even more secure when the nominally civilian government of Thanin Kraivichian was replaced by General Kriangsak Chomanan's administration in 1977.

If these state policies of fragmentation and disruption of working class (and peasant[103]) movements are compared to the promotional attitudes of state officials towards organisation within the bourgeois class (e.g. trade associations, chambers of commerce, Board of Trade),[104] then it is again clear that the state has deliberately represented the interests of capital. Repression of the working class has been one of the state's essential political and economic tasks in providing a climate conducive to the accumulation of capital.

3 Concluding remarks

To note that the international capitalist system is extremely complex is to acknowledge the obvious. At times, though, the obvious needs to be emphasised, for far too often there have been attempts to provide generalised explanations of Third World development which tend to obscure this obvious fact. Thailand, as one, small part of this complex system may or may not be a representative case, but this chapter has, I believe, shown that the Thai state has operated in the interests of those fractions of the bourgeoisie representing large-scale financial and industrial capital. This has been especially so since 1958.

Political and economic intervention by the state has allowed the bourgeoisie to expand its accumulative base to the extent that it has moved from a reliance on trade and petty commodity production to financial and industrial activities. While state intervention has also enhanced the position of foreign capital, Thai capitalists were prepared to pay this price.

Clearly, the Thai bourgeoisie is not merely a comprador bourgeoisie, and the state has not acted as a mere intermediary between domestic and international capital. While some Thai capitalists do cooperate with foreign capital, this is a necessary role to be filled in the modern, international, capitalist system, even in the advanced industrial societies. And, the same can be said for the role of the Thai state. In all capitalist societies the state plays a more or less active role in economic affairs, and this necessarily involves foreign capital. The point I have tried to make in this chapter, however, is that the Thai state has not just taken a passive, intermediary role, but has actively promoted domestic capital. Indeed, through the BoI and other state institutions, the state has sought to regulate the conditions under which foreign capital operates while, at the same time, being mindful of the fact that the Thai bourgeoisie operates within an expanding international system. No capitalist or capitalist state can afford to ignore this fact.

Notes

I am grateful to the editors of this book, and to Tony Diller, Vacharin McFadden, Suthy Prasartset, B.J. Terwiel and John Girling for advice, criticism and encouragement while I was researching this chapter. Of course, I am responsible for the final product and any errors it might contain. My thanks also to the School of Human Communication, Murdoch University, and the Faculty of Asian Studies, Australian National University, for providing the facilities necessary for the completion of this chapter.

1 The works referred to are: David A. Wilson, *Politics in Thailand*, (Ithaca, Cornell University Press, 1962); William J. Siffin, *The Thai Bureaucracy: Institutional Change and Development*, (Honolulu, East-West Center Press, 1966); and Fred W. Riggs, *Thailand: The Moderniz-ation of a Bureaucratic Polity*, (Honolulu, East-West Center Press, 1966).

2 This summary cannot do full justice to these writers. Riggs in particular

produced a novel structural-functionalist analysis – see D.C. O'Brien, 'Modernisation, Order and the Erosion of a Democratic Ideal: American Political Science 1960-1970', *Journal of Development Studies*, 8(4), (1972), pp.351-78.

3 Examples of dependency theory applied to Thailand are: Peter F. Bell, *The Historical Determinants of Underdevelopment in Thailand*, Yale Economic Growth Center, Discussion Paper No. 84, 1970; and Malcolm Caldwell, 'Thailand: Towards the Revolution', *Race & Class*, 18(2), (1976), pp.129-53.

4 See the introductory chapter in this book, and Nicola Swainson, 'State and Economy in Post-Colonial Kenya, 1963-1978', *Canadian Journal of African Studies*, 12(3), (1978), pp.357-81. The important 'Kenyan debate' on the nature of development has been discussed in P.F. Chapman, *The Development Debate: Some Theoretical Implications of the Kenyan Case*, M.A. Thesis, Sussex University, 1980.

5 Richard Robison, 'Culture, Politics and Economy in the Political History of the New Order', *Indonesia*, No. 31, (1981), p.8.

6 James C. Ingram, *Economic Change in Thailand 1850-1970*, (Stanford, Stanford University Press, 1971), pp.94, 312.

7 T.H. Silcock, 'Economic Effects of Thai Policy at the End of World War II', *Australian Outlook*, 22(1), (1968), pp.41-4. For President Truman's assessment see Edwin F. Stanton, *Brief Authority*, (New York, Harper & Brothers, 1956), p.165. Stanton was appointed as US Ambassador to Thailand in 1946. It is interesting to note that prior to World War II the Japanese viewed Thailand as both a source of raw materials and a strategically important area – see Benjamin A. Batson, 'Siam and Japan: The Perils of Independence', in Alfred W. McCoy (ed.), *Southeast Asia Under Japanese Occupation*, (New Haven, Yale University Southeast Asia Studies, Monograph Series No. 22, 1980), p.273.

8 *East Meets West in Thailand*, (Washington D.C.: Mutual Security Agency, n.d. (c. 1952)), p.1. This statement is almost identical to a National Security Council memorandum of 1952 quoted in Mark Selden, 'America's Global Enterprise and Asia', *Bulletin of Concerned Asian Scholars*, 7(2), (1975), pp.21-2.

9 For some of the reasons behind this move see Silcock, *op. cit.*, and M.S. Venkataramani, 'The United States and Thailand: The Anatomy of Super-Power Policy-Making, 1948-1963', *International Studies*, 12(1), (1973), pp.57-110.

10 David A. Wilson, *The United States and the Future of Thailand*, (New York, Praeger Publishers, 1970), p.144; Marcia Brewster, 'The Role of U.S. Aid in the Economic Development of Thailand', *Bank of Thailand Monthly Review*, 11(3), (1971), pp.30-1; and Boonkong Hunchangsith, *Economic Impact of the U.S. Military Presence in Thailand*, Ph.D. Thesis, Claremont Graduate School, 1974, p.31.

11 *Bank of Thailand Monthly Report*, 1(1), 1961.

12 On this see Fred L. Block, *The Origins of International Economic Disorder*, (Berkeley, University of California Press, 1977), Chapters 3-4; and Cheryl Payer, *The Debt Trap*, (Harmondsworth, Penguin Books, 1974).

13 See Narongchai Akrasanee, 'Growth and Structural Change in the Manufacturing Sector in Thailand 1960-69', *The Developing Economies*, 11(4), (1973), pp.416-42.

14 *Thailand Investment Bulletin*, 5(1), (1980), pp.1, 7-11.

15 The quotations are from two BoI promotional brochures, *Welcome to Thailand*, and *Thailand Welcomes Foreign Investment*, n.d.

16 Sirilak Sakkriangkriaai, 'Ton gamnoet chonchan naithun nai prathet thai ph.s. 2398-2453', in Chatthip Nartsupha (ed.), *Wiwatthanakan thunniyom thai*, (Bangkok, Faculty of Economics, Chulalongkorn University, and the Economics Students Group, Thammasat University, 1980), pp.77-97; and Thawisin Supwatthana, 'Khwam phayayam khong chaonai thai nai kan longthun thang setthakit: suksa chapho karani phrachaoboromawongthoe khromphra Narathip Praphanphong', *Warasan Thammasat*, 9(1), (1979), pp.99-119.

17 *Ibid.*; and Chatthip Nartsupha and Suthy Prasartset (eds), *The Political Economy of Siam (1851-1910)*, (Bangkok, The Social Science Association of Thailand, 1976).

18 Sirilak, *op. cit.*, pp.98-110; and George William Skinner, *A Study of Chinese Community Leadership in Bangkok, together with an Historical Survey of Chinese Society in Thailand*, Ph.D. Thesis, Cornell University, 1954, pp.121-88.

19 Thawisin, *op. cit.*, pp.106-11; Chatthip and Suthy (eds), *op. cit.*, pp.17-19, 216-44.

20 Charles A. Leckie, 'The Commerce of Thailand in Relation to the Trade of the British Empire' (1894), reprinted in Chatthip and Suthy (eds), *op. cit.*, pp.92-3.

21 Toemsakdi Krishnamra, 'Commercial Banks in Thailand', *Warasan Phanitchayasat lae kan banchi*, 1(4), (1963), pp.17-18; and Skinner, *op. cit.*, pp.135-6.

22 Sirilak, *op. cit.*, p.96.

23 Ingram, *op. cit.*, pp.126-36.

24 Benjamin A. Batson, *The End of the Absolute Monarchy in Thailand*, Ph.D. Thesis, Cornell University, 1977, pp.222-3.

25 'Announcement of the People's Party' (24 June 1932), reprinted in Thak Chaloemtiarana (ed.), *Thai Politics: Extracts and Documents 1932-1957*, (Bangkok, The Social Science Association of Thailand, 1978), pp.4-7.

26 Prayoon Phamonmontri, 'The Political Change of 1932', in *ibid.*; and Batson, *The End, op. cit.*, p.276.

27 Economic nationalism had also begun to play a part in royalist thinking in the sixth and seventh reigns, but given the symbiotic relationship described above, it was extremely difficult for the monarchy to act decisively on these matters, as was also the case after 1932.

28 Ingram, *op. cit.*, pp.135-7; and Suthy Prasartset, *State Capitalism in the Development Process, Thailand 1932-1959*, (Tokyo, Institute of Developing Economies, 1979).

29 Yu Chung-hsun, 'Income and Investment Among Overseas Chinese', *The Developing Economies*, 13(2), (1975), p.133.

30 Bank of Thailand, *Thi raluk wan khrop rob bi thi yisip*, (Bangkok, Bank of Thailand, 1962), p.17.

31 T.H. Silcock, 'Thai Money: A Review Article', *The Malayan Economic Review*, 11(1), (1966), p.109.

32 Krirkkiat Phipatseritham, quoted in *Sayam nikon*, (16 July 1979), p.10.

33 Larry Sternstein, *Thailand. The Environment of Modernisation*, (Sydney, McGraw-Hill, 1976), p.178.

34 For example, in 1961 the Bangkok Bank alone financed almost 20 per cent of Thai imports and just over 26 per cent of exports – *Bangkok Bank Monthly Review*, 3(2), (1962), p.27.

35 Toemsakdi, *op. cit.*, p.25 for the 1946 figure, and *Bank of Thailand Monthly Report*, 2(10), (1962), for the 1961 statistics.

36 Cited in Amos Yoder, 'Patterns of Foreign Investment in Thailand', *Far Eastern Survey*, (November 1957), p.173.

37 Data from Suthy Prasartset, *The Impact of Transnational Corporations on Economic Structure in Thailand*, Paper given at Conference on Asian Peace Research in the Global Context, Yokohama, 1-5 December 1980, p.2.

38 *Bank of Thailand Statistical Bulletin*, 19(12), (1979).

39 See Seth S. King, 'US Money for Thailand Bases Spurs Expansion in Bangkok', *New York Times*, (13 February 1966), p.8; and Malinee Isaradej, 'Thai Economy at the Close of the Second U.N. Development Decade: Problems and Prospects', *Asian Profile*, 7(2), (1979), p.167.

40 *Thailand Investment Bulletin*, 3(11), (1979), p.23.

41 Interview with the managing director of a Thai-Australian engineering joint-venture who was also a member of the Australian-Thai Chamber of Commerce, Bangkok, May 1980.

42 *Business in Thailand*, (August 1976), p.60.

43 *Sayam rat sapda wichan*, (30 March 1980), p.6.

44 *Ibid.*, and the issues of this magazine published on 6 April, 13 April, and 20 April 1980, indicate these relationships. I have discussed this in 'The Financial Bourgeoisie in Thailand', *Journal of Contemporary Asia*, 11(4), (1981), pp.395-412. Data on the international connections of Thai business people are difficult to obtain, but see Rob Salamon, 'Chin Sophonpanich: The Bangkok Connection', *Insight*, (June 1978), pp.8-18.

45 On the Chinese see Skinner, *op. cit.*, pp.317ff. A general survey of the Thai-ification process is given in Eliezer B. Ayal, 'Thailand', in Frank H. Golay *et al.*, *Underdevelopment and Economic Nationalism in Southeast Asia*, (Ithaca, Cornell University Press, 1969), pp.267-340.

46 Amnuay Viravan, 'Economic Policy and Political Structure in Thailand', *Warasan phanitchayasat lae kan banchi*, 5(3), (1967), p.272. Data in Thuan Kanchananaga (compiler), *The Commercial and Economic Progress of Thailand 1949*, (Bangkok, Thai Commercial Development Bureau, n.d.), pp.89-94, suggests that the level of production in these government enterprises fell well short of imports in all areas except gunny bags.

47 John L.S. Girling, *Thailand: Society and Politics*, (Ithaca, Cornell University Press, 1981), pp.75-6.

48 This is not the place for a full discussion of the NEDCOL case, but see Chakrit Noranitpadungkarn, 'Thailand's National Economic Develop-

ment Corporation Limited: An Evaluation with Special Emphasis on the Political Implication(s)', *Thai Journal of Development Administration*, 9(4), (1969), pp.732-45.

49 Hewison, *op. cit.*

50 See Veeravat Karchanadul and Suphachai Sirisuwanakura, 'Thailand', in Nguyen-Truong (ed.), *The Role of Public Enterprise in National Development in Southeast Asia*, (Singapore, Regional Institute of Higher Education and Development, 1976), pp.260-6.

51 Bangkok Chamber of Commerce, *Directory, 1955-56*, (Bangkok, 1956), pp.A1-A2.

52 Sarit's political ideology cannot be expanded upon here. Excellent studies of this are: Toru Yano, 'Sarit and Thailand's Pro-American Policy', *The Developing Economies*, 6 (September 1963), pp.284-99; Thak Chaloemtiarana, 'Khwam khit thang kanmuang khong chomphon Sarit Thanarat lae rabop kanmuang baep phokhun upatham', in Sombat Chantornwong and Rangsan Thanaphonaphan (eds), *Rak muang thai*, Vol.1., (Bangkok, The Social Science Association of Thailand, 1976), pp.35-81; and Thak's *Thailand: The Politics of Despotic Paternalism*, (Bangkok, Thai Khadi Research Institute, 1979).

53 *Fortune*, (April 1958), p.232; on the political and economic objectives of US aid, Belford L. Seabrook, in an AID/United States Operation Mission (USOM) paper given at a Technicians' Staff Meeting on 'Industrial Development in Thailand', Bangkok, 24 September 1963, stated that the Kennedy administration, 'like its predecessors, is dedicated to the proposition that the foreign assistance effort cannot succeed without a substantial increase in the participation of private business both from the United States and from the countries whose economic and social development is a major goal .... The United States has a national interest in the maintenance ... of a significant measure of private initiative ... and in the avoidance of state control ...'.

54 International Bank for Reconstruction and Development (IBRD), *A Public Development Program for Thailand*, (Baltimore, the Johns Hopkins Press, 1959); W.L. van Rijnberk, *Industrial Development Policy and Planning in Thailand*, (New York, United Nations Department of Economic and Social Affairs, Report TAO/THA/14, 10 January 1961), for the Government of Thailand.

55 T.H. Silcock, 'Outline of Economic Development 1945-65', in Silcock (ed.), *Thailand Social and Economic Studies in Development*, (Canberra, Australian National University Press, 1967), p.20.

56 Amnuay, *op. cit.*, p.272.

57 Cited in Frank C. Darling, 'Marshal Sarit and Absolutist Rule in Thailand', *Pacific Affairs*, 33(4), (1960), p.354.

58 IBRD, *op. cit.*, pp.94-106.

59 The USOM involvement is noted in Jack Bailhe (Chief, Private Enterprise Division, USOM/Thailand), 'The Board of Investment', In-Depth Presentation at the Director's Staff Meeting, USOM, Bangkok, 13 March 1970.

60 BoI, *Promotion of Investment Act B.E. 2503 (1960 and Ministerial*

Regulation No. 1 and No. 2, (Bangkok, BoI, 1961).

61 Prior to the promulgation of the new Act two, 'Revolutionary' Party Announcements, Nos 33 and 47, had been in force, but these too had proved to be of little interest, especially to foreign investors – see *Fortune*, (October 1959), p.91.

62 *Bank of Thailand Monthly Report*, 2(2), (1962), pp.12-18 lists the important features of the Act.

63 Another deciding factor, especially for foreign investors, would have been the Kennedy administration's solid commitment to Thailand over the crisis in Laos, epitomised in the Thanat-Rusk joint agreement of 1962 – see Venkataramani, *op. cit.*, pp.100-10.

64 Pote Sarasin, 'Industrial Development Policy', *Foreign Affairs Bulletin* (Bangkok), 5(1), (1965), p.21.

65 It is not possible, in a chapter of this nature, to provide an adequate account of the development of class forces in Thailand, and especially of the competition between various fractions of the bourgeoisie. An indication of such competition may be seen in the *Bangkok Bank Monthly Review*, 3(6), (1962), pp.1-3, where protectionists are attacked by the powerful capitalists who thought of themselves as free traders. On the political influence of these big capitalists see Hewison, *op. cit.*

66 *Bangkok Bank Monthly Review*, 3(2), (1962), p.2.

67 Ingram, *op. cit.*, p.291. For the same period two-thirds of registered capital was said to be Thai.

68 BoI, *Industrial Development in Thailand*, (Bangkok, BoI, Office of the Prime Minister, n.d.), p.9.

69 *Bangkok Bank Monthly Review*, 4(3) (1963), pp.61-3.

70 National Economic Development Board (NEDB), *The National Economic Development Plan, 1961-1966. Second Phase: 1964-1966*, (Bangkok, Office of the Prime Minister, 1964), pp.10, 84-7.

71 National Economic and Social Development Board (NESDB), *Summary of the Third Five-Year Plan (1972-1976)*, (Bangkok, Office of the Prime Minister, 1972), p.9. USOM had been urging this change since 1970 at least, according to a USOM mimeo, 'Recent Economic Developments', August 1970, p.4.

72 H.V. Richter and C.T. Edwards, 'Recent Economic Developments in Thailand', in Robert Ho and E.C. Chapman (eds), *Studies of Contemporary Thailand*, (Canberra, Australian National University, Research School of Pacific Studies, 1973), p.35.

73 *Bangkok Bank Annual Report 1979*, (Bangkok, 1980), and *Sayam rat sapda wichan*, (30 March 1980), pp.4-7 and (13 April 1980) pp.3-4.

74 *Sayam rat sapda wichan*, (13 April 1980), pp.3-4; Krirkkiat, *op. cit.*, pp.330-440; and Hewison, *op. cit.*

75 *Bangkok Bank Monthly Review*, 4(12), (1963), pp.187-8.

76 This figure, which, given the ability of transnational corporations to disguise their capital flows, is obviously an underestimate, is derived from *Business Review* (Bangkok), (December 1972), p.116, and Suthy, *The Impact, op. cit.*, p.3.

77 Puey Ungphakorn, *The International Economic Position of Thailand*,

Address to the Thai Council on World Affairs and International Law, Bangkok, 20 October 1969, pp.3-4 of USOM translation. A similar view was expressed by the Bangkok Bank – see note 66.

78 IBRD, *op. cit.*, pp.103-4, 204-6.

79 NEDB, *op. cit.*, p.87.

80 *Bank of Thailand Bulletin*, 1(2), (1960), p.29.

81 See Chamlong Tohtong, 'Practice and Problems of the Industrial Finance Corporation of Thailand', *Bangkok Bank Monthly Review*, 5(2), (1964), pp.47-51; Chitti Tingsabadh *et al.*, *Credit and Security in Thailand*, (St Lucia, University of Queensland Press, 1974), Chapter 10; and *Business in Thailand*, (September 1976), pp.54-7.

82 IBRD, *op. cit.*, p.103.

83 IFCT, *Annual Report*, 1964 and 1978 issues; and Chitti, *op. cit.*, p.122.

84 *Business in Thailand*, (September, 1976), p.55.

85 NEDB, *op. cit.*, p.89.

86 *Bank of Thailand Monthly Report*, 4(4), (1964), p.23, and 4(9), (1964), p.22. Note, however, that a list of twenty-six ineligible small industries was attached.

87 Saeng Sanguanruang *et al.*, *Development of Small and Medium Manufacturing Enterprises in Thailand*, (Bangkok, ADIPA Research Project, Vol.1: Main Report, 1978), pp.131-48.

88 *Bank of Thailand Monthly Report*, 2(5), (1962), p.8.

89 *Ibid.*, 6(6), (1966), and *Bank of Thailand Statistical Bulletin*, 19(12), (1979).

90 *Bank of Thailand Monthly Report*, 3(1), (1963), pp.24-6.

91 See Bevars, D. Mabry, *The Development of Labor Institutions in Thailand*, (Ithaca, Cornell University, Southeast Asia Program, Data Paper No. 112, 1979), pp.45-7; and D. Insor (pseudonym), *Thailand. A Political, Social, and Economic Analysis*, (London, George Allen & Unwin, 1963), pp.96-7.

92 Jan Schut, 'Focus on labour: Are the laws at fault?', *The Investor* (Bangkok), (June 1975), p.8.

93 Thak, 'Khwam khit thang', pp.45-9.

94 Mabry, *op. cit.*, p.52.

95 *Bangkok Bank Monthly Review*, 5(5), (1964), pp.145-6.

96 Schut, *op. cit.*, p.8.

97 *Bangkok World*, (2 September 1971), p.2. The Thai government had used low wages as a means of attracting foreign investors – see BoI, Ministry of Industry, and the Agency for International Development, *Thailand. Private Investment Opportunities. A Summary of the Investment Climate and Economic Status of Thailand*, (Bangkok, 1968), pp.9-10, where it is stated that even the wages of highly skilled machine tool operators were only 400-600 *baht* per week.

98 Mabry, *op. cit.*, p.52; and Randy Stross, 'The Junta pursues Foreign Capital', *Southeast Asia Chronicle*, No. 60, (1978), p.20.

99 *Bangkok Post*, (5 December 1973), pp.9, 11.

100 James Leung, 'Nervous Thai money pouring into HK', *South China Morning Post*, (12 June 1975), p.1.

101 *Bangkok Post*, (29 May 1975), pp.1, 3, and various issues, 1 May – 13 June 1975.

102 *Ibid.*, (21 December 1976), pp.1, 3.

103 No attempt has been made to describe similar attacks on the peasant movement in 1973-6. On this see Andrew Turton, 'The Current Situation in the Thai Countryside', in Andrew Turton *et al.*, *Thailand. Roots of Conflict*, (Nottingham, Spokesman Books, 1978), pp.121-9.

104 On this see Montri Chenvidyakarn, 'Economic Interest Groups in Thailand: Some Observations on Legal Aspects, Public Policy and Political Process', *Social Science Review*, (Bangkok), No. 2, (1977), pp.224-77.

11 Class, capital and the state in New Order Indonesia

RICHARD ROBISON – *Murdoch University*

1 Approaches to the analysis of the New Order state

The New Order government of President Suharto has been a fascination for scholars and political commentators since its emergence in 1965. Yet the cause of this fascination, and the consequent analysis of power and conflict in contemporary Indonesia, differ fundamentally according to the theoretical and ideological frameworks within which these analyses are, consciously or unconsciously, located.

It is the intention of this chapter to draw out the theoretical inadequacies of existing interpretations of the New Order state and its role in the political economy of contemporary Indonesia. At the same time, I will develop a theoretical analysis which attempts to provide a systematic explanation of the relationship between class, economy and politics and to place them in an historical context.

Setting aside those works on Indonesian politics which simply concentrate on the day-to-day manoeuvrings of individuals and factions within the power structure, and make no attempt whatever to place politics in any form of social or economic context, analysis of the New Order has fallen into three theoretical/ideological categories:

a) The political order approach;
b) The economic technocracy approach;
c) The dependency approach.

In the first section of this chapter I will outline the basic features of these approaches and suggest a fourth possible approach which derives from the theoretical questions raised by the productionist critique of dependency theory and the work being done on the 'New International Division of Labour'.

a) The political order approach

This approach is developed in the works of Donald Emmerson, Karl

Jackson and Bill Liddle.[1] It draws upon the structural-functional analysis of politics and society developed by Talcott Parsons, the comparative politics analysis of such political scientists as Lucien Pye and Gabriel Almond, but more immediately, upon the political order approach of Samuel Huntington and Fred Riggs.[2] In general terms it deals with the creation of power and the integration of a social system. In specific terms it asks whether the New Order state has been able to develop political and bureaucratic organizations with sufficient complexity, flexibility and power to integrate a society and polity in a process of upheaval and transition.

Apart from the concern for the problems of generation of political power and administrative efficiency, the basic currency of analysis is, in keeping with the tradition of the behaviouralism of cultural politics, the cultural and psychological attachments of individual political actors. Like Riggs in his analysis of Thailand, the political order analysis of the New Order concludes that the fundamental contradiction in the Indonesian polity is that between modern political structures and traditional political culture. Because politics is conceived and structured in terms of personal relationships between clients and patrons, the increasingly complex and powerful political structures clearly developed by the New Order are harnessed to the needs of individual officials, political factions, patron-client groups and cultural streams rather than to the integration of social and political forces and the pursuit of the common good. The power and resources of the state are appropriated by state officials to further their personal and political advantage and that of their family, clique or political power base. In essence, this is another variation of the conflict between tradition and modernity.

b) The technocracy approach

The intellectual origins of this second approach are the 'end of ideology' analyses of North American political science[3] and development or growth economics which was applied to the Indonesian situation by economists such as Bruce Glassburner and Heinz Arndt. There are three important dimensions to this approach. First, it is assumed that state policy can be conceived and implemented by technocrats on the basis of criteria provided by objective and scientific theories of economics transcendental to and autonomous of social and political conflict. In this sense it is not in contradiction with the political order theory and public policy approaches discussed in detail in Chapter 1 of this book. Second, it is assumed that economic growth theory is non-political in that it seeks the common good in the long term. Third, it is argued, in the case of Indonesia, that the transition from the Sukarno period to the New Order was an inevitable movement from chaos to order, from ideology to objectivity.[4] Such an interpretation was confirmed in a very concrete way by the appointment of trained economists to positions of authority with responsibility for the planning and implementation of economic strategy. The fall of the Sukarno state was considered to be a consequence of the subordination of 'economics' to politics, involving the imposition of irrational and ideological constraints upon rational and scientific economic policy. The movement from the Old Order to the New Order in 1965 was therefore a logical, necessary and indeed, inevitable, retreat from economic ruin.

To the extent that the New Order state has implemented sound economic policy, it and the military who dominate its apparatus, shed their political and ideological identity to become part of a technocracy guided by an apparently objective and scientific logic, with the technocrats as the intermediaries between science and power.

For those who adopt this analysis the measure of success for the New Order state is its ability to implement economic growth strategies. At one level this means strict adherence to the prevailing economic orthodoxies emanating from the World Bank or the Bulletin of Indonesian Economic Studies. The primary conflict in the New Order becomes that between economics and politics; whether or not rational economic goals will be sacrificed to short-term political expedience to satisfy the demands of individual interest groups.[5] A secondary conflict lies at the bureaucratic rather than the political level and is concerned with structural obstacles to growth, including inefficiency, poor management, red tape and corruption.

c) The dependency approach

The most notable dependency interpretation of the New Order state was Rex Mortimer's 'Indonesia: Growth or Development' which appeared in his collection of dependency-oriented articles, *Showcase State*.[6] For Mortimer, the New Order state was one component of an alliance between foreign capital and indigenous politico-bureaucratic forces dominated by the military. In return for access to the largesse which was a by-product of foreign investment, the politico-bureaucrats of the New Order facilitated the entry of foreign capital and the outflow of surplus which constituted the basis for the perpetuation of underdevelopment.

Although Mortimer had written on the process of class formation and conflict in Indonesia, he was generally of the opinion that domestic classes were too weakly developed to constitute the basis of politics. Instead, he argued that traditional, patrimonial networks of patrons and clients, cutting across weakly-formed class structures, provided the real basis of political conflict and organization.

Despite Mortimer's gloomy prognosis for the prospects of revolution, other writers influenced by dependency theory, notably Anderson and Feith, have taken the position that the increasing inequality, misery and repression inherent in the underdevelopment process, together with the accompanying isolation of the ruling group, will provoke a middle-class-led reaction against the New Order state.[7]

d) The productionist critique of dependency theory and its implications for the study of the New Order state

Although it has not yet been welded into a systematic thesis, the Marxist critique of dependency theory has raised some critical theoretical points which have important implications for our conception of the form and function of the state in the Third World.

Most important it has been argued that development and underdevelopment are functions of the development of forms and relations of production rather than consequences of global patterns of exchange. Leys put this point most succinctly:

> What produces underdevelopment is not the 'transfer of surplus' appropriated by metropolitan capital from the periphery to the metropole, significant though this may be. Rather, such a transfer should be seen as an effect of structures at the periphery which militate against the productive investment of the surplus of the periphery. Speaking generally, these are class structures which permit absolute surplus labour to be appropriated, but prevent the realization of relative surplus value.[8]

This immediately throws the focus of analysis upon the development of capitalist relations of production and the development of a class of capital accumulators. The state now becomes crucial because of its strategic role in the process of class formation, class conflict and capital accumulation. Special important questions require resolution. To what extent does the state intervene in political conflict to secure the social and economic dominance of the emerging class of accumulators or to secure the dominance of any one fraction of a bourgeois alliance? To what extent does the state provide the conditions of accumulation through the provision of direct investment, economic infrastructure, protection, credit and monopolies, and a legal and administrative infrastructure? To what extent does the state resolve social, economic and political crises which attend the process of development of industrial capitalism? Such questions mean that the relationship between state and class must be theorized and, in the case of Indonesia, this is particularly crucial where the military rule and the normal channels of institutionalized class domination of the state apparatus do not exist. This leads to further and more specific questions. Is the state autonomous? Do the military bureaucrats constitute a state class? How useful is the Bonapartist notion of the state? How helpful is a structural approach to the understanding of the relationship between state and class?

A second focus of the productionist approach centres around the demands imposed upon the state by different stages of capitalist development. Here the work of Luckham is most useful.[9] He relates the state project to stages of capitalist development, from petty commodity production, to enclave export commodity production, import substitution industrialization and, finally, export-oriented industrialization. As the stages progress, Luckham argues, increasing demands are placed upon the state to provide economic, political, legal and fiscal infrastructure for an increasingly complex accumulation process and to intervene in the social and political conflicts and crises generated by capitalist development on behalf of the accumulators. Consequently, the old forms of direct rule by families, or by loose party alliances of landowners and national bourgeoisie, or by military strongmen, characteristic of merchant capitalism or commodity export economics, must give way to new, complex bureaucratic regimes, often politically dominated by the military but administered by technocrats.

With the emergence of a new international division of labour which is having the effect of relocating manufacture globally, the process of industrialization in the Third World has accelerated. As a result, we are seeing a new type of Third World capitalist economy and state; characterized by high rates of economic growth, rapid industrialization, the development of powerful national bourgeoisie, and strong, authoritarian regimes exhibiting corporatist or even totalitarian tendencies, and developing political ideologies which legitimize power in terms of economic growth and technocratic government. South Korea, Taiwan, Singapore, Brazil and Iran before 1979 are the archetypes of such new states.[10]

The implications for analysis of the New Order regime are clear. To what extent can we explain the structure of the New Order and its policies in terms of the increasing necessity for intervention in the accumulation process brought about by rapid economic growth and industrialization? Is the New Order state moving towards the model capitalist state variously categorized as 'techno-fascist', 'bureaucratic-authoritarian' or 'repressive-developmentalist'?

One problem must be cleared up before I move on to a specific discussion of the Indonesian case. I am not proposing that the nature of the state is determined by an autonomous progression of the economy from one stage to another but, rather, that certain state functions, political and economic, are necessary to specific stages in economic development. Indeed, it is the process of class formation and conflict, and of the development of appropriate political structures, which makes such economic transitions possible. Industrialization cannot progress until certain social and economic preconditions are met: the existence of a potential free wage labour force and of a state able to protect the political interests of capital and provide a minimum of infrastructure. Of course the process is mutually reinforcing and the state will find itself increasingly forced to meet the economic and political demands of the growing bourgeoisie, particularly the international corporations.

2 The origins of the New Order state

The New Order state cannot be explained as the consequences of the political victory of the military or the inevitable triumph of 'economics' over politics or the replacement of patrimonial with technocratic behaviour. It is instead the consequence of a protracted and complex process of social, economic, and political conflict, notably:

i) The weakness of social classes, most importantly the failure of a powerful national bourgeoisie to emerge, enabled the development of a state apparatus in which political power and bureaucratic authority were appropriated and integrated by the military, party and state officials themselves. In the course of the struggle for power amongst these political-bureaucratic groups it was the military which triumphed.

ii) The failure of the national state and the national bourgeoisie to reconstitute the Indonesian economy from a declining colonial agricultural export economy into a state-led manu-facturing economy through import-substitution industrializ-ation (ISI).

iii) The failure of forces of social revolution, comprising significant elements of labour, peasants and intellectuals under the political leadership of the PKI (Indonesian Communist Party), to wrest political power from conserva-tive forces, which included rural landlords, national bour-geoisie and petty bourgeoisie, the urban middle classes and the military.

a) The weakness of the national bourgeoisie

Perhaps the most cohesive and clearly defined, and certainly the most powerful segment of the domestic bourgeoisie, was the Chinese merchants. Until the mid-nineteenth century they had been used by both traditional Javanese and Dutch colonial rulers as tax farmers and operators of state trading monopolies. With the development of estate and small-holder commercial production they began to establish domestic trade and credit networks dealing in rice and small-holder produce, retailing, money-lending and processing of agricultural produce, including rice hulling and sugar milling. With the lifting of travel and residence restrictions in 1908 they began to spread down to the villages, eroding the grip of small Javanese and Sumatran traders. At the same time they moved into the small-scale manufacturing sectors traditionally dominated by indigenous petty commodity producers: textiles, batik and kretek. Despite attempts by political parties, the state and the indigenous bourgeoisie to politically constrain Chinese economic influence, their economic dominance has been consolidated in the post-colonial period, especially after the departure of the Dutch, largely because their economic competitors, both private and state, were so weak.[11]

The power of the Chinese, however, was limited by several factors. Despite their general economic dominance, they were essentially a merchant petty bourgeoisie focused around the extended family with an economic position firmly embedded in the colonial export agricultural economy. Hence, they were unable to provide the basis of capital accumulation and corporate organization for industrialization in Indonesia. Equally important, the Chinese have been unable to secure access to public exercize of political power because of the social hostility of the indigenous population. Whilst they have been politically influential as individuals and economically indispensible as a group they have been forced to secure their interests indirectly through indigenous politico-bureaucrats.

Neither did an indigenous bourgeoisie form the social basis for political transformation of the social and economic order. The bulk of indigenous businessmen under colonial rule were petty commodity producers and small-scale traders in small-holder crops. By 1949, only a handful had expanded their activities to trade on a national level or to factory production employing wage and piece labour and replacing hand with mechanical production processes. Political and economic organization of the indigenous bourgeoisie, beginning from the formation of the *Sarekat Dagang Islam* in 1911 attempted to meet the Chinese challenge by securing control of trade, especially in the field of batik and textiles. By the early 1930s, after some early success, the surge had exhausted itself, not only because they had failed to secure control of trade but because economic power was now increasingly located in capital investment, i.e. industrial and finance capital was beginning to challenge merchants' capital. In the traditional areas of indigenous manufacture (kretek cigarettes, textiles, batik, beverages and foodstuffs) the indigenous producers found themselves increasingly outweighed by the superior capital resources of Chinese and international capital.[12]

Although private land title and increasing commercialization of agricultural production were introduced from the mid-nineteenth century, no economically dominant, landowning class emerged to constitute a politically cohesive force at the national level. The traditional Javanese ruling class had not converted their rights to agricultural produce into private landownership but instead became salaried officials of the Dutch – an agrarian bureaucracy rather than a class of hacienda owners.[13] At the village level the concentration of landownership was a slow and fitful process whilst politics was not defined by rival camps of landed and landless but by complex patron-client networks which mediated the conflicting social interests of different classes. The structure of the rural classes remained a confused amalgam of landlords, tenants and independent peasant proprietors and the real process of class development and capitalist transformation of rural society was to begin after independence and only accelerate in the 1960s and 1970s.

So from 1949 to 1965, the state operated in a vacuum of social power. However, there began a tentative crystallization of a new capitalist ruling class around the state, which proved to be the only concentration of political and economic power with the potential to develop national capitalism. A crucial element in this development was the relatively small group of party leaders and state officials who appropriated the state apparatus, fusing political power and bureaucratic authority. Parties, factions of parties and military commands secured control of various strategic sections of the state apparatus, dividing amongst themselves government departments, banks, state corporations controlling trade, economic policy, resources, credit and contracts. Economically strategic offices were filled with party and military officials who used the resources and power of office to finance the political operation of party and military factions and to enlarge the personal wealth of individual politico-bureaucrats. Using appropriated power to allocate licenses, concessions, credit and contracts, the politico-bureaucrats were able to construct economic alliances with the major Chinese and indigenous business groups.[14]

The most important implication of the weak and fragmented class structure, however, was the weakness and strength it simultaneously imposed upon the state. No class was able to impose its authority on the state, in either an instrumentalist sense (through the institution of a political party) or structuralist sense (through the exercize of structural imperatives), by virtue of highly developed social or economic power. Consequently, the state was both relatively free of the dominance of social forces and forced to play a central role in the process of capital accumulation. But at the same time, the weakness of classes meant that the power of the state was not embedded in deeply entrenched social and ideological structures developed by a dominant class upon the institutions of land or capital and institutionalized in party structures. It was a civil and military bureaucracy perched upon an uncertain, fragmented and unstable social structure.

b) The failure of Import Substitution Industrialization (ISI)

The new Indonesian Republic inherited a colonial, export-oriented, agrarian economy based on Dutch corporate investment in plantation production and trade. During the early years of independence, the Indonesian state was confronted with the enormous difficulties of interfering with this colonial economy. State revenue, foreign exchange earnings and the existing social order were predicated upon agricultural and mineral exports financed and managed by Dutch and Chinese bourgeoisie. Many centres of political-bureaucratic power and their Chinese and indigenous business associates indeed developed interests in the colonial economy by selective establishment of monopoly positions within its framework, particularly in the import sector. But at the same time, other forces were pushing for appropriation of the Dutch interests. These included the PKI, labour unions, economic nationalist elements within the PNI (Indonesian National Party), and even indigenous business associations who hoped to step into the shoes of the departing Dutch. The military also took a leading role in the process of nationalization, initially because of its alarm at the unilateral seizure of the Dutch corporations by labour unions, but in the long term because the appropriated Dutch plantations and trading houses promised and provided the military with valuable sources of revenue.[15]

Economic nationalism not only involved appropriation of the colonial economy but an attempt to build a national import substitution industrial section. The economic policies known as Guided Economy provided a blue print for state-led capitalist development involving the use of foreign exchange earnings from oil, mineral and agricultural exports as a basis for investment in industry together with varying degrees of state protection and credit for national industrial capital. Large-scale overseas borrowing was also undertaken to provide for investments in such capital goods industries as steel mills and shipyards.[16]

The drive to ISI failed for a variety of reasons. The attempt to industrialize suffered from the same problem which had confronted industrialization plans in the 1950s and which had led to the state assuming the dominant role in direct corporate investments as well as financing and policy-making; the Indonesian bourgeoisies, both Chinese and indigenous, were essentially merchant bourgeoisies unable to generate the process of accumulation necessary for industrialization.[17] Indeed, the weakness of the national bourgeoisies was a major factor in the move towards state-led national capitalism in the late 1950s. But the state apparatus was also unable to administer the accumulation process, largely because of the inexperience and inefficiency of the new military managers of state enterprise and their general misuse and misappropriation of state resources. Capital stock, including the plantings in the crucial plantation sector, were allowed to degenerate and little new investment was made.[18] As a result, the export earnings from agricultural products in particular declined sharply causing serious balance of payments problems which eventually rendered Indonesia incapable of servicing its existing debts. Such decline was already under way during the colonial period. Sugar, for example, had been virtually wiped out as an export crop during the depression.[19] A most important consequence was that planned accumulation for purposes of industrial investment did not take place.

By the early 1960s, it was obvious that the state-led national capitalist experiment was foundering. Inflation increased to over 600 per cent; by 1965, the flow of imported consumer goods and spare parts ground to a halt and the economic infrastructure fell into increasing disrepair. Because of declining export income, a stage was reached in 1965 where foreign debts could not be serviced under existing arrangements.[20] This dislocation affected with greatest intensity those elements of society most fully integrated with the previously Dutch-dominated economy: the state officials, the urban middle classes and the domestic bourgeoisie. For these people and the military, the solution appeared increasingly to lie in the reconstitution of capitalist economy with foreign capital as the primary basis of accumulation and organization.

c) The failure of social revolution

These events must be considered together with a process of social and political conflict. This conflict was often confused by ideological and political attachments cutting across class lines. Indeed, the revolutionary party, the PKI, used these non-class divisions for purposes of mobilization and found itself caught between alliance with the politico-bureaucrats and the bourgeoisie in the context of client-patron political structures and revolutionary action based upon a mass base of peasant and proletarian support.

Nevertheless, there is little doubt that class conflict was taking place, occurring with greatest intensity in the countryside. Out of this class conflict emerged a virulent counter-revolutionary move-ment – that of the indigenous petty bourgeoisie and landlords whose opposition to the PKI was defined not only by its material interest in the preservation of capital and private ownership of land but also in its ideological opposition to the PKI as an atheistic and anti-muslim party.[21] Nor was this conflict a recent phenomenon. It stretched back to the political struggles within Indonesia's first nationalist political movement, the *Sarekat Islam*, in the early 1920s.

In reality, the Sukarnoist state cannot be described as a socialist state; it was a state which constituted the interests of national capital and the politico-bureaucrats. Where the state did attempt to implement legislation of a reformist nature, such as the land reforms of 1960, it was frustrated and obstructed at every turn by its own officials and by the power of vested class interests. In a very important sense, the crucial flaw of the Sukarnoist state was its political inability to act decisively in the context of deepening polarization of class conflict, and secure the political victory of either of the antagonists.

The decisive element in the defeat of the PKI was the power of the military. In one sense military opposition to the PKI was the consequence of a history of political and institutional struggle between the only two political forces with the potential to rule Indonesia, stretching back to the period of the anti-Dutch struggle of the late 1940s. But deeper than this lay the military's interest in maintaining its economic appanages and, in the final analysis, in maintaining a social order in which its political dominance was secured.

Much has been written on the reasons for the failure of the PKI and the social revolution in Indonesia,[22] however, two points emerge. The PKI committed serious tactical political errors in sacrificing an emphasis on ideological and organizational cohesion to the mobilization of large numbers whose attachment to the party in many cases was not defined by a commitment to class struggle. But in a very important sense this may have been unavoidable. The potential revolutionary classes, peasants and workers, were weak because of the very weakness of capitalism. Peasant society was a complex and confused mass of small landlords, independent peasant owners, tenants and landless, tied together by various feudal and exchange networks of political and economic obligation. The working class was minute. Neither the political parties nor the Sukarno state could be said to base their authority upon any clearly defined class alliance, but the military, in contrast, found itself beginning to constitute the political expression of a loose, structural alliance of bourgeoisie, petty bourgeoisie and landowning class, increasingly aware of their economic interests and of the implications of the PKI challenge.

In this sense, the military came to power at the head of a counter-revolution. It is this political victory of a specific set of class interests, and not any objective logic of economics, which sets the course for the development of the New Order state and its economic policies in the years from 1965 to 1982.

3 The political structure of the New Order

In formal terms it is the military who rule in New Order Indonesia. During the twenty years since President Suharto secured power, the military has progressively entrenched and centralized its own power and excluded its allies, the students and intellectuals, the muslim petty bourgeoisie and the landlords, from any meaningful political role and has largely managed to muzzle even public criticism of the government. For those outside the military, access to even the outer circles of power and influence is confined to informal patron-client networks or to government-controlled and sponsored corporatist organizations such as *Golkar* (the state political party) and the myriad of state organizations for business, labour, public servants and other 'functional groups'.

This dominance has been made possible, not only because of the political success of the military in establishing these corporate structures and repressive apparatus, or to the social weakness of classes, but because the state occupies a strategic position in the economy. The dominant sources of wealth – oil, gas and minerals – do not produce profits for a national bourgeoisie but revenue for the state who participates in the exploitation of these resources in production-sharing agreements with international corporations. If we add to this the substantial amounts of foreign loans and aid channelled into the government, a picture of considerable financial autonomy from national sources emerges.[23]

Whereas the Sukarno regime justified its authoritarian form as most effectively crystallizing the popular consensus of the masses, the New Order has justified its refinement and extension of the same authoritarian structures as constituting a necessary element in the march towards economic development. This is one reason why the technocrats are important to the regime. The New Order defines itself as a modernizing, developmentalist state, its rule legitimized by the process of economic development. Using the type of arguments used in Huntington's concept of political order, the New Order further explains its monopoly of power and authoritarian rule as a necessary imposition of control over disintegrative and destructive social and political forces during the fragile interregnum between tradition and modernity.[24]

The social forces upon which the New Order state rests have become increasingly well-formed, well-defined and stronger, largely because international finance and industrial capital, largely absent during the Sukarno years, were reintegrated into a broad economic and political alliance. Most important, it is international capital, not of the old Dutch merchant variety but industrial and finance capital. In the seventeen years since the rise of the New Order, capital investment, both national and international, has expanded dramatically; industry now accounts for 13 per cent of GNP[25] and capitalist relations of production are beginning to establish a tentative hold in the countryside.[26] Petty capital has expanded far beyond the ranks of the traditional muslim merchants and petty commodity producers. Large national business groups have emerged, both Chinese and indigenous. Increasingly, the New Order state can be regarded as a capitalist state rooted in the social power of a growing bourgeoisie and consequently much stronger than the fragile, factionalized Sukarnoist state.

How can the New Order state be described as a capitalist state and as constituting the interests of a bourgeois coalition when it is the military, not the bourgeoisie who rule? The answer lies in a structuralist approach to the question. That is, we must look at structural relationships, not motives or formal political relationships. The New Order state does not operate as the instrument of the bourgeoisie or any of its factions (although I am not arguing that a state may not be the virtual instrument of a specific class in specific circumstances) nor does it *represent* their interests. Instead the state *constitutes* the general interests of this coalition (once again, this is a coalition only in a structural sense, not necessarily in the sense that they are bound by formal political agreements or common institutional frameworks) by providing political, ideological and even economic conditions for their existence and for the process of capital accumulation. This can be seen by examining the policies of the state. Most important amongst these has been the elimination of the

PKI and the removal of this most fundamental threat to private property. Land reform has been effectively abandoned, trade unions kept under tight control, finance and infrastructure provided for business. Development has been sought in the consolidation of existing class structures and in the concentration of wealth and power rather than in social change.

Why does the state provide the conditions for the escalation of capitalist transformation and therefore the consolidation of those classes whose dominance is embedded in such a social structure? Here we must leave the structuralist perspective and descend to the concrete and specific circumstances of the Indonesian case because, whilst we can speak of the 'state' as constituting something and functioning in a specific way, we cannot reify the state and attribute motives to it. Therefore, we must examine the specific political and class structures of Indonesia.

Despite the fact that the military have been gradually able to construct a state apparatus which excludes the landowning and bourgeois allies from direct and public exercize of power they nevertheless rule with the support or acquiescence of these classes. Amongst landlords, middle classes, bourgeoisie and petty bourgeoisie, opposition to authoritarian rule by the military and absence of the rule of law is tempered by the fact that the New Order state has provided conditions which have so far enhanced their economic prosperity. Continuing economic development therefore assumes a special significance for the New Order. Through the development budget and such projects as *Bimas*, (providing credit for the introduction of agrarian development packages including new seed varieties, pesticides and fertilizers), the state has provided investment finance, infrastructure, subsidies and contracts.[27] As a basic level, therefore, the structural political alliance between state and bourgeois/landowning class alliance in Indonesia is one forged out of mutual necessity, mutual benefit, and out of a fear of alternatives.

In reality, the military had little choice in the way they set about the reconstruction of the economy. Given the ideological, social and political nature of the counter-revolutionary movement, socialist reconstruction was obviously unacceptable as an option. The state and the national bourgeoisie had proven unable to generate national capitalist development so reintegration within the international capitalist division of labour was, in hindsight, an unavoidable option. The adoption of the growth policies of the technocrats must be seen as a consequence of political and class conflict, not of the intrinsic superiority of economics. The generals embraced the Berkeley technocrats because they offered the policies most integral to the interests of the counter-revolutionary coalition. They were ideologically acceptable to the foreign powers to whom the New Order was turning for assistance in economic rehabilitation, aid and investment. (Of course, as we shall see, foreign corporations and international financial institutions were later to be irritated that the initial enthusiastic, almost obsequious stance of the Berkeley technocrats developed into a much more cautious and ambivalent one.) Equally important, however, the Berkeley technocrats offered a vision of economic development in which the existing social order could be maintained and entrenched. Economic growth was not to be predicated upon social reform or redistribution of wealth but upon increased capital investment, upon technology, upon concentration of economic and social power and upon the assumption that the demonstration effect and the process of trickle down would spontaneously diffuse the growth process.[28]

There is one final factor which cements the military-dominated New Order state to the bourgeois coalition. As will be discussed in much greater detail later, individuals and factions within the state apparatus have been drawn into concrete economic and business partnerships with national and foreign capital. Indeed, the major business groups which have emerged in Indonesia are generally constituted by alliances between international capital, national capital (often Chinese), and indigenous politico-bureaucrats representing themselves or political factions, and state capital. Consequently, politico-bureaucrats have developed a direct proprietary interest in the process of capital accumulation.

4 State and capital under the New Order

a) The state as investor and financier

Because of the weakness of the national bourgeoisie, the accumulation process in Indonesia throughout the post-colonial period has been focused upon the state as an investor and financier as well as a provider of general policies necessary for private capital accumulation. The major source of capital for investment derives from revenues from oil and mineral production and export and from foreign aid. In 1980, oil revenues constituted 70 per cent of foreign exchange earnings and 62 per cent of state revenues. In 1980-1, the state development budget was Rp. 5,916.1 billion of which 42 per cent came from loan funds and the remainder from state savings.[29] We can see how important this is if we compare it to the approved domestic investment which totalled Rp. 3,942.6 billion from 1967-79, and Rp. 688.7 billion in 1979.

The development budget primarily provides funds for projects both through government departments and through local and regional level programmes. These projects are a major source of contracts for private capital both for construction and supply. Direct finance for private and state capital through project loans and government loans is the other major component of the development budget. To December 1980, credit extended by domestic bankers totalled Rp. 7,548 billion (US$12,580 million) of which 29.4 per cent consisted of loans from the Bank of Indonesia, 56.0 per cent from state-owned commercial and investment banks, 7.4 per cent from private domestic banks, and 5.3 per cent through foreign banks in Indonesia.[30] Indeed, the amount of credit available from the state to private capital exceeded the capacity to absorb it. Of the target for investment credit by state banks to the end of 1977, only 65.93 per cent was realized.[31]

The state also invests directly in production and economic organization through state-owned corporations. Various categories of state corporation provide different functions:

a) State banking corporations.
b) State corporations in the resources sector provide infrastructure, act as terminals for the allocation of oil, forestry and minerals concessions, supervize production-sharing agreements and collect taxes and royalties.
c) State corporations involved in direct investment in production, often in joint-ventures, in property, construction, resources and, most important, import substitution industrialization, notably in cement, petrochemicals and steel. The 1974-5 manufacturing figures show state corporations constituting about one-fifth of total output and value added. State firms produced 75.2 per cent of cement, 51.9 per cent of paper and paper products, 40.4 per cent of food manufacturing and 52 per cent of machinery.[32] Since then, extensive state investments have been made in both cement and petrochemicals.
d) State corporations which organize the process of distribution, storage and pricing of basic necessities and therefore mediate social and economic crises. The procurement agency Bulog is the obvious example here, coordinating in particular the politically sensitive area of rice procurement, distribution and pricing.

The role of the state in the process of capital accumulation under the New Order clearly continues the Guided Economy objective of securing national ownership and control of strategic sectors of the economy, and building a national import substitution industrial sector. However, it may increasingly be seen as establishing the preconditions for private capital accumulation, both foreign and domestic. The general point to be made here is that the function of the state in capitalism is defined by the structure of social and political power specific to the society. A comparative look at state capitalism in the Third World would tend to indicate that where the dominant political force is an alliance of national bourgeoisie and nationalist political forces with some popular base, as was the case with the Sukarno state, the result tends to be state-led ISI. Where this political alliance breaks down, the national bourgeoisie and petty bourgeoisie, usually under the political leadership of the military, attempt to secure their political and economic interests within a larger bourgeois coalition including international capital. In this situation, the state will be more concerned with providing infrastructure and credit for private capital, investing in sectors not sufficiently profitable for private capital and mediating a complex process of integration between different sectors of the bourgeois alliance.[33]

b) The state and international capital

Whereas the dependency theorists viewed the state in peripheral or underdeveloped economies as politically facilitating exploitation and economic dominance by foreign capital where the national bourgeoisie was too weak to generate a national capitalist revolution, Warren[34] argued that Third World societies were reproducing the same national, capitalist, industrial revolutions which had taken place in Europe and North America. Clearly, dependency theorists were placed under pressure by mounting evidence that industrial development was taking place in the Third World, that strong national bourgeoisies were emerging and that Third World states were confronting international capital in the interests of protecting and expanding the accumulation of national capital and the economic power of the national bourgeoisie.

Leys has demonstrated, in the case of Kenya, that the state became bound into the process of national capital accumulation:

> The essential function of the state was to displace monopolies enjoyed by foreign capital and substitute monopolies for African capital and also supplement individual African capitals with state finance, capital and state secured technology, to enable them to occupy the space created for them in the newly accessible economic sectors.[35]

However, as Alavi[36] points out, a national bourgeoisie cannot be dismissed as a natural enemy of the international bourgeoisie and, indeed, if a national bourgeoisie is to expand beyond a certain limit it will need to integrate with international corporate capital to gain access to the capital, organizational and technological resources which cannot be developed at the national level. In this situation the state will be required to mediate the process of integration.

It is a fruitless exercise, therefore, to consider the function of the state in the context of an inherent conflict between national and international capital. A national bourgeoisie will generally wish to secure protection and subsidy in those sectors where its capital base enables it to operate alone, but will require the state to mediate its integration with international capital in sectors where its capital resources are inadequate, i.e. in high technology, capital intensive sectors such as oil, mining and the more complex manufacturing processes. International capital will generally demand freedom of movement for capital, profits and goods, and prefer to operate without the requirement that they accept significant national equity in their operations.

The specific configuration of the accommodation between national and international capital and the role of the state in this accommodation will depend upon:

a) The pattern of class power and conflict in the society concerned, most crucially the development of the economic and political power of the national bourgeoisie.
b) The location of the economy concerned in the international division of labour; whether or not it is attractive to international capital and in what sectors.

In the case of Indonesia, the New Order quickly implemented an economic policy based upon maximization of economic growth and the infusion of international capital. In order to attract an inflow of investment and aid, existing foreign debts were negotiated and a new foreign investment law (hereafter PMA) was promulgated in 1967, offering inducements to new foreign investors in the form of tax holidays and guarantees of profit repatriation.[37] There were also, of course, the political inducements for investors offered by a regime which had stamped out radical political forces, including organized labour, with such vigour.

Opposition to the technocrats' early open door policy came from several sources. The first were liberal intellectuals using a dependency-based approach critical of the outflow of profits and damaging effect on local industry but their capacity for effective political action was limited by almost total lack of a power base.[38] A more interesting critique came from the CSIS group (Centre for

Strategic and International Studies – a Chinese Catholic-dominated secretariat/think tank associated with General Ali Murtopo) which argued that national capital is unable to develop effectively within the framework of an open door policy. They argued not for exclusion of foreign capital or isolated, self-reliant development, but for systematic state coordination of the development of national capital. This was to take place within the framework of nationally integrated economic units with the state providing coordination, protection and finance but with capital ownership remaining largely private. Integration of foreign capital was to be subject to wider requirements of planned national capitalist development. Such a concept borrowed heavily from models established by the Meiji state, the present Singapore state and even from the principles which underlay government attempts to coordinate and plan industrial production under Guided Economy.[39]

The nationalist, right-wing corporatism envisaged by CSIS has not found many supporters among the ranks of the major domestic bourgeoisie who have generally managed to either integrate profitably with foreign capital or hide behind state protection of national industry which began to develop in the 1970s. In any case, the type of coordination proposed by CSIS is of such complexity that it is clearly beyond the administrative capacity of the New Order state, not to mention the fact that it offers few inducements to the various military factions whose support would be needed to push such a strategy.

But the role of the New Order state mediating in the relationship between national and international capital was not determined by ideologies but by concrete economic and political conflicts and tensions which derived from the development of capitalism. Ultimately, it has been the power of national capital which proved decisive. On the one hand, the larger national bourgeoisie is anxious to benefit from the financial, capital and technological resources brought by the international corporations and in this objective its interests were served by legislation requiring foreign investors to take local partners. On the other hand, however, it requires protection from foreign capital in selected sectors, such as auto-assembly, construction, and cement manufacture where it felt it had sufficient capital resources to make large and profitable investments.

As mentioned earlier, these big national business groups have been able to secure state protection for a variety of reasons. In most cases such groups are partly owned by generals, ministers and other leading political and state officials whose interest in national capital accumulation has become proprietary rather than simply ideological. They have also been able to benefit from nationalist and anti-foreign sentiment which was an important component of the conflicts culminating in the 1974 Jakarta riots. Ironically, the economic nationalism expressed by the smaller indigenous petty bourgeoisie had been directed against the big conglomerates in general, including not only international capital but the business groups of the generals and their Chinese partners.

Following the 1974 riots, the government tightened regulations concerning the entry of international capital and by the mid-1970s, a whole range of sectors was closed to foreign investments where it was considered that national capital could operate without foreign partners. Foreign investors were required to take local partners and, within a period of ten years, to transfer 51 per cent of shares to these local partners.[40] However, as mentioned, it was not the small indigenous bourgeoisie, on whose behalf these nationalist moves were obviously taken, who benefited but the big national conglomerates. Apart from these restrictions imposed on foreign capital investment, national capital was also nurtured through protection and subsidy, particularly in the import substitution manufacturing sector.[41]

As Glassburner[42] has pointed out, the technocrats cannot be simply dismissed as agents of foreign capital. Their policies in the 1970s did place increasingly strict requirements upon international investors. This was not because of any ideological preference for national capital, indeed, the technocrats generally adhered to a policy of favouring those who could best generate growth and this usually meant big capital. However, after the oil crisis of 1973-5 and the explosion of oil-generated revenue, their increased bargaining position led the technocrats to pursue vigorously a policy of obtaining the best possible production-sharing arrangements with foreign oil and mineral producers, to place pressure on foreign investors to move into areas of higher value added investment. The most important example of the latter policy occurred in the forestry industry where cut logs were permitted to constitute only 30 per cent of export value, forcing companies into plywood production and other higher value added processing.[43]

By the late 1970s the backlash from international capital was well advanced. Specific complaints were made about the difficulties of investment in Indonesia – dealing with inefficient and corrupt officials, convoluted regulations and inadequate infrastructure. But most important, international capital objected to attempts by the Indonesian government to determine what sort of investment was to be made in Indonesia by means of protection and subsidy of national capital and the establishment of priority and closed sectors for international capital investment. This fundamentally contradicted the logic of the international division of labour within which international corporate capital freely located its investments on the basis of such factors as labour costs. Increasing pressure was placed upon Indonesia to reduce its regulation of international investment, to end subsidy and protection of import substitution industrialization and move to export-oriented industrialization.[44]

International corporations did not simply talk, they acted decisively by investing their capital elsewhere, especially in the field of manufacture. Total non-oil foreign investment declined from a peak of US$633.9 million in 1974 to US$346.6 million in 1980. In 1975, foreign investment in manufacture was at a peak of US$392.4 million but by 1980 had declined to US$235.4 million.[45]

The New Order state therefore found itself caught between the competing demands of national economic forces, particularly those powerful business groups in the ISI sector, and international capital. But there are signs emerging which suggest that resistance to the demands of international capital may be weakening. From 1975 to 1981, the government's increasing ability to impose specific demands on foreign capital and to capitalize the growth of national capital derived from increasing oil receipts. However, the 1980s have seen a rather disturbing downturn in Indonesian foreign exchange earnings from oil and non-oil exports.[46]

c) The state and national capital

The Indonesian national bourgeoisie and petty bourgeoisie may be divided into several categories:

    i) A category of medium- and large-scale business groups which integrate finance and industrial capital and often taking the form of partnerships between indigenous politico-bureaucratic power, indigenous and Chinese capital.

    ii) A category of small- to medium-scale indigenous bourgeoisie and petty bourgeoisie within which we may identify two categories:

        1) Long-established, muslim-oriented capitalists involved in traditional sectors of indigenous enterprise: trade in agricultural products, manufacture of textiles, batik, kretek, foodstuffs and beverages.

        2) Newer enterprises, with access to state contracts and credits, often with links to officials or state political organizations, (*Golkar*), operating in the transport and service sectors as well as manufacture.

iii) A small- to medium-scale Chinese bourgeoisie and petty bourgeoisie involved in trade, processing of agricultural products, workshop manufacture and the service industry.

One of the most significant developments under the New Order has been the growth of state-sponsored private business groups. Their emergence cannot be explained in terms of the normal processes of capital accumulation, and their relationship to the state cannot be explained in terms of interaction between 'state' and 'capital' expressed through public policy. Instead, the relationship has, to a significant degree, linked specific centres of politico-bureaucratic power to specific business groups. At the heart of this type of relationship is the capacity of politico-bureaucrats to appropriate state authority, resources and powers for private use.

In the late 1960s, individual generals, political cliques, military commands, ministers and governors established or expanded business groups, generally with Chinese partners, based upon their capacity to appropriate and provide privileged access to public credit and various monopolies, concessions, contracts and licenses. To a large degree these early business groups were opportunist dealers in contracts, monopolies and concessions or, at the very best, depended upon windfall profits from politically secured strategic positions in the import sectors, in forestry or in contracting to the state.[47]

However, this 'cargo cult'[48] approach to accumulation subsequently developed, during the 1970s, into the basis for increasingly consolidated and large-scale business groups involved in the process of capital accumulation, particularly in the industrial sectors. The Liem Sioe Liong/Suharto group, for example, is now a major regional corporate group with interests in banking and finance, industry, trade and property.[49] A sufficient proportion of the windfall profits derived from extortion appear to have been reinvested to transform what we might term primitive accumulators into capitalists. Whilst the initial accumulation of capital was made possible by the exercise of political power, the accumulation process, once under way, is now following a more normal path of accumulation through the generation of profits by capital investment. This is not to deny that the major business groups still enjoy politically secured and privileged access to state-controlled contracts and concessions.

Two persistent conflicts internal to the national bourgeoisie have been those between large and small capital and between indigenous and Chinese capital. Under the New Order we may say that this conflict has slowly evolved into one between a declining indigenous petty bourgeoisie and the larger national bourgeoisie as constituted within the major business groups. Although the political protest of the indigenous petty bourgeoisie has tended to manifest itself in anti-Chinese action, it is in reality addressed to the total alliance of big capital: the generals in business, their Chinese partners, the political and economic relations which bind them to the broader economic strategies of the technocrats which are not sympathetic to small capital.

In 1965, the indigenous petty bourgeoisie constituted a frustrated, poorly organized and economically battered class. Political independence had not arrested the continued deterioration of their economic position. State programmes and policies of subsidy and protection for domestic capital had primarily benefited state corporations, the larger Chinese business groups and the indigenous politico-bureaucrats.[50] Indigenous bourgeoisie and petty bourgeoisie also proved less able to escape from or cope with the inflation, shortages and infrastructure collapse which characterized the 1950s and early 1960s.[51] Policy-makers, both radical and conservative, also tended to be unsympathetic to introducing any cohesive policy of protection or financing small, indigenous capital.

Ultimately, their failure was a consequence of their very political and economic weakness and we may simply argue that these petty bourgeoisie represent a vanishing remnant of an earlier merchant/ petty commodity production phase of capitalism. However, such petty bourgeoisie have generally proven persistent and resilient during the drawn out process of transition to capitalism throughout the Third World. In political terms, this class has proven a constant irritant in Indonesia to a state which has been dominated by a Javanese civil and military bureaucracy.

A virulent anti-Chinese tradition has characterized petty bourgeois political movements in Indonesia. It characterized the Sarekat Islam movement of the 1910s and 1920s and was resurrected in the late 1950s by the Asaat movement.[52] But the indigenous petty bourgeoisie does not only represent or symbolize anti-Chinese sentiment, it also constitutes a most important and complex politico-cultural challenge: Islam against the Javanism of the officials, the outer islands against Java, the countryside against Jakarta. In short, the muslim petty bourgeoisie may never have been able to pose a serious threat to the Indonesian state but has always had the potential to mobilize sentiments or prejudices with a popular appeal and, for this reason, the state has been forced to treat this class with caution.

With the introduction of the Domestic Capital Investment Law (PMDN) in 1968, domestic investors were given a variety of tax and import duty concessions, priority in certain sectors of investment and access to state credit. The indigenous bourgeoisie and petty bourgeoisie, hard hit by inflation, found their liquid assets inadequate, not only for expansion of their capital base but for collateral requirements for investment credit. By 1973, only 17 per cent of state investment credit allocated under PMDN was being directed to indigenous businesses, and it was estimated that only 20 per cent of private capital invested under PMDN was indigenous.[53] Of course, the vast bulk of the indigenous petty bourgeoisie operated outside the PMDN provisions and therefore at considerable disadvantage to PMDN and PMA investors who enjoyed tax concessions and access to cheaper imports of raw materials and technology.

The protest of the indigenous petty bourgeoisie gathered strength in the early 1970s, parallel with the movements associated with growing student discontent with military rule and the direction of economic strategy. Muslim newspapers, *Abadi* and *Nusantara* voiced the concerns of the indigenous petty bourgeoisie that the resources and policies of the state were being channelled into building major economic alliances between generals and big Chinese business groups. Such resentment, associated specifically with the increasing difficulties of indigenous textile producers and more generally with the ever present social tension between indigenous Indonesians and Chinese, was a contributing factor in the Bandung riots of October 1973, and the Jakarta riots of January 1974.[54]

Following the Jakarta riots, the government moved to defuse the tensions by introducing a series of regulations designed to redress the perceived imbalances between indigenous, Chinese and foreign capital. These included:

1) A requirement that state bank credit be made available only to indigenous companies.
2) A requirement that, within ten years, companies investing under PMDN be 75 per cent owned by indigenous investors, or 51 per cent where management was in indigenous hands.
3) A requirement that 51 per cent ownership of companies investing under PMA be in the hands of national investors within ten years.
4) Expansion of state credit schemes and advisory programmes for indigenous small business.

These regulations constituted a direct confrontation with the normal logic of the process of capital accumulation. The indigenous petty bourgeoisie had previously received a small share of state bank credit, not only because they exercised little political influence but because in terms of normal banking criteria, they were a poor credit risk. Since the introduction of the requirement that bank credit be directed to the national bourgeoisie, it has been demonstrated that only a proportion of the national business firms possess the existing capital or organizations resources to use this credit effectively for purposes of accumulation. Credit targets remain unfulfilled and a low proportion of loans are repaid. Nevertheless, state credit programmes have continued to channel finance to the indigenous petty bourgeoisie and state banks have been ordered to accept the low rates of repayment.[55]

As far as the proposed transfer of equity from foreign to national and indigenous shareholders is concerned, neither the state nor the indigenous bourgeoisie or petty bourgeoisie possessed the finance to purchase the equity which came within the scope of such regulations. In effect, foreign and Chinese corporations were being asked either to provide credit for indigenous partners to purchase equity, or simply to hand over the equity.[56] Despite relaxation of the strict terms of the schedule, the government has maintained its pressure upon the principle of transfer to a surprising degree. General policies of protection for the petty bourgeoisie have also been introduced since 1974, most important were the Keppres (Presidential Decisions) 14, 14a, 18 and 20, introduced in 1980 and 1981, giving preference to small indigenous contractors in tendering for government contracts below the value of Rp.100 million.[57]

Quite clearly, however, the state has avoided moving against foreign and Chinese capital to the extent that the muslim petty bourgeoisie would have liked. Both are indispensable to the structure of capitalism in Indonesia and, in any case, are bound to the major centres of politico-bureaucratic power by concrete business alliances. If we take into account the experience of the past, we must also expect that a sizeable proportion of the credit, transferred equity and preferential contracts will not go to the traditional muslim bourgeoisie but to indigenous business groups owned by politico-bureaucrats and their clients and associates.

Although no comprehensive studies have been made of the indigenous petty bourgeoisie it has manifestly not been wiped out by big capital, indeed, in the service sectors, particularly transport[58] it would appear to thrive. But there may be a significant change in the political nature of this petty bourgeoisie involving a decline amongst old muslim trading and petty commodity production sections (especially in textiles and batik), and a rise of new petty capitalists who derive their finance from state credits and salary savings. There are clear indications that a nascent kulak/absentee landowning class is being constituted around capital invested by urban civil and military officials rather than capital accumulated by traditional, muslim landowners from rental income. In short, the new petty bourgeoisie and landowner/kulaks are much more likely to be tied into networks of patronage emanating from *Golkar* and the military rather than the remnants of the muslim parties, and much more dependent upon access to fertilizer subsidies, state bank credits, *Bimas* credits, contracts for local *Inpres* and *Banpres*[59] programmes than upon income from rents.

5 Political and economic tensions within the New Order state

a) Economic growth – fiscal crisis and political order

As we have seen earlier it has been argued by Anderson that the seeds of political instability in Indonesia are being created by the very success of the New Order in excluding opponents from power as well as centralizing and consolidating power within the ruling military group itself. It is true that there is considerable evidence of a pervading resentment of the privileges appropriated by the military, of the authoritarian nature of military rule, and the corruption of political leaders and the arbitrary application of law, felt by those former supporters and allies shouldered aside by the military, notably the urban middle classes: the managers, technicians, civilian bureaucrats, students and intellectuals. Publicly and privately, student leaders and intellectuals have long argued for termination or modification of the economic and political role of the military, the regularization of the state apparatus, the liberalization of politics and the rule of law.[60] In the last few years they have been joined by former military officers and political leaders including generals Nasution, Sadikin, Dharsono and Jassin, all losers in the process of increasing centralization of economic and political power.[61] But opposition to or support for the state is not determined solely by inclusion or exclusion from political power; a crucial factor is whether or not the government is able to produce conditions of economic prosperity for at least the strategic social and economic forces.

Despite the considerable frustrations and the open criticisms by important elements of the urban middle class in Indonesia, they have generally done well out of the type of capitalist development which has occurred under the New Order. Civil service salaries rose over 1,000 per cent in the 1970s, employment opportunities have been created with foreign and state enterprises, imported consumer goods and better housing have become increasingly available for the upper echelons of managers and officials. In the present situation, therefore, it is unlikely that they would support any moves for a radical restructuring of society or reallocation of wealth, nor could they be expected to willingly accept the privations or suffer the upheavals necessarily associated with the implementation of policies of radical economic nationalism. In short, their quiescence in the New Order is a function of the continuing development of their relative prosperity which is in turn based upon continuing economic growth.

In specific terms, the state has directly ensured that the social groups structurally necessary to the political dominance of the military have been major beneficiaries of the process of growth. This is achieved largely through the development budget and the regular budget in the following ways.

  a) Subsidies for purchases of pesticides, fertilizers and seed by farmers.
  b) Opportunities for contractors and suppliers to participate in development projects implemented through government departments, or special *Inpres* and *Banpres* schemes at the regional and village level.
  c) Provision of credit for indigenous business, in particular the special schemes for low interest credit.[62]

There have, however, emerged clear signs of strains upon the capacity of the state to maintain economic growth and levels of state expenditure through the budget. Foreign exchange earnings from oil are levelling off and earnings from non-oil exports have shown a sharp drop. Consequently there was a total revenue increase of 12.3 per cent for 1982-3 compared with an increase of 31.7 per cent for the previous year. This was due to a rise in oil revenues of only 6 per cent compared with more than 50 per cent in 1981-2. The state has dealt with this problem by slashing subsidies for fuel and basic commodities to the value of Rp.750 billion. In this way, an increase of 35 per cent in the development budget has been made possible, although a decrease of 7 per cent was necessary in the regular budget.[63]

The state has responded to the fiscal crisis by reducing its expenditure on its legitimation functions rather than interfering with the level of its support for the accumulation process. The immediate question posed by this strategy is whether or not the increase in price of basic commodities, coming on top of substantial increases associated with the devaluation of 1978 will impose intolerable hardships upon the ordinary peasants and workers, rural landless and urban unemployed who will bear the brunt of the new costs.

In any case, these cuts do not solve the basic problem, which is a decline in export earnings and of foreign investment in the non-oil sector. If the rate of increase of revenue and investment from these sectors continues to fall, which appears likely, the government will have to go further than cutting subsidies. A second option involves capitulation to the IBRD demands in the hope that a massive injection of foreign capital will replace lost oil revenue with export earnings from manufactures. This of course would alienate those sectors of the national bourgeoisie in the ISI sector. A further possible measure is to increase the amount of domestic revenue collected, a feat of considerable magnitude which would involve transforming the efficiency, honesty and powers of the tax collection apparatus.[64]

Essentially, I am arguing here that the maintenance of political order and the dominance of the military is not as reliant, as political order theorists would suggest, upon direct incorporation of various social power groups into the apparatus of the state, in a formal, institutional way or through informal client-patron arrangements. Undoubtedly, the incorporation of non-military groups into the power structure as ministers, officials of *Golkar* and members of patronage groups does impose a kind of corporatist cement. But it is the capacity of the state to constitute the interests of dominant social groups which is crucial, and for this we must examine not who occupies the state apparatus, but what the state does. Indeed, this is how the New Order sees the problem and it is in these terms that it seeks to legitimate its rule. The failure of the state to carry out this structural task increases the likelihood of social forces attempting to seize the state to ensure that their interests are served. It is in the light of these considerations that the fiscal pressures upon the state become of political significance.

b) The state and the regularization of authority

The power of the military rulers of Indonesia is, to a significant degree, built upon their capacity to appropriate state power and bureaucratic authority. These appropriated powers are used in two ways: to secure large sources of income from non-budgetary sources to finance their political survival, and to distribute largesse or economic opportunities to political clients and family members. The ruling groups within the New Order are well placed to do this because of the strategic economic position of the state. Through various state corporations and departments it controls the allocation of forestry and oil drilling concessions, the allocation of distributor-ships of basic commodities, and the allocation of import and export licenses, sole agencies and bank credit. Through the development budget, in turn channelled through departments and development projects, it controls the allocation of contracts for supply and construction. Indeed, no business can be established under PMA or

PMDN regulation without state approval.[65]

Since the New Order came to power there have been continuing political and economic pressures to regularize authority and impose the rule of law – in Weberian terms, to transform the form of bureaucratic power from patrimonial to legal-rational.

The first of these pressures is political. Corruption has become one of the most volatile political issues of the New Order period and one of the most constant and visible remainders of the absolute power of the rulers and of the frustration of those excluded from power.

Although it has been claimed by many liberal Western observers that corruption is culturally acceptable to Indonesians, this is both inaccurate and, to be quite blunt, rather racist. Corruption is not acceptable to Indonesians, apart from those engaged in it, for the very same reasons it is not acceptable to the average Westerner; it penalizes the poor, the politically weak and corrodes confidence and respect. Corruption is not a component of Indonesian culture but is an extra means of exploitation of the weak by the powerful, imposed by force. It may be argued that corruption has been a major focus of resentment and resistance of the 1970s. Indeed, the government has been forced to respond in form at least, carrying out several enquiries into corruption and several anti-corruption drives, all of which, however, have left the major terminals of corruption untouched.[66] Whilst middle-class opponents have not possessed the political power to impose the sovereignty of the law upon the generals, the state has come under far greater pressure from opposition generated by contradictions between corruption and capital accumulation.

In advanced industrial capitalist societies, the state most effectively provides the conditions for accumulation through fiscal and monetary policies which serve the general class interests of the bourgeoisie. The relationship is a general one between state and capital in which power is normally exercized publicly and in which discrimination is not normally made between companies. In Indonesia, however, the relationship between state and capital is, to a significant degree, a relationship between specific power groups and specific companies wherein the success or failure of individual companies is heavily dependent upon access to political patronage.

Those business groups which have flourished in Indonesia have so far benefited greatly from access to licenses, import monopolies, construction and supply contracts, credit, distributorships and forestry concessions allocated by power centres within the state apparatus.[67] Payoffs, contributions, equity and directorships for military units, generals and other officials and their families have become simply another operating cost.

Corruption may be argued to have two advantages; it makes action possible in a ramshackle, moribund and inefficient bureaucracy, and it facilitates the early stages of the accumulation process by guaranteeing certain groups generous access to monopolies, contracts and credit. Nevertheless, corruption interferes with the state's function in providing a legal and administrative framework for the regularized operation of business, particularly where large, long-term investments in industry are concerned. Capital is faced with uncertainty and insecurity where regulations, laws and agreements may be overridden by an informal network of politico-bureaucratic arrangements. The capriciousness of Jakarta palace politics becomes a central factor in the success or failure of investments. There is little doubt that this uncertainty has been a significant factor in the decline of foreign investment in industry in Indonesia since 1975.[68]

Whilst it is true that the major national business groups have benefited from integration with centres of politico-bureaucratic power, and whilst it is true that power has stabilized and concentrated over the last decade, there remains a constant threat of instability. Major national business groups continue to be subject to dramatic and immediate devastation by a change in political fortune attesting to the continuing importance of political pitfalls.[69] The continuation of appropriated state power is becoming a diminishing advantage to those major business groups which have already established themselves on a firm basis of accumulation, with large capital assets and developed corporate structures and, of course, have more to lose than a simple trading monopoly. As long-term profits for these groups become more clearly guaranteed and secured by the normal process of capital accumulation rather than by cultivating and paying off patrons, we may expect the national industrial bourgeoisie to become increasingly anxious about regularization of the state apparatus and establishment of the rule of law.

Indeed, the politico-bureaucrats themselves are being dragged into this contradiction. Whilst they remained simply dealers in licenses and concessions they had no necessary or structural interest in the survival of any one corporate group. However, politico-bureaucrats, their families and political associates, military commands and factions are establishing equity in the major business groups. As owners of capital, their interests have now become embedded in the accumulation process, and therefore potentially contradictory to their political interests in exerting a patrimonial influence over the economy. Generals whose families have been established as capital owners must now contemplate the economic consequences of their retirement.

Two final sets of contradictions remain. Firstly, those between the channelling of state funds into the construction of an effective physical infrastructure for capital accumulation, and the financial needs of those politico-bureaucratic groups who dominate the existing tendering process and who succeed in diverting a significant proportion of these funds.[70] Secondly, as we have mentioned earlier, there is the contradiction between corruption and the establishment of an effective tax revenue collection system. Ultimately, the resolution of the corruption question will depend upon:

a) The degree to which the politico-bureaucrats see the appropriation of state resources and the manipulation of economic policy as fundamentally damaging to the wider process of economic growth. This dilemma can best be illustrated by the reaction of the state to the Pertamina crisis of 1975-6. The massive debts incurred by the oil giant ($10.4 billion) forced the state to hand control of Pertamina over to the technocrats until the immediate threats of the crisis had been dealt with.

b) The degree to which the process of corruption contradicts the development of corporate capital and the extent to which corporate activity in Indonesia develops its capital base to the point where the risks of basing growth upon access to patronage as a generalized mode of operation outweigh the difficulties of competing within a regularized political and economic system.

Conclusion: paths of capitalist revolution and the future of the state in Indonesia

The present circumstances in Indonesia provide the logical preconditions for three likely paths of capitalist revolution and the development of the capitalist state. One of these is the technocratic, authoritarian developmentalist path of such countries as South Korea, Brazil and Singapore. A second is a nationalist, populist path, represented by the Peronist state, or, in its petty bourgeois variant, by the post-Shah Iranian state. Finally, we must consider the path of capitalist decline, and look to Vietnam under Diem or China under the Kuomintang as broad models.

In several important respects, the New Order state can be considered to be moving towards the model of an authoritarian developmentalist state currently epitomized by South Korea and Brazil. A military dominated and increasingly bureaucratic state apparatus exists in a relative vacuum of social and political power, reflected in an absence of influential and powerful political parties representing the interests of specific classes. The process of economic growth and industrialization is drawing the state further into the accumulation process, financing infrastructure and investment, securing social and political order and a disciplined, docile, low-wage labour force, and providing appropriate fiscal and monetary policies for capital investment. The move towards integration of the Indonesian economy within the New International Division of Labour is already reflected in increasing economic power of alliances of international corporate capital and those major Indonesian-based business groups which become linked into international corporate groups and the process of export-oriented manufacture. The already high levels of state reliance upon externally derived sources of revenue and political support have also guaranteed a significant degree of autonomy from mass-based domestic, political and social support.

However, we must remember that Indonesia has a far larger population (and predominantly peasant) than South Korea, Brazil or other similar Third World capitalist economies and a far lower base of industrialization. Foreign investment in the non-oil sector is not large.[71] The development of an industrial economy will take several decades of high growth rates. Fiscal problems confronted by the state in financing this growth, the general reluctance of foreign capital to invest in industry and the resistance of the national bourgeoisie entrenched in ISI manufacture to integration into the New International Division of Labour suggest that the path to strong corporate authoritarian developmentalist state power and export-oriented industrial capitalism is neither the inevitable nor even the most likely course.

Given the growing economic power of the larger national bourgeoisie, their economic and political incorporation with the military politico-bureaucrats and their success in securing state protection and subsidy for ISI manufacture, it is equally likely that capitalism will develop within a predominantly ISI framework. This may not make much difference to the demands upon the state to play a central role in the accumulation process or to impose a social order conducive to the needs of accumulation. The technocratic and authoritarian features of the state may be no different. But there is an increased likelihood that a bourgeois-dominated political party, perhaps in alliance with elements of the military, and even led by former generals, would replace the type of military rule now in existence. Given a greater emphasis upon protection and subsidy of domestic capital accumulation and revenue sources, a greater need for accommodation with domestic political and social forces would necessitate more populist or even democratic political forms. Perhaps the Petisi Limapuluh group discussed earlier is the clearest example of such a tendency.

Rather than concentrating upon a model of large-scale, capital-intensive development from above, led by the state and international capital, it may be important to consider capital accumulation from below, generated not only by the big national bourgeoisie but by small- and medium-scale business groups, the national petty bourgeoisie, and small- and medium-scale capitalist farmers. Little systematic research has been conducted on accumulation at this level but one of the most visible results of economic growth in the last decade has been the emergence of a relatively prosperous petty bourgeoisie and small- and medium-scale bourgeoisie in the service sector. If such a surge is expanded and sustained, the prospects for a new stage of political populism and economic nationalism are very real, based upon a far stronger class foundation than Guided Economy and Guided Democracy in the first half of the 1960s.

Finally, we must consider the possibility of stagnation and decline in capitalist development. As we have seen, the capacity of the state to generate growth and investment is very heavily predicated upon oil revenue. Given increased domestic consumption, lower rates of increases in production and prices, this source will need to be supplemented with other exports. However, given the extremely cautious attitude towards investment in Indonesia by foreign capital and the deepening international recession, export-oriented industrialization may not be able to fill this gap. Such difficulties will be compounded by demands upon servicing the mounting national debt.

A slowdown in growth implies an attendant impact upon living standards, job opportunities and business profitability which will severely damage, if not destroy, the compact between the state, the national bourgeoisie and the middle classes. Further, it will weaken the influence of the technocrats and strengthen the hand of military strongmen who operate at the head of patron-client networks. In this scenario an increasingly factionalized and corrupt state will confront revolt and resistance from populist social and political coalitions.

For the immediate future we must favour some sort of tension between the first two models. On the one hand, the impulse towards a centralized, military-dominated, corporate, authoritarian state presiding over an increasingly industrialized economy characterized by high growth rates. On the other, a populist but authoritarian regime of military and party forces presiding over a nationalist ISI economy with lower rates of growth and a burgeoning petty bourgeoisie and kulak class.

Notes

1 Donald K. Emmerson, *Indonesia's Elite: Political Culture and Cultural Politics*, (Ithaca, Cornell University Press, 1976); Karl D. Jackson, 'Bureaucratic Polity: A Theoretical Analysis of Power and Communications in Indonesia', and 'The Political Implications of Structure and Culture in Indonesia', in Karl D. Jackson and Lucien W. Pye (eds), *Political Power and Communications in Indonesia*, (Berkeley, University of California Press, 1978); R. William Liddle, 'Modernizing Indonesian Politics', in R. William Liddle (ed.), *Political Participation in Modern Indonesia*, (New Haven, Yale University Southeast Asian Studies, Monograph Series, No. 19, 1973). For a critique of these approaches see: R. Robison, 'Culture Politics and Economy in the Political History of the New Order', *Indonesia*, No.31, April 1981.

2 Fred W. Riggs, *Thailand: The Modernization of a Bureaucratic Polity*, (Honolulu, East-West Centre Press, 1968).

3 This aspect is developed by Ken Ward in 'Indonesia's Modernization: Ideology and Practice' in Rex Mortimer (ed.), *Showcase State*, (Sydney, Angus & Robertson, 1973) and by Peter Britton in 'The Indonesian Army: Stabiliser and Dynamiser', in Rex Mortimer (ed.), 1973.

4 The volume of economic growth-based political analysis is extensive. See: John M. Allison, 'Indonesia; Year of the Pragmatists', *Asian Survey*, Vol.9, No.2, 1969; Guy, J. Pauker, 'Indonesia: The Age of Reason?', *Asian Survey*, Vol.8, No.2, 1968; H.W. Arndt, 'Economic Disorder and the Task Ahead', in T.K. Tan (ed.), *Sukarno's Guided Indonesia*, (Brisbane, Jacaranda, 1967); H.W. Arndt, 'Development and Equality: the Indonesian Case', *World Development*, 1975; Bruce Glassburner, 'Indonesian Economic Policy after Sukarno', in Bruce Glassburner (ed.), *The Economy of Indonesia*, (Ithaca, Cornell University Press, 1971); Bruce Glassburner, 'Political Economy and the Suharto Regime', *Bulletin of Indonesian Economic Studies*, (henceforth *BIES*), Vol.XIV, No.3, November 1978.

5 Perhaps Peter McCawley's work on industrial policy best illustrates this concern. He sees the interests of state bureaucrats and a small group of national industrialists producing an import substitution industrial sector bolstered by protection and subsidy, thereby constituting an obstacle to efficient, export-oriented industrialization exploiting comparative advantage. See: Peter McCawley, *Industrialization in Indonesia*, (Canberra, Development Studies Centre Occasional Paper, No.13, Australian National University, 1979).

6 Mortimer's major piece on the New Order regime as a comprador patrimonial amalgam is, 'Indonesia: Growth or Development' in Rex Mortimer (ed.), 1973. The importance of patron-client political relationships and the weakness of class-based political relationships and the weakness of class-based political organization is discussed in Rex Mortimer, 'Class, Social Cleavage and Indonesian Communism', *Indonesia*, No.8, 1969.

7 Ben Anderson, 'Last Days of Indonesia's Suharto?', *Southeast Asia Chronicle*, Issue No. 63, July, August 1978; Herbert Feith, *The*

Class, capital and the state in New Order Indonesia

Indonesian Student Movement of 1977-78, Mimeo, Monash University, Centre of Southeast Asian Studies, 1978.

8 Colin Leys, 'Capital Accumulation, Class Formation & Dependency – the Significance of the Kenyan Case', *The Socialist Register*, (1978), p.245.

9 Robin Luckham, 'Militarism; Force, Class and International Conflict', *Institute of Development Studies Bulletin*, Vol.9, No.1, July 1977.

10 Herbert Feith, 'Repressive Developmentalist Regimes in Asia; Old Strengths, New Vulnerabilities', *Prisma*, No.19, December 1980.

11 Perhaps the best general overview of the development of the Chinese bourgeoisie and petty bourgeoisie is given by George Kahin in Chapter One of his *Nationalism and Revolution in Indonesia*, (Ithaca, Cornell University Press, 1952). The economic role of the Chinese in Indonesia since independence has not received the attention it deserves, possibly because of the politically sensitive nature of the topic, the necessarily secretive nature of Chinese business activity and, I would argue, the inadequate theoretical basis from which their position is usually analysed. For some insights see: K.D. Thomas and J. Panglaykim. *Indonesia – the Effect of Past Policies and President Suharto's Plans for the Future*, (Melbourne, Committee for Economic Development of Australia, 1973, pp.68-71); J.A.C. Mackie (ed.), *The Chinese in Indonesia*, (Melbourne, Nelson, 1976).

12 A useful overview of the indigenous bourgeoisie and petty bourgeoisie in the late colonial and early post-colonial period is to be found in J. Sutter, *Indonesianisasi* (Ph.D. Thesis, Cornell University, 1959, University Microfilms, Part I and Chapter VI of Part II). For a specific case study see: Lance Castles, *Religion, Politics and Economic Behaviour in Java: the Kudus Cigarette Industry*, (New Haven, Yale University Cultural Report Series No.15, Yale University Press, 1967).

13 Onghokham, *The Residency of Madiun, Priyayi and Peasant in the Nineteenth Century*, (Ph.D. Thesis, Yale University, 1975, University Microfilms, 1978, pp.109-50).

14 There are numerous sources on this, see: J. Elisio Rocamora, *Nationalism in Search of an Ideology*, Ph.D. Thesis, Cornell University, 1974, pp.180-5; J. Sutter, 1959, *op. cit.*, pp.997-1072.

15 Sanusi Achmad, *The Dynamics of the Nationalization of Dutch Owned Enterprises in Indonesia*, Ph.D. Thesis, Indiana University, 1963.

16 T.K. Tan, 'Sukarnian Economics', in T.K. Tan (ed.), 1967. K.D. Thomas and J. Panglaykim, 1973, Chapter III.

17 J. van der Kroef, 'Indonesia's Economic Future', *Pacific Affairs*, Vol.32, No.1, March 1959, pp.53-5; K.D. Thomas and J. Panglaykim, 1973, *op. cit.*, pp.56-9.

18 United States Survey Team to Indonesia, *Indonesia: Perspective and Proposals for United States Economic Aid*, New Haven, Yale University Southeast Asian Studies Centre, 1963, p.12; J.A.C. Mackie, 'The Indonesian Economy, 1950-63', in Bruce Glassburner (ed.), 1971, *op. cit.*, pp.28-34 and p.42.

19 J. Furnivall, *Netherlands India: A Study of Plural Economy*, (Cambridge

University Press, 1939, pp.317 and 436).

20 Heinz Arndt, 'Economic Disorder and The Task Ahead', in T.K. Tan (ed.), 1967, *op. cit.*, pp.130-1.

21 Rex Mortimer, *The Indonesian Communist Party and Land Reform*, (Melbourne, Monash University Centre of Southeast Asian Studies, Papers on Southeast Asia, No.1, 1972).

22 Rex Mortimer, 1969; Anonymous, 'A PKI Self-Criticism', in Herbert Feith and Lance Castles (eds), *Indonesian Political Thinking; 1945-65*, (Ithaca, Cornell University Press, 1970, p.270).

23 This question will be treated in some detail in part 4 of this chapter dealing with the state as an investor and financer.

24 Ali Moertopo, *The Acceleration and Modernization of 25 Years Development*, (Jakarta, CSIS, 1973).

25 The growth rate for manufacturing was 8.2 per cent from 1965-71 and 13.3 per cent from 1971-7, in comparison with 1.9 per cent from 1953-9 and 2.1 per cent from 1960-5. By 1980, manufacture comprised 13.4 per cent of GDP compared with 8.5 per cent in 1953. See: Ann Booth and Peter McCawley, 'The Indonesian Economy since the mid-Sixties', in Anne Booth and Peter McCawley (eds), *The Indonesian Economy During the Suharto Era*, Kuala Lumpur, Oxford University Press, 1981, pp.4 and 5; D.T. Healey, 'Survey of Recent Developments', *BIES*, Vol.XVII, No.1, March 1981, p.34; R. Daroesman, 'Survey of Recent Developments', *BIES*, Vol.XVII, No.2, July 1981, p.3.

26 Income distribution, the role of wage labour, landownership and capital investment have yet to be subjected to systematic analysis in terms of the development of capitalist class relationships. Nevertheless, the indications are that agrarian capitalism is at last emerging. See: Howard Dick, 'Survey of Recent Developments', *BIES*, Vol.XVIII, No.1, March 1982, pp.25-7; Arum Abey, Anne Booth and R.M. Sundrum, 'Labour Absorption in Indonesian Agriculture', *BIES*, Vol.XVII, No.1, March 1981; William L. Collier, *et al.*, 'Tebasan System, High Yielding Varieties and Rural Change', *Prisma*, 1, 1 May 1975.

27 Some idea of the significance of the government development expenditures is given by R. Daroesman, 1981, *op. cit.*, p.13. Some comments on the distribution of finance injected into the rural economy amongst social categories in made in Abey, Booth and Sundrum, 1981, *op. cit.*, and Dick, *op. cit.*, 1982.

28 A general statement of the economic philosophy of the technocrats is to be found in Mohammad Sadli, 'Reflections of Boeke's Theory of Dualistic Economies', in Bruce Glassburner (ed.), 1971, *op. cit.* The most detailed statement of the position of the technocrats is to be found in the collection of works entitled *Masalah-Masalah Ekonomi dan Factor-factor Ipolsos*, (Jakarta, LEKNAS – Lembaga Ekonomi dan Kemasjarakatan Nasional, 1965).

29 See figures for realized Repelita II and planned Repelita III Government Receipts and Expenditures; Ann Booth and Amina Tyabji, 'Survey of Recent Developments', *BIES*, Vol.XV, No.2, July 1979.

30 Taken from tables provided in: Peter McCawley, 'Growth and the

Industrial Sector', in Anne Booth and Peter McCawley, 1981, *op. cit.*, p.66; Boediono, 'Survey of Recent Developments', *BIES*, Vol.XVI, No.2, July 1980, p.29.

31 Indonesian Commercial Newsletter (henceforth ICN), Jakarta, No.112, 23.10.1978, pp.10-13 and *ICN* No.166, 26.1.81, pp.1,2.

32 Taken from figures provided in the 1975 industrial census, Jakarta, Badan Pusat Statistik.

33 Relationship between social and political structure and the nature of state capitalism is dealt with in: James Petras, 'State Capitalism in the Third World', *Journal of Contemporary Asia*, Vol.6, No.4, 1976; J. Leal, 'The Mexican State: 1915-1973, An Historical Interpretation', *Latin American Perspectives*, Vol.11, No.2, 1975; R. Munck, 'State, Capital and Crises in Brazil: 1929-1979', *The Insurgent Sociologist*, Vol.IX, No.4, 1980.

34 Bill Warren, 'Imperialism and Capitalist Industrialization', *New Left Review*, No.81, 1973.

35 Colin Leys, 1978, *op. cit.*, p.251.

36 Alavi states that:

> as the erstwhile 'national bourgeoisie' grows in size and aspires to extend its interest from industries which involve relatively unsophisticated technology (such as textiles) to those which involve the use of highly sophisticated technology (such as petrochemicals and fertilizers) they find that they do not have access to the requisite advanced industrial technologies. Their small resources and scale of operation keep the possibility of independently developing their own technology out of their reach . . . they have to turn for collaboration, therefore, to the bourgeoisies of the developed metropolitan countries or to the socialist states.
>
> The concept of a 'national' bourgeoisie which is presumed to become anti-imperialist as it grows bigger, so that its contradictions with imperialism sharpen further, is one which derives from an analysis of the colonial and not the post-colonial experience.

Hamza Alavi, 'The State in Post-Colonial Societies', in Gough, K. and Sharma, P. (eds), *Imperialism and Revolution in South Asia*, N.Y., Monthly Review Press, 1973, pp.164-5.

37 For an overview of the process of Indonesia's reintegration into the international capitalist economy see K.D. Thomas and J. Panglaykim, 1973, *op. cit.*, Chapter V.

38 Most of the liberal intellectual critics work for programmes of political and liberal reform from within the bureaucratic and political power structure and the press, hoping to influence the course of events through debate rather than active political alliance with workers or peasants. Given the highly developed intelligence and security apparatus of the regime it is of course difficult to establish such political alliances. Even criticism in the press has been subject to swift reprisals as in 1974 when five newspapers were closed. Student activity has almost been eliminated since Daud Jusuf was appointed Minister for Education. Critics of the

regime in business (as in the case of some of the signatories of the 'Petition of Fifty') may be denied work permits, import and investment licenses, state bank credits and exit permits. (See the statement of General Yoga Sudama, the Head of the Intelligence Coordination Body *(BAKIN)*, June 1980, in *Far Eastern Economic Review*, 27/6/80, p.26.

39 See: Jusuf Panglaykim, 'Origanisasi Bisnis Dalam Rangka Pembangunan Ekonomi di Asia Tenggara', in Persoalan Masa Kini, *Perusahaan Perusahaan Multi Nasional*, Jakarta, Yayasan Proklamasi, Centre for Strategic and International Studies, 1974; Jusuf Panglaykim, 'Structur Domestik Dalam Interdepensi Dunia', *Analisa Masalah Internasional*, Tahun II, No.12, 1973.

40 These requirements were made in a series of regulations issued in 1974. See: *Business News*, Jakarta, 23.1.74. Sectors open to foreign investment and the conditions applying to such investment are listed in: Investment Coordinating Board (BKPM), *Priority List for Foreign Investment 1981-1982*, Jakarta, 1981.

41 Peter McCawley, *Industrialization in Indonesia*, Canberra, Australian National University, Development Studies Centre, Occasional Paper No.13, 1979, pp.38-43; Martin Rudner, 'The Indonesian Military and Economic Policy', *Modern Asian Studies*, Vol.10, No.2, 1976, especially pp.270-5.

42 Bruce Glassburner, 'Political Economy and the Suharto Regime', *BIES*, Vol.XIV, No.3, November 1978.

43 New (third generation) mineral production-sharing agreements include a 10 per cent tax on the export of unprocessed minerals, a requirement that 51 per cent of shares be sold to Indonesians within ten years and a windfall profit tax. New oil production-sharing agreements lifted the Indonesian government's share of production to 85 per cent.

44 The most important statement of the position of international capital has been the World Bank Report on Indonesia for 1980. See: Guy Sacerdoti, 'Overdraft of Inefficiency', *Far Eastern Economic Review*, 29.5.81, pp.44-9; also Eduardo Lachica, 'Indonesia Investment Policy is too Rigid, U.S. Firms Say', *Asian Wall Street Journal*, 21.4.81, pp.1 and 4.

45 See the table on implemented foreign investment in *Indonesian Development News*, Vol.4, No.12, August 1981.

46 See Heinz Arndt's section on the 'Looming Resource Gap' in his 'Survey of Recent Developments', *BIES*, Vol.XVII, No.3, November 1981.

47 Richard Robison, 'Towards a Class Analysis of the Indonesian Military-Bureaucratic State', *Indonesia*, No.25, April 1978.

48 Richard Franke described the economic behaviour of politically powerful figures in the early period of the New Order in terms of a cargo cult mentality. See: Richard Franke, 'Limited Good and Cargo Cult in Indonesian Economic Development', *JCA*, Vol.2, No.4, 1972.

49 The structure of the Liem group to 1977 is outlined in Richard Robison, *Capitalism and the Bureaucratic State in Indonesia*, Ph.D. Thesis, Sydney University, 1977, (appendix B, pp.XVII-XIX).

50 The unsuccessful struggle of the traditional indigenous bourgeoisie in

the 1950s and 1960s is treated in: Lance Castles, 'Socialism and Private Business: the Latest Phase', *BIES*, No.1, 1966; R. Anspach, 'Indonesia', in F. Golay *et al.* (eds), *Underdevelopment and Economic Nationalism in Southeast Asia*, Ithaca, Cornell University Press, 1969.

51 The larger Chinese capitalists were best able to transfer money out of Indonesia because of a degree of integration with overseas Chinese financial networks. Indigenous capitalists often resorted to maintaining funds in the form of commodities (most lucrative were spare parts) but often found attempts to accumulate finance frustrated by inflation. See: Robison, R., *Capitalism and the Bureaucratic State in Indonesia, 1965-75*, Ph.D. Thesis, Sydney University, 1977, pp.98-105.

52 Probably the best general treatment of economic nationalist movements in this period is that of R. Anspach, 'Indonesia', in F. Golay *et al.* (eds), *Underdevelopment and Economic Nationalism in Southeast Asia*, (Ithaca, Cornell University Press, 1969). See also: Asaat, 'The Chinese Grip on Our Economy', in Herbert Feith and Lance Castles (eds), 1970, *op. cit.*, pp.343-5.

53 For an overview of the credit difficulties of the indigenous bourgeoisie and petty bourgeoisie in the early New Order period see: Robison, R., 1977, *op. cit.*, pp.133-5. Also the article: 'Kredit PMDN-Antara Koneksi dan Investasi', *Tempo*, 9.12.73.

54 Some interesting studies of the disintegration of indigenous bourgeoisie in the petty commodity production and small-scale manufacturing sector are to be found in the Indonesian press. See: *Tempo*, 2.12.72; *Topik*, 1.3.72; *Progress*, No. 7, 1972. For an overview, see: S. Joedoeno, 'Partisipasi Pengusaha Nasional Ekonomi Lemah', in S. Joedoeno *et al.* (eds), *Prospek Perekonomian Indonesia 1974*, LPEM, Fakultas Ekonomi, Universitas Indonesia, 1973.

55 See *Indonesian Commercial Newsletter* (*ICN*), No.166, 26.1.1981, pp.1 and 2.

56 Richard Robison, 1977, *op. cit.*, pp.442-4.

57 Contracts below Rp.50 million were to be reserved for the 'weak economic group' (i.e. indigenous) and from Rp.50-100 million the indigenous tenderer was to be given a 10 per cent margin. These regulations were an attempt to give indigenous contractors an increased share of the work generated at the regional level through such programmes as *Inpres*. For a summary of the regulations see: Ruth Daroesman, 'Survey of Recent Developments', *BIES*, Vol.XVII, No.2, July 1981, pp.14-16.

58 Some insights into the role of small capital in the urban transport sector are given by Howard Dick in 'Urban Public Transport', (parts I and II), *BIES*, Vol.XVII, Nos 1 and 2, March and July 1981.

59 *Inpres* (Instruksi Presiden – Presidential Instruction) and *Banpres* (Bantuan Presiden – Presidential Assistance) and the programme for development in the village and local levels, mostly in the form of grants for construction of schools, hospitals and public works. They are part of the development budget but it would appear that the process of allocating these grants is closely tied to patronage networks and is

subject to frequent allegations (both public and private) of corruption and manipulation.

60 See: *White Book of the 1978 Students Struggle*, (published under the auspices of the Students Council of the Bandung Institute of Technology, January 1978 and translated in *Indonesia*, No.25, April 1978).

61 This group of former military officers and political figures made a comprehensive statement concerning the increasing trend of political authoritarianism in the now well-known petition of fifty. See: *Pernyataan Keprihatian* (Statement of Concern – better known as Petisi Limapuluh – Petition of Fifty), Jakarta, 5 May 1980.

62 The KIK (Kredit Industri Kecil – Small Industry Credit) and KMKP (Kredit Modal Kerperluan Pribumi – Credit for Indigenous Capital Needs) are the main credit schemes involved. However, Ruth Daroesman reports that there are serious doubts about their success. Only 200,000 persons have benefited, most of these established businessmen, and repayment rates have been low. See: Ruth Daroesman, 'Survey of Recent Developments', *BIES*, Vol.XVII, No.2, July 1981, pp.17-20.

63 See: Howard Dick, 'Survey of Recent Developments', *BIES*, Vol. XVIII, No.1, 1982. For a review of the price rises generated by the subsidy cuts, see the article, 'Memang Sulit, Semua Harus Menanggun', *Tempo*, 9.1.82.

64 In the 1982-3 budget, oil company tax constituted Rp.9,122 billion out of the total of Rp.13,756 billion of domestic revenue. Income tax and company tax, normally the major component of direct taxes, contributed only Rp.1,079 billion, a little over half of foreign aid revenues.

65 Material on corruption is extensive. Two of the more comprehensive reports are: 'Korupsi-Mana ada Yang Bersih', *Tempo*, 31.10.81; 'Malik: Korupsi Sudah Epidemik', *Sinar Harapan*, 2.11.81.

66 Richard Robison, 1977, *op. cit.*, pp.354-70. See also: the Student White Book, translated in *Indonesia*, No.25, April 1978.

67 Richard Robison, 1977, *op. cit.*, chapters 6 and 7. An interesting article on the Suharto/Liem Sioe Liong Bogasari Flour milling group gives a recent insight into activities of politico-business alliances. See: Joseph P. Manguna and S. Karen Witcher, 'Suharto Relatives, Officials Gain Control of Indonesian Flour Trade', *Asian Wall Street Journal*, 23.11.81.

68 International business has consistently expressed its frustration not only at the cost of corruption in Indonesia but at the uncertainty it throws over the whole process of investment. The 1980 IBRD report was quite clear about the need to reduce corruption, and foreign business associations have been highly critical of the various levies and charges imposed by officials outside the legal apparatus. See, for example, the statements of the American Chamber of Commerce and Industry reported in *Asian Wall Street Journal*, 23.10.81.

69 Richard Robison, 1977, *op. cit.*, Chapter 5.

70 Corruption in tendering and contracting were specifically dealt with in the *Tempo* articles, 'Korupsi-Mana ada Yang Bersih?', (31.10.81) and 'Malik: Korupsi, Sudah Epidemik', (2.11.81). It is also significant that the latest regulations involving contracting require that all tenders for

contracts over Rp.200 million be submitted to the state Secretary's Office for final approval and allocation. This gives the President and the Secretary of State potential access to a massive source of patronage not formerly under their direct control.

71 The total to date is about $4,250 million implemented (*Indonesian Development News*, Vol.4, No.12, August 1981).

Index

Index

For Product Safety Concerns and Information please contact our EU
representative GPSR@taylorandfrancis.com
Taylor & Francis Verlag GmbH, Kaufingerstraße 24, 80331 München, Germany